The Investment Treaty Regime and Public Interest Regulation in Africa

INTERNATIONAL ECONOMIC LAW

Tania Voon is Professor at Melbourne Law School, the University of Melbourne.

The *International Economic Law* series, established by the late Professor John H. Jackson, addresses a range of issues in international economic law, which includes international trade law, international investment law, and the global financial order. The Series aims to encourage interest in the broad contours of international economic law, heightening awareness of its significance across the globe as well as its continuous interactions with other areas. The Series Editors encourage high-quality submissions from a wide range of perspectives, including doctrinal, theoretical, empirical, and interdisciplinary. Novel and cutting-edge research is particularly welcome, as are contributions from both emerging and established scholars from around the world.

ALSO PUBLISHED IN THIS SERIES

International Adjudication on Trial
The Effectiveness of the WTO Dispute Settlement System
Sivan Shlomo Agon

China's International Investment Strategy
Bilateral, Regional, and Global Law and Policy
Edited by Julien Chaisse

Emissions Trading Schemes under International Economic Law
James Munro

The Trade Policy Review Mechanism
A Critical Analysis
Mathias Kende

Mega-Regional Trade Agreements: CETA, TTIP, and TiSA
New Orientations for EU External Economic Relations
Edited by Stefan Griller, Walter Obwexer, and Erich Vranes

Small and Medium-Sized Enterprises in International Economic Law
Edited by Thilo Rensmann

Domestic Law in International Investment Arbitration
Jarrod Hepburn

Treaty Shopping in International Investment Law
Jorun Baumgartner

The Investment Treaty Regime and Public Interest Regulation in Africa

DOMINIC NPOANLARI DAGBANJA
The University of Western Australia Law School
Crawley, Western Australia

OXFORD
UNIVERSITY PRESS

OXFORD
UNIVERSITY PRESS

Great Clarendon Street, Oxford, OX2 6DP,
United Kingdom

Oxford University Press is a department of the University of Oxford.
It furthers the University's objective of excellence in research, scholarship,
and education by publishing worldwide. Oxford is a registered trade mark of
Oxford University Press in the UK and in certain other countries

First Edition published in 2022

Impression: 1

Published in the United States of America by Oxford University Press
198 Madison Avenue, New York, NY 10016, United States of America

British Library Cataloguing in Publication Data

Data available

Library of Congress Control Number: 2021951895

ISBN 978–0–19–289617–9

DOI: 10.1093/oso/9780192896179.001.0001

Printed and bound by
CPI Group (UK) Ltd, Croydon, CR0 4YY

In memory of my Father, Mr Dagbanja Bokpi, and Mother, Mrs Yoombei Dagbanja, and to my brother, Mr Kwame Dagbanja

Series Editor's Preface

In the last decade, concerns have grown about the intrusion of international investment law, and particularly investor–state dispute settlement (ISDS), into the sphere of sovereign regulatory autonomy. Responses to these and related concerns about the legitimacy of international investment law have taken different forms. For example, some commentators have called for the application of public law principles to procedural and substantive aspects of international investment law, using the framework of comparative public law.[1] Some states, such as Canada in its 2021 Model Foreign Investment Promotion and Protection Agreement, have inserted 'right to regulate' clauses in international investment agreements recognising the right of each party to regulate within their territory to achieve legitimate policy objectives.[2] In relation to ISDS, in 2015 the European Union proposed a multilateral investment court in a project that continues today.[3] Ongoing work is also being undertaken by Working Group III of the United Nations Commission on International Trade Law (UNCITRAL) on ISDS reform. In 2021, UNCITRAL and the International Centre for Settlement of Investment Disputes (ICSID) released a second draft code of conduct for adjudicators in international investment disputes.

This book addresses the problematic intersection between international investment law and regulatory sovereignty from a different angle, building on the existing literature and taking account of continuing reforms. The book focuses on the relationship between domestic constitutional norms and international investment law, asking not only whether international investment law aligns with such norms but also whether these norms provide a valid legal basis for entering international investment agreements such as bilateral investment treaties (BITs) in the first place. Noting constitutional requirements to comply with certain international treaty obligations, Dagbanja designates a thematic focus on human rights, environmental rights, and the right to development that extends to international obligations in these fields.

The book's regional focus is on Africa, a continent that has been underexplored in the literature on international economic law to date. The African International Economic Law Network of the Society of International Economic Law was established in 2008. James Thuo Gathii's book on African regional trade agreements was

[1] See, for example, Stephan W Schill (ed), *International Investment Law and Comparative Public Law* (OUP 2010).

[2] Canada's 2021 Foreign Investment Promotion and Protection Agreement (FIPA) Model, Article 3.

[3] European Commission, *Concept Paper: Investment in TTIP and Beyond—The Path for Reform* (5 May 2015).

published in 2011.[4] Interest in the area has grown, with a special issue of ICSID Review on Africa's contribution to ICSID and ISDS in 2019,[5] and a symposium issue of the Manchester Journal of International Economic Law on Africa's participation in international economic law in 2020.[6] In this book, Dagbanja adopts as case studies the countries of Cameroon, Egypt, Ghana, Kenya, Nigeria, and South Africa. He points out that 'Africa has been part of the investment treaty regime since its inception', with the first BIT signed in Africa on 16 May 1961.[7]

Dagbanja's theoretical framework is outlined in Chapter 2. He identifies as 'imperatives' arising from both constitutional and general international law 'the various fundamental human rights, including the right to life, health, development, healthy environment, food, water and cultural rights ... and corresponding obligations of states.' According to his imperatives theory, the making and interpretation of BITs must conform to these imperatives such that African states are unable to conclude BITs that are contrary to them. That brings into question the validity of existing African BITs and their future treatment. In Chapter 6, Dagbanja suggests that some African BITs may be procedurally unconstitutional (where they failed to comply with procedural requirements in the relevant constitution) while others may be substantively unconstitutional (where they are substantively inconsistent with the constitution or general international law). He recognises the limited possibilities for resolving a dispute as to the validity of a BIT, where the states parties do not agree on its validity.

The book's conclusion that Africa's investment treaty obligations are inconsistent with constitutional and general international law norms (in particular the right to regulate in the public interest) leads to some controversial proposals. For example, Dagbanja calls for the abolition of ISDS in future African BITs, because of the incompatibility of ISDS with the supremacy of local courts under domestic constitutions. He maintains that prohibitions on indirect expropriation should similarly be abolished, including because of constitutional recognition of compensatory payments only for instances of direct expropriation. He also argues against the inclusion of provisions requiring national treatment, most-favoured-nation treatment, and (unless limited in scope) fair and equitable treatment. As regards existing BITs, Dagbanja proposes their renegotiation and their interpretation in a manner consistent with constitutional and general international law principles with respect to the public interest. He suggests that the latter may require reconsideration of

[4] James T Gathii, *African Regional Trade Agreements as Legal Regimes* (CUP 2011). See also Fola Adeleke, *International Investment Law and Policy in Africa: Exploring a Human Rights Based Approach to Investment Regulation and Dispute Settlement* (Routledge 2017).

[5] 'Special Focus Section: Africa and the ICSID Dispute Resolution System' (2019) 34(2) ICSID Review.

[6] 'Symposium Issue: Africa's Participation in International Economic Law in the 21st Century' (2020) 17(1) Manchester Journal of International Economic Law.

[7] *Traité entre la République fédérale d'Allemagne et la République Togolaise relatif à l'encouragement des investissements de capitaux* (signed 16 May 1961, entered into force 21 December 1964).

tribunals' 'design and structure', something that could perhaps form part of existing institutional reform activities mentioned above.

Dagbanja's book makes a significant contribution to the literature on Africa and international economic law as well as the literature exploring the intersection between domestic and international law in the context of international investment law. While its focus is on several African countries, it has potential implications for other countries in Africa with similar constitutional frameworks linked to international treaties, as well as other countries around the world, particularly developing countries. The book continues critical explorations of international investment law and the legitimacy of that law in limiting states' exercise of regulatory power.

Tania Voon
May 2021

Foreword

In this important book, Dr Dominic Dagbanja persuasively argues that African states are subject to a set of fundamental constitutional and general international law obligations that forms the baseline for the kind of rights they should avail foreign investors. These fundamental obligations that African states have towards their citizens, Dr Dagbanja argues, impose limitations on the competence of African states to agree to absolutist standards of investment treaty protection. Proceeding from that premise, this book makes the case for rethinking the making and reform of investment treaty law and arbitration in Africa. For this reason, this book is a major regional case study of international investment law that has significant comparative lessons for other regions. In addition, the research for this book is very thorough and well written.

A central argument that threads through this important new book centres on reversing the neo-liberal foundations of investment treaties because of the way they restrain public interest regulation and instead privilege investment protection. Dr Dagbanja refers to this central argument as the imperatives theory. According to this theory, the autonomy to regulate in the public interest cannot be retained or effectively recaptured without ensuring that the norms pertaining to human rights, environment, development, and the jurisdiction of national courts form the pre-eminent bases for determining what states can or cannot do both domestically and in international economic relations. In an era characterised by the rising importance of national law in the context of international investment law, this book could not have come at a better time.

Drawing examples from Ghana, South Africa, and Egypt, among other African countries, the book focuses on the interplay of their investment treaty obligations on the one hand, and public interest obligations under national constitutions and general international law on the other. In Dr Dagbanja's view, conflicts between domestic law and international investment law should be resolved by deference to the values embodied in constitutional and domestic law of the host state including the right to regulate in the public interest. For this reason, a host state should not protect foreign investors at the expense of constitutional principles governing the exercise of its powers in the public interest. The public interests that the book is most concerned about include rights enshrined in national constitutions as well as in international human rights treaties and environmental treaties, including the right to development. These rights and corresponding duties of states, which Dr Dagbanja describes as *constitutional-general international law imperatives*, are the foundations of the imperatives theory.

The originality of the book's argument lies in how it derives the imperatives theory from the values of human rights, environment, and development. The book also makes a compelling case for the pre-eminence of the jurisdiction of national courts over investor–state dispute settlement (ISDS). Dr Dagbanja's claim is that human rights, environmental values, and the right to development bind African governments not to enter into investment treaties that abridge these values. In other words, Dr Dagbanja does not advocate for a repudiation of the international investment regime, rather that international investment law should adjust to the values of the imperatives theory. The book is, therefore, premised on the view that constitutional law and general international law are not merely formal analytical categories but embodiments of underlying values against which the making and validity of investment treaties and decisions based on them must be judged. It is thus the separation between domestic and international law that forms the terrain against which the book is written.

Dr Dagbanja's argument takes seriously the purpose of a state—particularly one with citizens with many basic needs unmet, to safeguard the rights of its people, their environment, and their economic well-being, and not to compromise these public interests when they conflict with the interests of foreign investors.

To buttress his arguments further, Dr Dagbanja argues in favour of a definition of investment that results in a tangible contribution to development; for doing away with indirect expropriation; for excluding national treatment, most-favoured-nation treatment, and ISDS in future investment treaties involving African countries; for limiting the boundaries of fair and equitable boundaries to preserve regulatory autonomy; and for restricting repatriation of transfers in the interest of financial stability and economic development. These proposals with the suggestions for re-negotiating and interpreting existing investment treaties that African countries have signed make the book an important scholarly contribution. Even more, it is a highly significant and welcome book for everyone involved in the review and reform of international investment law in Africa and beyond.

Professor James Thuo Gathii
Loyola University Chicago School of Law
Evanston, Illinois
27 June 2021

Preface

The idea of undertaking research on international investment law and public interest regulatory autonomy dawned on me in 2009 when I attended a training workshop organised by the Ministry of Justice and Attorney-General's Department for state attorneys in Accra, Ghana. I was then an Assistant State Attorney. One of the topics treated at the workshop was titled 'The Law Regulating Foreign Direct Investment,' which was handled by my former Lecturer in International Law at the premier University of Ghana, Professor Emmanuel Yaw Benneh. Based on the materials I read from this workshop, especially Benneh's 'International Law, Sovereign Rights and Foreign Direct Investment: Directions from the Jurisprudence of International Arbitral Tribunals' (2000–2002) XXI University of Ghana Law Journal 1, I framed two topics I thought were worth scholarly attention. One of the topics was 'The Legal and Regulatory Frameworks for the Control, Promotion and Protection of Foreign Investment in Ghana: Striking a Balance between Investor Protection and National Sovereignty Prerogatives'. This title reflects the thinking that informed my decision to undertake research on the issues underlying this book.

There is extensive literature on conflict of legal norms and interests in international investment law. The dominant discourse is on the implications of treaty-based investment protection for sovereign public interest regulatory autonomy. However, the legal status of investment treaties has been taken for granted in international investment law scholarship. Little systematic attention has been paid to the capacity of states to conclude investment treaties and the obligations states can or cannot agree to under those treaties in light of their public interest obligations. Yet, this issue is of fundamental importance for at least three reasons. First, the case for states' regulatory autonomy arises out of their primary duties to regulate in the public interest. These duties have their legal justification in or are sourced from national constitutions and general international law. This is the reason states commonly rely on national constitutions and international human rights and environmental treaties to defend regulatory measures challenged in investment treaty arbitration. Second, treaty obligations are founded on the existence of legal norms necessary for a treaty to come into existence and which define the juridical consequences attached to the conclusion of a treaty. These matters are also determined by constitutions and general international law. Third, the limitations inherent in state-specific defences or justifications in investment disputes settlement compel a proactive rethink of the conclusion of investment treaties and how they should be interpreted.

The questions this book address include does a state that is legally required to act both under the terms of its constitution and public international law in the public interest have the capacity to conclude investment treaties that expressly prevent or abridge the exercise of its public interest regulatory powers, and how should treaties adopted in breach of these obligations be interpreted? How might constitutional law *and* international law which are often treated as antinomic in investor–state arbitration simultaneously fight for states' autonomy to regulate in the public interest? To address these questions, four areas of public interest regulation that have featured prominently in investment arbitration served as case studies: the jurisdiction of municipal courts, environmental protection, human rights protection, and development policy. Based on the impact and potential limitations of standards of investment protection on regulation in these areas, the book argues that some investment treaties' terms are incompatible with the public interest regulation obligations of African states such as Cameroon, Egypt, Ghana, Kenya, Nigeria, and South Africa under their constitutions as well as international human right treaties and international environmental treaties to which they are parties. This book argues that the legal source and public purpose of the states' powers from national constitutions and general international law prevent them from concluding agreements that directly prohibit public interest regulation or indirectly achieve that effect. Accordingly, the book proposes that the express and implied limitations on the duties to regulate in the public interest placed on investment treaty-making powers of the states must inform the making of investment treaties and their interpretation. By its approach, this book establishes legal, principled, and normative bases for reflection on the limits to the capacity of African states, exemplified by those used as case studies, to conclude investment treaties and on how they should be interpreted.

Academics and domestic and international institutions have made various proposals as to how states can recapture or retain regulatory autonomy in international economic law. However, existing scholarship does not directly address the issue of the constitutional law *and* general international law limitations on the capacity of African states to execute investment treaties and how such limitations should inform investment treaty interpretation. This book's focus on the constitutional law and general international law limitations on the making of investment treaties in Africa adds vital new insights to international investment law scholarship. By its approach, the book contributes to ongoing discussion on where and how to draw the line between national regulation and policy measures aimed at protecting the public interest, for which compensation to foreign investors must not arise, and regulation and policy measures affecting foreign investment for which compensation may be required. The research issues underlying this book are timely because concerns over the limits investment treaties place on the jurisdiction of municipal courts, environmental protection, development policy choices, and human rights protection in preference for the activities of multinational business entities, are now very high on the public policy agenda of states, business, and international organisations. By giving considerable attention to the limits that the fundamental environmental rights and human rights and corresponding duties of African states towards the public place on the investment treaty-making powers of the states, this book addresses the issue of conflict of legal norms and interests in international investment law from its roots, rather than from its impacts or resultant effects alone.

Existing scholarship rightly points out that there is little understanding of the effects of investment treaties in developing countries. While the constitutionality of investment treaties has been studied in developed countries, including Canada and United States, people within the developing countries are hardly concerned with investment treaties even though their governments conclude them. Thus, there is a pressing need for legal scholarship that can contribute to an understanding of the nature and effects of investment treaties for domestic public interest values protected under national constitutions and international law from a perspective that incorporates developing countries' legal norms and interests in the discourse. Similarly, existing scholarship acknowledges that international investment rule-making poses particular challenges for developing countries and that there is a need for policy research and analysis that can help them to assess the implications of different policy options as they make decision on entering into new treaties. A legal, principled, and normative basis for that reflection is crucial and this book is a contribution to that. The issue addressed in this book is one that should engage the attention of African states and the developing countries in the future, as it should developed countries.

The pressing need to reform investment treaties to bring them in line with sustainable development imperatives has been very well acknowledged in the academic literature and recent global investment policy initiatives. This book is a contribution to *why*, *what*, and *how* to reform the investment treaty regime to meet these imperatives. Its message is that the reform of international legal regime on foreign investment cannot be meaningfully and effectively made without addressing the *a priori* question of whether states can, under national constitutions and international law, limit their right to regulate in the public interest in the manner they do under investment treaties. Ongoing reforms of international investment legal architecture to accommodate the right to regulate afford opportunity to raise and address the question as to the shared role of *both* municipal law and general international law in the conclusion and interpretation of investment treaties that requires serious and introspective engagement. This book does that.

Dr DN Dagbanja
The University of Western Australia Law School
Crawley, Western Australia
7 July 2021

Acknowledgements

I worked on this book over a span of ten years. During this period, I leaned on the giants in the field and beyond to all of whom I so much owe debts of gratitude.

This book built on and significantly expanded a PhD thesis I submitted to the University of Auckland in 2015 after four full years of research, commencing in June 2011. I was blessed and privileged to have a wonderful, profoundly dedicated, and supportive team of supervisors: Professor Elizabeth Jane Kelsey and Associate Professor Christopher Gerald Noonan. I thank them immeasurably for all their time, effort, thought, guidance, and support without which I could not have completed the research at the high level of quality required for a PhD in Law. Without Professor Kelsey's interest in my research proposal and guidance to develop it for admission while I was still in Ghana, I would not have enrolled in the PhD programme. The initial books and journal articles she recommended were most foundational and appropriate and I have had to constantly refer to them. Professor Kelsey's profound involvement in my research right from the time I started developing the proposal for admission was most engaging and challenging. It remained so throughout the four years of the research. She read every word of my submissions and critically evaluated the soundness, solidness, coherence, consistency, comprehensiveness, and balanced nature of each submission. She achieved this through in-depth, critical, and objective reviews and comments on the content and structure of each submission, often bluntly rejecting some chapters as not being good enough for a PhD. Her academic jealousy to maintain the standards to be reached for a PhD cannot be forgotten. By rejecting almost every draft as substandard for a doctorate, she helped me produce research output that I am personally satisfied with and which the examiners judged as original and highly ambitious, well written, and comprehensively researched. I am most grateful to her for devoting so much of her time, effort, and thought into this research. Associate Professor Noonan provided fresh perspective and input that would have been missing without the benefit of a co-supervisor. Both have also supported me with various research assistantships that came with generous financial benefits and work experience.

The examiners of my PhD thesis, Professor James Thuo Gathii of Loyola University Chicago and Dr Richard Joyce of Monash University, provided profound feedback which I embraced in revising the manuscript. The depth and quality of this book reflect the inputs they made through the examination. The *viva voce* Examination Panel consisted of Dr Richard Joyce (Oral Examiner), Professor Judy Parr (Independent Chair), and Associate Professor Amokura Kawharu (Head of School Nominee). I thank them for the able and professional manner in which they conducted the *viva voce* and the report for revision produced following the examination. I have maintained professional contacts with both Dr Joyce and Professor Gathii who have supported this book throughout.

I was able to work on the thesis as a full-time researcher because I received funding from the University of Auckland Doctoral Scholarship without which I could not have given the PhD the time and thought it most needed. I am grateful to the University of Auckland and its scholarship committees both at the Faculty of Law and the university levels who found merit in my application and made a decision in my favour. I am very grateful to the Ghana Institute of Management and Public Administration (GIMPA) for granting me study leave with pay which enabled me to maintain the family back home in Ghana. Before I left for the programme, I worked under Professor Franklyn Manu who was then the Dean of GIMPA Business School, and later the Rector of GIMPA. He supported my decision to leave for the PhD right from the beginning and recommended that I be granted study leave. I am very grateful for his foresight and support. Professor Agyeman Badu was the Rector of GIMPA at the time and I am thankful to him for the support I received from his administration, especially the decision to grant me study leave with pay.

I received feedback on a number of draft chapters of the book from Professor Gathii and Professor Yengkong Ngangjoh Hodu of the University of Manchester School of Law. The book proposal was edited by Dr Tanya Lyons. I also received feedback on an earlier version of the book proposal from Professor Christopher Thornhill of the University of Manchester School of Law. Professor Kelsey, Professor Gus Van Harten of York University, Emeritus Professor Muthucumaraswamy Sornarajah of the National University of Singapore, Emeritus Professor Ernst-Ulrich Petersmann of the European University Institute and Dr Richard Joyce all blessed this book with academic reviews and endorsements. Thanks so much to each of you for your support.

I submitted the book proposal to the Series Editors of the International Economic Law Series, Professor Tania Voon and Professor Andrew Mitchell, in 2018. I thank them for recognising the gap in the literature that the book fills and their support through the peer review and decision-making processes. I am also very grateful to Ms Merel Alstein (Senior Commissioning Editor), Mr Jack McNichol (Assistant Commissioning Editor), Ms Jordan Burke (Senior Project Editor), the Delegates of the Press, Janet Walker (Copy Editor), Ashirvad Moses (Production Editor/Project Manager), Lakshmi Amritha, Mark Ajin, and other members of the production team and everybody at Oxford University Press who has been involved in the development and completion of this book. Thanks so much to Arokia Anthuvan Rani of Newgen KnowledgeWorks Pvt. Ltd for professionalism and excellent work managing the production of this book. I am very grateful to the anonymous reviewers for decisions reached and the feedback and suggestions made.

Professor Kojo Yelpaala has been a wonderful social father, mentor, and adviser since I studied under him at the University of the Pacific McGeorge School of Law in Sacramento, California in 2007/2008. He was instrumental in my admission to the LLM programme there. He also introduced me to Foreign Investment and Development and International Business Transactions. We have engaged in conversation from the beginning and intermittently in the course of my research. His advice and written materials have been invaluable. He recommended me for admission into the programme and supported me with a recommendation letter for the scholarship. I am extremely thankful for his time and effort in support.

Various parts of this book which were originally on Ghana, but now expanded to include five other African countries, were published in volume 6(3) *Transnational Legal Theory*; volume 17(1) *Oxford University Commonwealth Law Journal*; volume 21 *African Yearbook of International Law*; volume 12(2) *Manchester Journal of International Economic Law*; and *Yearbook on International Investment Law and Policy:2014-2015*. I am grateful to Taylor & Francis, Electronicpublications.org Ltd, and Oxford University Press for the copyright permissions to reproduce revised versions of these publications in Chapters 2, 3, 4, and 5.

I thank everybody else, both in and outside Ghana who variously contributed towards the completion of this book. Above all, I thank my wife Lady Talata Dagbanja (Mrs) and children, Ndoombe, Wumborti, and Nignentim, and the entire Dagbanja Family without whose love, understanding, support, and sacrifice I would not have been able to complete the research leading to this book.

Dr DN Dagbanja

Contents

List of Abbreviations

ACA	Arbitration and Conciliation Act
AfCFTA	Agreement Establishing African Continental Free Trade Area
AGRA	Alliance for a Green Revolution in Africa
AMTC	American Manufacturing & Trading, Inc
AU	African Union
BELG	Balkan Energy Ltd (Ghana)
BIT	bilateral investment treaty
BLEU	Belgo-Luxembourg Economic Union
CCJA	Common Court of Justice and Arbitration
CECNA	Commission for Environmental Cooperation of North America
CETA	Comprehensive Economic and Trade Agreement
CHRJA	Commission on Human Rights and Administrative Justice
CIL	customary international law
CJEU	Court of Justice of the European Union
COMESA	Common Market for Eastern and Southern Africa
CP	Construction Pioneers
CRCICA	Cairo Regional Centre for International Commercial Arbitration
CRI	Community Rules on Investment
CSACC	Council of State Administrative Court of Cairo
DSB	Dispute Settlement Body
DTI	Department of Trade and Industry
ECJ	European Court of Justice
ECOWAS	Economic Community of West African States
EMCA	Environment Management and Coordination Act 1999
EPA	Economic Partnership Agreement
EPA	Environmental Protection Agency
EU	European Union
FDI	foreign direct investment
FET	fair and equitable treatment
FPS	full protection and security
GAFI	General Authority for Investment and Free Zones
GATS	General Agreement on Trade in Services
GIMPA	Ghana Institute of Management and Public Administration
GIPC	Ghana Investment Promotion Centre
GIPCA	Ghana Investment Promotion Centre Act 2013
GSPA	Gas Supply and Processing Agreement
GTCL	Ghana Telecommunications Company Limited
HDI	Human Development Index
HDSAs	historically disadvantaged South Africans

ICC	International Chamber of Commerce
ICESCR	International Covenant on Economic, Social and Cultural Rights
ICJ	International Court of Justice
ICS	Investment Court System
ICSID	International Centre for Settlement of Investment Disputes
IET	international environmental treaty
IHRT	international human rights treaty
IIA	international investment agreement
ILC	International Law Commission
IMF	International Monetary Fund
ISDS	investor–state dispute settlement
JRP	Joint Review Panel
JVA	Joint Venture Agreement
MAI	Multilateral Agreement on Investment
MDGs	Millennium Development Goals
MFHT	Most-Favoured-Home-Third States
MFN	most-favoured-nation
MPRDA	Mineral and Petroleum Resources Development Act 2002
MTBE	methyl tertiary-butyl ether
NAFTA	North American Free Trade Agreement
NDPC	National Development Planning Commission
NIEO	New International Economic Order
NT	national treatment
OECD	Organisation for Economic Cooperation and Development'
OHADA	Organisation for the Harmonisation of Business Law in Africa
OPSO	operating and performance standards and obligation
P&ID	Process and Industrial Developments Ltd
PAfIC	Pan-African Investment Code
PCB	polychlorinated biphenyl
PCIJ	Permanent Court of International Justice
PIA	Protection of Investment Act 2015
PMRA	Pest Management Regulatory Agency
PPA	power purchase agreement
ROB	reciprocity of benefit
ROO	reciprocity of obligation
SADC	Southern African Development Community
SADC FIP	Southern African Development Community Protocol on Finance and Investment
SAHRC	South Africa Human Rights Commission
SCC	Supreme Constitutional Court
TFEU	Treaty on the Functioning of the European Union
TMB	Telekom Malaysia Berhad
TRIMs	Trade-Related Investment Measures
TRIPs	Trade-Related Intellectual Property Rights
TTIP	Transatlantic Trade and Investment Partnership Agreement

UNCITRAL	United Nations Commission on International Trade Law
UNCTAD	United Nations Conference on Trade and Development
UNDP	United Nations Development Programme
UNESCO	United Nations Education, Science, and Culture Organization
UK	United Kingdom
UNECA	United Nations Economic Commission for Africa
US	United States
VCLT	Vienna Convention on the Law of Treaties
WCED	World Commission on Environment and Development
WTO	World Trade Organization

1

The Intersection of Investment Treaty Law and Arbitration and Public Interest Regulation in Africa

1.1 Introduction

What limits, if any, do, or should, the principles, of constitutional governance and the right to regulate in customary international law (CIL) as well as under international environmental treaties (IETs) and international human rights treaties (IHRTs) place on the authority of African states in entering into investment treaties? Might a case for reclaiming or retaining the right to regulate in international investment regulation be better or more effectively made by addressing the *a priori* question of the limitations states' right to regulate in the public interest place on their competence to conclude investment treaties in the first place? This book is concerned with these fundamental questions.

In *World Investment Report 2012: Towards a New Generation of Investment Policies*, Ban Ki-moon, former Secretary-General of the United Nations, stated that the '[p]rospects for foreign direct investment ... continue to be fraught with risks and uncertainties'.[1] These 'risks and uncertainties' relate, in part, to the range of policies and regulatory actions that stand to be challenged by foreign investors as breaching treaty-based standards of investment protection. Indeed, from its inception, international investment law has generated debates among scholars and policy-makers about the applicable law, standards of investment protection, and the challenge the regime poses to states' regulatory autonomy. Existing scholarship in international investment law predominantly focuses on how investment treaties and arbitration limit regulatory autonomy. For example,[2] Muthucumaraswamy Sornarajah ably describes and analyses the nature of conflict and change in international investment protection founded on treaties. However, no systematic

[1] Ban Ki-moon, Preface to United Nations Conference on Trade and Development (UNCTAD), *World Investment Report 2012: Towards a New Generation of Investment Policies* (United Nations 2012) iii (hereafter, UNCTAD, *World Investment Report 2012*). On the protection of the public interest in international investment law see: Stephan W Schill and Vladislav Djanic, 'Wherefore Art Thou? Towards a Public Interest-Based Justification of International Investment Law' (2018) 33(1) ICSID Review 29.

[2] Muthucumaraswamy Sornarajah, *Resistance and Change in the International Law on Foreign Investment* (CUP 2015).

The Investment Treaty Regime and Public Interest Regulation in Africa. Dominic Npoanlari Dagbanja, Oxford University Press.
 DOI: 10.1093/oso/9780192896179.003.0001

attention has been paid to states' powers to enter into such treaties and the implications of that for existing and future treaties.

National constitutions are supreme in the hierarchy of legal norms within the domestic context, and governmental actions in Africa, including the making of investment treaties, are governed by these fundamental legal norms. Do, or should, national constitutions and the rights they preserve limit the powers of African states in investment treaty-making? This book explores this question with particular reference to Cameroon, Egypt, Ghana, Kenya, Nigeria, and South Africa as case studies. Constitutional rights and duties in Africa require specific actions and African governments have inherent discretion as to the sort of measures that can be adopted to fulfil their constitutional obligations towards citizens. Most African countries are also parties to IETs and IHRTs which make a case for the protection of the public interest in the areas of human rights, environmental rights, and the right to development. These treaties have been constitutionalised in Africa in the sense that African constitutions require states to abide by international treaty obligations on the environment and human rights. Thus, the obligations to observe these IETs and IHRTs derive not only from international treaty law but also from African constitutions themselves. These IHRTs and IETs, therefore, reinforce the constitutions of many African countries as to the duties of these states in the protection of the public interest.

In order to address these questions it is necessary to examine in the first place whether or not investment treaties with African countries are capable of constraining or have the potential to constrain policies, legislative enactments, and the discretion needed to meet constitutional, CIL, international environmental treaty, and international human rights treaty requirements pertaining to the protection of the public interest in Africa. It is only by establishing the constraining effects of investment treaties on public interest regulation that the issue of whether African constitutions permit such constraining effects arises. In this regard, Section 1.2 analyses the substantive standards of investment protection in Africa and their adverse impact on the right to regulate. Chapters 3, 4, and 5 provide comprehensive case studies on the actual and potential impacts of investment treaty law and arbitration on the right to regulate in Africa.

To address the question of the constitutional, CIL, international environmental treaty, and international human rights treaty implications for the making of investment treaties and their implementation in Africa, the book develops the *imperatives theory* based on an analysis of the constitutions of Cameroon, Egypt, Ghana, Kenya, Nigeria, and South Africa. The basic premise of the *imperatives theory*, which is applicable to these selected African countries and other countries within and outside of Africa with similar constitutional imperatives, is that the primary role of the states under their constitutions, CIL, IETs, and IHRTs is to protect the public interest or the interests of their citizens. Thus, these legal norms are the sources of the authority and the powers of these states. Therefore, these norms must determine what the states can or cannot do with those powers and the legal and juridical consequences to be attached to the states acting outside of those norms or in a manner that prevents them from attaining the purposes for which the authority and powers are vested in or entrusted to them. The legal validity or effect of legal enactments made or legal commitments undertaken by African states, whether national or international, must be determined by how these legal instruments effectively deprive the states of their ability to act in fulfilment of the objectives of legal norms from which the states derive their authority and powers to regulate in the public interest.

I argue that African states' need for autonomy to regulate in the public interest in the areas of development, human rights, and the environment must limit the type of treaty-based standards of investment protection they can undertake. Accordingly, given their heavy constitutional responsibilities to put the public interest first in all their decisions and actions (including in international business relations), African states must not agree to investment treaties that directly or indirectly prevent or constrain them from performing functions constitutionally required in the public interest.

I propose that the express and implied limitations placed on the investment treaty making powers of African states by their duties to regulate in the public interest must inform the interpretation of investment treaties. I argue that the search for regulatory autonomy in international investment law will elude African states, and all states for that matter, unless they stop concluding investment treaties completely or only make those treaties that respect and uphold the legal norms which justify the right to regulate. If African states enter into investment treaties in disregard of their effects on the rights of citizens and the states' corresponding obligations to fulfil those rights, they cannot at the same time reasonably expect to retain their regulatory autonomy. Citizens' constitutional rights and the states' corresponding obligations to fulfil them matter, and these must come first, including in international economic relations. Granting foreign investors absolute and unqualified rights puts them and their covered investments interests first, contrary to national constitutions which require the public interest to be the overriding consideration in all governmental actions in Africa. Equally, the resolution of investment disputes (especially by arbitral tribunals) cannot guarantee African states that autonomy unless the legal norms that govern foreign investment reserve the autonomy of states to regulate in the public interest.

The challenge is how these imperatives can be implemented in relation to existing and future treaties, given the constraints of the law of treaties and customary international law.

1.2 Treaty-Based Standards of Investment Protection in Africa

1.2.1 Africa and Investment Treaty Law

Lauge Poulsen's book is a useful reading of why African countries and other developing countries enter into investment treaties.[3] Chapter 5 of this book addresses this issue. Particular attention is paid in this book to the texts of investment treaties and their conflicting relationship with constitutions in Africa.

Charles Shea in *The Calvo Clause: A Problem of Inter-American and International Law and Diplomacy* articulated the nature of conflict of legal norms and interests in international investment protection. According to Shea, international law 'like all systems of law, evolves to meet conflicts of interests. In few areas of relations in the international level is there a more real clash of interests than in the relations between the state and citizens of foreign states.'[4] Similarly, Sornarajah notes that the international law governing the relation between the host state and foreign citizens and their property has been 'one of the most highly controversial',[5] being engulfed by conflict over the standards of investment protection since its beginning.[6]

In most parts of the world, investment protection took place in the context of colonisation and there was no question as to the law that governed the regulation of imperial investors within the colonies: imperial laws of the colonisers were pre-eminent. The principle that international law trumps municipal law in the event of conflict between them is traceable to colonisation, imperialism, and neo-colonisation.[7]

In other parts of the world, investment protection was very much regional in character; for example, being confined to investment relations between the United States of America (US) and Latin America. That encounter resulted in conflict over standards of investment protection and the applicable law. The United States externalised the norms that governed aliens and their property by arguing that there existed an international minimum standard of customary international law in accordance with which aliens and their property were to be protected.[8] In contrast,

[3] Lauge Poulsen, *Bounded Rationality and Economic Policy: The Politics of Investment Treaties in Developing Countries* (CUP 2015).

[4] Charles Shea, *The Calvo Clause: A Problem of Inter-American and International Law and Diplomacy* (University of Minnesota Press 1955) 3.

[5] ibid.

[6] Muthucumaraswamy Sornarajah, 'Evolution or Revolution in International Arbitration? The Decent into Normlessness' in Chester Brown and Kate Miles (eds), *Evolution in Investment Treaty Law and Arbitration* (CUP 2011) 631, 634, 3 (hereafter, Sornarajah, 'Evolution or Revolution').

[7] Antony Anghie, *Imperialism, Sovereignty and the Making of International Law* (CUP 2005) (hereafter, Anghie, *Imperialism and International Law*).

[8] Muthucumaraswamy Sornarajah, *The International Law on Foreign Investment* (3rd edn, CUP 2010) 36 (hereafter, Sornarajah, *Law on Foreign Investment 2010*). See also Muthucumaraswamy Sornarajah, *The International Law on Foreign Investment* (4th edn, CUP 2017) 46–48 (hereafter Sornarajah, *Law on Foreign Investment 2017*).

Latin American countries denied the existence of any such customary international law minimum standard and asserted that foreign investors were not entitled to greater or better protections than those accorded to domestic investors under municipal law.[9] The dominant proponent of 'no more favourable' treatment of foreign investors and the proposition that 'a government's liability can be no greater toward foreigners than that which it has toward its own subjects'[10] was Carlos Calvo, whose writings gave birth to what is today described as the 'Calvo Doctrine'.[11]

That conflict was made universal following decolonisation, as the former colonial powers subscribed to the 'customary international law minimum standard' and the newly independent states supported regulation of foreign businesses based on domestic law.[12] International investment law since then has 'never been settled because of the interests at conflict',[13] as reflected in the current controversy in international investment protection now founded largely on investment treaties. As international investment law is largely founded on investment treaties, the question arises whether states have a case to complain if they agree to standards of investment protection that are inconsistent with their constitutional duties to regulate in the public interest. In the following passages in Subsection 1.2.2, these core treaty-based standards of investment protection are discussed.

Political independence brought about the development of the bilateral investment treaties (BITs) with African countries, making BITs instruments of neo-colonialism.[14] A number of African countries gained political independence from the late 1950s onwards, for example Ghana in 1957 and Nigeria in 1960. The acquisition of independence and sovereignty by the new states changed the nature of foreign direct investment (FDI) protection in the former colonies. Foreign companies now had to be regulated by the municipal law of the newly independent states which asserted control over their natural resources.[15] This historic epoch marked an important phase in the development of investment treaties. European countries started 'negotiations' and conclusion of investment treaties with some of their former colonies. European countries began to enter into investment treaties with their former colonies in Africa from the 1960s.

[9] Surya P Subedi, *International Investment Law: Reconciling Policy and Principle* (Hart Publishing 2012) 12–18; Sornarajah, *Law on Foreign Investment 2017* (n 8) 46–48.

[10] Alwyn V Freeman, 'Recent Aspects of the Calvo Doctrine and the Challenge to International Law' (1946) 40(1) American Journal of International Law 121, 132.

[11] Carlos Calvo, *International Law of Europe and America in Theory and Practice* (5th edn, A Rousseau 1868); and Carlos Calvo, *Le Droit International Theorique Et Pratique* (vol 1, Nabu Press 2012).

[12] Sornarajah, 'Evolution or Revolution' (n 5) 634.

[13] ibid.

[14] Kwame Nkrumah, *Neo-colonialism: The Last Stage of Imperialism* (Panaf Books 1974/2004).

[15] Anghie, *Imperialism and International Law* (n 7) 224; Permanent Sovereignty over Natural Resources, GA Res 1803 (XVII), 17 UN GAOR Supp (No 17) 15 UN Doc A/5217 (1962); Charter on Economic Rights and Duties of States, UNGA Res 29/3281 (1974) UNGA 29th Session Agenda Item 48 UN Doc A/RES/29/; and Declaration on the Establishment of a New International Economic Order (UNGA Resolution 3201 S-VI, 1 May 1974).

The first BIT in Africa to have legal effect is the Niger–Switzerland BIT which was signed on 28 March 1962 and entered into force on 17 November 1962,[16] two years after Niger gained independence. On 18 November 1962, the Côte d'Ivoire–Switzerland BIT which was signed on 26 June 1962 also entered into force as the second BIT to have legal force in Africa.[17] This BIT also came into being two years after Côte d'Ivoire's independence in 1960. The first BIT to be *signed* in Africa is the Togo–Germany BIT, signed on 16 May 1961 but it did not enter into force until 21 December 1964. Cameroon signed its first BIT with Germany on 29 June 1962, which entered into force on 21 November 1963, and between that year and 1989 nine BITs between Cameroon and Germany (1963), Switzerland (1964), the Netherlands (1966), Belgium–Luxembourg Economic Union (1981), Romania (1981), the United Kingdom (UK) (1985), and the United States (1989) came into force. The Guinea–Switzerland BIT, which was signed on 26 April 1962, came into force on 29 July 1963. Therefore, this is the third BIT to enter into force in Africa. Other BITs that entered into force between 1964 and 1966 are Congo–Sweden BIT (1964),[18] Guinea–Italy BIT (1964), Liberia–Switzerland BIT (1964), and Tunisia–Switzerland BIT (1964). In 1966, Niger–Germany, Sierra Leone–Germany, Côte d'Ivoire–Sweden, Côte d'Ivoire–Netherlands, and Togo–Switzerland BITs came into force. Both the Chad–Switzerland and Congo–Germany entered into force in 1967. Thus, Africa has been part of the investment treaty regime from its early stages which started with the Germany–Pakistan BIT of 1959.

These early treaties dealt 'exclusively with foreign investment',[19] but some of them did not make provision for investor–state arbitration. It was only after decolonisation and the dissolution of colonial empires that the need for BITs in the manner known today came to be felt by the former colonial and Western powers, which now became the 'exporters' of capital to Africa.[20] The idea that former colonial powers and Western countries at the inception were, and are still, described as *capital exporting* countries suggests that those that 'received' the investment or capital were not 'exporting' capital, that is they were not investing abroad. This begs the question as to the *bilateral* and *reciprocal* nature of BITs intended for the

[16] *Accord de commerce, d'investissements et de coopération technique entre la Confédération Suisse et la République du Niger*, signed 28 March 1962, entered into force 17 November 1962.

[17] *Accord de commerce, de protection des investissements et de coopération technique entre la Confédération Suisse et la République de Côte d'Ivoire*, signed 26 June 1962, entered into force 18 November 1962.

[18] *Accordde commerce, de protection des investissements et de coopération technique entre la Confédération Suisse et la République du Congo-Brazzaville*, signed 18 October 1962, entered into force 11 July 1964.

[19] Jeswald Salacuse, *The Law of Investment Treaties* (OUP 2010) (hereafter, Salacuse, *Law of Investment Treaties*) 94.

[20] Sornarajah, *Law on Foreign Investment 2010* (n 8) 21.

reciprocal promotion and protection of investment in the territory of each contracting party.[21]

The size of investment treaties reached 3,360 in 2020 (2,943 BITs and 417 treaties with investment provisions). Of these investment treaties 2,646 entered into force by the end of 2020.[22] Together, African countries are parties to nearly 900 of these treaties accounting for about 26 per cent of them, some of which entered into force as far back as 1960s.[23] These investment treaties involving African countries consist of BITs between individual African countries and non-African countries, regional investment agreements and a continental free trade agreement, and intra-Africa BITs.[24] The stated aim of investment treaties is to create favourable conditions to attract foreign investors to bring about increased economic prosperity and development, and to stimulate productive use of resources and strengthen cooperation between the contracting parties.[25] There is a voluminous literature on the

[21] Dominic N Dagbanja, 'The Limitation on Sovereign Regulatory Autonomy and Internationalisation of Investment Protection by Treaty: An African Perspective' (2015) 60(1) Journal of African Law 56, 75–76, 80.

[22] UNCTAD, *World Investment Report 2021: Investing in Sustainable Recovery* (United Nations 2021) 122–23. See also UNCTAD, *World Investment Report 2020: International Production Beyond the Pandemic* (United Nations 2020) 106 (hereafter, UNCTAD, *World Investment Report 2020*); UNCTAD (March 2019) 21 *Investment Policy Monitor* (UNCTAD/DIAE/PCB/INF/2019/2) 1; UNCTAD (December 2018) 20 *Investment Policies Monitor* 5; UNCTAD, *World Investment Report 2018: Investment and New Industrial Policies* (United Nations 2018); and UNCTAD, *World Investment Report 2017: Investment and the Digital Economy* (United Nations 2017) at xii.

[23] Detailed reading on Africa and investment treaties include: Dominic Dagbanja, 'Africa' in Markus Krajewski and Rhea Hoffmann (eds), *Research Handbook on Foreign Direct Investment* (Edward Elgar Publishing 2019) ch 11; and Richard Karugarama Lebero, *The International Law Framework for Foreign Investment Protection: An Analysis of African Treaty Practice* (PhD thesis, Submitted in Fulfilment of the Requirements for the Degree of PhD in Law School of Law, University of Glasgow 2012).

[24] On the reforms see: Olabisi D Akinkugbe, 'A Critical Appraisal of the African Continental Free Trade Area Agreement' in Kholofelo Kugler and Franziska Sucker (eds), *International Economic Law from a (South) African Perspective* (JUTA Law 2021) 283; Olabisi D Akinkugbe, 'Reverse Contributors? African State Parties, ICSID and the Development of International Investment Law' (2019) 34(2) ICSID Review—Foreign Investment Law Journal 354; Olabisi D Akinkugbe and others, 'Africa's Participation in International Economic Law in the 21st Century: An Introduction' (2020) 17(1) Manchester Journal of International Economic Law 1; Hamed El-Kady and Mustaqeem De Gama 'The Reform of the International Investment Regime: An African Perspective' (2019) 34(2) ICSID Review—Foreign Investment Law Journal 482; Makane Moïse Mbengue, 'Africa's Voice in the Formation, Shaping and Redesign of International Investment Law' (2019) 34(2) ICSID Review—Foreign Investment Law Journal 455; Antonio R Parra, 'The Participation of African States in the Making of the ICSID Convention'(2019) 34(2) ICSID Review—Foreign Investment Law Journal 270; Won Kidane, 'The Culture of Investment Arbitration: An African Perspective' (2019) 34(2) ICSID Review—Foreign Investment Law Journal 411; Meg Kinnear and Paul Jean Le Cannu, 'Concluding Remarks: ICSID and African States Leading International Investment Law Reform' (2019) 34(2) ICSID Review—Foreign Investment Law Journal 542; Makane Moïse Mbengue, 'Africa and the Reform of the International Investment Regime' (2017) 18 Journal of World Investment and Trade 371;and Okechukwu Ejims, 'The 2016 Morocco–Nigeria Bilateral Investment Treaty: More Practical Reality in Providing a Balanced Investment Treaty?' (2019) 34(1) ICSID Review—Foreign Investment Law Journal 62.

[25] See the preambles to: Belgo–Luxembourg Economic Union and United Republic of Cameroon Convention concerning the reciprocal promotion and protection of investments, Signed at Brussels on 27 March 1980, entered into force on 1 November 1981 (Cameroon–Belgo–Luxembourg Economic Union (BLEU)) Investment Treaty; Agreement on Encouragement and Reciprocal Protection of Investments between the Kingdom of the Netherlands and the Republic of Ghana, signed 31 March 1989, entered into force 1 July 1991; Agreement between the Government of Canada and the Government of

standards of investment protection by treaty.[26] For the purposes of this book, the focus is on the legal interpretations of investment treaties as applied by various investment tribunals and in particular on their conflict with African states' public interest obligations.

As international investment law is largely founded on investment treaties, supposedly freely entered into, it is arguable whether states have a case to complain about these agreements limiting their right to regulate since they 'agree' to standards of investment protection that are inconsistent with their constitutional, CIL, international environmental treaty, and international human rights treaty obligations to regulate in the public interest. The standards of investment protection in African investment treaties include fair and equitable treatment, full protection and security, national treatment, most-favoured-nation (MFN) treatment, expropriation, repatriation of investment and returns, and provision for investor–state arbitration.

1.2.2 The Substantive Standards of Investment Protection in Africa

1.2.2.1 Fair and Equitable Treatment

The obligation to accord investments fair and equitable treatment (FET)[27] is 'vague and ambiguous ... Its undefined and potentially elastic nature has made it a favourite of aggrieved investors.'[28] The FET has been equated to either the customary

the Arab Republic of Egypt for the Promotion and Protection of Investments, signed 13 November 1996, entered into force 3 November 1997 (Egypt–Canada Investment Treaty); Agreement between the Government of the United Kingdom of Great Britain and Northern Ireland and the Government of the Republic of Ghana for the Promotion and Protection of Investments signed 22 March 1989, entered into force 25 October 1991 (Ghana–United Kingdom Investment Treaty); Agreement between the Government of Japan and the Government of the Republic of Kenya for the Promotion and Protection of Investment, signed 28 August 2016, entered into force 14 September 2017 (Kenya–Japan Investment Treaty); Treaty between the Federal Republic of Germany and the Federal Republic of Nigeria Concerning the Reciprocal Promotion and Protection of Investment, signed 28 March 2000, entered into force 20 September 2007 (Nigeria–Germany Investment Treaty); and Agreement Between the Government of the People's Republic of China and the Government of the Republic of South Africa concerning the Reciprocal Promotion and Protection of Investments, signed 30 December 1997, entered into force 1 April 1998 (South Africa–China Investment Treaty).

[26] Salacuse, *Law of Investment Treaties* (n 19); Kenneth J Vandevelde, *Bilateral Investment Treaties: History, Policy, and Interpretation* (OUP 2010); Rudolf Dolzer and Christoph Schreuer, *Principles of International Investment Law* (OUP 2008); and Reinisch August (ed), *Standards of Investment Protection* (OUP 2008).

[27] Cameroon–BLEU Investment Treaty (n 25) art 3(1); Egypt–Canada Investment Treaty (n 25) art II(2)(a); Ghana–United Kingdom Investment Treaty (n 25) art 3(1); Kenya–Japan Investment Treaty (n 25) arts 5(1) and 10(3); Nigeria–Germany Investment Treaty (n 25) art 3(2); and South Africa–China Investment Treaty (n 25) art 3(1).

[28] Salacuse, *Law of Investment Treaties* (n 19) 218.

international law minimum standard of treatment of aliens[29] or an autonomous standard additional to protection under general international law.[30] There is no unitary jurisprudence on this issue, especially as investment tribunals are not bound by strict precedent.

Some investment tribunals have ruled that a failure to provide a stable and predictable legal environment for business breaches the legitimate expectations of investors that the actions, conduct, laws, policies, and regulations investors relied on to make investment will not subsequently be changed to their detriment.[31] This means for example that amendments to existing laws could be found to breach the FET. Other elements used to determine a breach include: a state's failure to act transparently towards an investor;[32] arbitrariness and discrimination towards investors or covered investment;[33] denial of justice and due process of law;[34] actions taken in bad faith;[35] and a wilful neglect of duty or an insufficiency of action to protect investment.[36] The FET obligation is, therefore, very broad. Its scope of application may cover all forms of measures and regulation that impair investment, whether intentional or unintentional.

The case for the stability and predictability of the legal environment for foreign investment assumes that the economic, political, and social conditions in the host state remain constant. As this is not the case, founding the FET obligation on an investor's expectation of a stable and predictable legal environment is neither justifiable nor reasonable. Governments have an inherent right to make new laws and to amend or repeal existing ones. Foreign investors are aware of these inherent functions of governments. Their 'legitimate' expectation must be consistent with the responsibility of governments to make new laws and amend or repeal existing laws as the economic, political, and social conditions of the time demand, provided states are not doing so merely to affect the interests of an investor.

Even if there has been a formal promise not to change the law on which the investor relied to make an investment, the case should not be that the law cannot be

[29] ibid 222–23; *Genin v Estonia*, Case No ARB/99/2, Award, 25 June 2001, [367]; and *Occidental Exploration and Production Co v Ecuador*, LCIA Case No UN3467, Award, 1 July 2004, [189]–[190].

[30] Salacuse, *Law of Investment Treaties* (n 19) 226–28; *Azurix Corporation v Argentina*, ICSID Case No ARB/01/12, Award, 14 July 2006, [345] and [361] (hereafter, *Azurix v Argentina*).

[31] *International Thunderbird Gaming Corporation v The United Mexican States*, UNICITRAL, 26 January 2006 [147]–[148]; *CME Czech Republic B.V. (The Netherlands) v Czech Republic*, UNCITAL, Partial Award, 13 September 2001, [611]; and *Tecnicas Medioambientales Tecmed SA v The United Mexican States*, Case No ARB (AF)/00/2, Award, 29 May 2003, [88], [122], and [154].

[32] *Metalclad Corporation v The United Mexican States*, Case No ARB(AF)/97/1 Award, 30 August 2000 [99]–[100].

[33] *Genin v Estonia*, Case No ARB/99/2, Award, 25 June 2001 [371]; *LG & E Energy Corporation v Argentina*, ICSID Case No ARB 02/1, Decision on Liability, 3 October 2006 [155]–[160].

[34] Jan Paulsson, *Denial of Justice in International Law* (CUP 2005); *Metalclad Corporation v The United Mexican States*, Case No ARB(AF)/97/1 Award, 30 August 2000 [91]; and *Middle East Cement Shipping and Handling Co SA v Egypt*, Arbitration ARB/99/6, Award, 12 April 2002 [147].

[35] *Mondev International Ltd v United States of America*, Award, ICSID Case No ARB(AF)/99/2, 11 October 2002, [116]; and *Genin v Estonia*, Case No ARB/99/2, Award, 25 June 2001 [371].

[36] ibid [367].

changed because of that promise where there is a compelling reason to do so. If, for example, such a promise was made during a stable economic and financial situation, it should not bind a government's response to an unpredictable economic and financial crisis that affects everybody and demands governmental action to restore the society to normalcy. Not to make or amend the law in such circumstances would be unfair and inequitable. Strengthening justice for foreign investors must not undermine justice for all. Where there is compelling need for legislation that affects the value of investment, compensation to an affected investor, if any, must take account of that need.

1.2.2.2 Full Protection and Security

African states also have an obligation to provide *full protection and security* (FPS) to investors and investments, typically in the same treaty provision as the obligation to provide FET.[37] This standard of investment protection is also open to varying interpretations.[38] Some tribunals have interpreted the FPS as protecting foreign investors and covered investments from *physical* injury or harm (eg, injury to the investor or looting or forceful seizure of property) by governments, government agents, or third parties.[39] That obligation means that a host state must exercise due diligence, taking reasonable and well-administered measures to prevent physical harm to an investor or investment.[40] The scope of the FPS extends to 'an obligation to provide adequate mechanisms and legal remedies for prosecuting the State organs or private parties responsible for the injury caused to the investor'.[41]

Other tribunals have expanded the FPS to include protection of foreign investors and their investment from non-physical injury.[42] In *Biwater Gauff Ltd v Tanzania*, the Tribunal stated that FPS 'implies a State's guarantee of stability in a secure environment, physical, commercial and legal'.[43] In *Azurix Corporation v Argentina* the Tribunal stated that it was:[44]

> persuaded of the interrelationship of fair and equitable treatment and the obligation to afford the investor full protection and security. The cases ... show that full protection and security was understood to go beyond protection and security

[37] Egypt–Canada Investment Treaty (n 25) art II(2)(b); Ghana–United Kingdom Investment Treaty (n 25) art 3(1); Kenya–Japan Investment Treaty (n 25) art 5(1); and Nigeria–Germany Investment Treaty (n 25) art 3(2).

[38] Salacuse, *Law of Investment Treaties* (n 19) 132.

[39] ibid; *BG Group v Argentina*, Final Award, 24 December 2007 [324]–[326]; *Elettronica Sicula S.p.A. (ELSI)*, (*US v Italy*), ICJ Reports 1989 [108]; and *Suez, Sociedad General de Aguas de Barcelona SA v Argentina*, ICSID Case No ARB/03/19, Decision on Liability, 30 July 2010, [162]–[163] and [179].

[40] *Suez, Sociedad General de Aguas de Barcelona SA v Argentina*, ICSID Case No ARB/03/19, Decision on Liability, 30 July 2010 [163].

[41] ibid [173].

[42] *Siemens AG v Argentina*, ICSID Case No ARB/02/8, Award, 6 February 2007 [303].

[43] *Biwater Gauff (Tanzania) Ltd v Tanzania*, ICSID Case No ARB/05/22, Award, 24 July 2008 [729].

[44] *Azurix v Argentina* (n 30) [408].

> ensured by the police. It is not only a matter of physical security; the stability afforded by a secure investment environment is as important from an investor's point of view … [W]hen the terms 'protection and security' are qualified by 'full' and no other adjective or explanation, they extend, in their ordinary meaning, the content of this standard beyond physical security.

1.2.2.3 National Treatment

The *national treatment* standard requires that foreign investors and investments be treated no less favourably than domestic investors and their investments.[45] The standard thus focuses on nationality. It seeks to prevent differential treatment that is adverse to the investor, for example, where governments provide assistance, such as tax exemptions, to domestic businesses or other advantages through laws, policies, regulations, or administrative actions that are not made available to foreign businesses protected under the applicable investment treaty. The goal is to place covered investors and their investments on at least the same footing in terms of competition or some other business advantage as domestic investors.

The application of national treatment depends on the articulation of the obligation in the treaty and facts of each case. To determine whether the host state has breached the national treatment clause, the Tribunal in *Total SA v Argentina* said the investor.[46]

> (i) has to identify the local subject for comparison; (ii) has to prove that the claimant-investor is in like circumstances with the identified preferred national comparator(s); and (iii) must demonstrate that it received less favourable treatment in respect of its investment, as compared to the treatment granted to the specific local investor or the specific class of national comparators … Different treatment between foreign and national investors who are similarly situated or in like circumstances must be nationality driven. Accordingly, a foreign investor who is challenging measures of general application as *de facto* discriminatory has to show a *prima facie* case of nationality-based discrimination.

Some investment tribunals also consider the policy justification for measures that have a discriminatory effect. If the measure is not intended to give preferential treatment to domestic investors, a tribunal may find no breach of national treatment.[47] The Tribunal in *Pope and Talbot Inc v Canada* stated that:[48]

45 Cameroon–BLEU Investment Treaty (n 25) art 3(3); Egypt–Canada Investment Treaty (n 25) art II(3)(a); Ghana–United Kingdom Investment Treaty (n 25) art 4(1); Kenya–Japan Investment Treaty (n 25) art 3; Nigeria–Germany Investment Treaty (n 25) art 4; and South Africa–China Investment Treaty (n 25) art 5(1).

46 *Total SA v Argentina*, ICSID Case No ARB/04/1, Decision on Liability, 27 December 2010, [211]–[212].

47 *Pope & Talbot v Canada*, NAFTA, Award on the Merits of Phase 2, 10 April 2001, [79].

48 ibid [78].

> [d]ifferences in treatment will presumptively violate [national treatment] unless they have a reasonable nexus to rational government policies that (1) do not distinguish on their fact or *de facto*, between foreign-owned and domestic companies, and (2) not otherwise unduly undermine the investment liberalizing objectives.

The national treatment standard is extremely broad in terms of the investments it seeks to protect, the nature of the treatment of the investments that is prohibited, and the subject matter of governmental regulation that may come under the standard. The typical provision as reflected in Article 4(1) of the Ghana–United Kingdom investment treaty states that '[n]either contracting party shall in its territory subject investments or returns of nationals or companies of the other Contracting Party . . . to treatment less favourable than that which it accords to investments or returns of its own nationals or companies or to investments' or 'as regards their management, maintenance, use, enjoyment or disposal of their investments'. The investment treaties also entitle foreign investors as regards restitution, indemnification, compensation, or other settlement to treatment 'no less favourable' than that accorded to nationals whose investments suffer losses owing to war or other armed conflict, revolution, a state of national emergency, revolt, insurrection, or riot.[49]

The phrases 'no less favourable treatment' and consequential 'losses suffered' have been interpreted by arbitral tribunals very broadly. In *Asian Agricultural Products Ltd v Sri Lanka*,[50] for example, a claim was made for compensation for the total loss of the investor's investment in Sri Lanka. It was alleged that the loss resulted from a military operation by governmental forces against an insurgent group. The claim was made under the 1980 Sri Lanka–United Kingdom investment treaty. Article 4 required compensation or settlement on terms *no less favourable* than the host country accorded its own nationals for *losses suffered* from the specified events. The Tribunal interpreted the phrase 'losses suffered' as including 'all property destruction which materializes due to any type of hostilities enumerated in the text'.[51] According to the Tribunal, the mere fact that such losses existed was by itself sufficient to render the provision 'applicable, without any need to prove which side was responsible for said destruction, or to question whether the destruction was necessary or not'.[52] The investment treaty had no restriction on the scope of application of national treatment. The Tribunal interpreted 'no less favourable treatment' under the treaty to 'cover all possible cases in which the

[49] Ghana–United Kingdom Investment Treaty (n 25) art 5; and Kenya–Japan Investment Treaty (n 25) art 11(1).

[50] *Asian Agricultural Products Ltd v Sri Lanka*, ICSID Case No ARB/87/3, Final Award, 27 June 1990.

[51] ibid [65].

[52] ibid.

investments suffer losses owing to events identified as including 'a state of national emergency, revolt, insurrection, or riot'.[53]

The national treatment requirement in the earlier investment treaties does not specify the industry or subject matter in respect of which it may apply. The treaties also do not define phrases like 'losses suffered' and 'no less favourable treatment'. This can lead to a situation where any form of regulation in favour of the domestic industry being attacked by foreign investors if such favourable regulation is not extended to foreign investors who may feel disadvantaged.

The effect of national treatment is to require changes in existing laws and policies favouring domestic business entities or 'discriminating' against foreign investors.[54] It also has chilling effect on the adoption of prospective laws and policies that might be intended to address the specific situation of domestic businesses only (if there are foreign investors in like circumstances). Thus, national treatment in investment treaties is most significant:[55]

> because host state measures that discriminate in favour of domestic firms are often tied closely to national development goals and are politically very sensitive. Most host states have some programmes that grant advantages exclusively to domestic businesses in order to encourage their growth and their ability to compete with foreign investors.

The national treatment standard limits the discretion of states to implement policies and measures the way they deem fit for the benefit of citizens. The standard also places extra regulatory and resource burdens on states by expanding their roles towards citizens to include foreign investors engaged in the same or similar business or making like investments. By requiring the extension of treatment accorded to domestic businesses and investors to foreign investors and covered foreign investments, the national treatment standard allows foreign investors to take or enjoy the benefits of citizenship without having to formally acquire citizenship. This standard thus confers *de facto* citizenship on foreign investors contrary to formal requirements for the acquisition of citizenship under national legislation.

1.2.2.4 Most-Favoured-Nation Treatment

The MFN seeks to prevent discrimination between foreign investors from different countries operating in the same host state by demanding that foreign investment

[53] ibid [66].

[54] Salacuse, *Law of Investment Treaties* (n 19) 246.

[55] J Anthony VanDuzer, Penelope Simons, and Graham Mayeda, *Integrating Sustainable Development into International Investment Agreements: A Guide for Developing Countries* (Commonwealth Secretariat August 2012) 112 (hereafter, VanDuzer, Simons, and Mayeda, 'Integrating SSD into IIAs').

or investment returns of the applicable treaty partner shall be treated no less favourably than foreign investors and investments and returns of any third state.[56]

By the MFN provisions, a country that is not able to negotiate a desired standard of treatment with a treaty partner may gain the protection of that standard for its investors and their investments if the treaty partner grants that higher standard of protection to investors and investments of a third country in another investments treaty.[57] The obligation is established by reference to the host state's treatment of third state foreign investors and covered investments so that any new and more favourable treatment of third state foreign investors increases the level of treatment that the host state must provide to a contracting party's foreign investors and covered investments.[58] This standard, therefore, broadens the scope of the host state's obligations as to the volume of the measures and number of foreign investors and covered who or which may claim rights from the host state. The 'level of protection for foreign investors who benefit from an MFN provision may increase over time as the treatment of foreign investors from other countries improves'.[59]

By its very nature, this standard of investment protection can defeat the very purpose for which a state did not agree to a particular investment treaty term with a particular treaty partner. For example, country A entered into an investment treaty with country B and the treaty did not provide for the FET standard because A objected to its inclusion in the treaty and B agreed. However, A and C entered into an investment treaty which contains the FET standard. If A accords FET to the investors and investments from C, then by virtue of the MFN clause in A's investment treaty with B, A will be under obligation to extend FET to investors and investments from country B even though for some reason A had objected to the inclusion of the FET in its investment treaty with B.

1.2.2.5 Expropriation

Investment treaties also prohibit states from directly or indirectly expropriating investments or subjecting them to measures that have an effect equivalent to expropriation, except when this is done for a public purpose, under due process of law, and subject to the payment of compensation.[60] Some investment treaties extend this protection to domestic companies in which foreign investors have interests

[56] Cameroon–BLEU Investment Treaty (n 25) arts 3(3) and 5(3); Egypt–Canada Investment Treaty (n 25) art II(3)(b); Ghana–United Kingdom Investment Treaty (n 25) art 4(1); Kenya–Japan Investment Treaty (n 25) art 4; Nigeria–Germany Investment Treaty (n 25) art 4; and South Africa–China Investment Treaty (n 25) arts 3(2) and 5(1).

[57] Salacuse, *Law of Investment Treaties* (n 19).

[58] VanDuzer, Simons, and Mayeda, 'Integrating SSD into IIAs' (n 55) 127.

[59] ibid.

[60] Cameroon–BLEU Investment Treaty (n 25) art 4; Egypt–Canada Investment Treaty (n 25) art VIII; Ghana–United Kingdom Investment Treaty (n 25) art 7(1); Kenya–Japan Investment Treaty (n 25) art 10; Nigeria–Germany Investment Treaty (n 23) art 5(2); and South Africa–China Investment Treaty (n 25) art 4.

through ownership of shares.[61] The treaties do not specify the level of share ownership that must be met before this requirement will apply.

Expropriation has been interpreted very liberally to cover measures that directly or indirectly have a substantial adverse effect on the economic value of investment. A classic statement on the scope of expropriation is contained in *Telenor Mobile Communications AS v Hungary*:[62]

> Expropriation can take various forms. Direct expropriation involves the seizure of the investor's property. But expropriation may also be indirect, as where, without the taking of property, the measures of which complaint is made substantially deprive the investment of economic value. Moreover, it is not necessary to show a single act or group of acts committed at one time ... [T]here may be 'creeping' expropriation involving a series of acts over a period of time none of which is itself of sufficient gravity to constitute an expropriatory act but all of which taken together produce the effects of expropriation. Phrases such as 'equivalent to expropriation' and 'tantamount to expropriation' ... are usually taken to indicate that the BIT covers indirect as well as direct expropriation, thus looking at the substance of the measures in question rather than the label attached to them by government, and the same is true of 'measures having a similar effect.'

The Tribunal in *Santa Elena v Costa Rica* stated that:[63]

> there is a wide spectrum of measures that a state may take in asserting control over property, extending from limited regulation of its use to a complete and formal deprivation of the owner's legal title. Likewise, the period of time involved in the process may vary—from an immediate and comprehensive taking to one that only gradually and by small steps reaches a condition in which it can be said that the owner has truly lost all the attributes of ownership ... There is ample authority for the proposition that a property has been expropriated when the effect of the measures taken by the state has been to deprive the owner of title, possession or access to the benefit and economic use of his property.

The scope of expropriation depends on the specific wording of the provisions and any interpretive annex. The key elements of expropriation include the permanence of an interference with investment and the impact of a measure on investment.[64] The expropriation standard illustrates the desire of the investment

[61] Ghana–United Kingdom Investment Treaty (n 25) art 7(3); Ghana–Netherlands Investment Treaty (n 25) art 6(1)(a).

[62] *Telenor Mobile Communications AS v Hungary*, ICSID Case No ARB/04/15, Award, 13 September 2006 [63].

[63] *Compañía Del Desarrollo De Santa Elena, SA v Costa Rica*, Case No ARB/96/1, Final Award, 17 February 2000 [76].

[64] Jane Kelsey, 'How the Trans-Pacific Partnership Agreement Could Heighten Financial Instability and Foreclose Governments' Regulatory Autonomy' (2010) 8 New Zealand Yearbook of International Law 41 57.

treaty regime to protect foreign investment against regulation that may adversely affect the value of investment. The effect of expropriation on regulatory autonomy has led to a more qualified wording of recent model investment treaties.[65]

1.2.2.6 Repatriation and Transfer of Investment and Returns

Provisions on the repatriation of investment and returns, or transfer which is broader in scope, guarantee foreign investors the right to transfer their investments and returns to the country where they reside or their home countries or to another country. Typically, transfers are permitted in respect of profits, dividends, interests, technical assistance and technical fees, proceeds from the total or partial liquidation of any investment, and funds in repayment of borrowings and loans. They also include the net earnings and other compensation of investors and foreign persons who are employed and allowed to work in connection with an investment. Further, transfers must be allowed in respect of royalties and funds necessary for the acquisition of raw or auxiliary materials or to replace capital assets in order to safeguard the continuity of an investment.

Transfers of currency must be made in the convertible currency in which the investment has been made or in any currency agreed by the investor, and at the official rate of exchange at the date of transfer. Transfers are to be permitted without unreasonable or undue delay. While some of the investment treaties permit unrestricted right to transfer investment and returns, others guarantee the right of transfer subject to conditions that may be imposed by municipal laws, regulations, and policies.[66] Recent model investment treaties permit state parties to prevent a transfer provided that the prevention is done equitably, is non-discriminatory, and in good faith.[67]

1.2.2.7 The Settlement of Investment Disputes

Beyond the foregoing substantive standards of investment protection, investment treaties also provide for the settlement of investor–state disputes related to covered investments.[68] If an investor's complaint cannot be resolved through mutual

[65] SADC Model Bilateral Investment Treaty Template with Commentary (Southern African Development Community, July 2012) <https://www.iisd.org/itn/wp-content/uploads/2012/10/sadc-model-bit-template-final.pdf> accessed 28 December 2020; and 2012 US Model Bilateral Investment Treaty, art 6(5), <http://www.ustr.gov/sites/default/files/BIT%20text%20for%20ACIEP%20Meeting.pdf> accessed 28 December 2020.

[66] Cameroon–BLEU Investment Treaty (n 25) art 5; Egypt–Canada Investment Treaty (n 25) arts VIII(1) and IX; Ghana–United Kingdom Investment Treaty (n 25) art 8; Kenya–Japan Investment Treaty (n 25) art 13; Nigeria–Germany Investment Treaty (n 25) arts 5(2) and 6; and South Africa–China Investment Treaty (n 25) art 6.

[67] Ghana Model BIT 2008, art 7(6), https://investmentpolicy.unctad.org/international-investment-agreements/treaty-files/2866/download (accessed 28 December 2020); and 2012 US Model Bilateral Investment Treaty (n 65) art 7(4).

[68] Ghana–United Kingdom Investment Treaty (n 25) art 10; Kenya–Japan Investment Treaty (n 25) art 14; Nigeria–Germany Investment Treaty (n 25) arts 10 and 11; South Africa–China Investment Treaty (n 25) arts 9 and 10.

discussion with the state within a specified period, it has to go to international arbitration. The available arbitral forums are usually specified in the treaty. The most common are the International Centre for Settlement of Investment Disputes (ICSID)[69] and *ad hoc* arbitration tribunals appointed under either the Arbitration Rules of the United Nations Commission on International Trade Law[70] (UNCITRAL) or the Arbitration Institute of the Stockholm Chamber of Commerce.[71] The Agreement Establishing the African Continental Free Trade Area prefers state-to-state dispute settlement.[72]

An investor–state dispute is any dispute between a contracting state and a national of the other contracting state 'concerning an obligation ... in relation to an investment'.[73] The jurisdiction of investment tribunals is limited to disputes concerning alleged breaches of the standards of investment protection and, where applicable, an umbrella clause which requires states to observe any other agreements that they may have entered into with investors. The tribunals are, therefore, required to apply the treaties and not to determine their validity.

Investment tribunals must resolve disputes *within* their mandates, which means they should interpret investment treaties and apply relevant principles of CIL in a manner that leads to a fair, equitable, and even-handed resolution of investor–state disputes. Disputes between contracting parties concerning the validity of treaties can be resolved only by domestic courts, state-to-state dispute investment tribunals established for that purpose, or the International Court of Justice (ICJ), as the case may be.[74] Investment treaties provide that state-to-state disputes between contracting parties are limited to those related to the *interpretation* or *application* of the treaties and are to be settled through diplomatic channels, failing which they can be settled by an arbitral tribunal specifically established to handle state-to-state disputes.[75] It can be argued then that an issue concerning the validity of an investment treaty can be settled through state-to-state dispute mechanisms including an arbitral tribunal the contracting parties may establish specifically for that purpose.

[69] See *Convention on the Settlement of Investment Disputes between States and Nationals of Other States*, 18 March 1965, 4 ILM 524 (entered into force 14 October 1966).

[70] See UNCITRAL Arbitration Rules (GA Res 65/22), (United Nations, 2010) entered into force on 1 January 2010.

[71] ibid.

[72] Decision (Assembly/AU/Dec.394 (XVIII)) on the Establishment of a Continental Free Trade Area.

[73] Cameroon–BLEU Investment Treaty (n 25) art 10; Egypt–Canada Investment Treaty (n 25) art XIII; Ghana–Malaysia Investment Treaty art 7(1); Agreement between the Kingdom of Denmark and the Government of the Republic of Ghana Concerning the Promotion and Protection of Investments, signed 13 January 1992, entered into force 6 January 1995 art 10(1); Ghana–Netherlands Investment Treaty (n 25) art 9(1); and Ghana–United Kingdom Investment Treaty (n 25) art 10(1).

[74] Alfred von Verdross, 'Forbidden Treaties in International Law: Comments on Professor Garner's Report on "The Law of Treaties"' (1937) 31 American Journal of International Law 571 (hereafter, Verdross, 'Forbidden Treaties').

[75] Ghana–United Kingdom Investment Treaty (n 25) art 11; Kenya–Japan Investment Treaty (n 25) art 14; Nigeria–Germany Investment Treaty (n 25) art 10; and South Africa–China Investment Treaty (n 25) art 8.

The primary purpose of the substantive standards of investment protection, supplemented by investor–state dispute settlement, is to ensure that governmental regulation and action accommodate the interests of foreign investors and covered investments by restricting governmental regulation and action that will adversely affect the value of investments. These investor protections and enforcement powers in investment treaties turn to conflict with states' public interest obligations.

1.3 Africa and Investment Treaty Arbitration

1.3.1 Investor–State Arbitration and the Right to Regulate: Global Context

As can be seen from Section 1.2, investment treaties are generally premised on two related rationales. The first conventional supposition is that foreign investment leads to development and that investment treaties are necessary to protect and thereby attract foreign investment.[76] The text of the first investment treaty, reached between Germany and Pakistan in 1959, was premised on the states' conviction that it was likely to promote investment, encourage private industrial and financial enterprises, and increase the prosperity of both states.[77] The Convention on the Settlement of Investment Disputes between States and Nationals of Other States of 1966 (ICSID Convention) was founded on the idea that there was a need for international cooperation and private international investment for the attainment of economic development.[78] According to Kofi Annan, former United Nations Secretary-General, foreign investment 'is a vital factor in the long-term economic development'[79] of developing countries because it has the potential to create jobs, raise productivity, enhance exports, and transfer technology. Annan also states that foreign investment offers an additional avenue for developing countries to link up to global markets and production systems. These investments, if managed properly, could help firms to access markets, natural resources, foreign capital, technology, or various intangible assets that are essential to their competitiveness.[80]

Investment treaties, it is claimed, can attract foreign investment by establishing the standards of investment protection analysed in Subsection 1.2.2. To ensure that these standards are 'effectively' enforced, investment treaties make provision for

[76] Sornarajah, *Law on Foreign Investment* (n 8).

[77] Pakistan and Federal Republic of Germany Treaty for the Promotion and Protection of Investments, signed at Bonn, on 25 November 1959, preamble.

[78] *Convention on the Settlement of Investment Disputes between States and Nationals of Other States*, 18 March 1965, 4 ILM 524 (entered into force 14 October 1966), preamble [1].

[79] Kofi Annan, 'Foreword' in UNCTAD, *World Investment Report 2003. FDI Policies for Development: National and International Perspectives* (United Nations 2003) iii.

[80] ibid.

investment arbitration which is used to settle disputes between states and foreign investors. In 1965, the Executive Directors of the World Bank stated that:[81]

> [t]he creation of an institution designed to facilitate the settlement of disputes between States and foreign investors can be a major step toward promoting an atmosphere of mutual confidence and thus stimulating a larger flow of private international capital into those countries which wish to attract it.

Sornarajah states that the internationalisation of investment protection by concession agreements, joint ventures, production sharing agreements, management and service contracts, and investment treaties have all been influenced by the neoliberal idea that foreign investment leads to development.[82] Today, investment treaties have become the dominant international legal mechanisms for the protection of investment.[83]

The growth in the number of investment treaties shows how dominant this perception has become. For example, in 2007 Ghana and the European Union (EU) entered into a Stepping Stone Economic Partnership Agreement[84] and in February 2014 sixteen West African states concluded 'negotiations' with the EU for an Economic Partnership Agreement (EPA) to promote trade between the two regions. The Heads of State of the Economic Community of West African States endorsed the EPA at a summit in Accra, Ghana, in July 2014.[85] As at 2 February 2022, Ghana had twenty-eight investment treaties, nine of which were in force and one terminated. Most of Ghana's investment treaties in force including with China,[86] Denmark,[87] Malaysia,[88] Netherlands,[89] and United Kingdom,[90] are in

[81] *Report of the Executive Directors on the Convention on the Settlement of Investment Disputes between States and Nationals of Other States* [9] <https://oxford.universitypressscholarship.com/view/10.1093/acprof:oso/9780199660568.001.0001/acprof-9780199660568-appendix-5> accessed 28 December 2020.

[82] Muthucumaraswamy Sornarajah, *The Pursuit of Nationalized Property* (Martinus Publishers 1986) 42 (hereafter, Sornarajah, *Nationalized Property*).

[83] Andrew Guzman, 'Why LDCs Sign Treaties That Hurt Them: Explaining the Popularity of Bilateral Investment Treaties' (1997) 38 Virginia Journal of International Law 639, 640.

[84] European Commission, *Economic Partnership Agreement (EPA) Ghana—European Union: A New Partnership for Trade and Development* (April 2014).

[85] Authority of ECOWA Heads of State and Government, Forty-Fifth Ordinary Session of the Authority of ECOWA Heads of State and Government: Final Communique (Done at Accra, 10 July 2014) [15]–[17 <https://www.ecowas.int/wp-content/uploads/2015/02/45th-ECOWAS-Summit-Ghana-10-Dec-20141.pdf> accessed 22 December 2021. See also Dagbanja, 'Africa' (n 23) 356–57.

[86] Agreement between the People's Republic of China and the Government of the Republic of Ghana Concerning the Encouragement and Reciprocal Protection of Investments (signed 12 October 1989, entered into force on 22 November 1991).

[87] Agreement between the Kingdom of Denmark and the Government of the Republic of Ghana Concerning the Promotion and Protection of Investments (signed 13 January 1992, entered into force 6 January 1995).

[88] Agreement between the Government of the Republic of Ghana and the Government of Malaysia for the Promotion and Protection of Investments (signed on 8 November 1996, entered into force 18 April 1997).

[89] Agreement on Encouragement and Reciprocal Protection of Investments between the Kingdom of the Netherlands and the Republic of Ghana (signed 31 March 1989, entered into force 1 July 1991).

[90] Ghana–United Kingdom Investment Treaty (n 25).

English.[91] Of the other countries involved in this study, as at 2 February 2022, Cameroon had eighteen BITs, eleven of which were in force; Egypt had 115 BITs, seventy-two of which were in force and fourteen terminated; Kenya had twenty BITs, eleven of which were in force and one terminated; Nigeria had thirty-one BITs, fifteen of which were in force and one terminated; and South African had fifty BITs, twelve of which were in force and twelve terminated. These countries are also parties to African regional investment treaties.

The preambles to these treaties suggest they were intended to create favourable conditions to attract foreign investors and investments to bring about increased economic prosperity and development, to stimulate productive use of resources, and to strengthen cooperation between each of the African states and its contracting parties. These conventional views are seriously suspect. Studies show that other reasons drive foreign investment.[92] Further, the claims fail to acknowledge that the decision to enter into a treaty may be influenced by factors, such as the unequal power of the states involved. Most important for this book, the views do not address the negatives associated with the protection of foreign investment by treaties, such as their restraint on the right to regulate in the public interest.[93]

The second argument is that host states' judicial systems cannot provide adequate protection for foreign investors. It had been argued that local bias is a serious barrier to obtaining redress in some host-country courts. International arbitration was, therefore, meant to serve as an insurance against local prejudice.[94] Efficiency of local courts was identified as another of the many concerns of foreign investors, because 'developing countries' supposedly 'lack responsive, robust legal systems capable of effectively adjudicating complex claims'.[95] Such a claim is ethnocentric in the sense that the proponents of the view are judging the judiciary in the 'developing' world by standards of the 'developed' world. The claim is also overgeneralised because it does not speak to the reality of how the judiciary functions in each developing country.

The United Nations Conference on Trade and Development (UNCTAD) points out that investor–state arbitration has become 'the most controversial issue in international investment policymaking'.[96] States and policy-makers are mainly concerned about the range of policy issues, the volume of cases being initiated against them and the amount of damages. At the end of 2018, about 60 per cent of decisions on the investor–state dispute settlement (ISDS) decisions on the merits were decided in favour of the investor and the rest of the 40 per cent either settled

[91] United States Department of State, *Investment Climate Statement—Ghana* (June 2012).

[92] Karl Sauvant and Lisa Sachs (eds), *The Effect of Treaties on Foreign Direct Investment: Bilateral Investment Treaties, Double Taxation Treaties, and Investment Inflows* (OUP 2009).

[93] Sornarajah, *Nationalized Property* (n 82) 45–47 and 88–90.

[94] Christopher Dugan and others, *Investor–State Arbitration* (OUP 2008) 13.

[95] ibid 15.

[96] UNCTAD, *World Investment Report 2014: Investing in SDGs: An Action Plan* (United Nations 2014), 126.

or decided in favour of the state.[97] As of January 2021, the total number of publicly known ISDS claims (from 1987) reached 1,104 with 124 countries as respondents to one or more ISDS claims. By the end of 2020, at least 740 ISDS proceedings had been concluded.[98]

There is a long list of policy and regulatory measures which may be considered essential for development and the protection of the environment and human rights which have been challenged under investment treaties. They include: regulating ownership in joint ventures in the interest of local populations;[99] abolition or modification of tariffs set in contracts for utilities;[100] regulation of management structures of business entities in which foreign investors have interest;[101] revocation of banking licenses;[102] the exercise of regulatory and administrative authority;[103] revocation of free trade zone certificates or licenses;[104] enactment[105] and amendment[106] of legislation that affects investment; restrictions on free transfer of funds;[107] requisition of concessionaires and the revocation of concession contracts;[108] the imposition of tax on investment operations;[109] denial of duty exemptions;[110] refusal to grant or revocation of licenses and permits;[111] re-zoning land;[112] the termination of service agreements and modification of a contractual relationship;[113] suspending work for lack of a permit;[114] and granting other businesses

[97] UNCTAD, Fact Sheet on Investor–State Dispute Settlement Cases in 2018 (IIA Issues No 2, May 2019) 4.

[98] UNCTAD, *World Investment Report 2021* (n 22) 121 and 130; and UNCTAD, *Investor–State Dispute Settlement Cases: Facts and Figures 2020* (IIA Issues Note 4, United Nations, September 2021) 1. See also UNCTAD, *World Investment Report 2020* (n 22) 110.

[99] *Tradex Hellas SA v Albania*, ICSID Case No ARB/94/2, Award, 29 April 1999.

[100] *Compañía de Aguas del Aconquija SA v Argentina*, ICSID Case No ARB/97/3, Award, 20 August 2007; and *BG Group Plc v Argentina*, UNCITRAL, Final Award, 24 December 2007.

[101] *Wena Hotels Limited v Arab Republic of Egypt*, ICSID Case No ARB/98/4, Award, 8 December 2000.

[102] *Genin v Republic of Estonia*, ICSID Case No ARB/99/2, Award, 25 June 2001.

[103] *PSEG Global Inc v Turkey*, ICSID Case No ARB/02/5, Award, 19 January 2007; and *Siemens v Argentina*, ICSID Case No ARB/02/8, Award, 6 February 2007.

[104] *Goetz v Burundi*, ICSID Case No ARB/95/3, Award on Liability and Amicable Settlement 10 February 1999; and *Middle East Cement Shipping and Handling Co SA v Egypt*, ICSID Case No ARB/99/6, Award, 12 April 2002.

[105] *ADC Affiliate Limited v Hungary*, CSID Case No ARB/03/16, Award, 2 October 2006; and *Wintershall Aktiengesellschaft v Argentina*, ICSID Case No ARB/04/14, Award, 8 December 2008.

[106] *Archer Daniels Midland Company v United Mexican States*, ICSID Case No ARB(AF)/04/5, Award, 21 November 2007; and *BG Group Plc v The Republic of Argentina*, UNCITRAL, Final Award, 24 December 2007.

[107] *Joy Mining Machinery Limited v Egypt*, ICISD Case No ARB/03/11, 6 August 2004.

[108] *Gemplus v United Mexican States*, ICSID Case Nos ARB(AF)/04/3 and ARB(AF)/04/, Award, 16 June 2010.

[109] *Cargill, Incorporated v United Mexican States*, ICSID Case No ARB(AF)/05/2, Award, 18 September 2009; and *Feldman v Mexico*, ICSID Case No ARB (AF)/99/1, Award, 16 December 2002.

[110] *Duke Energy Electroquil Partners v Ecuador*, ICSID Case No ARB/04/19, Award, 18 August 2008.

[111] *RSM Production Corporation v Grenada*, ICSID Case No ARB/10/6, Award, 10 December 2010.

[112] *MTD Equity Sdn v Chile*, ICSID Case No ARB/01/7, Award, 25 May 2004.

[113] *CME Czech Republic BV (the Netherlands) v Czech*, Partial Award, 13 September 2001.

[114] *Biloune v Ghana Investments Centre and the Government of Ghana*, Award on Jurisdiction and Liability, 29 October 1989.

opportunities in an area related to foreign investor's area of operation without granting the same to foreign investors and covered investments.[115]

These measures have applied to diverse areas where governments have public interest responsibilities including agricultural activities;[116] tourism, hospitality, housing and real estate development;[117] banking, financial services, and securities;[118] the utilities and energy sector;[119] minerals and mining;[120] highways and air transport;[121] national identification cards;[122] media and broadcasting services;[123] wood and wood production;[124] insurance;[125] and waste management and sanitation services.[126]

Crippling monetary awards, legal costs, and compound interest that flow from the cases can have devastating impacts on development. The highest known monetary award in the history of investor–state dispute settlement was made in *Yukos Universal Limited v Russia*[127] where Russia was found to be liable to pay unprecedented damages for seizing and transferring Yukos assets and interfering with the management of the company. Russia was also ordered to bear the costs of the jurisdiction and merit phases of the arbitration which amounted to EUR8.44 million.[128] The costs for legal representation and assistance of the investor amounted to USD79.63 million and Russia was ordered to pay USD60 million of these costs to the investor.[129] In total, Russia was ordered to pay USD50 billion to cover the damages, costs of arbitration, and the investor's costs for legal representation. Russia puts it its own legal costs at USD27 million.[130] This award is a major burden for Russia; it would be unbearable for any African country.

Other massive awards have been made against very poor countries. The second highest known monetary award was made in *Occidental Petroleum Corporation and Occidental Exploration and Production Company v Ecuador*,[131] involving an amount of USD1.77 billion for termination of a concession contract. The third,

[115] *Waste Management v Mexico*, Case No ARB(AF)/00/3, Award, 30 April 2004.
[116] *Gustav F W Hamester GmbH & Co KG v Ghana*, ICSID Case No ARB/07/24, Award, 10 June 2010.
[117] *Wena Hotel v Egypt* (n 101).
[118] *Joy Mining v Egypt* (n 107).
[119] *Duke Energy v Ecuador* (n 110).
[120] *Goetz v Burundi* (n 104).
[121] *ADC Affiliate Limited v Hungary* (n 105).
[122] *Biloune v Ghana* (n 114).
[123] *CME v Czech* (n 113).
[124] *Pope & Talbot Inc v Canada*, UNCITRAL, Award on Merits, 10 April 2001.
[125] *Continental Casualty Company v Argentina*, ICSID Case No ARB/03/9, Award, 5 September 2008.
[126] *Jan de Nul NV Dredging International NV v Egypt*, ICSID Case No ARB/04/13, Award, 6 November 2008.
[127] *Yukos Universal Limited v Russia*, PCA Case No AA 227, Final Award, 18 July 2014.
[128] ibid [1866] and [1869].
[129] ibid [1887].
[130] ibid [1874].
[131] *Occidental Petroleum Corporation and Occidental Exploration and Production Company v. Ecuador*, ICSID Case No ARB/06/11, Award, 5 October 2012.

awarded in *Abdulmohsen Al-Kharafi & Sons Co v Libya*[132] for cancellation of a land-lease for development of a resort, amounted to USD935 million plus interest.

The range of issues that foreign investors have challenged and the amount of compensation involved which has to be paid out of public funds support the proposition that claims for breach of investor protections involves elements of the public interest. Foreign investment may be directly connected to environmental and human rights issues. The challenge of investment protection by treaty and arbitration to regulatory autonomy has raised legitimate concerns among advocacy groups, academic commentators, and governments about the extent to which the investment treaty regime prioritises investment protection over the right of states to regulate in the public interest. Therefore, there is a reason for each state that is party to this treaty-based investment protection regime to be concerned about the regime's limitations on its autonomy to regulate in the public interest.

1.3.2 Investor–State Arbitration and the Right to Regulate in Africa

1.3.2.1 Ghana and Arbitration

A number of known investor–state cases involving African countries illustrate the nature of the limitations of investment treaties and other international agreements on regulatory autonomy in Africa. The most direct confrontation with African states' powers and responsibilities under their constitutions involved the cases of *Balkan Energy Limited (Ghana) v Ghana*,[133] *Bankswitch Ghana Ltd (Ghana) v Ghana*,[134] and *Waterville Holdings (BVI) Limited v Ghana*.[135]

Balkan Energy v Ghana concerned a foreign investor's claim of the state's breach of a power purchase agreement (PPA) for the refurbishment and commissioning of fired (diesel and gas) barge and associated facilities. *Bankswitch v Ghana* concerned an agreement for an investor to provide a secure document management system for the government of Ghana. *Waterville v Ghana* was about contracts for the construction of stadia in Ghana. These disputes involved international agreements that provided for the settlement of disputes by arbitration, so they are relevant to investment treaty arbitration.

In *Balkan Energy v Ghana* the state argued that the PPA was not valid because it had not received parliamentary approval in accordance with Article 181(5) of the

[132] *Abdulmohsen Al-Kharafi & Sons Co v Libya*, Final Arbitral Award, 22 March 2013.

[133] *Balkan Energy Limited (Ghana) v Ghana*, UNCITRAL, PCA Case No 2010-7, Interim Award, 22 December 2010; and *Balkan Energy Limited (Ghana) v Ghana*, UNCITRAL, PCA Case No 2010-7, Award on the Merits, 1 April 2014.

[134] *Bankswitch Ghana Ltd (Ghana) v Ghana*, PCA Case No 118294, UNCITRAL, Award Save as to Costs, 11 April 2014.

[135] *Waterville Holdings (BVI) Limited v The Republic of Ghana*, ICC Arbitration Case No 205.61/TO, Partial Award on Jurisdiction, 20 March 2017.

Constitution of the Republic of Ghana 1992, which requires an 'international business or economic transaction' to be approved by Parliament. A similar issue arose in *Bankswitch v Ghana* and *Waterville v Ghana*, namely whether the agreements between the state and the companies constituted an international business or economic transaction and had to be approved by Parliament.

The interpretation of the Supreme Court of Ghana of the meaning of an 'international business or economic transaction' under Article 181 of the Constitution of Ghana was disregarded by both investment tribunals, even though they found the Court's approach was one possible way of interpreting the provision. The tribunal adopted their own interpretations and by doing so not only usurped the judicial powers of the Supreme Court under the Constitution but also sought to render the Court's decisions otiose. These three cases are analysed fully in Chapter 3.

Previous known disputes had mixed outcomes. In 1996, Telekom Malaysia Berhad (TMB), a Malaysian telecommunication company, invested USD38 million in Ghana Telecommunications Company Limited (GTCL) and acquired 30 per cent of shares, and control over and management GTCL. In 2001, a dispute arose between the parties as to TMB's interest in GTCL and TMB initiated arbitration proceedings for purported breaches by Ghana of its BIT with Malaysia. The investor claimed damages for expropriation of its investment in GTCL. The case was settled on terms that are not public.

In *Biloune v Ghana*,[136] the state was found liable for expropriation for terminating an agreement with a Syrian national for the construction of a hotel resort complex in Accra. The state claimed the investor had not procured a construction permit. Damages were awarded against Ghana in the following terms: payment to Biloune of USD334,637, GBP61,811, and DM430; payment of USD100,000 to counsel for the investor; and payment of arbitration costs and fees of USD84,781.

In *Vacuum Salt Products Ltd v Ghana*,[137] the claimant was incorporated in Ghana under the Companies Act 1963 (Act 179). Twenty per cent of the shares in the company were held by a Greek national. The company entered into a thirty-year lease agreement with the government in 1988 for salt production and mining in Ada-Songor Lagoon. The company instituted arbitration proceedings against the government alleging it 'suffered both a breach and progressive expropriation of its contractual rights' to produce the salt when the government continuously breached and subsequently terminated the lease agreement.[138] The government objected to the jurisdiction of the Tribunal on the ground that the company was a national of Ghana and not of Greece. In 1994, the Tribunal upheld Ghana's submission and dismissed the claim for want of jurisdiction. The Tribunal decided each

[136] *Biloune v Ghana* (n 114). For an analysis of this case see: Emmanuel Laryea and Oladapo Fabusuyi, 'African Countries and International Investment Law: Right to Regulate or Appropriate Regulation or Both?' (2019) 40(2) Australasian Review of African Studies 27.

[137] *Vacuum Salt Products Ltd v Ghana*, ICSID Case No ARB/92/1, Award, 16 February 1994.

[138] ibid [2].

party was to bear its own expenses in connection with the proceedings and the fees and expenses of the arbitration were to be borne in equal shares.

Gustav FW Hamester GmbH & Co KG v Ghana[139] concerned a dispute submitted to ICSID based on an investment treaty between Germany and Ghana and a Joint Venture Agreement (JVA) between a German investor and Ghana Cocoa Board. The dispute related to this joint facility for processing of cocoa beans, shea nuts and related products. The investor claimed damages for alleged breaches by Ghana of the fair and equitable treatment, full protection and security, and national treatment standards. The investor claimed the state had imposed a ban on the export of the company's products and a price agreement on the company and had usurped the management of the company in which it had made the investment.[140] The Tribunal held that Ghana Cocoa Board was a separate legal entity whose acts could not be attributed to the State. The Tribunal also held that acts such as police investigation and the export ban which were attributable to Ghana did not violate the BIT. Each party had to pay arbitration costs of USD305,000 and its own legal and other costs expended in connection with this arbitration.[141]

In December 1996, the government of Ghana and Construction Pioneers (CP) entered into an agreement by which CP was to construct and rehabilitate some roads in southern Ghana. The agreement provided that the parties would submit disputes between them to arbitration before the International Chamber of Commerce (ICC). The law of Ghana was the governing law and Accra in Ghana was the venue for arbitration proceedings. In 2001, a new government took power in Ghana. The new government began an investigation into alleged fraud surrounding the previous government's dealings with CP. The government later that year suspended payments to CP based on the alleged fraud. This action resulted in CP initiating arbitration proceeding, *CP Construction Pioneers Baugesellschaft Anstalt v The Government of the Republic of Ghana*, in March 2002 with the ICC Arbitral Tribunal against the government seeking payment under the contract. The government objected to the jurisdiction of the Tribunal relying on section 27(2) of the repealed Arbitration Act 1961 of Ghana. According to that provision, where a difference gave rise to a dispute between the parties involved the issue whether one of the parties was guilty of fraud, a court had powers to declare the agreement to arbitrate void and to give leave to revoke the authority of any arbitrator appointed based on of the agreement. While the jurisdictional issue was pending, in April 2003 the government submitted an application to the High Court to revoke the authority of the Tribunal. Both parties appeared in a hearing before the High Court on the matter.

139 *Gustav FW Hamester GmbH & Co KG v Ghana*, ICSID Case No ARB/07/24), Award 18 June 2010 [1]
140 ibid [70]–[74].
141 ibid [361].

The High Court ordered that the agreement to arbitrate had no effect and granted leave to the government to revoke the authority of the arbitrator. In May 2003, the government informed the Tribunal that there were no further proceedings pending before it. The Tribunal nevertheless went ahead and issued a partial award to the effect that it had jurisdiction, reasoning that the decision of the High Court was arbitrary. Then in August 2004, the Tribunal issued a partial final award of approximately EUR24 million and GHC22 billion (Ghanaian currency) in favour of CP. The government later submitted an application to the High Court to set aside this partial award. While this case was pending, CP filed a petition in the US District Court for the District of Columbia to confirm the partial award against the Government. That case was adjourned under Article VI of the Convention on the Recognition and Enforcement of Foreign Arbitral Awards of 1959. The US court reasoned that adjournments pending the completion of set-aside proceedings were an integral part of such proceedings and that since the case involved Ghana law the issue could more properly be decided by a court in Ghana.[142]

A Commission of Inquiry established in 2012 by the government of President John Mahama to inquire into payments made from public funds arising from judgment debts, arbitration awards, and negotiated settlements. The Commission found that as at October 2002, the total outstanding claim by CP against the Government arising out of the arbitration awards had reached DM55,092,545 and GHC2,747,166, a total equivalent of EUR27,547,272. This was in addition to an amount of DM117 million which the government had to pay to CP as an out-of-arbitration settlement in respect of a different dispute involving Accra City Roads Project. The Commission found that the government, because of the suspicion of either fraud or corruption or both, refused to settle the amount made in favour of CP until it lost power in 2009. By that time the liability of the state had grown to EUR162,609,600.89 and was accruing interest at the rate of EUR12,787 a day. The Attorney-General negotiated for a settlement of the amount down to EUR94 million. Payment of two final instalments on this amount was suspended in 2012 because the Parliamentary Public Accounts Committee was undertaking hearings on payments made out of the public accounts. The non-payment of these instalments also became a subject of arbitration in which CP claimed the outstanding amount and interest thereon.[143] As the government itself has noted, 'there is a limit to how much the Government can pay' and these 'judgments against the State are invariably judgments against the Ghanaian taxpayer'.[144]

[142] As contained in *Construction Pioneers v Government of the Republic of Ghana*, Civil Act No 1:04-01564 (LFO), <https://jenner.com/system/assets/assets/4919/original/CPC_20v_20Ghana_20Aug_2012_20decision.pdf?1320332149> accessed 28 December 2020.

[143] *White Paper on the Report of The Commission of Inquiry into Payments from Public Funds Arising from Judgment Debts & Akin Matters (C.I. 79/2012)* 35–36 <https://media.peacefmonline.com/docs/201511/46495893_35731.pdf> accessed 28 December 2020.

[144] ibid 46. There are other cases brought against Ghana which space will not allow analysing. In *West Africa Gas Limited (BVI) v The Government of The Republic of Ghana*, LCIA Arbitration No 194422, Final Award, 15 January 2021 which involved a claim for recovery fees upon the termination of a gas

1.3.2.2 The Democratic Republic of Congo, Burundi, Algeria and Arbitration

American Manufacturing & Trading, Inc v Republic of Zaire was instituted by an American company incorporated in Delaware against Zaire (now Democratic Republic of Congo) under United States–Zaire BIT.[145] American Manufacturing & Trading, Inc (AMTC) held 94 per cent stocks in a subsidiary company based in Zaire, Industrielle Zairoise Societe, a private limited liability company. This company produced and sold automotive and dry cell batteries and imported and resold consumer goods and foodstuffs. The AMTC alleged that in September 1991 and January 1993, the armed forces of Zaire caused destruction to the properties and installations of Industrielle Zairoise Societe. It was alleged that the armed forces destroyed and took away property of the subsidiary company. It claimed it sustained losses because of the destruction and looting by the army. The AMTC said Zaire failed to fulfil its obligations of protection under Articles II of the United States–Zaire BIT and asked for damages and compensation cover the losses sustained.

Article II of the BIT guaranteed the right to enjoy protection and security no less than recognised by international law. The Tribunal interpreted the FPS as an obligation of vigilance, meaning the contracting parties had an obligation to take all measures necessary to ensure the full enjoyment of protection and security of investments and could not invoke domestic law to detract from this obligation. This meant that Zaire had an obligation to show that it had taken all measures of precaution to protect the investments.[146] The Tribunal interpreted the obligation of protection and security no less than accorded under international law as requiring the 'minimum standard of vigilance and of care required by international law'.[147] The Tribunal came to the conclusion that Zaire breached this standard because it failed to take any measure whatsoever to ensure the protection and security of the investment in the face of disastrous consequences arising from the actions of the militia. The company was awarded USD9 million. Similarly, in *Mitchell v Congo*[148] which was founded on the same BIT, Congo was founded to have breached the

sales agreement, USD68,584,623.37 was awarded against Ghana with simple interest at annual rate of 6.5 per cent on the sum awarded dating back to 22 April 2019 until payment. However, in *Dunkwa Continental Goldfields Limited (Ghana) v The Government of the Republic of Ghana*, ICC Case No 18294/ARP/MD/TO, Final Award, 30 July 2015, the Government of Ghana was successful in the claim against it.

[145] Agreement between the United States of America and the Republic of Zaire concerning the Encouragement and Reciprocal Protection of Investments signed 3 August 1984, entered into force on 28 July 1989.

[146] *American Manufacturing & Trading Inc v Republic of Zaire*, ICSID Case No ARB/93/1, Award, 21 February 1997, [6.05].

[147] ibid [6.06].

[148] *Patrick Mitchell v Democratic Republic of the Congo*, ICSID Case No ARB/99/7, Award, 9 February 2009.

expropriation standard for the military's seizure of the premises of Mitchell's legal consulting firm and documents.

The *Orascom TMT Investments Sàrl v Algeria*[149] case was brought under Algeria–Belgo–Luxembourg Economic Union BIT,[150] alleging interference and harassment by the Algerian government against a local telecommunications company in which the investor made investments. The acts alleged to constitute interference and harassment were tax reassessments and an attempt to sell of part of the local company. The claim was dismissed as inadmissible.[151] The investor was asked to reimburse Algeria the costs of the arbitration and to pay USD2,842,811.01 plus EUR58,382.16 to Algeria as a contribution to the legal fees and other expenses which Algeria had incurred in connection with the arbitration.

Algeria has also been a party to an investor–state claim under the Algeria–Denmark BIT[152] which arose out of the imposition of a windfall tax collected by an Algerian national oil company. This was alleged to contravene a production sharing agreement concluded between the investor and the national oil company. The case was settled.[153] Algeria has been challenged under Algeria–Egypt BIT for a court judgment against an investor, which imposed a fine of approximately USD1.3 billion and a criminal sentence on a senior executive.[154] This claim was settled before the decision on liability. In *Consorzio Groupement LESI-DIPENTA v Algeria*,[155] the investor alleged breach of indirect expropriation, FPS, and guarantees against unreasonable and discriminatory measures provisions under the Algeria–Italy BIT for alleged prolonged stoppage of work and cancellation of a contract for the construction of a dam. The Tribunal declined jurisdiction noting that following the signing of the contract, the investor had entered into a consortium resulting in a situation where the parties that signed the contract were not identical to the party that submitted the request for arbitration.[156]

Houben v Burundi[157] concerned an alleged *de facto* expropriation of land. The case was that Burundian government allowed occupation of Houben's property but

[149] *Orascom TMT Investments Sàrl v People's Democratic Republic of Algeria*, ICSID Case No ARB/12/35, Award, 31 May 2017.

[150] Belgo–Luxembourg Economic Union and the People's Democratic Republic of Algeria on the Reciprocal Promotion and Protection of Investments, signed 24 April 1991, entered into force 17 October 2002.

[151] *Orascom v Algeria* (n 149) 546.

[152] Agreement between the Government of the Kingdom of Denmark and the Government of The People's Democratic Republic of Algeria Concerning the Promotion and Reciprocal Protection of Investments, signed 25 January 1999, entered into force 15 July 2005.

[153] *Mærsk v Algeria Mærsk Olie, Algeriet A/S v People's Democratic Republic of Algeria*, ICSID Case No ARB/09/14.

[154] *Orascom Telecom Holding v Algeria Orascom Telecom Holding SAE v People's Democratic Republic of Algeria*, PCA Case No 2012-20.

[155] *Consortium Groupement LESI—DIPENTA v People's Democratic Republic of Algeria*, ICSID Case No ARB/03/8, Award, 10 January 2005.

[156] ibid [37].

[157] *Joseph Houben v Republic of Burundi*, ICSID Case No ARB/13/7, Award, 12 January 2016.

without compensation. The claimant argued that Burundi breached indirect expropriation, FET, and FPS under the Burundi–Belgium–Luxembourg Economic Union BIT. The Tribunal found Burundi in breach of indirect expropriation and FPS provisions of the BIT.

Antoine Goetz and other Belgian investors instituted *Goetz v Burundi*.[158] They were investors in a company involved in the production and marketing of precious metals. The company was granted a certificate of free zone in 1993, which gave the investors tax and customs exemptions. In 1995, Burundi withdrew the certificate saying the free zone regime was no longer applicable to companies involved in extracting and selling ore. This withdrawal resulted in losses to the Belgian investors. While the proceedings were ongoing, the parties entered into negotiations with a view to reaching a settlement agreement. Because of this, the Tribunal rendered a decision on liability holding that the withdrawal of the certificate was tantamount to expropriation under Article 4 of the BIT. The parties reached settlement agreement by which Burundi agreed to reimburse the taxes and custom duties of nearly USD3 million the company had paid. Burundi also agreed to create another free zone.[159]

1.3.2.3 Egypt and Arbitration

Egypt has had a long list of arbitral cases brought against it. In *Wena Hotels Limited v Egypt*, Egypt was found to be in breach of indirect expropriation, FET, and FPS under Egypt–United Kingdom BIT.[160] The Tribunal found that the seizure and occupation of a hotel in respect of which the investor held a lease and the failure of Egypt to act to protect the investments breached these standards of investment protection.[161]

Unión Fenosa Gas SA v Egypt[162] was initiated when Egypt limited and subsequently suspended gas supplies to a liquefied natural gas plant which was operated by the investor. Because of the suspension, the plant did not operate for over a year. The case was brought under Egypt–Spain BIT, which provided for, among others, 'fair and equitable treatment of the investments' under Article 4(1). The Tribunal stated the FET requires the customary international law standard, which prohibits conduct that is unjust, arbitrary, unfair, discriminatory, or frustrates an investor's legitimate expectations.[163] The Tribunal was of the opinion that the shutdown of the plant favoured the supply of gas to other users and consumers in Egypt

[158] *Antoine Goetz et consorts v République du Burundi*, ICSID Case No ARB/95/3, Award embodying settlement, 10 February 1999.

[159] Summary relied on Eloïse Obadia, *Antoine Goetz and others v Republic of Burundi*, ICSID Case No ARB/95/3.

[160] Agreement between the Government of the United Kingdom of Great Britain and Northern Ireland and the Government of the Arab Republic of Egypt for the Promotion and Protection of Investments, signed 11 June 1975, entered into force 24 February 1976.

[161] *Wena v Egypt* (n 101) [47], [77], [80], [84], [110], and [131].

[162] *Unión Fenosa Gas SA v Arab Republic of Egypt* ICSID Case No ARB/14/4, Award, 31 August 2018.

[163] ibid [9.51].

while targeting the plant's commercial interest, given the higher prices of the plant compared to the lower prices for the subsidised Egyptian electricity sector.[164] The Tribunal found this to be discriminatory[165] and in breach of the FET and the legitimate expectations of the investor.[166]

Siag v Egypt commenced when Egypt cancelled an investor's contract and seized the property. The investors held majority shares in two local companies. The two companies acquired a parcel of oceanfront land for the development of a tourist resort. The ownership of land was formally transferred from Siag Touristic to the government of Egypt. Defining direct expropriation as occurring 'when the title of the owner is affected by the measure in question', the Tribunal held that Egypt directly expropriated the investments contrary to Egypt–Italy BIT.[167] In finding breach of the FPS, the Tribunal held that the conduct of Egypt 'fell well below the standard of protection' that the investors 'could reasonably have expected, both in allowing the expropriation to occur and in subsequently failing to take steps to return the investment' to the investors when Egyptian courts had ruled that the expropriation was illegal.[168] The Tribunal was of the opinion that the FET included such notions as acting in good faith, transparency, protection of legitimate expectations, due process, freedom from discrimination, coercion, and harassment, and denial of justice.[169] Egypt was found to be in breach of the due process and denial of justice of the FET by refusing to obey its domestic court decisions.[170]

Middle East Cement Shipping and Handling Co SA v Egypt[171] arose out of the enactment of a decree prohibiting the investor from importing grey Portland cement even though a licence had previously been granted the investor to carry out this activity. The Tribunal held that the actions of Egypt amounted to expropriation. The Tribunal reasoned that indirect expropriation arose when 'measures are taken by a State the effect of which is to deprive the investor of the use and benefit of his investment even though he may retain nominal ownership of the respective rights being the investment'.[172] Egypt has also been sued and decisions made in its favour for: modification by a bank's credit policy towards investors, assessment of customs duties and taxes against the investors, and criminal proceedings initiated against the investors;[173] enactment of legislation to privatise and liberalise

[164] ibid [9.135]–[9.138].
[165] ibid [9.140].
[166] ibid [9.144]–[9.146].
[167] *Waguih Elie George Siag and Clorinda Vecchi v Arab Republic of Egypt*, ICSID Case No ARB/05/15, Award, 1 June 2009 [427].
[168] ibid [448].
[169] ibid [450]–[452].
[170] ibid [453].
[171] *Middle East Cement Shipping and Handling Co SA v Arab Republic of Egypt*, ICSID Case ARB/99/6, Award, 12 April 2002.
[172] ibid [107].
[173] *Ahmonseto Inc and others v Arab Republic of Egypt*, ICSID Case No ARB/02/15, Award, 18 June 2007.

the cotton trade;[174] and rescission of a contract to construct and operate an international airport.[175]

These cases help to establish the nature of regulatory and administrative actions that have been the subject of investor–state arbitration in Africa and highlight the need for African countries to be mindful of entering into investment treaties. Among the regulatory and other actions that have been the subject of investor–state suits are tax and customs duties assessment, imposition of a fine, stoppage of work, cancellation of a contract, repossession and occupation land previously granted to an investor, withdrawal of a free zone certificate, suspension of service supply, introduction of subsidies, and changes in banking policies.

1.3.2.4 Kenya, Nigeria and Arbitration

In *WalAm Energy LLC v Kenya*,[176] the investor alleged that Kenya breached Kenyan geothermal legislation and customary international law by revoking a geothermal resources licence issued to the investor. The investor argued that the revocation of the licence amounted to unlawful expropriation and violated the minimum standard of treatment of foreign investors. It was argued that the expropriation was unlawful because Kenya failed to provide fair and effective compensation, the licence was taken not for a public purpose, the investor was not accorded due process and there was discrimination.[177] In dismissing the claim, the Tribunal reasoned that Article 40(3) of the Constitution of Kenya expressly prohibited expropriation of interests in property and that there was no scope for the operation of international law. In the opinion of the Tribunal, the forfeiture of the licence was consistent with the terms and the statutory framework under which it was issued and that there were factual bases to support the forfeiture.[178] As to the claim for breach of international minimum standard of customary international law, the Tribunal found that the Kenya government's actions were not arbitrary, discriminatory, or unfair, and did not lack due process.[179] This case comes as good news for regulatory autonomy under domestic law.

The facts of *Process and Industrial Developments Ltd v Ministry of Petroleum Resources of Nigeria*[180] are that the parties entered into a written Gas Supply and Processing Agreement (GSPA) under which the government of Nigeria agreed to make to available to Process and Industrial Developments Ltd (P&ID) wet gas. P&ID would then process the gas and to return about 85 per cent by volume to the government in the form of lean gas. P&ID instituted arbitration alleging that the

[174] *Champion Trading Company and Ameritrade International, Inc v Arab Republic of Egypt*, ICSID Case No ARB/02/9, Award 27 October 2006.
[175] *Malicorp Limited v Arab Republic of Egypt*, ICSID Case No ARB/08/18, Award, 7 January 2011.
[176] *WalAm Energy LLC v Republic of Kenya*, ICSID Case No ARB/15/7, Award, 10 July 2020.
[177] ibid [334], [529]–[538].
[178] ibid [548]–[550].
[179] ibid [551]–[561].
[180] *Process and Industrial Developments Ltd v The Ministry of Petroleum Resources of the Federal Republic of Nigeria*, Part Final Award on Liability, 15 July 2015.

government breached its obligations by failing to provide wet gas by the agreed dates or not providing any wet gas at all. It was also argued the government failed to ensure that the pipelines, infrastructure, and arrangements with third parties were in place to facilitate the implementation of gas processing. P&ID claimed USD6 billion damages for lost profits.[181] The government argued that the GSPA was illegal and contrary to public policy because the promise of various permits, licences, and approvals for five years was not within the remit of the Ministry of Petroleum Resources. The Tribunal found that the GSPA was a contract with the federal government of Nigeria, not the Ministry, and concluded that the government repudiated its obligations under the GSPA. Therefore, P&ID was entitled to terminate the contract and claim damages for the government's failure to perform its side of the bargain.[182] In the end, USD6,597,000,000 together with interest at the rate of 7 per cent was awarded against Nigeria in favour of P&ID.[183] As at October 2020, the sum amounted to about USD9.6 billion, representing about 20 per cent of Nigeria's foreign reserves.[184]

1.4 Fundamental Rights of Citizens and Corresponding Obligations of African States

The African constitutions under study not only recognise or endorse the principle that sovereignty resides in people, they also require the powers of government to be exercised to promote the welfare of the people.[185] This book focuses on four areas of African constitutions and legislation: the supreme authority of the courts in a system based on separation of powers, environmental protection, human rights protection, and development policy.

These African constitutions vest the judiciary with exclusive jurisdiction in all matters, civil and criminal, and over all legal persons, foreign and domestic within the state. It is, therefore, within the province of the courts of these African

[181] ibid [3], [5], and [60].

[182] ibid [77]–[78].

[183] *Process and Industrial Developments Ltd v The Ministry of Petroleum Resources of the Federal Republic of Nigeria*, Part Final Award on Liability, 31 January 2017 [112].

[184] Ohio Omiunu and Oludara Akanmidu, 'Lessons from Nigeria and Process & Industrial Developments Limited (P&ID)' <https://www.afronomicslaw.org/2020/10/12/lessons-from-nigeria-and-process-industrial-developments-limited-pid> accessed 19 October 2021; Ohio Omiunu and Oludara Akanmidu, 'Reflections on Nigeria v. Process & Industrial Developments Limited' (2021) 53 New York University Journal of International Law and Politics 110.

[185] Constitution of the Republic of Cameroon 1972 (with Amendments through 2008), art 2(1) (hereafter, Constitution of Cameroon); Constitution of the Arab Republic of Egypt 2014, art 4 (hereafter, Constitution of Egypt); Constitution of the Republic of Ghana 1992 art 1(1) (hereafter, Constitution of Ghana); Constitution of the Republic of Kenya 2010, preamble and art 10 (hereafter, Constitution of Kenya); Constitution of the Federal Republic of Nigeria 1999, s 14(1) (hereafter, Constitution of Nigeria); and Constitution of the Republic of South Africa 1996, ss 1(a) and 7 (hereafter, Constitution of South Africa).

countries to decide upon legal disputes relating to constitutional rights and matters even when foreign legal persons are involved.[186]

The constitutions recognise the importance of environmental and natural resources to human existence and development and provide for the right to a clean and healthy environment.[187] They assert national ownership of natural resources and require the states to take appropriate measures to protect and safeguard the environment for posterity and to cooperate with other states and bodies to protect the wider international environment.[188] The constitutions vest minerals in the president or people and require relevant state institutions to regulate and manage the utilisation of natural resources, namely minerals, forestry resources, and fisheries for the public good.[189] These constitutions also provide for the protection of various fundamental human rights for whose enjoyment and full realisation the exercise of governmental powers is necessary. These human rights include the right to life, clean and healthy environment, health, security of person, dignity, and a standard of living adequate for health and well-being.[190] Environmental protection and the jurisdiction of municipal courts are fundamental for the realisation of these rights.

The constitutions guarantee the right to development and preserve certain economic and social values that are pertinent to development. They require the states to manage the economies to maximise the rate of economic development and secure the maximum welfare, freedom and happiness of citizens and provide adequate means of livelihood, suitable employment, and public assistance to the needy. The states are to take all necessary steps to establish a sound and healthy economy that assures the necessities of life and take appropriate measures, to promote the development of agriculture and industry, afford equality of economic opportunity to all citizens, and guarantee the health, safety, and welfare of all persons in employment.[191]

[186] Constitution of the Republic of Cameroon (n 185) arts 37–41, 46–47, and 50; Constitution of Egypt (n 185) arts 184–197; Constitution of Ghana, arts 125–143; Constitution of Kenya (n 185), arts 164–165; Constitution of Nigeria (n 185) ss 4, 6, and 251; Constitution of South Africa (n 185) ss 167–168.

[187] Constitution of Cameroon (n 185) preamble and art 65; Constitution of Egypt (n 185) arts 29 and 46; Constitution of Ghana (n 185) arts 24(1) and 36(9); Constitution of Kenya (n 185) arts 42 and 69–70; Constitution of Nigeria (n 185) s 20; and Constitution of South Africa (n 185) s 24.

[188] Constitution of Cameroon (n 185) preamble and arts 26(6)(d)(5); Constitution of Egypt (n 185) arts 30, 32, and 43–44; Constitution of Ghana (n 185) arts 257–269, 24(1), and 36(9); Constitution of Kenya (n 185) arts 69–72; Constitution of Nigeria (n 185) s 17(2)(d); and Constitution of South Africa (n 185) ss 24(b)(iii) and 25(4)(a).

[189] Constitution of Cameroon (n 185) preamble and arts 26(6)(d)(5); Constitution of Egypt (n 185) arts 32 and 44–45; Constitution of Ghana (n 185) arts 257(6) and 269(1); Constitution of Kenya (n 185) art 62(1)(f); and Constitution Nigeria (n 185) s 44(3).

[190] Constitution of Cameroon (n 185) preamble and arts 55(2) and 56(1); Constitution of Egypt (n 185) arts 13, 18–19, and 78–79; Constitution of Ghana (n 185) arts 12, 13, 15, 17, 26, 30, and 37(2) (n 185); Constitution of Kenya (n 185) arts 19–59; Constitution of Nigeria (n 185) ss 33–44; and Constitution of South Africa (n 185) ss 7–39.

[191] Constitution of Cameroon (n 185) preamble and arts 55(2), 56(2), and 65 read together; Constitution of Egypt (n 185) preamble and arts 27–28, 38, 41, 46, and 236; Constitution of Ghana (n

The obligations also arise in general international law. Borrowing from Elihu Lauterpacht, I use the concept of general international law to refer to 'the body of rules of conduct ... which confer rights and impose obligations primarily ... upon sovereign states as expressed in custom and treaties',[192] in particular as they pertain to the jurisdiction of municipal courts, the environment, development, and other fundamental human rights. In this broad sense, I use the concept then to include customary international law principles relevant for the right to regulate in international investment law.[193] In a narrower sense, general international law in this book consists of IETs and IHRTs to which African states are parties which provide for the protection of environmental and human rights and impose corresponding duties on the states similar to the constitutional protection and guarantee of these rights and values as detailed in Chapters 2, 4, and 5. The right to development, a clean and healthy environment, and other fundamental human rights and corresponding obligations thus derive both from African constitutions and general international law because African states are parties to IETs and IHRTs and indeed, African constitutions require African states to respect and uphold IETs, IHRTs, and other international agreements they have entered into.[194] This informs the choice of the concept of *constitutional-general international law imperatives* to describe fundamental human rights of citizens and corresponding obligations of African states deriving from constitutions, CIL, IETs, and IHRTs as legal sources collectively.

1.5 The Object and Contribution of the Book

1.5.1 The Research Questions Explored

African governments must regulate in the public interest by acting constructively and decisively to protect constitutional rights and values, relating to the environment, human rights, and development. They must also preserve the independence and the jurisdiction of domestic courts. Yet, in order to secure the protection of foreign investment, investment treaties impose constraints on the ability of

185) arts 36 and 86–87; Constitution of Kenya (n 185) arts 10(2), 19(1), and (2), 43, 46, 56–57, and 74(f); Constitution of Nigeria (n 185) ss 7(3), 16(1), and(2) and Fourth Schedule, clause 1; Constitution of South Africa (n 185) ss 24, 152–153, 187, and 195(c).

192 Elihu Lauterpacht (ed) *International Law: The General Works: Being the Collected Papers of Hersch Lauterpacht* (vol 1, CUP 1970) 9.

193 See for example Patrick Dumberry, *The Formation and Identification of Customary International Law in International Investment Law* (CUP 2016).

194 Constitution of Cameroon (n 185) preamble, arts 5(2) and 43–45; Constitution of Egypt (n 185) arts 93 and 151; Constitution of Ghana (n 185) arts 40, 73, and 75; Constitution of Kenya (n 185) art 2(6); Constitution of Nigeria (n 185) ss 12 and 19(d); and Constitution of South Africa (n 185) arts 39(b) and 231–233.

African governments to act within national constitutions and legislation by prohibiting specified measures (eg taking measures in favour of nationals or imposing performance requirements in the national interest). Investment treaties also constrain domestic policy space by requiring the award of damages in favour of foreign investors for the adoption of measures that substantially reduce the value of that investment, even if the measure is required under domestic law and justified in general international law

It is the duties of African states to make policies, enact laws, and take all measures to protect society at large. The very essence of government is the protection of the public interest. Jean-Jacques Rousseau underscored this point when he posed and disposed of a fundamental question: 'What is the object of any political association? It is the protection and the prosperity of its members.'[195] This edict is reflected in Article 1(1) of the Constitution of Ghana which states that '[t]he Sovereignty of Ghana resides in the people of Ghana in whose name and for whose welfare the powers of government are to be exercised in the manner and within the limits ... in this Constitution'. It is also reflected in Article 4 of the Constitution of the Arab Republic of Egypt 2014 which states in succinct terms that sovereignty 'belongs to the people alone, which exercises it and protects it. They are the source of power'. According to the Constitution of the Federal Republic of Nigeria 1999, Section 14(2)(a), sovereignty 'belongs to the people of Nigeria from whom government through this Constitution derives all its powers and authority'. Similar expressions are contained in Article 1(1) of the Constitution of the Republic of Kenya 2010 and Article 2 of the Constitution of the Republic of Cameroon 1972. Therefore, African governments must retain regulatory autonomy to meet their public interest obligations relating to human rights, environment, and the right to development when they pursue business-related policy objectives with other states and multinational business entities.[196]

I explore the actual and potential legal implications of the constitutional and general international law obligations of African states to protect the public interest for their investment treaty regime. I emphasise the central role of the states for several reasons.

First, the constitutions put the fundamental rights of citizens and corresponding obligations of African states above everything, as overriding considerations, in all governmental decision-making and actions. Thus the negotiation, entering into, and performance of international obligations must revolve around their positive contribution to the realisation of basic rights of citizens. As the public interest must be put first, absolute investment protection that prohibits or limits the efficacy of justified constitutional and legislative measures in the public interest reverses the

[195] Jean-Jacques Rousseau, *The Social Contract* (Maurice Cranston tr, Penguin Books Ltd 2004) 99.
[196] Commission on Human Rights, *Guiding Principles on Business and Human Rights: Implementing the United Nations 'Protect, Respect and Remedy' Framework* (United Nations 2011) Principle 9.

order of prioritising competing interests as constitutionally required in Africa. African states may only enter into investment treaties that are consistent with the realisation of these fundamental rights, but not the ones that suppress or undermine their realisation. The public interest must be prioritised in public–private international economic arrangements and agreements. I shall call this the *public interest prioritisation principle* in international economic relations.

Second, development theories that advocate a one-size-fits-all development policy, with macroeconomic policies that are linked to liberalisation and privatisation and investment openness, have failed. That is well documented, in light of major financial crises and economic stagnation or even the economic collapse of willing adherents such as Argentina.[197] The 2008 financial crisis has revitalised the legitimate role of the state in the economy.[198] According to UNCTAD, governments 'have become decidedly less reticent in *regulating* and *steering* the economy. Governments are moving away from the hands-off approach to economic growth and development that prevailed previously.'[199] There are growing calls for what Albert Cho and Navroz Dubash describe as 'heterogeneous and strategic development policies'[200] and 'domestic institutional innovations',[201] so the idea that FDI is the panacea for development can no longer be taken for granted.

Third, governments, the public's expectations and preferences, and development policies change over time. The state must be free to act because every reduction of its legal authority, as stated by Jane Kelsey, 'limits future domestic political control … and exposes governments who wish to change direction to potentially crippling economic, legal and moral sanctions'.[202]

I review and analyse the compatibility of these African states' investment treaty obligations with their constitutional and general international law obligations. I also examine the stated goals of these states' investment treaties, how much policy and regulatory autonomy are retained under them, and whether the standards of investment protection by treaty can constrain the exercise of constitutional powers relating to judicial sovereignty, environmental protection, development policy-making and implementation, and human rights. More fundamentally, I assess whether or not African states, to borrow from Kojo Yelpaala, have 'treaty making authority to waive, undermine or abrogate positive or negative constitutional

[197] Albert Cho and Navroz Dubash, *Will Investment Rules Shrink Policy Space for Sustainable Development? Evidence from the Electricity Sector* (South Centre Trade Related Agenda Development and Equity Working Paper 16, December 2003) 4 (hereafter, Cho and Dubash, *Will Investment Rules Shrink Policy Space*); and Joseph Stiglitz, 'Challenging the Washington Consensus—An Interview with Lindsey Schoenfelder' (2003) 9 The Brown Journal of World Affairs 33, 40.

[198] UNCTAD, *World Investment Report 2012* (n 1) 99.

[199] ibid at 100 (emphasis in the original).

[200] Cho and Dubash, *Will Investment Rules Shrink Policy Space* (n 197) 4.

[201] ibid.

[202] Jane Kelsey, *The New Zealand Experiment: A World Model for Structural Adjustment?* (Auckland University Press with Bridget Williams Books 1995) 367 (hereafter, Kelsey, *New Zealand Experiment*).

protections to life, health and safety of its citizens'[203] in favour of investment protection. There are five interrelated key research questions:

1. Are African states' treaty-based standards of investment protection compatible with the states' obligations to protect the public interest under their constitutions, CIL, IETs, and IHRTs?
2. Can African governments bargain away their obligations under constitutions, CIL, IETs, and IHRTs with respect to development policy-making and implementation, and the protection of fundamental human rights and the environment in pursuit of foreign investment?
3. Does the constitutional need to put the public interest first and attain development goals in Africa require some restrictions or qualifications on the standards of investment promotion and protection in investment treaties or even on the competence of African states to enter into investment treaties?
4. Under their constitutions, do African states have the competence to agree to a mechanism that exempts foreign investors from the jurisdiction of municipal courts?
5. How can these issues be addressed within the constraints of treaty law and customary international law, as embodied in the Vienna Convention on the Law of Treaties, in relation to existing investment treaties and the entry into any future investment treaties?

1.5.2 The Contribution of the Book

There currently exists no single book examining the intersection of national constitutions and international economic law in Africa. Indeed, this volume is the first of its kind focusing on its subject matter from a regional perspective. This book contributes to ongoing discussion on where and how to draw the line between national regulation and policy measures aimed at protecting the public interest, for which compensation to foreign investors may not arise, and regulation and policy measures affecting foreign investment for which compensation may be required. The research issues underlying this book are timely because Africa has no choice but to rise legally, economically, politically, and socially and thus be truly independent. Moreover, concerns over the implications of investment treaties for the jurisdiction of municipal courts, environmental and development policy choices, human rights, and over the activities of multinational business entities, are now very high on the public policy agenda of states, business, and international organisations.[204]

[203] Kojo Yelpaala, 'Fundamentalism in Public Health and Safety in Bilateral Investment Treaties Part I' (2008) 3(1) Asian Journal of WTO and International Health Law and Policy 235, 240.

[204] John Ruggie, *Report of the Special Representative of the Secretary-General on the Issue of Human Rights and Transnational Corporations and other Business Enterprises Business and human*

I argue that African states' investment treaty obligations are largely incompatible with their legal obligations to protect the public interest under national constitutions and general international law and have been pursued without due regard to the treaties' restraining effects on policy space and the right to regulate in the public interest. This compatibility is measured by assessing existing and prospective policies and legislative requirements which, if implemented or undertaken to protect the public interest, could conflict with investment treaties. I identify actual and potential points of friction between investment treaties and constitutions in Africa.

Academics have made various proposals as to how states can recapture or retain regulatory autonomy in international investment law.[205] The focus of this book on the constitutionality of investment treaties, and more broadly the intersection of national constitutions and international investment law in Africa, adds new insights to international investment law scholarship. There is a lack of comprehensive and systematic country-specific and regional-specific studies on the compatibility of standards of investment protection by treaty with constitutional *and* general international law standards on public interest regulation, and on the nature of the standards of investment protection that states can or cannot undertake in investment treaties. This book's regional focus on Africa, makes it a pioneering study of its kind, and it is a much-needed book given that constitutions are the bedrock of governance in Africa.

Kojo Yelpaala does address the issue of the constitutional and general international law implications for the making and interpretation of investment treaties.[206] Yelpaala strongly argues that there is the need to '*return to first principles of sovereignty, constitutionalism and international law on the issues of sovereign authority with respect to domestic policy relating to security and other critical social policies*'.[207] His core concern is the situation where a state's authorities lack the competence to commit a state to obligations under treaties such as investment treaties, which restrain the state from adopting measures in the interest of public health.

Rights: Towards operationalizing the 'Protect, Respect and Remedy' Framework (2009) (A/HRC/11/13) [30].

[205] Muthucumaraswamy Sornarajah and Leo Trakman, 'A Polemic: The Cases for and Against Investment Liberalization' in Leon Trakman and Nicola W Ranieri (eds), *Regionalism in International Investment Law* (OUP 2013) 499, 500 (hereafter, Sornarajah and Trakman, 'Polemic'); Sornarajah, *Law on Foreign Investment 2010* (n 8) 110, 275, and 296–97; Kelsey, 'How the Trans-Pacific Partnership Agreement Could Heighten Financial Instability and Foreclose Governments' Regulatory Autonomy' (n 64) 41 at 75; Gas Van Harten, *Investment Treaty Arbitration and Public Law* (OUP 2007) 152 and 168; David Schneiderman, *Resisting Economic Globalization: Critical Theory and International Investment Law* (Palgrave Macmillan 2013) 1–13; David Schneiderman, *Constitutionalizing Economic Globalization: Investment Rules and Democracy's Promise* (CUP 2008) 225 and 235; and Philippe Sands, 'Searching for Balance: Concluding Remarks' (2002–2003) 11 New York University Environmental Law Journal 198, 202.

[206] Kojo Yelpaala, 'Fundamentalism in Public Health and Safety in Bilateral Investment Treaties Part II' (2008) 3(2) Asian Journal of WTO & International Health Law and Policy 465.

[207] ibid (emphasis in the original).

Yelpaala's starting point is the fundamental rights protected by a constitution, although the issue can be addressed from an international law perspective as well.[208]

However, Yelpaala's study is rather general, being a grand theory and not being specific to Africa. As he states, 'a casual examination of the relevant issues concerning the relationship between constitutional law doctrines and theories of BITs provisions suggests complexity deserving deeper analysis than can be undertaken in this study'. Yelpaala's goal was to raise the 'larger and more fundamental questions in the interpretation of BITs provisions when constitutional law questions are implicated' in order 'to redirect the debate to the fundamental constitutional law issues so far not addressed in the emerging debate over the implications of BITs'.[209] In order to engage the issues in a more specific yet deeper, detailed, comprehensive, systematic, and practical manner, this book focuses on specific constitutions, CIL, IETs, IHRTs, and international investment treaties to which specific African states are parties.

With particular reference to Africa, the book questions whether national constitutional and general international law obligations do or should regulate the conduct of African states in investment treaty-making. It does this with reference to the jurisdiction of municipal courts, human rights, the right to a clean environment and the right to development in Africa. By giving considerable attention to the limits that the duties of African states towards the public places on the investment treaty-making powers in Africa, I address the issue of conflict of legal norms and interests in international investment law from its roots. For this book, the discussion of the limitations of international investment law on the right to regulate must start from *a priori* question of how that right to regulate limits the competence to conclude investment treaties.

This book is original not only in approach but also because it uses the specific case of Africa to add new insights, perspectives, and value to existing discourse on international investment law and the right to regulate. The legal and regulatory issues associated with international investment protection by treaty have not been explored since the 1960s when African countries began to enter into investment treaties with former colonial powers and Western nations. An analysis of the kind undertaken in this book is a prerequisite for rethinking those legal and normative relationships.

With reference to 'developing' countries generally, Sornarajah points out that 'there is little understanding of the effects of treaties that are entered into at the instigation of international organizations that may make such treaties a condition for assistance'.[210] According to him, while the constitutionality of investment treaties

[208] ibid 475 and 479. For related seminal works see: Ernst-Ulrich Petersmann, *Multilevel Constitutionalism for Multilevel Governance of Public Goods: Methodology Problems in International Law* (Hart Publishing 2017).

[209] ibid.

[210] Sornarajah and Trakman, 'Polemic' (n 205) 509.

has been studied in developed countries including Canada and United States, '[p]eople within the developing states are seldom concerned with low visibility instruments such as investment treaties'.[211] Ordinary people on the streets in the developing world do not know that their countries have tied up their sovereignty in order to protect foreign investment which may not come with tangible public benefits. Developing country elites who supposedly do know may stand to profit from the system and may be less inclined to challenge it.[212] Thus, there is a pressing need for legal scholarship in Africa and the developing world generally that can contribute to an understanding of the nature and effects of investment treaties and arbitration for domestic public interest values protected under national constitutions and general international law. The UNCTAD emphasised the importance of this approach in 2007 when it stated: 'international investment rulemaking poses particular challenges for developing countries. One consequence of this situation is the growing need for policy research and analysis ... to help developing countries in assessing the implications of different policy options before entering into new agreements.'[213] This monograph fills that gap.

1.6 The Scope and Methodology

As reflected in the title of this book and referenced throughout, investment treaties have been treated as a 'regime'. What makes them constitute a 'regime'? According to Stephen Krasner, regimes in the international plane 'are ... principles, norms, rules, and decision-making procedures around which actor expectations converge in a given issue-area'.[214] Jeswald Salacuse also says an international regime 'is essentially a system of governance in a particular area of international relations'.[215] Donald Puchala and Raymond Hopkins also define a regime as

> a set of principles, norms, rules, and procedures around which actors' expectations converge. These serve to channel political action within a system and give it meaning ... Regimes constrain and regularize the behavior of participants, affect which issues among protagonists move on and off agendas, determine which activities are legitimized or condemned, and influence whether, when, and how conflicts are resolved.[216]

[211] ibid 512.

[212] ibid.

[213] UNCTAD, *International Investment Rule-Setting: Trends, Emerging Issues and Implications* (United Nations 2007) [56] (hereafter, UNCTAD, *International Investment Rule-Setting*).

[214] Stephen D Krasner, 'Structural Causes and Regime Consequences: Regimes as Intervening Variables' (1982) 36(2) International Organization 185

[215] Jeswald Salacuse, *The Law of Investment Treaties* (2nd edn, OUP 2015) 6 (Salacuse, *Law of Investment Treaties 2015*).

[216] Donald J Puchala and Raymond F Hopkins, 'International Regimes: Lessons from Inductive Analysis' (1982) 36(2) International Organization 245, 245–46.

Investment treaties consist of bilateral investment treaties and other treaties such as free trade agreements with investment provisions. Investment treaties constitute a 'regime' because collectively they 'represent a convergence of expectations by states as to how host governments will behave towards investments from other regime members. The norms and rules embodied in investment treaties are intended to constrain and regularize such behaviour in order to fulfil those expectations.'[217] At least three components of investment treaties as a regime can be identified: (1) investment treaties themselves; (2) conventions, institutions, and rules of procedure that regulate the conduct of investment treaty arbitration; and (3) the body of rules and principles that emerge from the decisions of arbitral institutions responsible for the resolution of investment disputes.[218]

The protection of foreign investment by treaty and arbitration raises a number of questions which are of policy and practical significance. These include whether investment treaties attract foreign investment at all; whether foreign investment leads to development; how policy coherence can be established in investment treaties with overlapping obligations and with national legal and policy frameworks; and how a state might address any incompatibilities between its public interest obligations under its constitution and general international law and investment treaty obligations.

The last two issues in particular are addressed herein. The book focuses on the jurisdiction of municipal courts, environmental and human rights protection, and development policy effects and implications of international investment law as case studies because they are core functions constitutionally assigned to African governments and are the areas of public interest regulation that raise the most significant concerns in the international investment regime. The *public interest* is defined here as interests members of a community or state have in common, with particular reference to environment, development, human rights, and national institutional autonomy.[219] Ordinarily, measures that are not captured by constitutional text or international environmental and human rights treaties can fall within the concept of the public interest. This is the reason I qualified this rather broad view of the public interest by defining it with particular reference to environment, development, and human rights. These were chosen in view of the fact that these are areas of governmental regulation most members of the public have in common, and yet which have been the direct areas that have been the subjects of investor–state suits. Therefore, a measure that cannot be justified in constitutional law and relevant international treaties as a measure of the public interest cannot qualify for recognition and protection under relevant constitutional laws

[217] Salacuse, *Law of Investment Treaties 2015* (n 215) 6.

[218] Jonathan Bonnitcha, Lauge Poulsen, and Michael Waibel, *The Political Economy of the Investment Treaty Regime* (OUP 2017) 3.

[219] Barry M Mitnick, 'A Typology of Conceptions of the Public Interest' (1976) 8(1) Administration & Society 5.

and international treaties even though in a different context it might be matter of interest to the public.

The job of a lawyer is *interpretive* in nature: determining the meaning, scope, and legal effect of the words and phrases used in a legal text. Ronald Dworkin made this point when he stated that 'legal practice is an exercise in interpretation not only when lawyers interpret documents or statutes but also generally'.[220] Interpretation involves a number of legal activities. The first is resolving contradictions or real doubts and ambiguities in a given legal text. This involves imparting meaning to legal texts which requires resolving internal contradictions *within the text itself*.[221]

Second, interpretation comprises the art of resolving contradictions or conflicts between *different legal texts* either on the same normative level or on a different normative level, such as constitution and statute, statute and contract, contract and will, and international law and municipal law.[222] Giving meaning to legal texts either alone or in relation to another legal text constitutes an interpretive activity.[223] Third, interpretation may be understood as filling a lacuna or gap in a legal text.[224]

The legal texts and sources analysed in this book are six African constitutions, statutes, investment treaties, CIL, IETs, IHRTs, and case law. When examining the actual and potential contradictions between investment treaties and the rest, the method is doctrinal, interpretive, analytical, and evaluative. The book draws heavily on theories of constitutionalism and the role of public institutions in a constitutional democracy, theories of the law of treaties and the relationship between municipal law and international law,[225] and theories on the role of law and institutions in society.[226]

There are limited known arbitral awards involving African countries and foreign investors that are relevant to this book. However, selected African countries' investment treaty terms are substantially the same as those of other countries involved in the arbitral cases selected for analysis because they directly involved similar policy issues and measures to those required by constitutions and domestic legislation in Africa. There have been specific arbitral cases touching on constitutional cases involving Ghana in which the jurisdiction of arbitral tribunals and

[220] Ronald Dworkin, 'Law as Interpretation' (1982) 60(3) Texas Law Review 529.
[221] Aharon Barak, *Purposive Interpretation in Law* (Princeton University Press 2005).
[222] ibid 5.
[223] ibid.
[224] ibid.
[225] Verdross, 'Forbidden Treaties' (n 74); and Ernst-Ulrich Petersman, *International Economic Law in the 21st Century: Constitutional Pluralism and Multilevel Governance of Interdependent Public Goods* (Hart Publishing Ltd 2012).
[226] Thomas Aquinas, *The Summa Theologica* (vol 2, Fathers of the English Dominican Province tr, Encyclopaedia Britannica Inc 1952); John Finnis, *Natural Law and Natural Rights* (2nd edn, OUP 2011); Thomas Pogge, *Politics as Usual: What Lies Behind the Pro-Poor Rhetoric* (Polity Press 2010); Thomas Pogge, *World Poverty and Human Rights: Cosmopolitan Responsibilities and Reforms* (Polity Press 2002); John Rawls, *A Theory of Justice* (rev edn, OUP 1999); and John Rawls, *Justice as Fairness: A Restatement* (Erin Kelly ed, Harvard University Press 2001).

domestic courts clashed which serve as perfect cases studies on constitutional issues and investor–state arbitration in Africa.

The study resulting in this book initially focused on Ghana. The choice of Ghana was informed by the author's familiarity with the key legal instruments and the importance of these issues for the nation, Africa, and the developing world. Recent arbitral disputes revealed the tension between investment treaty obligations and constitutional obligations of Ghana. The fact that Ghana's investment treaties do not make exception for public interest regulation without the need to pay compensation to foreign investors increases the potential for the investment treaty regime to limit the state's regulatory autonomy. The status of the Constitution of Ghana as the supreme law of Ghana has been argued by the state in defence of measures challenged by foreign investors. Given this context, it became imperative to ascertain the extent to which Ghana needed to comply with its Constitution in entering into investment treaties.

In order to expand this book to address the relationship between international investment law and national constitutions in the broader context of Africa, five other African countries have been selected to cover the five regional groupings of Africa, namely central Africa, east Africa, northern African, southern Africa, and west Africa. This explains the addition of Cameroon, Kenya, Egypt, South Africa, and Nigeria to represent each of the regions. Therefore, six African countries are represented in this book. The constitutions of these countries are generally similar in terms of their focus on the public interest obligations of states and their positions on the relationship between municipal law and international law. There are similarities in the constitutional jurisdiction of the courts in all the selected countries. There are also similarities in the substantive terms of investment treaties studied in the book, which all make provisions for investor–state arbitration. This selection allows for the theme of the constitutional-general international law limitations on African states to enter into investment treaties in light of their public interest obligations to be pursued coherently and in depth using relevant constitutional texts, domestic legislation and international treaties.

South Africa and Nigeria (southern African and west Africa) were selected as the largest economies in Africa and because of the relevance of their constitutional texts on the subject of analysis of the book. As stated, Ghana (west Africa) was the original focus of the study giving rise to the book. Ghana is the only country, at the time of writing, where there has been a clash between the *constitutional* jurisdiction of domestic courts and arbitral tribunals. The key cases on Ghana involved constitutional issues and the exercise of the jurisdiction of the Supreme Court of Ghana under the *Constitution*, which eventually ended up in arbitration. The remaining countries of Cameroon, Egypt, and Kenya (central Africa, east Africa, and north Africa) were selected based on the relevance of their constitutional texts and to represent their respective three regions. Egypt has the largest number of investment treaties in Africa and thus becomes a relevant subject of study on international investment law and policy in Africa. Regional and continental international agreements on investment and trade of relevance have also been analysed to broaden and justify the scope of the focus on Africa. The arbitral cases reviewed in Subsection 1.3.2 also broadens the books coverage of Africa.

The book is presented as a composite analysis of each of the countries represented to allow for a general point about these countries collectively or about Africa in general to be made rather than being presented as individualised case studies. The findings on the relationship between investment treaties and arbitration and national constitutions are thus arguably applicable to all African constitutions *with similar* constitutional obligations and which have borrowed heavily from international human rights treaties in developing their own constitutional jurisprudence on human rights and corresponding obligations of states. The findings and conclusions may not be generalisable across all African states, which are all vastly different. The findings and conclusions may apply to these countries *mutatus mutandis*. How the *constitutional-general international law imperatives* developed using these countries might be met in relation to future treaties and different states, and what can be done about existing treaties, raise different but related legal arguments. This inquiry is of broader practical value given the debates happening around the investment treaty regime and regulatory autonomy and ongoing efforts of states to reform investment treaties to accommodate public interest regulation.[227]

The book develops the common theme of the fundamental constitutional and general international law obligations of African states with respect to the public interest areas such as human rights, the right to development, and the right to a clean and safe environment, and how those obligations determine the capacity of these states to conclude investment treaties (without ignoring known constitutional differences that matter). The analysis suggests that there are major similarities when it comes to the centrality of the public interest and the corresponding constitutional and general international law obligations of the selected African countries towards the public or their citizens. None of the selected constitutions allows for situations where constitutional public interest protections could be derogated from in order to further the interests of private individuals, whether domestic or foreign. Therefore, while constitutional practice will vary in each of the jurisdictions and across the continent, I did not find any practice, based on any of the constitutions, that allows for a significant point of difference to be articulated. However, textually there are differences in the constitutional requirements for concluding treaties. These differences would affect arguments about the validity of concluded treaties. Nevertheless, a close reading of those texts suggests that the requirements for concluding treaties were stipulated in each jurisdiction to ensure

[227] UNCTAD, *International Investment Rule-Setting* (n 213).

that the power to make treaties is not exercised in a manner that is adverse to the exercise of constitutional powers in the public interest.

This book uses investment treaties and investor–state arbitration as a case study. The fundamental argument made based on investment treaties, constitutional law, and general international law analysis applies to and raises profound implications for all other forms of international business (including trade) agreements and even domestic legislation and policies that make provision for state–private actor disputes to be resolved by international arbitration when the disputes have implications for the protection of the public interest. For example, in Ghana the authorisation of the development of mineral resources requires parliamentary ratification as a matter of constitutional law. To the extent that such authorisation comes with environmental and human rights concerns, the constitutionality of the authorisation comes into play as revealed from the analysis in Chapter 4. However, a predominantly domestic measure that leads to violations of human rights, but which is not subject to an investment treaty, does not result in the same controversy as the same measure which is subject to an investment treaty. Disputes arising from measures subject solely to domestic law can be resolved as a matter of domestic law in domestic courts. A dispute concerning a measure that affects a right protected by an investment treaty arbitration has to resolved in accordance with the terms of the applicable investment treaty even if domestic law is implicated.

1.7 The Organisation of the Book

African constitutions under study acknowledge the source of sovereignty in the people. The powers of African governments derive from and are to be exercised within constitutional limits primarily in the public interest. These constitutions provide for various fundamental rights of citizens: the right to development, a clean and healthy environment, and other fundamental human rights. African states have primary responsibilities to fulfil these rights by taking appropriate legislative and policy measures. So long as such measures are consistent with the applicable constitution, the state concerned has the latitude to pursue those measures. The obligations to protect these rights of citizens also derive from CIL, IETs, and IHRTs to which Africa states are parties. African constitutions specifically require that states shall abide by their international environmental and international human rights treaty obligations. Therefore, the obligation to protect fundamental human rights and environment is a *constitutional-general international law imperative* because the source of that obligation derives from *both* national constitutions and general international law. The *imperatives theory* derives from this premise.

Based on these premises, I argue that as the constitutions are supreme in the hierarchy of legal rules within the domestic context, just as peremptory norms of general international law are on the international plane, the competence of African states to conclude investment treaties and the legal effect of treaties so made must be judged in terms of the effects of those treaties for public interest regulation. Therefore, in interpreting investment treaties, normative priority should be given to constitutions and general international law when they both protect public interest pursued by the measure giving rise to the dispute since African states derive their powers from these norms for the public good. In such a case, the states must not be liable for adopting the measure concerned. If regulation is justified and liability arises nevertheless, the award of damages must have regard to that justification in terms of mitigating any damages. Building on these themes as the foundation, the book is presented in four substantive chapters and a concluding one as follows.

Chapter 2 develops the *imperatives theory* as the theoretical and analytical framework applied in the book based on theories on constituent power and constitutionalism and the role of the state. The Imperative Theory is a theory of law on the effects and implications of fundamental human rights and corresponding duties for the exercise of the powers of states. The Chapter reviews and interprets the basic right and corresponding duties of various African states under their constitutions and IETs and IHRTs. The analysis makes it clear the nature of the potential conflict between the states' obligations under the investment treaty regime and obligations under constitutions, CIL, IETs, and IHRTs. It also assesses the limitations inherent in state-specific defences and justifications, such as the principle of proportionality, the defence of necessity, and margin of appreciation to justify the need for alternatives.

The chapter then introduces the theories of constituent power and constitutionalism, which emphasise the sources of powers to govern and constitutional guarantee and recognition of fundamental rights, and the corresponding obligations of the states to fulfil those rights in the public interest, and the limits to the exercise of governmental powers in Africa. Drawing on theories on constitutionalism and the role of the state, the chapter emphasises the central role of African governments in protecting the public interest, which must limit their competence in investment treaty-making. In general, it argues the problem of international investment law in terms of the challenge it poses to regulatory autonomy lies squarely in states concluding investment treaties without having regard for the effects they have on constitutional norms and other national interests which govern the exercise of the powers of governments. It argues at the core that the competence of African states to conclude investment treaties must be guided by their duties to regulate in the public interest as guaranteed under their constitutions and recognised in general international law. Based on this, the chapter develops the *imperatives theory* to explain the legal and normative limits to the power of African states to conclude investment treaties.

Chapter 3 analyses how investment treaty arbitration can affect the exercise of judicial authority of the courts in Africa. It questions whether African states have the competence to agree to investor–state arbitration, which permits foreign investors to bypass municipal courts. This is because African constitutions assign original, appellate, and final jurisdiction over legal disputes to municipal courts. The chapter also establishes that foreign investors do not have an automatic and direct right in CIL to access international dispute resolution, that is, without at least an attempt to exhaust local remedies. Therefore, the direct right to investment arbitration cannot be justified in CIL, without showing by empirical evidence that foreign investors cannot have effective remedy before municipal courts. In this regard, the chapter questions the capacity of African states to agree to international arbitration in light of CIL and national constitutions. The right of international arbitration under existing treaties must be interpreted as arising only when foreign investors have legitimately made a case that they do not have remedy before municipal courts. This imperative requires that foreign investors commence their actions before domestic courts in the first place.

In addition, given the right to appeal within domestic legal systems in Africa, once an investor commences legal action or submits to the jurisdiction of domestic courts, it must exhaust local remedies as required under the applicable legal system. Recourse to international arbitration in those circumstances can be justified only if it is established that it would be futile to continue with the domestic legal process. The principles of constitutional governance, especially on accountability of governments through the judiciary, transparency, rule of law, and putting citizens first all prohibit automatic and absolute preferential treatment to foreign investors, especially when they are not making better contribution to the economy compared to domestic investors in like circumstances. The proposal for the future is that constitutional norms with respect to the jurisdiction of the courts must guide the African states in making decision whether to agree to investor–state arbitration, given its potential to undermine judicial independence and potency of the courts' decisions.

Chapter 4 focuses on human rights and environmental regulation of foreign investment. The environment and human rights are protected, in part, by the enforcement of environmental and human rights laws and policies and by the enactment of new legislation. The African constitutions, IETs, and IHRTs to which African states are parties guarantee, recognise and provide for the protection of fundamental human rights and the right to a healthy environment. They also impose corresponding obligations on African states to fulfil these rights. However, evidence shows that the activities of businesses (including foreign investors) in the mining industry have contributed to environmental damage in Ghana, Nigeria, and South Africa, among other African countries, threatening people's right to food, health and wellbeing. In those circumstances, African states have constitutional and general international law obligations to act to protect human rights and the environment.

The chapter assesses how investment treaties restrict the adoption of measures aimed at protecting environment and human rights in Africa. The main legal means by which environmental and human rights laws and regulations are enforced include the termination, cancellation and suspension of environmental permits and imposition of fines for non-compliance with environmental regulations. These measures can be challenged as breaching various standards of investment protection under investment treaties. In this regard, the investment treaties stand to compromise environmental and human rights protection and the realisation of the right to a clean and safe environment. This chapter argues that the duties to protect the environment and human rights emanate from constitutions, IETs and IHRTs. Therefore, fundamental human rights and the right to a clean and safe environment and corresponding duties of African states place limitations on the standards of investment protection by treaty the African states can undertake. Where a human right or an environmental right measure is justified under domestic law and IETs or under domestic law and IHRTs, the adoption of such a measure must not give rise to state liability given the combined force of the legal sources for the adoption of the measure.

Chapter 5 explores the constitutional right to development and the potential effects of investment treaties for development policymaking and implementation in Africa. The chapter shows that there is a right to development in Africa and corresponding duties of African states to adopt policy and regulatory measures to ensure the realisation of this right. Although development is claimed to be an objective of the investment treaty regime, the actual terms of the treaties can conflict with the adoption of broader development policies when they affect an investment interest, even though investment per se does not always come with tangible benefits to the state. Specifically, the standards of investment protection, such as national treatment and guarantees on repatriation of investment and returns, limit the constitutional powers of African states to adopt targeted social, economic, and industrial policies and to regulate foreign exchange transactions for currency stability to promote development. The adoption of these measures can result in investment treaty claims for breach of the applicable investment treaty standards as evidenced by relevant arbitral case law. This chapter argues that the right to development and corresponding duties to make and implement development policies under the constitutions, IETs, and IHRTs limit the competence of African states in investment treaty-making and must guide the states in concluding investment treaties, taking into consideration their effects for the autonomy to regulate in discharge of those duties.

Chapter 6 concludes that there is the need for the treaty-based standards of investment protection to be reconciled with the constitutional and general international law duties of African states to protect the environment and human rights and to initiate and implement development policy and in light of judicial sovereignty. It is only by being guided by constitutional norms which justify regulatory autonomy in making investment treaties that that autonomy can be reclaimed or retained. This means that African states must not enter into investment treaties at all or the treaty terms must be effectively qualified to accommodate the right to regulate. Existing investment treaties must be revised and certain terms must be excluded from them or qualified to make room for the exercise of the right to regulate.

African states must always put the interests of their citizens first in international economic relations. In so stating, I acknowledge, as pointed out by Sornarajah, that '[t]here is an absence of perfect equality in knowledge, negotiating power, and lack of coercion to support the view that there is voluntary surrender of sovereignty'[228] in disregard of constitutional law and general international law guaranteeing that sovereignty. However, it is equally the case, as Kelsey states, that '[t]he globalisation of national economies is, at least, a fact of life. *But there is choice in how far* a particular state embraces it, and how much room that leaves for manoeuvre if (or when) the expansion of trans-national enterprise proves ecologically, economically, politically or socially unsustainable.'[229]

[228] Sornarajah and Trakman, 'Polemic' (n 205) 509.
[229] Kelsey, *New Zealand Experiment* (n 202) 369 (emphasis added).

2
Reclaiming Regulatory Autonomy from the Investment Treaty Regime in Africa
The Imperatives Theory

2.1 Introduction

A plurality of legal norms on national and international planes often gives rise to conflict between or among those norms. This happens particularly where municipal law and international legal norms cover, deal with, or regulate the same subject matter. This is the case, for example, between treaties on foreign investment protection and municipal law from which the right of states to regulate foreign investors and their covered investments is sourced.[1] As Ernst-Ulrich Petersmann remarks, 'states, governments and international organizations justify themselves by their collective supply of public goods (PGs) demanded by citizens'.[2] This justification is sourced or derived from an amalgam of national constitutions, domestic legislation as well as general international law, and customary international law. As the sources of the powers of states to regulate in the public interest, what do these norms or must these norms play in states' negotiation and conclusion of investment treaties which turn to constrain states' exercise of public interest powers? Human rights, constitutional and democratic governance 'proceed from the assumption that citizens, as democratic "principals" of all governance agents, ought to be in a position to judge government decisions so as to hold governments democratically accountable and defend their constitutional rights if government agents fail to protect and promote the collective 'public interest' of citizens'.[3] Do the rights of citizens under national constitutions and in general international law and the corresponding obligations of states limit the competence of states in any way when states conclude investment treaties? What are the legal and/or normative consequences where states surrender their right to regulate in the public interest under

[1] Michel Rosenfeld, 'Rethinking Constitutional Ordering in an Era of Legal and Ideological Pluralism' (2008) 6 International Journal of Constitutional Law 415, 45–416 (hereafter, Rosenfeld, 'Rethinking Constitutional Ordering').

[2] Ernst-Ulrich Petersmann, *Multilevel Constitutionalism for Multilevel Governance of Public Goods: Methodology Problems in International Law* (Hart Publishing 2017) 1.

[3] Ernst-Ulrich Petersmann, 'Constitutional Theories of International Economic Adjudication and Investor-State Arbitration' in Pierre-Marie Dupuy, Ernst-Ulrich Petersmann, and Francesco Francioni (eds), *Human Rights in International Investment Law and Arbitration* (OUP 2009) 136.

The Investment Treaty Regime and Public Interest Regulation in Africa. Dominic Npoanlari Dagbanja, Oxford University Press.
 DOI: 10.1093/oso/9780192896179.003.0002

investment treaties in order to secure absolute protection for foreign investment? The imperatives theory, developed in this chapter and which is the theoretical foundation for the analyses in this book, addresses these questions with a focus on African states as case studies.

From the very inception of the legal regime of foreign investment protection, there has been concern and contestation among states, investment scholars, policy-makers, and international organisations about standards of investment protection under international law and municipal law. The concerns relate to the restraining effects of treaties on the making and implementation of regulatory measures aimed at protecting human rights, the environment, and other public welfare interests.[4] The issue is the extent to which governments may adversely affect the value of foreign investors' property by regulation, particularly in the context of general regulation for a public purpose, without having to compensate an affected foreign investor.[5] On one hand, there is the need to protect legitimate foreign investment. On the other hand, if states are required to pay compensation in all cases in which regulation adversely affects foreign investment, they may not only lose huge sums of public money, but regulation for public purposes may also be restrained by the fear of international arbitration. In such a case, international investment law would become an instrument for the exploitation of host states.[6] In light of these issues, '[m]uch rethinking will need to be done on recapturing the regulatory space that has been sacrificed as a result of the treaties and the encroachments on this space made by arbitral tribunals'.[7] How is this to be done?

International investment law scholarship on the subject of conflict between international investment law and the right to regulate as well as domestic policy choices might be divided into two broadly opposing camps. On the one hand, there are those who believe that a liberalised investment regime will spur development in countries with otherwise bleak development prospects. They seem to equate foreign investment with development. Ignaz Seidl-Hohenveldern, for example, is of the view that 'there must be private foreign investment to meet the needs of newly-developing countries' and that they 'must encourage the flow of such investments by making them more secure'.[8]

[4] OECD, *International Investment Law: A Changing Landscape: A Comparative Volume to International Investment Perspectives* (OECD Publishing 2005) 44.

[5] ibid.

[6] Muthucumaraswamy Sornarajah, 'The Case against a Regime on International Investment Law' in Leon Trackman and Nicola Ranieri (eds), *Regionalism in International Investment Law* (OUP 2013) 475, 501, and 506 (hereafter, Sornarajah, 'Case against Investment Law').

[7] Muthucumaraswamy Sornarajah, *The International Law on Foreign Investment* (3rd edn, CUP 2010) 82 (hereafter, Sornarajah, *Law on Foreign Investment*).

[8] Ignaz Seidl-Hohenveldern, 'The ABS–Shawcross Draft Convention to Protect Private Foreign Investment: Comments on the Round Table' (1961) 10 Journal of Public Law 100.

Conventional works on international investment promotion and protection 'seek to analyse this area as if there is nothing wrong that is taking place'.[9] Yet there is 'no evidence to show that investment treaties have led to greater inflows of foreign investment into states making them'[10] which is the reason the international law on foreign investment has been described as the 'law of greed'.[11] This is because 'it is built on accentuating only one side of the picture of foreign investment so as to benefit the interests of multinational corporations which exist to seek profits for their shareholders'.[12] The 'case for an international body of investment law can be made only on the basis that there is but one way towards economic development that serves all mankind. Unfortunately, neither in practice nor in economic theory can such a case be made.'[13]

On the other hand, there are scholars who seriously caution against the use of investment treaties and arbitration to protect foreign investment, given their limiting impact on public interest regulation.[14] Jane Kelsey, argues that '[t]he current orthodoxy of ... investment liberalization leaves no space to talk of social and environmental justice, indigenous rights, healthy communities, eradicating poverty or redistributing power'.[15] The investment treaty regime constrains governments from pursuing a range of legislative strategies that significantly impair investment interests. The investment agreements place binding limits on what governments can and cannot do. The restraining effects of investment treaties are attributable to their constitutional characteristics in the sense that they seek to regulate the exercise of public power much like constitutions do.[16] The system of investment arbitration is a method of public law adjudication since it resolves regulatory disputes between individuals and the state as opposed to reciprocal disputes between private parties or between states. The use of private arbitration in the regulatory sphere 'conflicts with the cherished principles of judicial accountability and independence

[9] Muthucumaraswamy Sornarajah, 'Evolution or Revolution in International Arbitration? The Decent into Normlessness' in Chester Brown and Kate Miles (eds), *Evolution in Investment Treaty Law and Arbitration* (CUP 2011) 631, 656.

[10] Sornarajah, *Law on Foreign Investment* (n 7) 299.

[11] Muthucumaraswamy Sornarajah, 'A Law for Need or a Law for Greed?: Restoring the Lost Law in the International Law of Foreign Investment' (2006) International Environmental Agreements 329, 331.

[12] ibid 331.

[13] Sornarajah, Case against Investment Law (n 6) 504.

[14] Jane Kelsey, 'Global Economic Policy-Making: A New Constitutionalism?' (1999–2000) 9 Otago Law Review 535; Jane Kelsey (ed), *No Ordinary Deal: Unmasking the Trans-Pacific Partnership Free Trade Agreement* (Bridget Williams Books Ltd 2010); David Schneiderman, *Constitutionalizing Economic Globalization: Investment Rules and Democracy's Promise* (CUP 2008) (hereafter, Schneiderman, *Constitutionalizing Economic Globalization*); Gus Van Harten, *Investment Treaty Arbitration and Public Law* (OUP 2007) (hereafter, Harten, *ITA and Public Law*).

[15] Jane Kelsey, 'International Economic Agreements and Environmental Justice' in Klaus Bosselmann and Benjamin J. Richardson (eds) *Environmental Justice and Market Mechanisms: Key Challenges for Environmental Law and Policy* (Kluwer Law International 1999) 154.

[16] Schneiderman, *Constitutionalizing Economic Globalization* (n 14) 41.

in democratic societies; in effect, it taints the integrity of the legal system by contracting out the judicial function in public law'.[17]

International investment and trade law scholars have written extensively on the limiting impact of investment treaties and arbitration on regulatory autonomy of host states and made various proposals for the reform of investment and trade treaties.[18] One of the basics that has not been comprehensively and coherently considered in this scholarly inquiry is the question of the capacity of states to execute investment treaties and the obligations states can or cannot assume under these treaties in light of states' public interest obligations under national constitutions and general international law. This issue has not been explored in Africa. Yet, such an inquiry is of fundamental importance because as Alfred von Verdross stated:[19]

> each treaty presupposes a number of norms necessary for the very coming into existence of an international treaty. *These are the norms determining which persons are endowed with the capacity to act in international law, what intrinsic and extrinsic conditions must be fulfilled that an international treaty may come into*

[17] Harten, *ITA and Public Law* (n 14) 3.

[18] Kojo Yelpaala, 'Fundamentalism in Public Health and Safety in Bilateral Investment Treaties Part I' (2008) 3(2) Asian Journal of WTO & International Health Law and Policy 235; and Kojo Yelpaala, 'Fundamentalism in Public Health and Safety in Bilateral Investment Treaties Part II' (2008) 3(2) Asian Journal of WTO & International Health Law and Policy 465 (hereafter, Yelpaala, 'Fundamentalism in Public Health Part II'); David Schneiderman, *Resisting Economic Globalization: Critical Theory and International Investment* Law (Palgrave Macmillan 2013); James Gathii, 'Third World Approaches to International Economic Governance' in Richard Falk, Balakrishnan Rajagopal, and Jacquelin Stevens (eds), *International Law and the Third World: Reshaping Justice* (Routledge-Cavendish 2008) 255; James Gathii, 'International Justice and the Trading Regime' (2005) 19 Emory International Law Review 1407; and James Gathii, *African Regional Trade Agreements as Legal Regimes* (CUP 2011); Boris Rigod, *Optimal Regulation and the Law of International Trade: The Interface between the Right to Regulate and WTO Law* (CUP 2015); Makane Mengue and Stefanie Schacherer, 'The "Africanization" of International Investment Law: The Pan-African Investment Code and the Reform of the International Investment Regime' (2017) 18(3) The Journal of World Investment & Trade 414; Makane Mengue and Stefanie Schacherer 'Africa and the Rethinking of International Investment Law: About the Elaboration of the Pan-African Investment Code' in *Comparative International Law* (OUP 2018); Jonathan Bonnitcha, *Substantive Protection under Investment Treaties: A Legal and Economic Analysis* (CUP 2014); Michael Waibel and others (eds), *The Backlash against Investment Arbitration: Perceptions and Reality* (Kluwer Law International 2010); Emmanuel Laryea, Nokuhle Madolo, and Franziska Sucker (eds), *International Economic Law: Voices of Africa* (Siber Ink 2012); Boris Rigod, *Optimal Regulation and the Law of International Trade: The Interface between the Right to Regulate and WTO Law* (CUP 2015); Berk Demirkol, *Judicial Acts and Investment Treaty Arbitration* (CUP 2018); Laurence Boulle and Emmanuel Laryea (eds), *International Economic Law and African Development* (Siber Ink 2014); Charlotte Sieber-Gasser, *Developing Countries and Preferential Services Trade* (CUP 2016); Sonia E Rolland, *Towards Development-Oriented Rules at the WTO: Some Proposals* (OUP 2012); Ryan Reetz and Pedro Martinez-Fraga, *Public Purpose in International Law: Rethinking Regulatory Sovereignty in the Global Era* (CUP 2015); Eric De Brabandere, *Investment Treaty Arbitration as Public International Law: Procedural Aspects and Implications* (CUP 2013); Kate Miles, *The Origins of International Investment Law: Empire, Environment and the Safeguarding of Capital* (CUP 2013); Jorg Viñuales, *Foreign Investment and the Environment in International Law* (CUP 2012); and Jonathan Bonnitcha, Lauge Poulsen, and Michael Waibel, *The Political Economy of the Investment Treaty Regime* (OUP 2017).

[19] Alfred von Verdross, 'Forbidden Treaties in International Law: Comments on Professor Garner's Report on "The Law of Treaties"' (1937) 31 American Journal of International Law 571, 572, (emphasis added) (hereafter, Verdross, 'Forbidden Treaties').

> *existence, what juridical consequences are attached to the conclusion of an international treaty*. These principles concerning the conditions of the validity of treaties cannot be regarded as having been agreed upon by treaty; they must be regarded as valid independently of the will of the contracting parties. That is the reason why the possibility of *norms of general international law, norms determining the limits of the freedom of the parties to conclude treaties*, cannot be denied a *priori*.

Do norms such as national constitutions and general international law necessary for the coming into being of investment treaties place legal limitations on the authority of states in terms of investment treaty terms to agree to? The conflict between investment treaty norms, on the one hand, and municipal law and international legal duties concerning the protection of the public interest, on the other, is both about the lack of protection in investment treaties for the right to regulate and the capacity of states to execute investment treaties undertaking any type of obligation thereunder, irrespective of its effect on regulatory autonomy. The conflict is also about interpretation; that is, whether in settling investor–state disputes investment tribunals should interpret investment treaties as excluding or abridging the right to regulate and giving rise to state liability for compensation when in fact the treaties do not expressly exclude or abridge that right. An analysis of conflict of legal norms and interests in international investment law must start with an examination of the limits to the legal obligations states can assume under investment treaties. I do this analysis with particular reference to African countries with similar constitutional public interest obligations, but the conclusions drawn can have implications for all countries with similar constitutional norms.

African countries have constitutions which create and define the framework for governance and the protection of basic human rights.[20] Most African states are also parties to the major international environmental treaties (IETs) and international human rights treaties (IHRTs) and other norms on development and good governance. For example, by the Constitution of the Republic Ghana 1992, the state has the legal authority to make policies and laws and implement and enforce them in the public interest. Article 35(1) of this Constitution states that the 'sovereignty of Ghana resides in the people of Ghana from whom Government derives all its powers and authority through this Constitution'. Articles 1 and 73 require the government of Ghana to promote the welfare of the people, exercise governmental powers within constitutional limits, and conduct its international affairs in accordance with accepted principles of public international law.

[20] Chris Thornhill, *A Sociology of Constitutions: Constitutions and State Legitimacy in Historical-Sociological Perspective* (CUP 2013).

In investment arbitration, states commonly invoke their powers to regulate in the public interest under their constitutions *and* general international law, including customary international law (CIL), IETs, and IHRTs to justify their non-liability for adopting measures challenged by foreign investors.[21] This fact shows that states recognise their right to regulate in the public interest as deriving from constitutional and public international legal norms. I make the *a priori* argument that in the first place these legal norms and the higher values of society contained in them concerning the public interest must determine and shape the investment treaty-making powers of African states.[22]

Based on *constitutional-general international law imperatives*, I develop the imperatives theory as a framework for explaining and dealing with this conflict of legal norms and interests in international investment law. The issue addressed by the imperatives theory is whether the fundamental obligations of African states towards citizens under their constitutions, CIL, IETs, and IHRTs do limit or should limit their competence to enter into investment treaties. This *a priori* and fundamental question cannot be left to be addressed at the point of dispute and investor–state arbitration. I conclude that constitutional and general international law norms on public interest regulation do limit the capacity of African states in the making of investment treaties for several reasons.

First, African states derive their powers from the people through their constitutions (or equivalent law) to be exercised in the name of and for the good of the people and within constitutional limits. The public source of African states' powers and public purpose for which the powers to govern are entrusted to the states limit them from entering into legal agreements that directly and explicitly restrain or have the effect of restraining sovereign regulatory autonomy. For example, national treatment and most-favoured-nation treatment directly and explicitly limit the regulatory autonomy of states by requiring them to extend treatment accorded to domestic investors to foreign investors of a contracting party or third state when

[21] See for example, *CMS Gas Transmission Company v Argentina*, ICSID No ARB/01/8, Award, 12 May 2005 [113]–[114]; *Continental Casualty Company v Argentina*, ICSID Case No ARB/03/9, Award, 5 September 2008, [74]; *Tecnicas Medioambientales Tecmed SA v Mexico*, Case No ARB (AF)/00/2, Award, 23 May 2003 [70]; *Saluka Investments BV (The Netherlands) v Czech Republic*, Partial Award, 17 March 2006 [289]; and *Compañía Del Desarrollo De Santa Elena, SA v Costa Rica*, Case No ARB/96/1, Final Award, 17 February 2000 [35], [40], and [62]; *Biwater Gauff (Tanzania) Ltd. v United Republic of Tanzania*, ICSID Case No ARB/05/22, Award, 24 July 2008; *Balkan Energy Limited (Ghana) v Ghana*, UNCITRAL, PCA Case No 2010-7, Award on the Merits, 1 April 2014; *Balkan Energy Limited (Ghana) v Ghana*, UNCITRAL, PCA Case No 2010-7, Interim Award, 22 December 2010; and *Bankswitch Ghana Ltd (Ghana) v Ghana, PCA 118294, UNCITRAL*, Award Save as to Costs, 11 April 2014; *Philip Morris Brands SÀRL, Philip Morris Products S.A. and ABAL Hermanos S.A. v Oriental Republic* of Uruguay ICSID Case No ARB/10/7, 08 July 2016, [218] and [227]; and *Yukos Universal Limited (Isle of Man) v The Russian Federation*, UNCITRAL, PCA Case No AA 227, Final Award, 18 July 2014, [113], [696], [1314], and [1315].

[22] Sornarajah, *Law on Foreign Investment* (n 7) 231.

under national legislation the rights and activities of foreign investors can be curtailed and special treatment can be accorded to domestic investors without the obligation to extend the same treatment to foreign businesses. Expropriation requirements also directly limit regulatory autonomy by requiring compensation even for general regulation when national laws do not impose an obligation to pay compensation for such regulation.

Second, investment treaties presuppose the existence of norms necessary for them to come into existence and to have legal effect. The African constitutions under discussion and general international law specify who has the capacity to make treaties and the procedures for treaty-making. As investment treaties are required to be made in accordance with national constitutions and general international law and not just for investment protection *per se*, their validity and legal effect should be determined within the terms of these constitutions and general international law.

The remainder of this chapter is organised as follows. Section 2.2 reviews and analyses the nature and scope of African states' obligations to protect the public interest to outline clearly the core obligations at the centre of the research questions.

Section 2.3 discusses existing state-specific defences and justifications or principles that have been canvassed or applied by investment scholars and tribunals to address the conflict of legal norms and interests in international investment law. It concludes that these defences and justifications do not guarantee states success in investor–state arbitration. Therefore, there is the need for alternatives.

Section 2.4 develops the imperatives theory for addressing the challenge posed by international investment law for states' regulatory autonomy. The imperatives theory focuses on whether public interest regulation, such as for purposes of human rights and environmental protection or to advance a specific development objective, should limit the competence of African states in investment treaty-making in light of the fact that these states' primary obligations are owed towards citizens.

Section 2.5 distils the basic postulates of the imperatives theory which are a set of theoretical implications based on constitutional analysis on how to address the challenge international investment law poses to regulatory autonomy. The limitations of investment treaty law and arbitration on the right to regulate are treated in Chapters 3, 4, and 5 with specific case studies on the jurisdiction of municipal courts, environmental protection, and development policy. Building on the theme of constitutional-general international law imperatives, each of these case studies establishes a point about constitutional and general international law limitations on the capacity of African states to execute investment treaties and agreeing to absolute standards of investment protection

Section 2.6 concludes that treaty-based standards of investment protection must be reconciled with the right to regulate in the public interest.

2.2 The Public Interest Obligations of African States

The municipal law and international legal duties of African states to regulate in the public interest necessarily implies some measure of discretion in the exercise of the powers to perform those duties. For example, the Constitution of Ghana states in Article 1 that:

> [t]he Sovereignty of Ghana resides in the people of Ghana in whose name and for whose welfare the powers of government are to be exercised in the manner and within the limits laid down in this Constitution.
>
> This Constitution shall be the supreme law of Ghana and any other law found to be inconsistent with any provision of this Constitution shall, to the extent of the inconsistency, be void.

Within the domestic context, this emphasises the supremacy of the Constitution of Ghana over all laws (including treaties) made by the legislature and the executive. It also underscores the source of sovereignty and purpose of public power entrusted to the government of Ghana, namely the people, in whose name and for whose interests the powers of government shall be exercised. Article 1 expresses a constitutional meta-norm expressed in Latin by Marcus Cicero[23] as *ollis salus populi suprema lex esto*, meaning 'let the safety or good of the people be the supreme law'.[24] Similar provision is found in Article 1(1) of the Constitution of the Republic of Kenya 2010,[25] wherein it is stated that '[a]ll sovereign power belongs to the people of Kenya and shall be exercised only in accordance with this Constitution'. The Constitution of the Federal Republic of Nigeria 1999[26] states in Article 14(1)(a) and (b) that 'sovereignty belongs to the people of Nigeria from whom government through this Constitution derives all its powers and authority' and that 'the security and welfare of the people shall be the primary purpose of government'. According to the preamble to the Constitution of the Republic of South Africa 1996, South Africans adopted the Constitution in order to '[l]ay the foundations for a democratic and open society in which government is based on the will of the people' and to '[i]improve the quality of life of all citizens and free the potential of each person'. The express foundational values of the Constitution of South Africa in Section 1(a) and (c) are '[h]uman dignity, the achievement of equality and the advancement of human rights and freedoms' and '[s]upremacy of the constitution and the rule of law'. Under the Constitution of the Federal Republic of Cameroon 1972,[27] the people resolved in the preamble to harness Cameroon's

[23] Marcus Cicero, *de Legibus* III <https://www.loebclassics.com/view/marcus_tullius_cicero-de_legibus/1928/pb_LCL213.467.xml> accessed 04 November 2020.

[24] Bryan A Garner (ed-in-chief), *Black's Law Dictionary* (9th edn, Thomson West 2009) 1870.

[25] Constitution of the Republic of Kenya 2010.

[26] Constitution of the Federal Republic of Nigeria 1999.

[27] Constitution of the Republic of Cameroon 1972 with Amendments through 2008.

natural resources 'in order to ensure the well-being of every citizen without discrimination, by raising living standards, proclaim [their] right to development'. Article 2(1) of the Constitution of Cameroon and Article 4 of the Constitution of the Arab Republic of Egypt *2014*[28] provide that sovereignty is vested in the people.

In effect, the people are at the centre stage in the making of at least these constitutions and the promotion of their welfare is the reason for the constitution of governments in Africa. In this regard, the positions of John Locke and Jean-Jacques Rousseau provide relevant background to the specific point about the African states' constitutional obligations I analyse in this book. In his *Second Treatise of Government*, Locke treats *salus populi* as the *basic norm* for governance and the exercise of governmental powers. According to Locke, political power is the 'right of making laws ... for regulating and preserving of property and of employing the force of the community in the execution of such laws ... *all this only for the public good*'.[29] Rousseau underscored this point about the role of government when he posed and disposed of a fundamental question: 'What is the object of any political association? It is the protection and the prosperity of its members.'[30]

Constitutions in Africa protect fundamental human rights and freedoms, including the right to health and life, and require state institutions and all natural and legal persons (which includes foreign investors) to uphold and respect these fundamental human rights.[31] African states have constitutional responsibilities to ensure the realisation of basic human rights, a healthy economy, the right to work, the right to good healthcare, and the right to education.[32] It is also the responsibilities of African states to enact and enforce laws to assure the protection and promotion of human rights and freedoms.[33] African states must take all necessary action to ensure that their economies are managed in a manner that maximises development and secures the maximum welfare, freedom, and happiness of every person and to provide adequate means of livelihood and suitable employment.[34] African states must take steps to safeguard and protect their environments. These constitutional imperatives place the public interest at the centre of the exercise of

[28] Constitution of the Arab Republic of Egypt 2014, adopted 15 January 2014, entered into force 15 January 2014.

[29] John Locke, *Two Treatises of Civil Government* (JM Dent and Sons 1924) at 118 (emphasis added).

[30] Jean-Jacques Rousseau, *The Social Contract* (Maurice Cranston tr, Penguin Books Ltd 2004) 99.

[31] Constitution of Cameroon (n 27) preamble and arts 1(2), 55(2); Constitution of Egypt (n 28) preamble and arts 5, 24, 46, 79, 91, 93; Constitution of the Republic Ghana 1992, art 12(1); Constitution of Kenya (n 25) arts 19 and 26–56; and Constitution of the Republic of South Africa 1996, ss 7–39.

[32] Constitution of Cameroon (n 27) art 55(2); Constitution of Egypt (n 28), art 79; Constitution of Ghana art (n 31) art 34(2); Constitution of Kenya (n 25) art 43; and Constitution of South Africa (n 31) ss 7–39.

[33] Constitution of Cameroon (n 27) art 26; Constitution of Egypt (n 28) art 101; Constitution of Ghana (n 31) art 37(2)(b); Constitution of Kenya (n 25) art 21(2) and (4); Constitution of Nigeria (n 26) ss 16–18; and Constitution of South Africa (n 31) ss 24(b).

[34] Constitution of Ghana (n 31) art 36(1); Constitution of Kenya (n 25) art 21; and Constitution of Nigeria (n 26) s 17(3).

the powers of governments in Africa.[35] This public interest must be prioritised in Africa's international economic relations with other countries.

Most African states are also parties or signatories to a number of IETs, IHRTs, and declarations, including the Charter of the United Nations,[36] the International Covenant on Civil and Political Rights,[37] International Covenant on Economic, Social and Cultural Rights,[38] the Universal Declaration of Human Rights,[39] the African Charter on Human and Peoples' Rights,[40] and African Convention on Conservation of Nature and Natural Resources.[41] These international legal instruments directly or indirectly recognise or guarantee various fundamental human rights, including the right to development and the right to a clean environment, and impose corresponding obligations on the states. Article 33(5) of the Constitution of Ghana extends fundamental human rights and corresponding duties of Ghana to include those rights inherent in a democracy and intended to secure the freedom and dignity of human beings. The Supreme Court of Ghana held in *Republic of Ghana v High Court, Ex Parte the Attorney-General* that ratified international conventions which have been 'incorporated into Ghanaian law by appropriate legislation'[42] have legal effect and are enforceable as internal law in Ghana.[43] This demonstrates the obligation of Ghana to respect and uphold IETs and IHRTs to which it is a party. For Kenya, the 'general rules of international law' and ratified treaties 'shall form part of the law of Kenya'.[44]

African governments in their dealings with other nations have constitutional obligations to promote and protect the national interests, promote respect for international law and treaty obligations, and conduct international affairs in accordance with the accepted principles of public international law.[45] Accepted principles of

[35] Constitution of Ghana (n 31) art 36(9); Constitution of Kenya (n 25) art 42; and Constitution of Nigeria (n 26) s 20.

[36] Charter of the United Nations, signed in San Francisco, 26 June 1945, entered into force 24 October 1945.

[37] International Covenant on Civil and Political Rights, International Covenant on Economic, Social and Cultural Rights, General Assembly Resolution 2200A (XXI) of 16 December 1966, entry into force 23 March 1976.

[38] International Covenant on Economic, Social and Cultural Rights, General Assembly resolution 2200A (XXI) of 16 December 1966, entry into force 3 January 1976.

[39] Universal Declaration of Human Rights, proclaimed by the United Nations General Assembly in Paris on 10 December 1948, General Assembly Res 217 A (III).

[40] African Charter on Human and Peoples' Rights, adopted 27 June 1981, OAU Doc CAB/LEG/67/3 rev 5, 21 ILM 58 (1982), entered into force 21 October 1986.

[41] African Convention on Conservation of Nature and Natural Resources, adopted 15 September 1968, entered into force 16 June 1969, revised and adopted 11 July 2003.

[42] *The Republic of Ghana v High Court, Ex Parte the Attorney-General; NML Capital & the Republic of Argentina*, Case No J5/10/2013, Judgment of 20 June 2013, 2 <https://ghalii.org/gh/judgment/supreme-court/2011/31> accessed 4 November 2020 (hereafter, *Ex Parte: Attorney-General*).

[43] ibid 5 and 7.

[44] Constitution of Kenya (n 25) art 2(5) and (6).

[45] Constitution of Cameroon (n 27) preamble and arts 44–45; Constitution of Egypt (n 28) preamble and arts 93 and 151; Constitution of Ghana (n 31) art 40(a) and (c) and art 73; Constitution of Kenya (n 25) art 21(4); Constitution of Nigeria (n 26) s 19(d); and Constitution of South Africa (n 31) ss 37(4)(b)(i), 39(1)(b), 99(5), 201(2)(c), and 231.

public international law include IETs and IHRTs to which African states are parties as well as CIL. African constitutions place primacy on fundamental human rights of citizens and corresponding obligations of states *both* as contained in the respective constitutions *and* in general international law conventions on human rights and the environment.[46] The constitutions of Egypt, Ghana, and Nigeria specifically place the *national interest* at the centre of their foreign policies and international relations.[47] These constitutional principles on the public interest and governments in Africa are the foundation of the imperatives theory.

National constitutions in Africa seek to retain states' regulatory autonomy in relation to foreign investment. Article 36(4) of the Constitution of Ghana states that '[f]oreign investment shall be encouraged within Ghana, subject to any law for the time being in force regulating foreign investment in Ghana'. This provision requires the entry of foreign investment and its substantive protection thereafter to be conducted in consonance with laws in force governing foreign investment in Ghana. Those laws include the Constitution of Ghana, which in Article 17(4)(c) empowers Parliament to enact laws 'reasonably necessary for the imposition of restrictions on the acquisition of land by persons who are not citizens of Ghana or on the ... economic activities of such persons and for other matters related to such persons'. So, the admission and substantive protection of foreign investment in Ghana must be consistent with the Constitution of Ghana and other domestic legislation on foreign investment, including the Ghana Investment Promotion Centre Act 2013 (Act 865), the primary legislation on foreign investment. In the same way, the Constitution of Nigeria states in Article 16(2)(c), that the state shall direct policy towards ensuring that the economic system 'is not operated in such a manner as to permit the concentration of wealth or the means of production and exchange in the hands of few individuals or of a group'. According to Article 66(2) of the Constitution of Kenya, Parliament 'shall enact legislation ensuring that investments in property benefit local communities and their economies'.

Clearly then the public interest must be prioritised in the promotion and protection of foreign investment in Africa whether this is done through international law or domestic law or both. This is the reason public interest obligations must determine the content of international investment agreements on trade and investment in Africa. Yet, the enactment of legislation or adoption of policies aimed specifically at citizens to give effect to these constitutional obligations could conflict with national treatment and expropriation provisions in investment treaties as illustrated in Chapter 5.

46 Constitution of Cameroon (n 27); preamble and art 55(2); Constitution of Egypt (n 28) art 79; Constitution of Ghana (n 31) arts 12–33, 36(9), 40, and 73; Constitution of Kenya (n 25) arts 21(4), 51(3)(b), 42, 69–70, and 72; Constitution of Nigeria (n 26) ss 19(d), 20, 21, and 33–34; Constitution of South Africa (n 31) arts 184 and 39(1)b) and (3), 184(3), 24.

47 Constitution of Egypt (n 28) art 151; Constitution of Ghana (n 31) arts 40(a), and 73; and Constitution of Nigeria (n 26) s 19(a).

The fundamental issue then is whether African states such as those involved in this book, the constitutions of which require them to act both within constitutional limits and in accordance with accepted principles of general international law with respect to public interest regulation, nevertheless have the capacity to enter into investment treaties that directly and explicitly abridge or confine their public powers, or require the payment of compensation for adopting measures required under the constitutions and/or general international law. I seek to make the case that the analysis of the effects of investment treaties on regulatory autonomy and the resolution of foreign investment disputes must be grounded or contextualised in the fundamental rights of citizens and the corresponding constitutional and general international law obligations of states, because it is these legal norms that define what African states can or cannot do with public power.

2.3 State-Specific Defences and Justifications in Investment Treaty Arbitration

2.3.1 The Scope and Efficacy of the Defences and Justifications

2.3.1.1 The Principle of Proportionality

International investment law scholars and tribunals have invoked the principle of proportionality, which they say can be used to strike a balance between the rights of investors and states' right to regulate in the public interest.[48] Caroline Henckels has engaged extensively with the efficacy of this defence.[49]

This principle as an interpretive tool and defence requires 'a reasonable relationship of proportionality between the charge or weight imposed' on 'the foreign investor and the aim sought to be realized ... by any measure'.[50] According to the Court of Justice of the European Union (CJEU), the proportionality principle 'requires that measures implemented ... be appropriate for attaining the ... objectives pursued by the legislation at issue and must not go beyond what is necessary to achieve them'.[51] Thus a tribunal must determine whether the means used by the state are suitable to achieve the aim pursued (*suitability*); the means adopted are necessary to achieve the aim involved (*necessity*); and the burden borne by the

[48] Jasper Krommendijk and John Morijn, 'Proportional' by What Measure(s)? Balancing Investor Interests and Human Rights by Way of Applying the Proportionality Principle in Investor–State Arbitration' in Pierre-Marie Dupuy, Ernst-Ulrich Petersmann, and Francesco Francioni (eds), *Human Rights in International Investment Law and Arbitration* (OUP 2009) 422, 450 (hereafter, Krommendijk and Morijn, *Balancing Investor Interests and Human Rights*).

[49] Caroline Henckles, *Proportionality and Defence in Investor–State Arbitration: Balancing Investment Protection and Regulatory Autonomy* (CUP 2015).

[50] *Tecmed v Mexico* (n 21) [122].

[51] Case C-58/08 *Vodafone Ltd v Secretary of State for Business, Enterprise and Regulatory Reform* [2010] ECR I-4999 [51].

individual is not excessive having regard to the benefits secured by the state (*proportionality stricto sensu*).[52]

Proportionality requires 'an identification and qualification of that which is to be balanced, that is, the rights and interest at stake'.[53] If there existed objective means of weighing those interests and the interests were of equal value, proportionality could provide a very fair way of evenly protecting the competing interests. However, the requirement for weighing is the fundamental weakness of proportionality theory.

The problem centres on how to weigh or place value on the competing interests. In some cases it is simply not possible to do so. It may be possible to assess the monetary value of an investment and how governmental regulation affects that value. However, it may not always be possible, for example, to assess or quantify environmental contamination and its effects on human health and life arising from the operations of a business entity, given both the immediate and long-term effects of such contamination. For example, in 1984 a gas leak from a facility owned by Union Carbide India Limited in Bhopal, India (with majority interest held by Union Carbide and Carbon Corporation of the United States, Union Carbide Corporation), led to the deaths of 4,000 human beings between 1984 and 1992. Between 30,000 and 40,000 people were maimed and about 200,000 people were estimated to have been affected by the disaster.[54] Many of the people affected by the disaster have not been compensated.[55] Moreover, the right of investors to make profit cannot be placed on the same level with the human right to health and life. Investment activities in natural resource extraction and industrial chemicals, for example, can have serious implications for the environment, water pollution, and human health as the Bhopal disaster illustrates and as shown in Chapter 4. As the sanctity and dignity of human life must precede everything, it sounds inappropriate to say that measures aimed at protecting human right to health and life must be weighed or balanced against the right to make profit for private gain.

The principle of proportionality does not address the problem of 'textual void' in international investment law. Investment treaties do not expressly make room for public interest regulation without the need to pay compensation to affected foreign investors. The investment treaties focus solely on investment protection. Even where exceptions are made in these treaties for public interest regulation, those exceptions are qualified in a manner that significantly reduces their efficacy. Since investment tribunals interpret these treaties based on the texts, 'in searching for

[52] N Jansen Calamita, 'International Human Rights and the Interpretation of International Investment Treaties: Constitutional Considerations' in Freya Baetebs (ed), *Investment Law within International Law: Integrationist Perspectives* (CUP 2013) 164, 175 (hereafter, Calamita, *Human Rights and Interpretation of IIAs*).

[53] ibid 175.

[54] ibid.

[55] Sornarajah, *Law on Foreign Investment* (n 7) 147.

a basis for the identification of rights and interests, which might be included in a balancing of textually identified investor rights ... one is left with a textual void'.[56]

By its insistence on the suitability and necessity of the measures taken and means adopted to implement the measures, proportionality subjects governmental decision-making to evaluation based on standards or preferences chosen by the investment tribunals, which themselves are not be suitably placed to make such evaluations and judgments. In addition, the fluid nature of the yardsticks of the proportionality principle means the boundaries of the principle cannot be known in advance of measures to be undertaken. In fact, Tribunals 'have adopted different approaches to the process of balancing and to the use of the proportionality principle'.[57] So governments cannot always predict the legality of their actions against the elements of proportionality.

'Balancing' does not exist if it always begins with the measures adopted by the government which must be scrutinised and not with the claims made by the foreign investor. To be even handed, tribunals would also need to begin with an assessment of the proportionality of the investors' claims against the measures giving rise to the claims. Proportionality as it stands now is, therefore, not proportional because it ignores questions as to how the weighing of interests is to be carried out and who gets the last word, the state or the investment tribunal (or the investor).[58] Proportionality is not an effective tool for deciding on the right to regulate and investor rights. On the basis of the foregoing analysis, the chapter adopts the perspective expressed by Jansen Calamita that:[59]

> Proportionality in the end is nothing more than a technical framework by which one may organise an argument. Absent an infusion of normative content from external sources [which infusion is largely absent in investment treaty arbitration], proportionality simply functions as a scale without weights. Thus, even if we assume that a rational and principled process of balancing is possible, and we are able to identify in general terms that which is to be balanced, we do not (and cannot) know how the balance called for by the principle of proportionality will be struck until we know the identity of the interests we intend to recognise, what weight they are to be given and to whom we intend to entrust the balancing ... Absent such criteria for determining what goes on the scales and what does not, we are beset with indeterminacy, subjectivity and an absence of consensual validation. Proportionality simply provides no answers to these concerns and, indeed, may actually obfuscate the importance of the political process of contesting and establishing constitutional values.

56 ibid.

57 Krommendijk and Morijn, *Balancing Investor Interests and Human Rights* (n 48) 439.

58 Evan J Criddle and Evan Fox-Decent, 'A Fiduciary Theory of Jus Cogens' (2009) 34 Yale Journal of International Law 331, 386 (hereafter, Criddle and Fox-Decent, 'Theory of Jus Cogens').

59 Calamita, 'Human Rights and Interpretation of IIAs' (n 52) 181.

2.3.1.2 The Defence of Necessity

Acts of a state illegal under international law entail the international responsibility of that state, except where some valid defence such as 'necessity' in general international law or in a specific treaty can be made.[60] Necessity shields states from the wrongfulness of acts which are not in conformity with an international obligation. Thus, in international investment law a state may place reliance on necessity as an excuse for not complying with an investment treaty obligation.

However, necessity provides limited scope as a defence mechanism by the very nature of its standards. Necessity under general international law may only be invoked if the act is the only way a state can safeguard an 'essential interest' against 'a grave and imminent peril'. Necessity is also permitted only if the carrying out of the act does not seriously impair an essential interest of any other state towards which the obligation exists or that of the international community as a whole.[61] It is not applicable if the international obligation in question excludes its application or where a state contributed to the situation that has given rise to the claim of necessity.[62]

Necessity does not apply in respect of any act which breaches an obligation arising under a peremptory norm of general international law, such as those on the slave trade.[63] Moreover, circumstances precluding the wrongfulness of state conduct do not necessarily free a state from paying compensation for any material loss caused by the conduct in question. It is for the investment tribunal to decide whether necessity excuses the state for an act that is otherwise wrongful in international investment law. Therefore, the discretion that states are supposed to enjoy even under the defence of necessity is subject to scrutiny by an investment tribunal.

Investment tribunals tend to emphasise the predictability and stability of the legal environment for business, even where necessity is invoked as a defence. Therefore, necessity has not proved to be an effective defence, even in economic and financial emergencies or changed circumstances that require the repeal or amendment of existing laws and policies governing foreign investment. A review of various cases in which Argentina invoked necessity as a defence in investment arbitration leads to the conclusion that 'necessity has not generally been a winning defence'.[64]

Thus, the uncertainty surrounding the scope and efficacy of necessity as a defence is exemplified by the situation of Argentina, which went through an economic

[60] International Law Commission, Draft Article on *Responsibility of States for Internationally Wrongful Acts* (International Law Commission 2001) art 1.

[61] ibid art 25(1).

[62] ibid art 25(2).

[63] ibid art 26.

[64] Daniel Kalderimis, 'Systemic Integration and International Investment Law—Some Practical Reflections', Society of International Economic Law Third Biennial Global Conference, National University of Singapore Faculty of Law Centre for International Law (Society of International Economic Law Working Paper No 2012/46, 6 July 2012, 7.

and financial crisis in the late 1990s and early 2000s. The Argentine government allegedly derogated from municipal law and investment treaty obligations in order to address the crisis. The government removed the parity between United States dollar and the Argentine peso and terminated the pegging of tariffs in government contracts to inflation-adjusted dollars.[65] Emergency laws and regulations were also made to give effect to these changes. These measures were said to have affected or disadvantaged foreign investors who made investments in the public sector, such as water concessions following privatisation in Argentina in the 1990s. The investors held extensive US dollar-denominated debts and were compelled to collect tariffs from customers in the Argentine peso, which had devalued. Following the crisis, and the adoption of these measures in response to the crisis, no fewer than fifty-three arbitral cases have been brought by foreign investors against Argentina.[66]

In defending arbitral suits against the adoption of these measures, Argentina argued that the measures were implemented in response to a national emergency resulting from a severe financial crisis which threatened its very existence as a country and the lives of very poor citizens. Argentina relied on the necessity defence and the treaty-based emergency exceptions.[67] Despite the large similarity in the facts, tribunals have differed in their findings on breach of the applicable investment treaties.[68] For example, *LG & E Energy Corporation v Argentina*[69] accepted Argentina's defence of necessity over the period beginning 1 December 2001 and ending 26 April 2003. The Tribunal reasoned that during the relevant period, the conditions in Argentina constituted an emergency which made it necessary for Argentina to enact measures to maintain public order, restore civil order, stop the economic decline, and protect its essential security interests within the meaning of the emergency clause under the applicable investment treaty.[70]

However, *CMS Gas Transmission Company v Argentina*,[71] *Sempra Energy International v Argentina*,[72] and *Enron Corporation Ponderosa Assets LP v*

[65] Christina Binder, 'Changed Circumstances in Investment Law: Interfaces between the Law of Treaties and the Law of State Responsibility with a Special Focus the Argentine Crisis' in Christina Binder and others (eds) *International Investment Law for the 21st Century: Essays in Honour of Christoph Schreuer* (OUP 2009) 608, 610 (hereafter, Binder, 'Changed Circumstances').

[66] United Nations Conference on Trade and Development, *Recent Developments in Investor–State Dispute Settlement* (Issue Note No 1, 7 April 2014), 8.

[67] *CMS Gas v Argentina* (n 21) [200]; *Enron Corporation Ponderosa Assets LP v Argentina*, ICSID Case No ARB/01/3, Award, 22 May 2007 para 288ff; and *Sempra Energy International v Argentina*, ICSID Case No ARB/02/16, Award, 28 September 2007, [325].

[68] Binder, 'Changed Circumstances' (n 65) 609.

[69] *LG & E Energy Corporation v Argentina, Decision on Liability*, ICSID Case No ARB 02/1, 3 October 2006.

[70] ibid [228]–[241].

[71] *CMS Gas v Argentina* (n 21). The decision of the Tribunal that Argentina failed to observe the obligations entered into with regard to the investment guaranteed was annulled in *CMS Gas Transmission Company v Argentina*, ICSID Case No ARB/01/8, (Annulment Proceeding), Decision of the Ad Hoc Committee on the Application for Annulment of the Argentine Republic, 25 September 2007, [163].

[72] *Sempra v Argentina* (n 67). The Sempra Award was annulled on the ground of manifest excess of powers in *Sempra Energy International Argentina*, ICSID Case No ARB/02/16, (Annulment

Argentina[73] found Argentina in breach of the applicable investment treaties. The *CMS Gas Transmission* Tribunal decided in favour of investor protection and found Argentina in breach of fair and equitable treatment (FET).[74] It reasoned that the standard requires the maintenance of a stable legal framework for investment and that the measures the investor complained of entirely transformed or dispensed with the legal and business environment under which the investments were made.[75] Another illustration of tribunals' contradictory decisions on the application of the defence of necessity is the disagreement of an annulment committee with the finding in *Enron Corporation v Argentina* that Argentina was not entitled to rely on the defence.[76]

These divergent positions on the defence of necessity illustrate the uncertainties surrounding its scope. More important for the purposes of regulatory autonomy, whether or not a measure is necessary is 'non-self-judging'. This means the state adopting the measures in question is not 'the sole arbiter of the scope and application of ... the invocation of necessity'.[77] It is for a tribunal to evaluate whether impugned measures are necessary[78] and to 'establish how grave an economic crisis must be so as to qualify as an essential security interest'[79] defence.

The necessity defence has the potential to provide some breathing space for states in the sense that their determination of the existence of a state of necessity may be affirmed by investment tribunals.[80] However, 'the application of the necessity doctrine's conditions is generally made in "black and white" terms' and 'portends the unjust failure of the necessity doctrine in many future cases'.[81] The defence of necessity is also of limited relevance because it applies only to emergencies and does not address the obligations on the state in general.

Proceeding), Decision on the Argentine Republic's Request for Annulment of the Award, 29 June 2010 [229].

[73] *Enron Corporation Ponderosa Assets LP v Argentina*, ICSID Case No ARB/01/3, Award, 22 May 2007.
[74] *CMS Gas v Argentina* (n 21) [281].
[75] ibid [274]–[275] and [277].
[76] *Enron Creditors Recovery Corp Ponderosa Assets, L.P v Argentina*, ICSID Case No ARB/01/3, (Annulment Proceeding), Decision on the Application for Annulment of the Argentine Republic, 30 July 2010 [359]–[395].
[77] *CMS Gas v Argentina* (n 21) [366].
[78] ibid [189].
[79] ibid [361].
[80] *BG Group Plc v The Republic of Argentina*, UNCITRAL, Final Award, 24 December 2007 [409]–[410].
[81] Avidan Kent and Alexandra R Harrison, 'The Plea of Necessity under Customary International Law: A Critical Review in Light of the Argentine Cases' in Brown and Miles (eds), *Evolution in Investment Treaty Law* (n 9) 246, 269.

2.3.1.3 The Margin of Appreciation Doctrine

International legal norms, including investment treaties, often give review powers to international tribunals and courts over national decision-makers. The margin of appreciation doctrine is applied in international dispute settlement to accommodate states' right to make and implement policies, decisions, and laws at the domestic level. The doctrine allows international courts and tribunals to scrutinise the decisions of states and their instrumentalities, but with a measure of deference. Two elements may be identified. The first is judicial deference, by which international courts and tribunals are expected to grant governments some degree of deference and to respect their discretion on how to execute their national and international law obligations. The second element is normative flexibility, which operates on the premise that international norms are open-ended or unsettled and provide limited conduct guidance for states. Therefore, these norms preserve space within which states are free to operate.[82]

However, 'the margin of appreciation afforded to states is never unlimited—i.e., there is no total deference to the national decision-making process'.[83] For the doctrine to apply, it must be shown that the state has exercised its discretion in good faith. More important, it is ultimately for tribunals to determine whether national decisions are reasonable. Reasonableness is measured by the conformity of a course of action selected by the state with the object of the governing norm.[84]

In investment arbitration, states have invoked the margin of appreciation doctrine to defend measures challenged by foreign investors. The doctrine does not guarantee with certainty that merely because a state is entitled to exercise discretion, its sense of judgment is final. At the end of the day, states' need for policy space and regulatory autonomy may or may not be guaranteed under the margin of appreciation doctrine.

This uncertainty is evidenced by *Quasar de Valores SICAV SA v Russia*,[85] where the investor claimed compensation under the Russia–Spain investment treaty for expropriation arising from tax enforcement measures. Russia defended its actions arguing that it was entitled to a wide margin of appreciation. The Tribunal stated that 'measures are bona fide, unless there is convincing evidence that, upon a true characterisation, they constitute a taking'.[86] However, it held that 'foreigners may invoke a higher standard of protection than nationals'.[87] While human rights conventions establish minimum standards to which all individuals are entitled, irrespective of any act of volition on their part:[88]

[82] Yuval Shany, 'Towards a General Margin of Appreciation Doctrine in International Law?' (2005) 16 European Journal of International Law 907, 909–10.
[83] ibid 910–11.
[84] ibid.
[85] *Quasar de Valores SICAV SA v Russia*, SCC, Award, 20 July 2012.
[86] ibid [181].
[87] ibid [21].
[88] ibid [22] and [179].

> investment-protection treaties contain undertakings which are explicitly designed to induce foreigners to make investments in reliance upon them. It therefore makes sense that the reliability of an instrument of the latter kind should not be diluted by precisely the same notions of 'margins of appreciation' that apply to the former.
>
> The notion that states have a considerable margin of discretion in enacting and enforcing tax laws should not lead to any confused idea that they have ... discretion as to whether or not to comply with an international treaty.

There is an extremely narrow window for the application of the margin of appreciation doctrine. In *Continental Casualty Company v Argentina*,[89] the Tribunal held that effective interpretation of a bilateral treaty founded on reciprocity requires an accommodation of the different interests and concerns of the parties to the treaty. In the Tribunal's view, there is the need for 'a significant margin of appreciation for the State applying the particular measure'[90] in 'a time of grave crisis'.[91] Nevertheless, the Tribunal stated that, although the provision in the Argentina–United States investment treaty allowing measures necessary for the essential security interests or public order[92]

> involves naturally a margin of appreciation by a party invoking it caution must be exercised in allowing a party unilaterally to escape from its treaty obligations in the absence of clear textual or contextual indications. This is especially so if the party invoking the allegedly self-judging nature of the exemption can thereby remove the issue, and hence the claim of a treaty breach by the investor against the host state, from arbitral review. This would conflict in principle with the agreement of the parties to have disputes ... settled compulsorily by arbitration.

2.3.2 Rethinking Regulatory Autonomy in International Investment Law

Various state-specific defences and justifications are thus available in international investment dispute settlement aimed at providing the bases for the recognition and accommodation of states' right to regulate. Where a defence or justification is successfully invoked, a state may not have to pay compensation to foreign investors for measures that adversely affect the value of their investments. These defences do not provide realistic, tangible, and easily measurable standards on which states can

[89] *Continental v Argentina* (n 21).
[90] ibid [181].
[91] ibid.
[92] ibid [187].

safely rely to assert their policy space and regulatory autonomy and not having to pay compensation to an affected investor. The defences are of limited scope and efficacy because their standards are uncertain and their applicability ultimately resides in the wisdom of the court or tribunal. Because of the inherent limitations of these defences or justifications, the core issue is whether states should continue to assume the currently applicable standards of investment protection. A legal and principled basis for responding to this issue is to critically examine the role of constitutions and general international law (including CIL, IETs, and IHRTs), constitutional-general international law imperatives, in Africa and beyond in the search for regulatory autonomy in international investment law.

The *constitutional-general international law imperatives test* I propose provides more clarity and objectivity than do its alternatives for deciding whether African states can or should assume certain investment treaty obligations and for the resolution of investment disputes. Two arguments can be advanced for this position.

The first is that the fulfilment of constitutional and general international law obligations to promote the welfare of the people must be the reason to enter into investment treaties because African states have primary obligations to put the public interests of their citizens first in all governmental decisions and actions.

The second is that investment treaties are premised on the theory that they are *sine qua non* for the attraction of investment, which it is claimed can advance a public interest objective such as development as shown in Chapter 1. It should follow then that if investment treaties are necessary for development, their terms must not be agreed to if they will undermine development objective.

Where the public interest regulation giving rise to investor–state dispute is justified by a constitution and general international law, the regulation should take precedence and command much more obedience than investment treaties which seek to limit even public interest regulation in order to attain absolute investment protection. Since IETS and IHRTs protect human rights, the environment, and the right to development, as do constitutions in Africa, these human rights and environmental treaties should take precedence over investment treaty obligations in the event of conflict. The legal validity and effect of investment treaties, given their absolute and sole focus on private investment interests, should be determined based on their limiting effect on the right to regulate in the public interest as required by national constitutions, IETs and IHRTs. Thus, Sornarajah questioned:[93]

> whether matters of international concern relating to the environment or human rights are *ius cogens* principles which trump the rights of foreign investors under investment treaties unilaterally to institute arbitral proceedings. The argument can credibly be made that there are some values in international environmental

[93] Sornarajah, *Law on Foreign Investment* (n 7) 231.

law and human rights law that are so fundamental that the propositions of investment treaties which are designed to protect large multinational corporations should give way to them.

The Vienna Convention on the Law of Treaties (VCLT)[94] provides for very limited scope for voiding treaties or escaping from their binding effect. Because of this, states can hardly free themselves from treaty obligations they have voluntarily entered into. This is the reason African states must be cautious as to treaty standards they agree to. I argue that public interest regulation is justified by national constitutions and general international law in Africa. These norms are the primary legal bases on which African states can claim that they are entitled to regulate in the public interest. At the same time, African states would justify entering into investment treaties based on their duties towards their citizens under their constitutions and general international law. Therefore, both the competence of African states to agree to certain terms in investment treaties and the validity and binding effect of those standards ought to be judged on the basis of the standards' limiting impact or effect on the exercise of those powers in the public interest. Unless in concluding investment treaties African states are restrained by the very legal norms which justify public interest regulation, and which states actually rely on as legal justification for challenged measures in investment arbitration, regulatory autonomy cannot be effectively recaptured or retained.

These arguments can hardly be accommodated in existing orthodoxy on the making of treaties and the validity and binding effect of those treaties once they have been entered into as reflected in the VCLT Articles 26–27, 46, and 53. The postulates I develop in this chapter and throughout the book are intended to provide a fundamental framework for rethinking the making and interpretation of investment treaties. In providing that framework, there would be the need to expand or stretch the argument beyond the contours of existing theory and discourse in order to provide fresh input into the debate.

2.4 The Capacity of African States to Execute Investment Treaties

This section sets out and interprets the analytical and theoretical foundations of the imperatives theory. The section establishes that constitutionalism is entrenched in a number of Africa states. Therefore, to retain their autonomy to regulate in the public interest, African states must act within the procedural and substantive

94 Vienna Convention on the Law of Treaties, concluded in Vienna 23 May 1969, entry into force 27 January 1980 (hereafter, 'VCLT').

constitutional limits governing the exercise of governmental powers and respect constitutional rights and obligations.

2.4.1 Constituent Power, Constitutionalism, and the Execution of Investment Treaties in Africa

The legal limits to the exercise of the powers of African states can be explained in terms of the concept of *constituent power*. According to Martin Loughlin, the primary function of the concept of constituent power 'is to specify in constitutional language the ultimate source of authority in the state'.[95] Constituent power[96]

> *rests on two conditions: recognition that the ultimate source of political authority derives from an entity known as 'the people'* and acceptance of the idea of a constitution as something that is created. The concept comes into its own only when the constitution is understood as a juridical instrument deriving its authority from a principle of self-determination: specifically, that the constitution is an expression of the constituent power of the people to make and re-make the institutional arrangements through which they are governed.

Thus, constituent power establishes a constitution and determines the nature of institutional arrangements to meet the purposes for which a constitution is established. Sovereign people define the mode of their political existence by adopting a constitution and allocating governmental powers to various institutions of government.[97] Constituent power creates agency and delegation in the sense that someone else (the constituted actor) is given the power to represent and make decisions on behalf of and for the benefit of the source of the power, the people. That real sovereignty, *majestas realis*, resides in or is vested in the people is reflected in Article 1(1) of the Constitution of Ghana wherein it is stated that the '[s]overeignty of Ghana resides in the people of Ghana in whose name and for whose welfare the powers of government are to be exercised in the manner and within the limits laid down in this Constitution'.

Indeed, like the Constitution of the United States of America 1787 and the Constitution of India 1949, the preamble to the Constitution of Ghana shows that 'the People of Ghana' adopted the Constitution in exercise of their 'natural and inalienable right to establish a framework of government which shall secure for [themselves] and posterity the blessing of liberty, equality of opportunity and

[95] Martin Loughlin, 'The Concept of Constituent Power' (2014) 13(2) European Journal of Political Theory 218, 219 (hereafter, Loughlin, 'Constituent Power').
[96] ibid.
[97] ibid 224 and 225.

prosperity'. The preambles to the Constitution of Kenya and the Constitution of Nigeria are to similar effect. Article 14(2)(a) and (b) of the Constitution of Nigeria states that 'sovereignty belongs to the people ... from whom government through this Constitution derives all its powers and authority'. Accordingly, the 'security and welfare of the people shall be the primary purpose of government'. Article 2(1) of the Constitution of Cameroon provides that national sovereignty 'shall be vested in the people of Cameroon who shall exercise same either through the President of the Republic and Members of Parliament or by way of referendum'. According to Article 4 of the Constitution of Egypt, sovereignty 'belongs to the people alone, which exercises it and protects it. They are the source of power.'

Thus, constituent power in these African countries 'forms part of an original and *pre-legal* wellspring for legitimate political order, in the exercise of which the sovereign subject of the people (or the nation) first enacts and authorizes laws (the constitution) by which the people is then publicly and objectively bound'.[98] Sovereignty, sovereign will, and constituent power have thus become 'submerged' in the concept of *the people* 'as an organic unity'.[99]

The representational nature of the status and authority of the constituted actors gives rise to what is described as the *paradox of constitutionalism*,[100] where a state as well as its agency is established through a constitutive process and yet it may become unaccountable to those who created it. Constituent power oscillates between unbound sovereignty and the force of a constitution.[101] The paradox of constitutionalism is reflected in the idea that the people who are the source of the constituent power cannot exercise sovereignty by themselves; governmental action is undertaken primarily by those who act in the name of the people so that the power the people possess can be exercised through constitutional forms.[102] The paradox of constitutionalism means governmental power ultimately derives from the people but is exercised through distinct individuals and institutions.[103]

It can be argued that in a state such as Ghana, the idea of unbound sovereignty is unknown in the sense that 'the tension between the constituent power of the sovereign people and constitutional forms that are intended to express and check this power'[104] is addressed by constitutional provisions restraining unbridled exercise

98 Chris Thornhill, 'Contemporary Constitutionalism and the Dialectic of Constituent Power' (2012) 1(3) Global Constitutionalism 369, 369–70.

99 Loughlin, 'Constituent Power' (n 95) 225.

100 Martin Loughlin and Neil Walker (eds), *The Paradox of Constitutionalism: Constituent Power and Constitutional Form* (OUP 2007) (hereafter, Loughlin and Walker (eds), *Paradox of Constitutionalism*).

101 Rainer Nickel, 'Private and Public Autonomy Revisited: Habermas' Concept of Co-originality in Times of Globalization and the Militant Security State' in Loughlin and Walker (eds), *Paradox of Constitutionalism* (n 100) 147, 148.

102 Martin Loughlin and Neil Walker, 'Introduction' in Loughlin and Walker (eds), *Paradox of Constitutionalism* (n 100) 1.

103 ibid. See also Denis J Galligan, 'The Paradox of Constitutionalism or the Potential of Constitutional Theory' (2008) 29(2) Oxford Journal of Legal Studies 343, 346.

104 Stephen M Griffin, 'Constituent Power and Constitutional Change in American Constitutionalism' in Loughlin and Walker (eds), *Paradox of Constitutionalism* (n 100) 49.

of powers by constituted actors and empowering citizens to challenge unconstitutional actions. The primacy of constituent power over the constituted actors is reflected in Article 1 of the Constitution of Ghana, Article 1 of the Constitution of Kenya, Sections 1 and 14(2)(a) and (b) of the Constitution of Nigeria and Sections 1(a), 2, and the preamble of the Constitution of South Africa which acknowledge the people as the source of the powers of government and the people's welfare as the purpose for the exercise of those powers and establish the supremacy of the constitutions over contravening governmental actions.

In Ghana, the limitation on the exercise of sovereign power provision is given practical significance by Article 2 of the Constitution which gives citizens the standing to bring an action in the Supreme Court if they believe that an enactment or any act or omission of any person is in contravention of a provision of the Constitution. The provision, which has given rise to a lot of litigation challenging the constitutionality of executive, parliamentary, and administrative actions and decisions,[105] empowers the Supreme Court to make orders and give directions so that effect can be given to any declaration the Court makes pursuant to legal action challenging the constitutionality of an act of government. Any person to whom an order or direction is addressed must duly obey and carry out the terms of the order or direction. A failure to do so is a high crime subject to appropriate penalties. In this regard, exercising governmental power in an unconstrained and unlimited manner in Ghana is inconsistent with the very source and purpose of the powers of government, particularly in relation to specific constitutional imperatives such as the protection of fundamental human rights.

The protection of constitutional rights could be weakened because of international agreements that states enter into, when those agreements may not come with present or future tangible benefits for the people. These agreements not only impose substantive legal obligations and constraints on states, they also provide for international dispute settlement mechanisms and require national courts to ensure compliance with transnational norms. If African constitutions are to retain their prime role in the regulation of the actions of constituted actors, these constitutions and the very rights, interests, and values they preserve should dictate the content of international agreements that African states enter into in the first place. The reform

[105] *New Patriotic Party v Attorney-General* [1993–94] 2 GLR 35; *Bilson v Attorney-General* [1993–94] 1 GLR 104; *New Patriotic Party v The Electoral Commission* [1993–94] 1 GLR 124; *New Patriotic Party v Rawlings* [1993–94] 2 GLR 193; *New Patriotic Party v Ghana Broadcasting Corporation* [1993–94] 2 GLR 354; *New Patriotic Party v Inspector-General of Police* [1993–94] 2 GLR 459; *Addy v Attorney-General [1997–98] 1* GLR 47; *Mensah v Attorney-General* [1997–98] 1 GLR 227; *Mensima v Attorney-General* [1997–98] 1 GLR 159; *Edusei v Attorney-General* [1997–98] 2 GLR 1; *Sam v Attorney-General (No 2)* [1999–2000] 2 GLR 336; *New Patriotic Party v National Democratic Congress [1999–2000]* 2 GLR 506; *Amidu v Kufuor* [2001–2002] 2 GLR 510; *National Democratic Congress v Electoral Commission* [2001–2002] 2 GLR 340; *Adofo v Attorney-General* [2003–2005] 1 GLR 239; *Mensah v Attorney-General* [1996–97] SCGLR 320; and *New Patriotic Party v National Democratic Congress* [2000] SCGLR 461.

of investment treaties must be positively and directly, not incidentally, informed by the dictates of national constitutions in Africa.

2.4.1.1 Constitutionalism and the Legitimacy of Public Institutions in Africa

At its most basic level, Albert Dicey defines a 'constitution' as comprising 'rules which directly or indirectly affect the distribution of or the exercise of the sovereign power in the state'.[106] Constitutions define the holders of sovereign power, regulate the relations among institutions of the state, and determine the manner in which sovereign power shall be exercised.[107] Hans Kelsen describes a constitution as 'the positive norm or norms which regulate the creation of general legal norms' and 'represents the highest level of positive law'.[108] Constitutional supremacy 'is the doctrine applied to written constitutions which create the various organs of government and mark out the limits of their respective powers'.[109] In Kelsen's language, a norm, such as a constitution, which is the reason for the validity of another norm, is called a '*basic norm (Grundnorm)*'[110] or 'higher norm'.[111]

In *Marbury v Madison*,[112] the Supreme Court of the United States held that it is the people who have the original right to establish for government the principles that are most conducive to their own happiness. The principles so established by the people are fundamental. Where the powers of government are limited, the limitations so imposed will not serve their purposes for the people or otherwise if they may be bypassed by those intended to be restrained.[113] The theory underlying the supremacy of the constitution is 'constitutionalism'. Constitutionalism is the principle that the exercise of political power is to be done within rules that determine the validity of legislative and executive actions.[114]

In Ghana, the principles of constitutional supremacy and constitutionalism are entrenched in the Constitution of Ghana. Article 1(2) states that the Constitution is 'the supreme law of Ghana and any other law found to be inconsistent with any provision of this Constitution shall, to the extent of the inconsistency, be void'. The preamble shows that the Constitution was enacted by the people of Ghana in the exercise of their 'natural and inalienable right to establish a framework of government which shall secure for [themselves] and posterity the blessings of liberty,

[106] Albert V Dicey, *Introduction to the Study of the Law of the Constitution* (10th edn, ECS Wade ed, Macmillan & Co 1959) 23.

[107] ibid.

[108] Hans Kelsen, *The Pure Theory of Law* (Max Knight tr, University of California Press 1967), 222 (hereafter, Kelsen, *Pure Theory of Law*).

[109] Leslie Rubin and Pauli Murray, *The Constitution and Government of Ghana* (Sweet and Maxwell 1961) 52.

[110] Kelsen, *Pure Theory of Law* (n 108) 8.

[111] ibid 193.

[112] *Marbury v Madison* 1 Cranch (US) 137 at 176–77.

[113] ibid 177.

[114] Stanley A de Smith, 'Constitutionalism in the Commonwealth Today' (1962) 4 Malaya Law Review 205.

equality of opportunity and prosperity'. The people, then, are the source of the legal validity of the Constitution of Ghana and the government of Ghana must work to advance the interests of the people and act within the limits laid down in the Constitution. In the celebrated case of *Tuffuor v Attorney-General*, the Supreme Court of Ghana, per Justice Sowah, underscored the supremacy and importance of the Constitution, stating that[115]

> [a] written Constitution ... is not an ordinary Act of Parliament. It embodies the will of a people. It also mirrors their history. Account, therefore, needs to be taken of it as a landmark in a people's search for progress. It contains within it their aspirations and their hopes for a better and fuller life ... It is the fountainhead for the authority which each of the three arms of government possesses and exercises. It is a source of strength. It is a source of power. The executive, the legislature and the judiciary are created by the Constitution. Their authority is derived from the Constitution. Their sustenance is derived from the Constitution.

Constitutions in Africa such as those represented in this book guarantee and protect various fundamental human rights, including the rights to life and health. The powers of African governments under study are to be exercised to give effect to the full realisation and enjoyment of these rights.[116] Governments shall exercise their powers in the name, and for the welfare, of the people in the manner and within constitutional limits. The established legal order in African states analysed in this book is constitutionalism; that is, governments not of absolute power that can do whatever pleases them, but those of limited power and must exercise their powers within legal limits and for the public good.[117] For example, the powers of the government of Ghana must be exercised within constitutional limits according to Article 1(1) of the Constitution.

This government of limited power is reflected in the constitutions of Africa that require that treaties entered into by the authority of the executive be ratified by parliament or the appropriate legislative body.[118] The requirement for parliamentary approval is intended both to bring about transparency and to ensure that treaties entered into by the states are consistent with the goals of the constitutions and the national interests. Accordingly, the executive does not have the power to conclude treaties that come into force without the need for parliamentary ratification.[119] In this regard, the concept of 'treaty' is broad, so as to capture all forms of international

[115] *Tuffuor v Attorney-General* [1980] GLR 637 at 647–48.
[116] Constitution of Ghana (n 31) art 34(2).
[117] Richard L Sklar, 'On the Study of Constitutional Government in Africa' in Okon Akiba (ed), *Constitutionalism and Society in Africa* (Ashgate Publishing 2004) 43.
[118] Constitution of Cameroon (n 27) preamble and arts 44 and 45; Constitution of Egypt (n 28) arts 93 and 151; Constitution of Ghana (n 31) art 75; Constitution of Kenya (n 25) art 2(6); Constitution of Nigeria (n 26) s 12(1); Constitution of South Africa (n 31) s 231(2) and (4).
[119] *Ex Parte the Attorney-General* (n 42) 2.

agreements, including loan agreements, memoranda of understanding, investment treaties, multilateral trade and investment agreements, and other international executive agreements to the extent that they seek to impose binding and enforceable international obligations on a state. In *France v Commission of the European Communities*,[120] the CJEU defined an 'agreement' within the context of Article 228 of the Treaty establishing the European Economic Community signed in Rome in 1957 as 'any undertaking entered into by entities subject to international law which has binding force, whatever its formal designation'.[121]

In *The Republic v High Court: Ex Parte Attorney-General*[122] the Supreme Court held that customary international law is part of the law of Ghana 'incorporated by weight of common law case law ... However, treaties, even when the particular treaty has been ratified by Parliament, do not alter municipal law until they are incorporated into Ghanaian law by appropriate legislation.'[123] The ratification of a treaty by Parliament does not mean that it is incorporated into Ghanaian laws. A treaty that has not been incorporated into municipal law 'may come into force and regulate the rights and obligations of the State on the international plane without changing rights and obligations under municipal law'.[124] There is 'need for legislative incorporation of treaty provisions into municipal law before domestic courts can apply those provisions'.[125] In particular, treaties cannot alter rights and obligations under domestic law unless the treaty is incorporated into domestic law by legislation.[126] The obligations of the state to promote respect for international law and treaty obligations and conduct its international affairs in consonance with accepted principles of public international law in Articles 40 and 73 of the Constitution of Ghana do not alter the dualist stance of Ghanaian law requiring the need to incorporate treaties into domestic law for them to have effect.[127] These provisions equally 'do not authorize the courts to enforce treaty provisions that change rights and obligations in the municipal laws without legislative backing. If the law were otherwise, it would give the Executive an opportunity to bypass Parliament in changing the rights and obligations of citizens.'[128]

However, since in some of these African states a president can enter into a treaty before parliamentary ratification and incorporation into domestic law, the treaty may have effect in international law without having effect in municipal law, that is, in terms of being recognised and adjudicated upon in municipal courts. To avoid a

[120] *France v Commission of the European Communities*, Case C-327/91, Judgment of the European Court of Justice, 9 August 1994.
[121] ibid [27].
[122] *Ex Parte the Attorney-General* (n 42).
[123] ibid 2.
[124] ibid 4.
[125] ibid 5.
[126] ibid.
[127] ibid 6–7.
[128] ibid 7.

situation where a treaty has effect in international law when the constitutional requirements for entering into treaties have not been fully complied with, parliamentary debate and approval of a treaty must come first before presidential execution of the treaty. This will allow for consensus on the constitutionality and compliance of the treaty with the national interests of the states before the treaty is entered into.

Articles 43 of the Constitution of Cameroon gives absolute authority to the President to ratify treaties but where a treaty covers an area within the exclusive legislative power of the Parliament under Article 26, then Parliament must authorise the President before the ratification of the treaty. Article 44 of the Constitution of Cameroon provides that where the Constitutional Council finds the provision of a treaty to be unconstitutional, authorisation to ratify the treaty and ratification of the treaty must come only after the Constitution of Cameroon is amended, meaning that if the Constitution is not amended then no authorisation or ratification is permitted. This essentially means a determination of the constitutionality of a treaty must be made before steps are taken to ratify it. In fact, Article 47(3) of the Constitution of Cameroon envisages the referral of treaties and laws to the Constitutional Council prior to their enactment. More specifically, Article 36(1) of the Constitution of Cameroon provides that the President may, upon consultation with relevant persons, submit to a referendum 'any reform bill which could have profound repercussions on the future of the Nation and national institutions'. The bills envisaged include 'bills to ratify international agreements or treaties having particularly important consequences'.[129]

Under Article 151 of the Constitution of Egypt, the President can only conclude treaties and ratify them 'after the approval of the House of Representatives'. Where a constitution requires parliamentary approval or ratification of a treaty before the treaty comes into force, it means that a president cannot enter into a self-executing treaty, that is, a treaty that is capable of judicial application municipally and internationally without implementing legislation or without the need for parliamentary endorsement.[130]

The central point of this Subsection, as elaborated in Subsection 2.4.1.3 later in this chapter, is that the power of African states exists for the benefit of the people. Public institutions in Africa derive their public authority through applicable constitutions to be exercised in the public interest. The exercise of authority (public or private) is directly linked to the legitimacy of the particular institution both in terms of the source of the authority and how that authority is exercised.[131] John Rawls defines institutions as:[132]

[129] Constitution of Cameroon (n 27) art 36(1)(b).

[130] On self-executing treaty see Lori Fisler Damrosch, 'The Role of the United States Senate Concerning "Self- Executing" and "Non-Self-Executing" Treaties' (1991) 67 Chicago-Kent Law Review 515.

[131] Christian Lund, 'Twilight of Institutions: Public Authority and Local Politics in Africa' (2006) 37(4) Development and Change 685 at 693.

[132] John Rawls, *A Theory of Justice* (rev edn, OUP 1999) 47–48.

> a public system of rules which defines offices and positions with their rights and duties, powers and immunities … These rules specify certain forms of action as permissible, others as forbidden … An institution may be thought of in two ways: first as an abstract object, as possible forms of conduct expressed by a system of rules; and second, as the realization in the thought and conduct of certain persons at a certain time and place of the actions specified by the rules.

An institution 'exists at a certain time and place when the actions specified by it are regularly carried out in accordance with a public understanding that the system of rules defining the institution is to be followed'.[133] In this regard, 'the constitutive rules of an institution, which establish its various rights and duties' and the 'strategies and maxims for how best to take advantage of the institution for particular purposes'[134] are interrelated and interdependent. Two ways to determine the legitimacy of public authority of public institutions then are to determine the source of the public authority (that is, the rules establishing the institutions) and whether those vested with public authority to act in the public interest actually do represent or act in the public interest and within the terms of the source of the authority. In part, this issue can be addressed by examining the constraining effects of international agreements a state enters into for the performance of functions essential for the realisation of the rights of members of the public. Whether state institutions which are required by a constitution to act in the public interest actually do represent the public interest can be determined, for example, by examining the legitimacy of the authority of state institutions to agree to certain terms under investment treaties in light of the potential effects of those terms for the discharge of public interest obligations. In this regard, various authorities have analysed the legitimacy of the investment treaty regime in relation to national constitutions.

Ernst-Ulrich Petersmann argues that 'international trade, financial, investment and environmental regulation remain dominated by government bureaucracies and their business advisors without adequate representation and legal protection of general citizen interest in consumer welfare and protection of fundamental human rights'.[135] For example, the Bretton Woods Articles of Agreement[136] establishing the World Bank and International Monetary Fund (IMF) focus on regulation of economic and financial policy issues such as international balance of payment, sovereignty over the issuance of money, international regulation of exchange rates, and development assistance.[137]

[133] ibid 48.

[134] ibid 49.

[135] Ernst-Ulrich Petersmann, *International Economic Law in the 21st Century: Constitutional Pluralism and Multilevel Governance of Interdependent Public Goods* (Hart Publishing Ltd 2012) 18 (hereafter, Petersmann, *International Economic Law*).

[136] *International Bank for Reconstruction and Development Articles of Agreement*, United Nations Monetary and Financial Conference, Bretton Woods, New Hampshire, 1–22 July 1944, entered into force 1945 (as amended effective 27 June 2012).

[137] Petersmann, *International Economic Law* (n 135) 18.

Diplomats of the World Bank and IMF, 'often justify their neglect for human rights and constitutional rights in intergovernmental economic regulation by the claim' that the Articles of Agreements 'focus on regulation of economic policy issues'.[138] James Gathii has argued that the World Bank:

> bases its position on its constituent instrument ... to support the view that human rights are a political issue which fall outside the Bank's mandate unless it can be defined in a technical or functional mode, to fit within the economic and financial goals of the Bank. This means that the Bank, as well as human rights supporters working within and outside the Bank, must reconcile human rights initiatives with the Bank's economic and financial goals.[139]

The Articles of Agreement are made by states, just like investment treaties are. Though creatures of the state, these treaties are interpreted to exclude public interest issues such as human rights which underlie them. Such a state of affairs manifests a failure of institutions vested with public powers to act for the common good for which the powers have been vested in them. It is in this regard that I argue that since it is constitutions that specify what the public interests are and the corresponding obligations of states in relation to them, then constitutional norms should determine the content of investment treaties which as they largely are now turn to limit public interest obligations of states.

The universal human rights obligations of members of the United Nations (UN) justify constitutional and judicial protection citizens' rights in international economic law.[140] The human rights obligations of UN Member States are based on universally recognised principles of justice. Thus there is the need to respect, protect, and promote the rights of citizens and people all over the world. Multilevel human rights 'constitute equal rights of citizens' and thereby 'limit the power of all governments as "agents," coordinate national and international legal regimes and promote "principled" conflict resolution, legal coherence and synergies among national and international government policies for the benefit of citizens'.[141]

Accordingly, 'economic regulation needs to be justified also in terms of ... constitutional ... theories'.[142] This means that as 'rules of and institutions for public goods shape the infrastructure and welfare of states, the production, design, enforcement and justification of international public goods cannot be left to intergovernmental power politics and piecemeal engineering'.[143] As 'multilevel governance

138 ibid.

139 James Thuo Gathii, 'Good Governance as a Counter Insurgency Agenda to Oppositional and Transformative Social Projects in International Law' (1999) 5 Buffalo Human Rights Law Review 107 at 120.

140 Petersmann, *International Economic Law* (n 135) 19.

141 ibid 23.

142 ibid 25.

143 ibid.

of interdependent international public goods has become the most challenging policy task in the twenty-first century . . . the current under-supply of international public goods requires embedding IEL into stronger constitutional, cosmopolitan and democratically justifiable foundations'.[144]

States' obligations to protect human rights 'also in international economic co-operation among citizens justify legal presumptions that . . . international guarantees of economic freedoms and transnational rule of law must be interpreted as protecting the rights of not only of governments (as agents with limited, delegated rights) but also of citizens as "primary legal subjects"' of international economic law.[145]

Rawls defines the parameters for legitimate exercise of the powers of government. According to Rawls:[146]

> Political power is legitimate only when it is exercised in accordance with a constitution (written or unwritten) the essentials of which all citizens, as reasonable and rational, can endorse in light of their common human reason. This is the liberal principle of legitimacy. It is a further desideratum that all legislative questions that concern or border on these essentials, or are highly divisive, should also be settled, so far as possible, by guidelines and values that can be similarly endorsed.

A society is 'well-ordered' if it is 'effectively regulated by a public conception of justice'[147] and Rawls states (hyperbolically in order to emphasise the importance of complying with constitutional norms) that 'if a political conception of justice covers the constitutional essentials, it is already of enormous importance even if it has little to say about many economic and social issues the legislative bodies must consider'.[148] A 'free market system must be set within a framework of political and legal institutions that adjust the long-run trend of economic forces so as to prevent excessive concentration of property and wealth'.[149] The justice of basic institutions and social policies should be judged in terms of how they promote and protect basic rights and liberties.[150]

In German constitutional law, the dignity of the human person 'is considered to be the highest value to be protected' because the 'ultimate aim of the state is to protect this value' and for this reason 'the exercise of *any public authority*, including

144 ibid.

145 Ernst-Ulrich Petersmann, '*Justice and Human Rights Require Cosmopolitan International Economic Law*' in Federico Lenzerini and Ana Filipa Vrdoljak (eds), *International Law for Common Goods: Normative Perspectives on Human Rights, Culture and Nature* (Hart Publishing Ltd 2014) 117, 118. See also ibid 120–21.

146 John Rawls, *Justice as Fairness: A Restatement* (Erin Kelly ed, Harvard University Press 2001) 41.

147 ibid 30.

148 ibid 28.

149 ibid 44.

150 ibid 45.

authority in the field of foreign relations, may be challenged on the basis of basic constitutional principles'.[151] Under Article 22(1) of the Constitution of Japan 1947, 'business activities can be restricted by law if the restriction is necessary for the purpose of promoting the public welfare'.[152]

I argue that as the legitimacy of African governments is founded on constitutions or equivalent legal norms, the very system of norms that impose obligations on states with respect to the protection of the public interest, the actions of governments such as the execution of investment treaties and the interpretation of those treaties should be judged within the terms of those norms. To the extent that the powers of a government which derive from the people through a constitution are limited for the public good, unlimited power to the state to enter into an investment treaty that can limit public interest regulation cannot co-exist with this constitutional limitation. Governments 'usually cannot directly produce welfare and economic wealth, but only a framework of rules that may encourage or impede the welfare of their citizens ... There is no constitutionally valid reason why the principle of limited delegation of powers should not also require to limit trade regulatory powers.'[153] In Rawls' view, such limitation is justified because:[154]

> [i]nternational guarantees of freedoms, non-discrimination, legal certainty, and transparency and use of proportionality policy instruments cannot fulfil their 'constitutional functions unless they are supplemented by effective 'enforcement mechanisms' and placed into a 'constitutional system' subjecting the interpretation, application and enforcement of the rules to institutional 'checks and balances'. Such constitutional framework can hardly be made effective within worldwide international organizations which recognize the national sovereignty and diversity of member states ... and provide no effective sanctions against mutually agreed 'rule departures' among governments ... For instance, the establishment of parliamentary and judicial 'checks and balances' at the level of worldwide international economic organisations appears hardly feasible. And, as illustrated by the example of the EEC, even the existence of international parliamentary and judicial bodies is no adequate safeguard against international 'protectionist

[151] Meinhard Hilf, 'Treaty-Making and Application of Treaties in International Trade Law: The Case of Germany' in Meinhard Hilf and Ernst-Ulrich Petersmann (eds), *National Constitutions and International Economic Law* (Kluwer Law and Taxation Publishers 1993) 211, 213 (hereafter, Hilf and Petersmann (eds), *Constitutions and Economic Law*).

[152] Mitsuo Matsushita, 'Constitutional Framework of the Major Trade Laws in Japan: In the Context of the Uruguay Round' in Hilf and Petersmann (eds), *Constitutions and Economic Law* (n 151) 149, 275, 277.

[153] Ernst-Ulrich Petersmann, 'Limited Government and Unlimited Trade Policy: Why Effective Judicial Review of Foreign Trade Restrictions Depends on Individual Rights' in Hilf and Petersmann (eds), *Constitutions and Economic Law* (n 151) 537, 542.

[154] Ernst-Ulrich Petersmann, 'National Constitutions and International Economic Law' in Hilf and Petersmann (eds), *Constitutions and Economic Law* (n 151) 48–49.

> collusion' among trade and agricultural ministers at the expense of domestic citizens. The experience with the often little success of customs unions, and free trade areas in Africa and Latin America further indicates that even comprehensive, international customs union and free area agreements are no guarantee for effective liberalisation of national trade barriers.

The justification for constitutional limitations on investment treaty-making capacity of African states is that they are constitutional democracies. For example, according to Article 35(1) of the Constitution of Ghana, 'Ghana shall be a democratic state dedicated to the realisation of freedom and justice; and accordingly, sovereignty resides in the people of Ghana from whom Government derives all its powers and authority through this Constitution'. Equivalent provisions are found in Articles 1 of the Constitution of Kenya, Section 14(2)(a) of the Constitution of Nigeria, and the preamble to the Constitution of South Africa.

A constitutional democracy requires, 'a reasonably just constitutional democratic government that serves fundamental interests'.[155] By a 'reasonably just ... constitutional democratic government', Rawls means that the government is effectively under the *people's*

> political and electoral control, *and that it answers to and protects their fundamental interests as specified in a written or unwritten constitution and its interpretation.* The regime is not an autonomous agency pursuing its own bureaucratic ambitions. *Moreover, it is not directed by the interests of large concentrations of private economic and corporate power veiled from public knowledge and almost entirely free from accountability.*[156]

Given the constitutional regimes in Africa, exemplified by the constitutions studied, which place the welfare and basic rights of the people at the centre of governance, the governments in these countries will be acting unconstitutionally if they enter into investment treaties that directly prohibit the undertaking of measures constitutionally required or necessary in the public interest or which indirectly achieve that effect. Constitutional obligations of states relating to human rights, including the right to development demand a limit to the exercise of governmental powers, including in the making of investment treaties and international economic law generally.[157]

155 John Rawls, *The Law of Peoples: with The Idea of Public Reason Revisited* (Harvard University Press 1999) 23.

156 ibid 24 (emphasis added).

157 Ernst-Ulrich Petersmann, 'Why Rational Choice Theory Requires a Multilevel Constitutional Approach to International Economic Law: A Response to The Case Against Reforming the WTO Enforcement Mechanism' (2008) 2008(1) University of Illinois Law Review 359, 366.

2.4.1.2 The Substantive and Procedural Constitutionality of Investment Treaties in Africa

There are two basic ways the constitutionality of treaties may arise in a constitutional democracy. First, as treaties have to be made in accordance with the constitutional procedures and by institutions empowered to do so, treaties may be constitutional or unconstitutional depending on whether they have been made in accordance with those procedures and by institutions empowered to make them. Treaties in this sense may be either *procedurally constitutional* or *procedurally unconstitutional* depending on whether or not they are made *in the manner* laid down in a constitution.

The Supreme Court of Ghana, for example, has held in *Attorney-General v Faroe Atlantic Co Ltd*,[158] *Attorney-General v Balkan Energy Ghana Ltd*,[159] and *Martin Alamisi Amidu v Attorney-General* cases[160] that international business or economic transactions such as power purchase agreements, international loan agreements, and international project implementation agreements that have not been laid before and approved by Parliament as required by Article 181 of the Constitution of Ghana are unconstitutional and the state cannot be required to pay damages for breach of such agreements. The principle reflected in these cases is appropriately stated in *Georgina Amartey v Winifred Iddrisu*, wherein Justice Dotse stated that 'once the entire process is void, it lacks legitimacy and no rule of practice can bring it back to life'.[161] Another way to put it is to say that once 'the procedural lapses are so fundamental, they go to the root' and any actions or decisions based on them cannot stand, they 'must fail'.[162] As stated by Lord Denning in *MacFoy v United Africa Co Ltd*, you 'cannot put something on nothing and expect it to stay there. It will collapse.'[163]

These Ghanaian cases about international contracts have the same legal consequences for investment treaties because Article 75 of the Constitution of Ghana requires that treaties executed by the President shall be ratified by Parliament just as Article 181 requires parliamentary approval of an international economic or business transaction. Six of Ghana's investment treaties (Ghana–Denmark and Ghana–Malaysia, Ghana-Germany, Ghana-Switzerland, Ghana-Serbia and Ghana-Burkina Faso BITs) came into force in between 1993 and 2003 respectively, after the Constitution of Ghana came into force in 1992. It is not clear from parliamentary debates or formal resolution of Parliament around the time whether these

[158] *Attorney-General v Faroe Atlantic Co Ltd* [2005–2006] SCGLR 271 (hereafter, *AG v Faroe*).
[159] *Attorney-General v Balkan Energy Ghana Ltd*, Judgment, 16 May 2012 (hereafter, *AG v Balkan*).
[160] *Amidu v Attorney-General, Writ No JI/15/2012, Judgment, 14 June 2013*; and *Amidu v Attorney-General, Writ No* JI/23/2012, Judgment, 21 June 2013 (hereafter, *Amidu v AG*).
[161] *Georgina Amartey v Winifred Iddrisu* Civil Appeal No J4/26/2007, Judgment, 29 April 2009, 11.
[162] ibid.
[163] *MacFoy v United Africa Co. Ltd* [1961] 3 All ER 1169 at 1172.

treaties were ratified by Parliament. If these investment treaties did not receive parliamentary approval, they are *procedurally unconstitutional.*

Secondly, treaties may be *substantively constitutional* or *substantively unconstitutional. Substantive constitutionality* arises where a treaty does not conflict with any of the substantive standards laid down in a constitution. Where a treaty expressly conflicts with any of the substantive standards in a constitution so that a state cannot protect substantive rights at all or with the most convenient measures required under a constitution, there is *substantive unconstitutionality.* For example, national treatment is arguably unconstitutional to the extent that it imposes an obligation on a state to extend treatment to foreign investment when the constitution of that states specifically requires that such treatment or measures be designed and accorded solely to domestic investors. Unreasonable restriction on the ability of state institutions to carry out a constitutionally mandated policy or requirements would be substantively unconstitutional. For example, the Supreme Court of Ghana has held in *Adofo v Attorney General*[164] that a statute that ousts the court of their jurisdiction is unconstitutional. By extension this can apply to investment treaties that provide for investor–state arbitration.

Substantive unconstitutionality may be *express*, in which case a law or treaty explicitly conflicts with a constitution by, for example, taking away or abrogating a substantive constitutional right.[165] For example, Article 151 of the Constitution of Egypt explicitly says 'no treaty may be concluded which is contrary to the provisions of the Constitution or which leads to concession of state territories'. A treaty that provides for otherwise than as contained in the Constitution of Egypt, such as providing for the concession of a territory in Egypt, would suffer from *substantive unconstitutionality.* Again, a treaty that provides for indirect expropriation when some constitutions of Africa expressly require and recognise only direct expropriation by law would be *substantively unconstitutional.*[166] Substantive unconstitutionality may also be *implicit* or *indirect* (*indirect unconstitutionality*). *Indirect unconstitutionality* arises where a treaty or other law or action, although not expressly taking away a substantive constitutional right or not directly conflicting with a constitutional stipulation, nevertheless achieves that effect if the treaty or law is implemented or if the action is undertaken. An example of this is where an investment treaty imposes damages against a state for adopting general measures that are required under a constitution or under a domestic law that gives effect to a constitution when the constitution does not require the payment of compensation. Although in this case the investment treaties do not expressly prohibit the adoption of the measures, they may achieve that effect since the state might roll back from

[164] *Adofo v Attorney-General* [2003–2005] 1 GLR 239 (hereafter, *Adofo v AG*).
[165] ibid.
[166] Constitution of Cameroon (n 27) preamble; Constitution of Egypt (n 28) art 35; Constitution of Ghana (n 31) art 20(2); Constitution of Kenya (n 25) art 40(3); Constitution of Nigeria (n 26) art 44(1); Constitution of South Africa (n 31) art 25(1).

adopting measures for fear of investor–state arbitration suits and ensuing compensation. In this sense, the obligation to pay compensation under the investment treaty can have the same legal effect as an express prohibition against adopting a constitutionally required measure.

By this analysis, a treaty may be procedurally constitutional if it has been made in accordance with the constitutional procedures, yet be substantively unconstitutional if, on its face, it abolishes or seriously undermines the realisation of a substantive constitutional right. Within the domestic context, laws made under municipal law by parliament are void if they conflict with a constitution. Therefore, a treaty will be substantively unconstitutional and should be treated as void if it substantially contravenes a substantive constitutional right because treaties should help realise constitutional rights and not abrogate them or compromise their realisation.

However, a treaty's unconstitutionality at the municipal plane does not necessarily render it unenforceable in international law. The implication is that an action that is unconstitutional under domestic law may not justify an act that is illegal under international law on the basis of *pacta sunt servanda* and the principle that international law prevails over municipal law in the event of conflict. Nevertheless, if in substance and procedure such a treaty could not have been made under municipal law then the treaty could be invalid and should not be legally binding if the conditions of Article 46 of the VCLT as interpreted in Subsection 2.4.1.4 are met.

2.4.1.3 The Legal Source and Public Purpose of Governmental Powers in Africa

One basis for arguing that constitutions of Africa substantively limit the treaty-making powers of the African states is to study the source and purpose of the powers of governments and the limits within which the powers must be exercised under the constitutions. For example, as noted, Article 1(1) of the Constitution of Ghana says that the sovereignty of Ghana resides in the people of Ghana. The powers of government are to be exercised in the people's name, for their welfare, and in the manner and within the limits laid down in the Constitution. It provides two such constitutional limitations.[167]

The first limitation may be called the *Broad Limitation Test*. To establish this test it must be shown that the particular exercise of the powers of government was neither done in the name of the people of Ghana nor to advance their welfare. Whether or not the exercise of the powers breaches the constitutional standard that the powers shall be carried out in *the name and for the welfare* of the people will depend on the circumstances of each case. For example, a decision to permit a mine to operate without any consideration of the obvious effects on the environment

[167] For equivalent provisions see arts 1 and 14(2)(a) of the Constitution of Kenya (n 25) and Constitution of Nigeria (n 26). Thus, the interpretations on the provision of the Constitution of Ghana should be relevant for the interpretation of these provisions as well.

or the welfare of the local community may well be unconstitutional given that the state has an obligation to protect the environment and the health of people.

Under this test governmental policies and actions can also be challenged as *not in the public interest*, even if the powers were exercised within the Constitution of Ghana, for the reason that they do not advance any public purpose. An example would be if an individual patently exercises public power to enter into an investment agreement with a state to advance specific interests of business cronies or specific government supporters for whom the agreement was a prerequisite to securing foreign finance. This limitation test thus focuses on the purpose for or motive behind the exercise of the powers of government in the face of a constitutionally mandated value.

The second limitation, the *Narrow Limitation Test*, requires that the powers of government be exercised *strictly within the parameters* set out in the Constitution of Ghana, both substantively and procedurally. Under this test, the exercise of the powers could, objectively, be in the public interest but nevertheless be unconstitutional because substantively or procedurally it does not comply with the constitutional provisions. For example, a treaty executed by the President that does not receive parliamentary approval is procedurally unconstitutional. A treaty that expressly denies citizens access to local courts to seek remedies for violations of human rights as required by the Constitution of Ghana will be substantively unconstitutional, even if it brings some public good. The Constitution of Ghana may only be amended by an Act.[168] The entrenched provisions of the Constitution of Ghana, including those on the supremacy and enforcement of the Constitution, fundamental human rights, the laws of Ghana, powers and structure of the executive, legislature, and judiciary can only be amended by special procedures outlined in the Constitution.[169] If these provisions are amended by any means other than by the specified approaches, the amendments will be unconstitutional, although the amendments may have been done in the public interest. This second limitation test focuses on the *legal limits* to the exercise of the powers of government.

Interpreted together, the *Broad Limitation Test* and the *Narrow Limitation Test* require that the exercise of the powers of the government of Ghana must be done both in the name of and for the welfare of the people and must in substance and procedure comply with the dictates of the Constitution of Ghana. This constitutes the core of the concept of constitutionalism in Ghana. Thus, given that this Constitution is the supreme law of Ghana,[170] the President and Parliament do not have the power to make treaties that substantively contravene it. Every treaty action the government takes will involve some limitation on its future freedom to act. However, certain limitations on rights (to individuals) or on the powers of the

[168] Constitution of Ghana (n 31) art 289.
[169] ibid art 290.
[170] ibid arts 1(2) and 11(1).

organs of the state under the investment treaties without qualification such as national treatment and the requirement under investment treaties to pay compensation to foreign investors even in situations of war and national emergency, are not in the public interest as that term is understood in the Constitution of Ghana. This is because they limit the powers of the state to act in the interest of citizens for whom the government is constituted if the same or similar treatment is not extended to foreign investors or in situations of emergency when the state may need to prioritise in favour of citizens. These standards require the state to expend its resources (time, money, and human capital) where the Constitution requires the contrary. For example, under Article 31(10) of the Constitution of Ghana, the right to compensation for actions that affect property rights may be denied in a state of emergency, such as natural disaster and war. If the state exercises its discretion against payment of compensation, investment treaty claims can be made against it even if it is acting constitutionally to refuse such compensation.

These interpretations apply *mutatis mutandis* to Cameroon, Egypt, Kenya, Nigeria, and South Africa because their constitutions derive from the people, acknowledge the people as the source of governmental powers and that those powers are to be exercised in the public interest and within constitutional limits. Thus, the powers to make treaties or enter into international agreements in these African states do not authorise the direct and indirect abridgment of the competences of the states and their institutions to such an extent that they are constrained or prevented from continuing to function in pursuit of these constitutional norms in the public interest. On the contrary, the power to make treaties is granted in order that the states can enter into treaties that will promote the core constitutional values and interests such as the promotion and protection of fundamental human rights, development, and environmental protection.[171] Where a treaty or enactment derives its legal validity from another legal source, the source from which it derives its legal validity takes precedence over the treaty or enactment. Kelsen espoused this point when he stated that[172]

> [t]he relation between the norm that regulates the creation of another norm and the norm created in conformity with the former can be metaphorically presented as a relationship of super- and subordination. The norm which regulates the creation of another norm is higher, the norm created in conformity with the former is the lower one.

National courts in Africa have jurisdiction in all or certain matters relating to the enforcement or interpretation of constitutions and to determine whether an

[171] *Polish Membership of the European Union (Accession Treaty)*, Polish Constitutional Court, Judgment K18/04 of 11 May 2005 para 8.

[172] Kelsen, *Pure Theory of Law* (n 108) 221.

enactment has been made in excess of the powers conferred on parliament or any other authority.[173] Based on this constitutional mandate, the courts can pronounce on the constitutionality of both domestic legislation and investment treaties and other international agreements as the Supreme Court of Ghana did in *Attorney-General v Faroe Atlantic Co Ltd*,[174] *Attorney-General v Balkan Energy Ghana Ltd*,[175] and *Amidu v Attorney-General* cases.[176]

In *New Patriotic Party v Attorney-General*,[177] the Supreme Court of Ghana stated that the Constitution of Ghana is the supreme law of Ghana and therefore 'laws, *municipal or otherwise*, which are found to be inconsistent with the Constitution, cannot be binding on the State whatever their nature. International laws ... are not binding on Ghana until such laws have been adopted or ratified by the municipal laws'.[178] It follows that as a matter of municipal law, all laws made in Africa, including treaties, must comply with constitutional laws both procedurally and substantively. Ratified treaties will be binding on the states to the extent that they are substantively consistent with the applicable constitutions. This is necessary to ensure accountability and that constitutional norms are not arbitrarily, capriciously, and flimsily disregarded. Justice Date-Bah delivering a unanimous decision of the Supreme Court stated in *Adofo v Attorney-General*:[179]

> The power to strike down legislation in conflict with any provision of the Constitution ... is one of the most important powers of this court. It is a power to safeguard liberty from encroachment by the legislature ... It is a power accorded this court by clear provisions in the Constitution ... whose exercise is ... mandated by binding precedent from this court. That binding precedent includes ... article 1(2) of the Constitution ... which provides as follows: 'This Constitution shall be the supreme law of Ghana and any other law found to be inconsistent with any provision of this Constitution shall, to the extent of the inconsistency, be void.' This constitutional provision unequivocally and authoritatively establishes a doctrine of supremacy of the Constitution ... in the Ghanaian jurisdiction. This doctrine implies that ... Parliament's enactments and those of previous legislatures are subject to the supremacy of the Constitution.
>
> The doctrine of the supremacy of the Constitution ... should logically imply the power of judicial review of the constitutionality of legislation in order to enforce that supremacy ... The power of judicial review of the constitutionality of legislation, which is explicitly conferred on this court by articles 2(1) and 130(1)

173 Constitution of Ghana (n 31) art 130(1); Constitution of Kenya (n 25) art 163(a); Constitution of Nigeria (n 26) ss 232–234; Constitution of South Africa (n 31) ss 232 and 233.

174 *AG v Faroe* (n 158).

175 *AG v Balkan* (n 159).

176 *Amidu v AG* (n 160).

177 *New Patriotic Party v Attorney-General* [1997–1998] 1 GLR 378 (SC).

178 ibid 412 and 413 (emphasis added).

179 *Adofo v AG* (n 164) 245–46.

> of the Constitution ... is one that should be vigilantly deployed by this court in discharge of the obligation of this court to uphold the Constitution.[180]

The executive powers in Cameroon, Egypt, Ghana, Kenya, Nigeria, and South Africa including in the making of investment treaties are to be exercised in accordance with the provisions of the constitutions.[181] The executive authority includes preparing and initiating legislation, the execution and maintenance of the constitution and other laws, and developing and implementing national policies.[182] Legislative power is vested in Parliament.[183] The treaty-making powers are vested in the president subject to parliamentary ratification. The exercise of these constitutional powers by the various institutions in Africa is *sine qua non* to promoting and protecting the welfare of the people in Africa, which I argue is the yardstick for the exercise of governmental powers. Also, in making and implementing policies and laws, governments are to be guided by the directive principles of state policy.[184] The directive principles require governments to take steps to bring about the realisation of basic human rights, a healthy economy, the right to good healthcare, and the right to education.[185] These are constitutional principles that limit the competence of African states from acceding to agreements that are incompatible with their constitutions because these constitutions put the people and their interests first even when African states enter into investment treaties.

2.4.1.4 Internal Law of Fundamental Importance and Binding Effect of Investment Treaties

Whether a treaty cannot be binding on a state because the expression of a state's consent to be bound by the treaty was expressed in violation of internal law depends in part on the interpretation of the VCLT.[186] Article 26 of the VCLT gives effect to the *pacta sunt servanda* principle in international law, namely that every treaty 'in force is binding upon the parties to it and must be performed by them in good faith'. The principle of the law of treaties as reflected in Article 27 of the VCLT is also that a 'party may not invoke the provisions of its internal law as justification for its failure to perform a treaty'. This principle is premised on the treaty in

[180] ibid.

[181] Constitution of Cameroon (n 27) art 5; Constitution of Egypt (n 28) arts 139 and 151; Constitution of Ghana (n 31) art 58(1); Constitution of Kenya (n 25) art 131; Constitution of Nigeria (26) s 5; and Constitution of South Africa (n 31) s 85.

[182] Constitution of Ghana (n 31) art 58(2); Constitution of Nigeria (n 26) art 5(1); and Constitution of South Africa (n 31) s 85(2).

[183] Constitution of Ghana (n 31) art 93(2); Constitution of Kenya (n 25) art 109; Constitution of Nigeria (n 26) s 4(1); Constitution of South Africa (n 31) s 44.

[184] Constitution of Ghana (n 31) art 34(1); Constitution of Kenya (n 25) art 10; and Constitution of Nigeria (n 26) ss 13–24.

[185] Constitution of Ghana (n 31) art 34(2).

[186] Anthony Aust, *Modern Treaty Law and Practice* (CUP 2007) 312–14 (hereafter, Aust, *Modern Treaty Law*).

question having been validly made in the first places since each treaty is preceded and regulated by norms that give states power to enter into investment treaties. Therefore, constitutions are the higher or superior norms and treaties and laws deriving from them are the subordinate or lower norms. Thus, the VCLT recognises that an expression of consent to be bound may be expressed in violation of internal law and that in such a case a state may not be bound by the treaty concerned. According to Article 46:

> [a] State may not invoke the fact that its consent to be bound by a treaty has been expressed in violation of a provision of its internal law regarding competence to conclude treaties as invalidating its consent unless that violation was manifest and concerned a rule of its internal law of fundamental importance. A violation is manifest if it would be objectively evident to any state conducting itself in the matter in accordance with normal practice and in good faith.

A constitution is an 'internal law of fundamental importance' because it is the supreme law of the land. It creates rights and governance institutions, defines the powers of governments and the limits to those powers, and protects fundamental rights of human beings. In this regard, constitutions give expression to fundamentals values of society and polity and reflect the collective identity and values of the people.[187]

Accordingly, where an expression of consent to be bound by a treaty is made contrary to substantive provisions of a constitution or its procedural requirements, a state may subsequently argue that its consent to the treaty was expressed in violation of its supreme law and is, therefore, not binding on it. In *Land and Maritime Boundary between Cameroon and Nigeria*,[188] Nigeria argued that its constitutional rules regarding the ratification of treaties were not complied with in respect of a declaration entered into between it and Cameroon and that the declaration was invalid.[189] Nigeria further argued that Cameroon knew, or ought to have known, that the head of state of Nigeria had no power legally to bind Nigeria without consulting the Nigerian government.[190] The International Court of Justice (ICJ) rejected these arguments on the basis that the signatures of the heads of Cameroon and Nigeria were sufficient to make the declaration binding without the need for ratification.[191] Accordingly, the ICJ held that the declaration was 'binding and as establishing a legal obligation on Nigeria'.[192] The Court reasoned further that:[193]

[187] Joseph HH Weiler, 'In Defence of the Status Quo: Europe's Constitutional *Sonderweg*' in Joseph HH Weiler and Marlene Wind (eds), *European Constitutionalism Beyond the State* (CUP 2003) 7, 15.

[188] *Land and Maritime Boundary between Cameroon and Nigeria (Cameroon v Nigeria: Equatorial Guinea intervening)* Judgment, (2002) ICJ Reports 303.

[189] ibid [258]–[259] and [265].

[190] ibid.

[191] ibid [264].

[192] ibid [268].

[193] ibid [265] and [266] (emphasis added).

> [t]he rules concerning the authority to sign treaties for a State are constitutional rules of fundamental importance... However, *a limitation of* a Head of State's *capacity* in this respect is not manifest in the sense of Article 46, paragraph 2 [of the VCLT], unless at least properly publicized. This is particularly so because Heads of State belong to the group of persons who, in accordance with Article 7, paragraph 2, of the Convention '[i]n virtue of their functions and without having to produce full powers' are considered as representing their State.
>
> [T]here is no general legal obligation for States to keep themselves informed of legislative and constitutional developments in other States which are or may become important for the international relations of these States.

Under Article 7(1) of the VCLT, a person is considered as 'representing a State for the purpose of adopting or authenticating the text of a treaty or for the purpose of expressing the consent of the State to be bound by a treaty if' the person 'produces appropriate full powers'. The production of full powers makes manifest the authority to adopt the text of the treaty or expression of consent to be bound. By Article 7(2), heads of state, heads of government, ministers for foreign affairs, and heads of diplomatic missions are, by virtue of their functions, considered as representing the state in treaty-making. They may, therefore, perform all acts relating to the conclusion of a treaty or can adopt the text of a treaty without having to produce full powers.

Article 7 is about *establishing* the *authority or capacity* to represent the state in the making of a treating[194] and the legal limitations on *how* the person so empowered to represent the state *should express a state's consent to be bound*. The fact that a person has full powers to represent a state in the making of a treaty as defined under the VCLT and not necessarily domestic law is not conclusive that the person has authority to agree to every term of the treaty or that the person will express a state's consent to be bound by the treaty in accordance with internal law of fundamental importance. Although persons such as the heads of state, heads of government, and ministers for foreign affairs are not required to produce appropriate full powers when performing acts relating to the conclusion of a treaty, it is still open and possible that they may perform the acts in question either in accordance with or against the dictates of internal law. Everybody within a constitutional form of government irrespective of their position or functions is supposed to exercise their powers within the confines of the law. International law must not authorise people to do that which is expressly forbidden by municipal law. Therefore, the authority of a head of state and other specified persons to conclude treaties without the need

[194] On competence to conclude treaties see: *Application of the Convention on the Prevention and Punishment of the Crime of Genocide (Bosnia and Herzegovina v Serbia and Montenegro)*, Provisional Measures, Separate Opinion of Judge Lauterpacht) 13 September 1993 ICJ Reports 1993, 325 [102]; and *France v Commission of the European Communities* (n 120) [42]–[43].

to produce full powers should be treated as a rebuttable presumption so that the functions of the person cannot override express and unambiguous internal law governing the exercise of that authority. The functions of a person should not be treated as more conclusive than the need to establish the competence to conclude a treaty in accordance with domestic law. There is the risk of a narrow interpretation of Article 7(2) of the VCLT focusing solely on the functions of the person expressing the consent leading to that conclusion.

It is questionable whether the ICJ is legally right when it held that 'a limitation of a Head of State's capacity ... is not manifest' unless the limitation is published because heads of state belong to the group of persons who can perform treaty conclusion acts without having to produce full powers. There is nothing in Articles 7 and 46 of the VCLT that suggests that the basis for determining whether an expression of consent to be bound by a treaty was expressed in violation of internal law is to be limited to the instrument authoring the expressing of consent or publication. So, if a constitution as a document is accessible and available for the whole world to read, it is arguable that its limitations are manifest. When a constitution is readily accessible to the parties negotiating to conclude a treaty, the limitation on capacity to inter into a treaty contained in the constitution is arguably published. Vigilant contracting parties would only need to pick at it, that is read the relevant parts dealing with the subject matter of the contract.

The instrument authorising the expression of consent to be bound by a treaty may not exhaust all factors that a person must take into consideration before expressing the consent to be bound. The instrument may only authorise the person to go and negotiate and agree to the terms of the treaty and may not contain the specifics of what terms to agree or not to agree to. In other words, while the instrument giving authorisation to express consent may deal with both the capacity to express consent and the extent of the person's powers in relation to the performance of this function, the instrument may be of limited scope in terms of the extent of that person's powers in the exercise of that representative function. If the instrument simply gives the person the capacity to conclude a treaty without specifying what the person may or may not agree to, which in practice seems to be the case, it will be out of context to argue that the person is thereby seized of the power to agree to any and every term, irrespective of its objective illegality under existing law, whether or not obvious at the time of concluding the treaty. If limitations on the expression of consent to be bound are to be judged solely on the basis of the instrument showing the full powers of the person to represent the state in the making of the treaty or on publication, then those who are not required to produce full powers could always make any and every type of treaty, in spite of any fundamental limitations in internal law which may not have been obvious at the time of concluding the treaty. In a situation where the instrument authorising a person to adopt the text of a treaty does nothing beyond simply authorising the person to express consent to be bound, the person's position will not be different from those who are not required to produce full powers.

The objectives of Article 46 are twofold: (i) to ensure that a state simply does not invoke non-compliance with internal law to avoid treaty obligations and thereby preserve the rights of the other contracting party which says the treaty is binding; and (ii) to cure violations of fundamental internal law in the making of a treaty in favour of the state which says its internal law has been violated in the making of the treaty. The right to say a violation of internal law was not manifest is to protect the rights of the state which says the treaty is binding. The right to say the treaty is not binding is for the other state to secure compliance with its internal law of fundamental importance. So, there has to be a balance between these competing objectives in interpreting Article 46. It will be lopsided to interpret Article 46 based on a predisposition to make a treaty binding. The requirement that violation of internal law be manifest if interpreted narrowly would lead to a situation where the second objective of Article 46 would always be defeated because violations of a constitution would be ignored.

Violation of internal law has to be manifest for Article 46 to apply. For example, violation of a constitution would be manifestly evident to a state signing investment treaties with another if the treaties were expressly to prohibit the courts from entertaining suits brought against foreign investors for violation of human rights in the latter state. A breach of a constitution is more likely to be manifest to another state where the breach would also amount to a breach of general international law obligations—in particular where both parties to the investment treaty are also parties to another treaty that imposes specific human rights or environmental obligation on the parties. In this regard, it is significant to note that most states which are parties to investment treaties are also members of the UN Organization and signatories or parties to the UN covenants on civil, political, economic, social, and cultural rights.

The objective to cure violations of internal law will be defeated if it were to be held that in each and every case, compliance with internal law is conclusive if the other state party had no reason to doubt it or if a treaty that does not comply with internal law anyway could nevertheless be valid and have legal effect because of the functions of the person who concluded the treaty. The objective of Article 46 will also be defeated if it is interpreted in such a manner that it becomes an instrument for violation or non-compliance with internal law by relevant persons in concluding international agreements. Thus it may be treated as conclusive if a state party has no reason to doubt compliance with internal law and capacity to make treaty can be presumed in order to protect the state which has no manifest reason to believe that the internal law of its contracting party had not been complied with. This must not, however, lead to a situation where the objective purpose of Article 46 for a state to excuse itself from the binding effect of a treaty for non-compliance with its internal law to be defeated each time the issue comes up. Accordingly, it is proposed that violations of internal law should be treated as manifest if it would be objectively manifest to the parties conducting themselves at the time of concluding a treaty that one contracting party could not ordinarily have entered into the treaty or agreed to a particular treaty term, for example because the treaty will undermine the protection of fundamental human rights in the territory of that party.

It is proposed that the nature of the obligations under the treaty, the basis of a claim of invalidity or non-binding nature of a treaty or its provision, and the accessibility of the internal law in question to the parties at the time of the conclusion of the treaty should also inform the determination whether expression of consent was expressed in manifest violation of internal law. If in substance, the obligation is one that a state could not have assumed in the first place then a state should not be bound by such obligation, irrespective of the status of the person who purportedly expressed the consent of the state to be bound. A determination of whether an expression of consent to be bound by a treaty was expressed in violation of internal law should not be based solely on the instrument authorising the expression of consent or publication. The language in Articles 7 and 46 does not seem to establish a rigid standard. It is arguable that a violation of internal law is manifest if the legal document bearing the limitation is readily accessible.

Violation of internal law may be manifest depending on the nature of the terms of the treaty. So the means for determining whether an expression of consent to be bound by a treaty should include the instrument authorising the expression of consent, internal law, and the terms of the treaty in question (whether those terms could objectively have been agreed). It is on the basis of these that a state may claim the binding effect of a treaty on the parties. It is the ICJ's position that a state does not have a general legal obligation to keep itself informed of legislative and constitutional developments in other states. However, since each state entering into a treaty is aware or ought to be aware that under Article 46 a contracting state may not be bound by a treaty if the expression of consent is made in manifest violation of internal law, a contracting party should not only comply with its internal law but also should at least in good faith and out of abundance of caution verify or seek confirmation (at least in its own interest) if the other party has complied with internal law, especially if that internal law is accessible. Doing this is one way a state can act to meet the requirement in Article 46 that states conduct themselves in good faith in concluding a treaty. The good faith obligation does not require a state to monitor another contracting party to ensure the latter contracting party complies with its internal law. However, it should be treated as requiring each contracting party to take prudent steps that protects its interests. That way, either state may be estopped from arguing that a violation of internal law is or is not manifest, as the case may be. This is consistent with international law. For example, the precautionary principle in international environmental law and international law generally reflects the value of risk avoidance.[195] Verification by a contracting state can help its contracting partner to discover violations of its internal law will be in the mutual benefit of both parties.

This position is espoused on the basis that each state must act to protect its interests in treaty-making. If a state's representatives enter into a treaty in disregard of the legal consequences attached to non-compliance with its internal law or non-compliance with the internal law of its treaty partner, then the state failing to do so should hardly be heard to say it was or was not manifest that internal law had not been complied with. Given the two objectives of Article 46 as set out in this Subsection, the burden should be on both states to act prudently in concluding a treaty. This is necessary to ensure that each of the contracting parties acts fairly, honestly, and in good faith towards each other in treaty-making treaties and implementation. More important, what Article 46 requires to be 'manifest' for an expression of consent to not bind a state is not the 'limitation of ... capacity' to express the consent, as the ICJ suggests, but rather 'violation of . . . internal law' resulting from the expression of consent. Thus, if in practice and in good faith a treaty's terms such as expropriation (in particular, indirect expropriation) will have a telling and obvious limiting effect on the right to regulate in the public interest under an internal law such as a constitution, the expression of consent to be bound would have been expressed in violation of internal law of fundamental importance and the state should not be bound by the treaty.

2.4.1.5 The Constitutionality of Treaties in Comparative Perspective: The Imperatives Theory as a Contrast

In the United States, scholars have argued in favour of constitutional supremacy over treaties. Under Article VI(2) of the Constitution of the United States, treaties and federal legislation made thereunder are the supreme laws of the land and are binding on states. While treaties are 'supreme', they remain subject to the Constitution. Even at the states level, there is evidence to the effect that state judges are

> harmonizing international law with state executive and legislative objectives, limiting the disruptive effect of treaties, using customary international law to advance state interests and applying international law where state citizens choose it to govern their contractual relationships. In short, state judges contribute an important structural safeguard of federalism vis-à-vis international law.[196]

[195] Andrew Jordan and Timothy O'Riordan, 'The Precautionary Principle: A Legal and Policy History' in Marco Martuzzi and Joel Tickner (eds), *The Precautionary Principle: Protecting Public Health, the Environment and the Future of our Children* (World Health Organization 2004).

[196] Sam Foster Halabi 'The Supremacy Clause as Structural Safeguard of Federalism: State Judges and International Law in The Post-Erie Era' (2012) 23 Duke Journal of Comparative and International Law 63, 118.

A treaty 'might be unenforceable in court because it is too vague, or otherwise calls for judgments of a political nature, or is unconstitutional, just as statutes ... might be'.[197] While treaties are the supreme law of the land, 'later in time statutes can supersede them. Thus Congress and the President can together supersede a Treaty adopted by the President and Senate alone'.[198] There are few subject-matter constitutional limitations on the power to conclude or agree to an international agreement in the United States, for example in relation to an international agreement that seeks to cede a US territory, abolish state militia, or modify the states' republican form of government. Such agreements might be held to be invalid.[199] The United States has moved from being a pioneer in treaty observance 'to being a country that, unlike some other Western democracies, puts increasing obstacles in the way of giving domestic effect to its international legal obligations'.[200]

Indeed, as far back as 1889 the United States Supreme Court held in *Chinese Exclusion*[201] that 'the Constitution does not bar Congress from enacting laws inconsistent with the international obligations of the United States and that the courts will give effect to an act of Congress inconsistent with provisions in an earlier treaty'.[202] Thus while the debate over the constitutionality of treaties continues unabated, the conclusion to draw is that in practice a treaty will be held unconstitutional and unenforceable domestically if it conflicts with a federal constitutional stipulation. In fact, according to Louis Henkin, 'treaties are subject to constitutional limitations'.[203] In the event of conflict between a treaty and an Act of Congress, the decisions of the Supreme Court dedicate that 'courts must give effect to an act of Congress that is inconsistent with a prior treaty obligation of the United States'.[204] It 'is unlikely' then that the Supreme Court 'would subordinate the Constitution to the law of nations and give effect to a principle of international law without regard to constitutional constraints'[205] so that a treaty that is inconsistent with the Constitution may be binding internationally 'but will not be enforced as law in the United States'.[206]

[197] Vázquez, Carlos Manuel, 'Treaties as Law of the Land: The Supremacy Clause and the Judicial Enforcement of Treaties' (2008) 122(2) Harvard Law Review 599, 605.

[198] Tom Ginsburg, 'Locking in Democracy: Constitutions, Commitment, and International Law' (2006) New York University Journal of International Law and Politics 707, 716.

[199] John H Jackson, 'US Constitutional Principles and Foreign Trade Law and Policy' in Hilf and Petersmann (eds), *Constitutions and Economic Law* (n 151) 66, 72.

[200] Thomas Buergenthal, 'Modem Constitutions and Human Rights Treaties' (1998) 36 Columbia Journal of Transnational Law 211, 212 (hereafter, Buergenthal, 'Constitutions and Human Rights Treaties').

[201] *Chinese Exclusion Case* 130 US 581 (1889).

[202] As summarised by Louis Henkin, 'The Constitution and United States Sovereignty: A Century of "Chinese Exclusion" and Its Progeny' (1986–1987) 100(4) Harvard Law Review 853 at 854.

[203] ibid 869.

[204] ibid 870.

[205] ibid 869–70.

[206] Louis Henkin, 'International Law as Law in the United States' (1983–1984) 82 Michigan Law Review 1555, 1562–63. For similar analysis see Lori Fisler Damrosch, 'The Role of the United States Senate Concerning "Self-Executing" and "Non-Self-Executing" Treaties' (1991) 67 Chicago-Kent Law Review 515; Michael J Glennon, 'The Constitutional Power of the United States Senate to Condition

With regards to the protection of public rights under the Constitution and general international law and its implications for the binding effect and efficacy of treaties which is of particular interest to this book, it is instructive to note that the practice in the United States dictates that constitutional rights prevail over conflicting treaty provisions. Peter Spiro posed and addressed the question of the constitutionality of treaties and whether constitutionally protected human rights prevail against international agreements in the United States:[207]

> Can a treaty override an individual right protected under the Constitution? In its 1957 decision in *Reid v. Covert*, the Supreme Court held that the 'obvious and decisive answer to this ... is that no agreement with a foreign nation can confer power on the Congress, or on any other branch of Government, which is free from the restraints of the Constitution.' There is perhaps no element of the foreign relations law canon more universally held than the proposition that constitutional rights prevail as against inconsistent international agreements; a consensus of commentators, courts, and other constitutional actors has long held that, in this respect, the Constitution stands supreme. Even as other elements of modem foreign relations law have come under vigorous assault, this constraint on the treaty power has gone unchallenged. Indeed, across the political spectrum, the rule is counted among those whose deep entrenchment eliminates the need for justification—so much so that it has attracted almost no scholarly attention in recent decades.

The practice with regards to the ranking of treaties in the scheme of municipal law varies from country to country. For example, in countries such as France, Costa Rica, Belgium, and Sweden, treaties at one time (if not now) had been given higher normative rank.[208] However, The proliferation of international human rights treaties giving jurisdiction to international tribunals over human rights issues and requiring domestic compliance with their decisions, a number of states have accorded 'a special or preferred status with a normative higher than that of other

Its Consent to Treaties' (1991) 67 Chicago-Kent Law Review 533; Stefan A Riesenfeld and Frederick M Abbot, 'The Scope of US Senate Control over the Conclusion and Operation of Treaties' (1991) 67 Chicago-Kent Law Review 571; John C Yoo, 'Globalism and the Constitution: Treaties, Non-Self-Execution, and the Original Understanding' (1999) 99(8) Columbia Law Review 1955; George A. Finch, The Need to Restrain the Treaty-Making Power of the United States within Constitutional Limits (1954) 48(1) American Journal of International Law 57; Pitman B Potter, 'Relative Authority of International Law and National Law in the United States' (1925) 2 American Journal of International Law 315; Louis Henkin, 'Treaties In A Constitutional Democracy' (1989) 10 Michigan Journal of International Law 406; and Detlev F Vagts, 'The United States and Its Treaties: Observance and Breach' (2001) 95(2) American Journal of International Law 313.

[207] Peter J Spiro, 'Treaties, International Law, and Constitutional Rights' (2003) 55(5) Stanford Law Review 1999, 2000 (hereafter, Spiro, 'International Law and Constitutional Rights').

[208] Buergenthal, 'Constitutions and Human Rights Treaties' (n 200) 216.

treaties and ordinary domestic law'.[209] Spain and a number of Latin American countries, including Argentina, fall into this category. In Costa Rica, the Supreme Court has set aside a number of laws it found to be inconsistent with the American Convention on Human Rights and other international human rights treaties.[210]

The preamble to the Constitution of Cameroon affirms fundamental freedoms and rights enshrined in the Universal Declaration of Human Rights and the African charter on Human and Peoples' Rights. It goes further, perhaps to the extreme, to provide in Article 45 that '[d]uly approved or ratified treaties and international agreements shall, following their publication, override national laws, provided the other party implements the said treaty or agreement'. Such a provision can lead to greater rights under human rights treaties being accorded to citizens. It can also lead to investment treaty rights and obligations being interpreted as overriding human rights and corresponding obligations under Cameroonian national laws. However, it may be that since specific mention is made of an obligation to observe international human rights treaties (and not investment treaties) only these human treaties may override national laws if they provide for greater rights for citizens from whom the government of Cameroon derives its powers.

According to Article 93 of the Constitution of Egypt, that country 'is committed to the agreements, covenants, and international conventions of human rights that were ratified by Egypt'. Article 40(a), (c), and (d) of the Constitution of Ghana provide that in in dealing with other nations the government must promote and protect the national interests and respect international law and treaty obligations, including those contained in the Charter of the United Nations, the Charter of the Organisation of the African Unity (now African Union), and the Treaty Establishing the Economic Community of West African States. Most of these treaties are human rights centred which suggests that the Constitution of Ghana accords significant and higher legal standing to these treaties than those on private interests. This is particularly the case when the Constitution places the 'national interests of Ghana' as a central pillar in the government's dealing with other nations and further requires it to seek the 'establishment of a just and equitable international economic and social order' in Article 40(b). An 'international economic order', which includes the regulation of foreign investment by treaty, will not be 'just and equitable' constitutionally if it subordinates the promotion and protection of human rights to private foreign investment interests that do not bring any public good. Similarly, in Kenya, general rules of international law and ratified treaties are part of the laws of Kenya by virtue of Article 1(5) and (6) of the Constitution of Kenya. So Kenya has an obligation to observe rules of general international law regarding human rights just as it has the same obligation under Articles 19–51 of its Constitution.

[209] ibid 216–17.
[210] ibid 218.

In South Africa the national executive is responsible for negotiating and signing 'international agreements', but an international agreement binds South Africa only after it has been approved by resolution in both the National Assembly and the National Council of Provinces and enacted into law by national legislation.[211] The preference in South Africa, according to Section 233 of the Constitution, is for 'reasonable interpretation of legislation that is consistent with international law over any alternative interpretation that is inconsistent with international law'. State institutions must act in compliance with the Constitution of South Africa, international agreements, and customary international law.[212] However, the event of conflict the Constitution takes precedence over international law and customary international and international agreements.[213]

The actions of African governments are no longer matters that are governed exclusively by domestic law alone. International law has an important role as well to play in the regulation of the conduct of national governments provided the legitimacy of such source of international law is not in dispute. This justifies the approach adopted in this book focusing on both the constitutional and public international law obligations of the selected African states and the implications of both legal norms for the execution and implementation of investment treaties.

The 'international human rights norms played an important part in the expanded conception of domestic civil right ... No account of twentieth-century constitutional rights is complete without international geopolitical referents' for where international law 'was once blind to individuals as such, today we find an increasingly consequential umbrella of individual rights protections in the form of international human rights norms'.[214] It follows that where states 'were once free to bargain away individual rights—for none were protected under international law itself—they now must account for them under other treaty and nontreaty norms'.[215] As the legal regime for the protection of human rights and other public interests now comprises international human rights norms and national constitutions as revealed in those analysed here, it is not just the doctrine of constitutional supremacy that establishes a basis for determining the validity and binding of effect of conflicting investment treaties but the combined legal force of both constitutional and international human rights treaty norms on the promotion and protection of human rights and the public interest. The concept of constitutional-general international law imperatives derives from this reality.

In the context of the European Union (EU), the issue has also arisen whether EU law is supreme over national constitutions of Member States or national constitutions retain sovereignty over EU law. Three approaches on how to accept EU law

211 Constitution of South Africa (n 31) s 231(1), (2), and (4).
212 ibid s 199(5).
213 ibid ss 2, 231(4), and 232.
214 Spiro, 'International Law and Constitutional Rights' (n 207) 2001 and 2002.
215 ibid.

have emerged. The first position, termed the primacy or constitutional supremacy of EU law by which the European Court of Justice legal decisions on EU law are accepted my Member States of the EU and their domestic courts.[216] The second approach insists on self-determination, the sovereignty national constitutional systems'[217] and emphasises the need for 'constitutional checks and balances' on EU law's application[218] The third approach, 'constitutional tolerance', posits that national constitutional courts can decide on the authority and reach of EU law, but that these courts have a commitment to recognise the special status of EU law. In deciding on the application of EU law they need to do so in a manner does not violate certain constraints of national constitutional law.[219]

Multi-layered legal pluralism creates both divergences and convergences.[220] Therefore, to 'sustain the rule of law in the face of plural legal orderings that cannot be subsumed, readily within a smoothly working legal hierarchical or unity',[221] it is important to focus on the convergence of legal norms. It is for this reason that Rosenfeld proposes the 'harmonization through the spread of a normative congruence that weaves together a plurality of legal regimes and of world views'.[222] The international constitutionalist approach 'lacks a reliable framework for assessing the exact, integral nature of the relations between national sovereignty and global law.'[223] State sovereignty 'cannot be pressed into a uniform legal category'.[224] On these bases, I emphasise instead the legal and normative approaches and values shared between national constitutions and general international law in the areas of human rights, the environment and development (the convergence on the role of the state in relation to the public) and how those *shared constitutional-international law public interests and values* should regulate the competence of states in the execution of investment treaties. I argue that the juridical consequences to be attached to investment treaties and the interpretation of those treaties by arbitral tribunals

[216] Damian Chalmers, Gareth Davies, and Giorgio Monti, *European Union Law: Cases and Materials* (2nd edn, CUP 2010) 190 (hereafter, Chalmers, Davies, and Monti, *EU Law*).

[217] ibid. See also *Polish Membership of the European Union (Accession Treaty)*, Polish Constitutional Court, Judgment K18/04 of 11 May 2005.

[218] Chalmers, Davies, and Monti, *EU Law* (n 216) 193. For further reading see Daniel Halberstam, 'Local, Global and Plural Constitutionalism: Europe Meets the World' in Gráinne de Búrca and Joseph Halevi Horowitz (eds), *The Worlds of European Constitutionalism* (CUP 2011) 150; Joseph HH Weiler and Marlene Wind (eds), *European Constitutionalism Beyond the State* (CUP 2003); Mattias Kumm, 'Who Is the Final Arbiter in Europe?: Three Conceptions of the Relationship German Federal Constitutional Court the European Court of Justice' (1999) 36 Common Market Law Review 351; and Mattias Kumm, 'The Legitimacy of International Law: A Constitutionalist Framework of Analysis' (2004) 15(5) European Journal of International Law 907.

[219] Chalmers, Davies, and Monti, *EU Law* (n 216) 194.

[220] Rosenfeld, 'Rethinking Constitutional Ordering' (n 1) 419.

[221] ibid 421.

[222] ibid 417.

[223] Chris Thornhill, 'National Sovereignty and the Constitution of Transnational Law: A Sociological Approach to Classical Antimony' (2012) 3(4) Transnational Legal Theory 394, 408.

[224] ibid.

should be guided by the dictates of African states' primary obligations under their constitutions and general international law towards the public.

2.4.2 General International Law and the Execution of Investment Treaties in Africa

2.4.2.1 Peremptory Norms of General International Law

Beyond an analysis founded on constitutionalism, it can similarly be argued that peremptory norms of general international law limit the treaty-making powers of states. The VCLT states in Article 53 that:

> [a] treaty is void if, at the time of its conclusion, it conflicts with a peremptory norm of general international law … [A] peremptory norm of general international law is a norm accepted and recognized by the international community of States as a whole as a norm from which no derogation is permitted and which can be modified only by a subsequent norm of general international law having the same character.

Human rights, such as the rights to life and health, access to justice, the right to water, the right to a clean and safe environment, and the right to development are universally recognised and accepted as fundamental for human existence and a life of dignity. They are rights *erga omnes*. I suggest that these rights should be recognised as constituting *jus cogens* in general international law and should inform investment treaty-making and interpretation. The ICJ held in the *Case Concerning East Timor (Portugal v Australia)*[225] that 'the right of peoples to self-determination, as it evolved from the Charter and from United Nations practice, has an *erga omnes* character [and] is irreproachable'. The recognition of genocide and slavery as constituting *jus cogens* underscores the importance of the basis on which the prohibition against these crimes derive (not merely the crimes themselves as such), namely the right to life, health, and human dignity. In the same way, the basic rights (including the right to development and environmental cleanliness) that are necessary for human health and a life of dignity should be regarded as *jus cogens* and should prohibit states from taking actions that prevent or undermine the realisation of these rights.

There is no agreement on the criteria to be used to identify norms of general international law that have a peremptory character.[226] However,[227]

225 *Case Concerning East Timor (Portugal v Australia)*, Judgment, ICJ Reports 1995, 90 [29].
226 Aust, *Modern Treaty Law* (n 186) 319.
227 Malcom N Shaw, *International Law* (6th edn, CUP 2008) 125–27 (emphasis added).

> [t]he concept of *jus cogens* is based upon an acceptance of fundamental and superior values within the system and *in some respects is akin to the notion of public order or public policy in domestic legal orders* ... Rules of *jus cogens* are not new rules of international law as such. It is a question rather of a particular and superior quality that is recognised as adhering in existing rules of international law ...Of particular importance ... is the identification of the mechanism by which rules of *jus cogens* may be created, since once created no derogation is permitted.
>
> A two-stage approach is here involved in light of article 53: first, the establishment of the proposition as a rule of general international law and, secondly, the acceptance of that rule as a peremptory norm by the international law community of states as a whole ... The appropriate test would thus require universal acceptance of the proposition as a legal rule by states and recognition of it as a rule of *jus cogens* by an overwhelming majority of states, crossing ideological and political divides. It is also clear that only rules based on custom or treaties may form the foundation of *jus cogens* norms.

African states are obliged by their constitutions to protect the fundamental human rights which are also protected in various IETs, IHRTs, and development-oriented agreements and declarations to which they are parties. These norms include the Universal Declaration of Human Rights,[228] International Covenant on Economic, Social and Cultural Rights, International Covenant on Civil and Political Rights, the African Charter on Human and Peoples' Rights, United Nations Convention on Climate Change,[229] Rio Declaration on Environment and Development,[230] African Convention on the Conservation of Nature and Natural Resources,[231] UN resolution on the human right to water and sanitation,[232] Declaration on the Right to Development,[233] and Charter on Economic Rights and Duties of States.[234] These conventions and declarations are, in one way or another, aimed at preserving human life and promoting human development generally as are protected under national constitutions in Africa. The rights, values, and interests they seek to protect or preserve are also reflected in national legal norms. The rights and interests they protect should be recognised as constituting *jus cogens*, from which derogation

228 Universal Declaration of Human Rights, 10 December 1948 UNGA Res 217A (III).

229 United Nations Framework Convention on Climate Change, 9 May 1992, 1771 UNTS 107, entered into force 21 March 1994.

230 Rio Declaration on Environment and Development, 13 June 1992, A/CONF.151/26 (Vol I), 31 ILM 874.

231 African Convention on the Conservation of Nature and Natural Resources, 15 September 1968, CAB/LEG/24.1, 1001 UNTS 3, entered into force 16 June 1969.

232 The human right to water and sanitation, UNGA Res 64/292 (28 July 2010).

233 Declaration on the Right to Development, UNGA Res 41/128 (4 December 1986).

234 Charter of Economic Rights and Duties of States, UNGA Res 29/3281 (1974) UNGA 29th Session Agenda Item 48 UN Doc A/RES/29/, art 1.

should not permitted since they are universally recognised. This will help promote good governance which is good both citizens and foreign investors.[235]

The constitutions of a number of African states require their governments to conduct their international affairs in consonance with the accepted principles of public international law and treaty obligations, specifically on human rights.[236] *Accepted principles of public international law* include customary international law, IHRTs, and IETs which have been ratified and incorporated into municipal law.[237] It is consistent with the national interest of African states that human rights and the environment be protected and that the people enjoy their right to development. The general international law duties to protect human rights and the environment and to make and implement development policies are also required of African states under their constitutions, so these rights and duties must guide states in entering into treaties in Africa. An investment treaty provision should be treated as void if it prevents a state from adopting measures to protect, for example, the right to clean water which is essential to human health and life and recognised under general international law.

In the following passages, I analyse selected theoretical frameworks that support the use of constitutionalism and general international law to address the issue of conflict of legal norms and interests in international investment law.

2.4.2.2 The Forbidden Treaties

It is settled in general international law that states have the capacity to enter into treaties. The VCLT states in Article 6 that every state 'possesses capacity to conclude treaties'. In 1923, the Permanent Court of International Justice (PCIJ) stated in the *Case of S. S. Wimbledon* that 'the right of entering into international engagements is an attribute of State sovereignty'.[238] However, do states have the capacity to make all kinds of treaties on any subject or assume any type of obligations whatsoever? Alfred Verdross' work[239] offers an illuminating theoretical model and foundations for my position on the role of general international law in treaty-making. Verdross acknowledged that 'as a matter of principle, states are free to conclude

[235] On public policy, good governance, and good faith in international economic law see: is Diane Desierto, *Public Policy in International Economic Law: The ICESCR in Trade, Finance and Investment* (OUP 2015); Andrew D Mitchell, Elizabeth Sheargold, and Tania Voon, 'Good Governance Obligations in International Economic Law: A Comparative Analysis of Trade and Investment' (2016) 17(1) Journal of World Investment Trade 7; and Andrew D Mitchell, Muthucumaraswamy Sornarajah, and Tania Voon, *Good Faith and International Economic Law* (OUP 2015).

[236] Constitution of Cameroon (n 27) preamble and arts 1(2) and 5(2); Constitution of Egypt (n 28) preamble and art 93; Constitution of Ghana (n 31) arts 40 and 73; Constitution of Kenya (n 25) art 1(5) and (6) and art 58(6)(a)(ii); Constitution of Nigeria (n 26) s 19(d); and Constitution of South Africa (n 31) s 39(1)(b); and s 231(1).

[237] Ex Parte Attorney-General (n 42) 2–7; Constitution of Ghana (n 31) art 75, Constitution of Kenya (n 25) art 1(6); and Constitution of Nigeria (n 26) s 12(1).

[238] *Case of the SS Wimbledon (UK v Japan)*, 1923 PCIJ (ser A) No 1 (17 August), *(Permanent Court of International Justice)* [35].

[239] Verdross, 'Forbidden Treaties' (n 19).

treaties on any subject whatsoever'.[240] However, he questioned whether this is an absolute rule or it admits of certain exceptions. If there is an exception to the rule, some treaties must be forbidden. His theory operates on the hypotheses that treaties are premised on norms necessary for them to come into force and that general international law contains rules which have the character of *jus cogens* which limit the capacity of states in treaty-making. Among the group of norms which constitute *jus cogens* is[241]

> the general principle prohibiting states from concluding treaties *contra bonos mores*. This prohibition . . . is the consequence of the fact that every juridical order regulates the rational and moral coexistence of the members of a community. No juridical order can, therefore, admit treaties between juridical subjects, which are obviously in contradiction to the ethics of a certain community.

A 'treaty norm is void if it is either in violation of a compulsory norm of general international law or *contra bonos mores*'.[242] Treaties are *contra bonos mores* if they 'restrict the liberty of one contracting party in an excessive or unworthy manner or . . . endanger its most important rights'[243] or if they prevent states 'from fulfilling the universally recognized tasks of a . . . state'.[244] Investment treaties as applied by most tribunals do not have such effect. However, indirect expropriation which provides investors with protection and assurance of compensation to them against general regulation not directly aimed harming foreign investors limits regulatory autonomy in an 'excessive or unworthy manner'. Foreign investors should be willing to accept inherent risks arising from legitimate regulation that has indirect adverse effects on their investments. According to Verdross, 'every positive juridical order has its roots in the ethics of a certain community, that it cannot be understood apart from its moral basis'.[245] Therefore, treaties are 'immoral' if they force a contracting state into a situation or position which contradicts the ethics of the community,[246] or if they undermine the performance of 'moral tasks states have to accomplish in the international community'.[247] There is an 'ethical minimum recognized by all the states of the international community',[248] which I argue includes the protection of the right to health and life, the right to development, and the right to environmental quality.

240 ibid 571.
241 ibid 573.
242 ibid 577.
243 ibid 574.
244 ibid 577.
245 ibid 576.
246 ibid 574.
247 ibid.
248 ibid.

Universally recognised tasks of a state includes the maintenance of law and order, defence against external attacks, care for the welfare of citizens, and protection of citizens abroad.[249] A treaty norm which expressly prevents a state from fulfilling one of these essential tasks is *contra bonos mores* and void.[250] When something is *contra bonos mores (et decorum)* it means that it is '[i]nconsistent with or contrary to preferred or sound practices, customs, public policy, or notions of equity'.[251]

Several examples of treaties as *contra bonos mores* may be cited. The first binds a state to reduce its police or its organisation of courts so that the state 'is no longer able to protect at all or in an adequate manner, the life, the liberty, the honor or the property … on its territory'.[252] The second is binds a state 'to reduce its army in such a way as to render it defenseless against external attacks'.[253] The third binds a state 'to close its hospitals or schools, to extradite or sterilize its women, to kill its children, to close its factories, to leave its fields unploughed, or in other ways to expose its population to distress'.[254] The content of these treaties is also void for being in violation of compulsory norms of general international law. Where a treaty is void, 'no obligation with such contents has ever come into existence'.[255] Verdross proposed that a dispute over the 'immorality' of a treaty norm should be submitted to the decision of the PCIJ, which today is the ICJ.

Verdross' theory provides a powerful tool for examining the limits that must be placed on states' treaty-making powers because it is founded on accepted principles of general international law and the public values and interests each individual state should protect internally. This is reflected in Verdross' emphasis on 'ethical minimum' of the community and 'universal tasks of a state', such as the duty to protect liberty, life, and property and to defend the state against external attacks. His examples show that human beings are entitled to certain basic rights and suggest that states must necessarily be performing certain basic and inherent corresponding functions in relation to those rights. This being so, a state should not have the capacity to make treaties that prohibit or have the effect of prohibiting it from performing basic functions in the interests of the public. The theory of forbidden treaties can be extended to investment treaties, which should be treated as *contra bonos mores* and should be void and not binding if they prevent the state from performing duties essential for the realisation of basic rights in society or 'expose the population to distress'. Investment treaties may not always have the direct effect of limiting the authorities of states as envisaged by Verdross. However, the chilling

[249] ibid 577.
[250] ibid 573 and 574.
[251] Aaron X Fellmeth and Maurice Horwitz, *Guide to Latin in International Law* (OUP 2009).
[252] Verdross, 'Forbidden Treaties' (n 19) 574.
[253] ibid.
[254] Ibid 575.
[255] Ibid 577.

effect of a possible arbitral award is that a state may not adopt a measure in the public interest if the state can reasonably foresee that measure being successfully challenged in investor–state arbitration.

Various renowned natural law theorists support the position I have advanced in this book that since the powers of a state derive from its constitution for the public good, it must be exercised to promote the common good of the people. A law that fails to promote or takes away the power of the state to act in the common good should not be obeyed. According to John Finnis the principal concern of natural law theory 'is to explore the requirements of practical reasonableness in relation to the good of human beings who, because they live in community with one another, are confronted with problems of justice and rights, of authority, law and obligation'.[256] Natural law theories seek to identify the principles and limits of the law and to trace the ways in which sound laws are to be derived.[257] Finnis' view on just and unjust laws and whether they are obeyed or not obeyed is influenced by his position on the source and public purpose of the authority to rule much similar to the position adopted in this book. For him:[258]

> [t]he ultimate basis of rulers' authority is the fact that they have the opportunity, and thus the responsibility, of furthering the common good by stipulating solutions to a community's coordination problems. Normally, though not necessarily, the immediate source of this opportunity and responsibility is the fact that they are designated by or under some authoritative rule as bearers of authority in respect of certain aspects of those problems. In any event, authority is useless for the common good unless the stipulations of those in authority (or which emerge through the formation of authoritative customary rules) are treated as exclusionary reasons, i.e. as sufficient reason for acting notwithstanding that subjects would not themselves have made the same stipulation and indeed considers the actual stipulation to be in some respect(s) unreasonable, not fully appropriate for the common good.

There are, in Finnis' view, 'human goods that can be secured only through the institutions of human law, and the requirements of practical reasonableness that only those institutions can satisfy'.[259] He identifies these human goods as life, knowledge, play, aesthetic, experience, friendship, practical reasonableness, and religion.[260] He argues that 'since authority is derived solely from the needs of the common good, the use of authority by rulers is radically defective if they exploit

256 John Finnis, *Natural Law and Natural Rights* (2nd edn, OUP 2011) 351.
257 ibid.
258 Ibid 351–52.
259 Ibid 4.
260 Ibid 90.

their opportunities by making stipulations intended by them not for the common good'.[261] Since the allocation of authority

> is normally determined by authoritative rules dividing up authority and jurisdiction, amongst separate office-holders, office-holders may wittingly or unwittingly exploit their opportunity to affect people's conduct, by making stipulations which stray beyond their authority. Except in 'emergency' situations in which the law (even the Constitution) should be bypassed and in which the source of authority reverts to its ultimate basis, an *ultra vires* act is an abuse of power and an injustice to those treated as subject to it.[262]

It

> may be commutatively unjust, by denying to one, some, or everyone an absolute human right, or a human right the exercise of which is in the circumstances possible, consistent with the reasonable requirements of public order, public health, etc., and compatible with the due exercise both of other human rights and of the same human rights by other persons.[263]

Any such law or action amounts to injustice.

In addressing the question whether injustice of any of this sort affects the obligation to obey the law, Finnis takes the position that 'the stipulations of those in authority have presumptive obligatory force ... only because of what is needed if the common good is to be secured and realized'.[264] Since rulers have authority 'for the sake of the common good ...if they use their authority to make stipulations against the common good, or against any of the basic principles of practical reasonableness, any such stipulation all together lacks the authority it would otherwise have'.[265] For this reason, 'stipulations made for partisan advantage, or ... in excess of legally defined authority, or imposing inequitable burdens or their subjects, or directing the doing of things that should never be done, simply fail, of themselves, to create any moral obligation whatever'.[266] The principle is that *lex injusta non est lex*, which helps address what Finnis describes as 'problems created for the conscience of reasonable citizens by unreasonableness in lawmaking'.[267]

St Thomas Aquinas is of the view that 'law must properly look to the relationship of universal happiness' since 'law properly speaking, regards first and foremost

[261] Ibid 352.
[262] Ibid.
[263] Ibid 354.
[264] Ibid 359.
[265] Ibid 359–60.
[266] Ibid 360.
[267] Ibid 62.

the order to the common good'.[268] The common good 'belongs either to the whole people, or to someone who is in the vicegerent of the whole people'.[269] According to St Aquinas,

> laws are ... just both from the end, when ... they are ordered to the common good; and from their author ... when the law that is made does not exceed the power of the law-giver; and from their form, when ... burdens are laid on the subjects according to an equality of proportion and with a view to the common good.[270]

Since law must be directed to the common welfare of human beings, if a case arises 'in which the observance of that law would be hurtful to the general welfare, it should not be observed'.[271] The force and reason of the law lie in its ability to promote the common good of people, *vim et rationem legis*. Therefore, if the law fails to advance that common good then it does not have the authority or capacity to bind, *virtutem obligandi non habet*.[272]

Applied in the context of investment treaty law, the promotion of private foreign investment must serve the interests of African states and their citizens and not just those of foreign private interests alone. This can be achieved if foreign investment actually makes a contribution to the development of the host state and the terms of investment treaties do not override public interest regulation. Where investment treaties fail to attain this objective they should not be enforced at the expense of the common good for which African states have entered into investment treaties. In that sense, therefore, they are unjust as imposing a disproportionate burden on the public, judged in terms of their restrictive effects on public interest regulation, in terms of a lack of an investment's contribution to the development of the host state and in terms of unqualified and unrestricted rights and privileges they confer on private foreign investors as against the lack of similar rights for states and their citizens. The protection of human rights, environment, and the taking of measures for the realisation of the right to development can only be secured through the actions of national institutions. States should not by any law, including investment treaties, unduly abridge their authority to perform these functions.

2.4.2.3 The Limitations and Qualifications Inherent in Statehood

Kojo Yelpaala examines the constitutional and *jus cogens* limitations on the competence of states in treaty-making, that is the extent to which the recognition of

[268] Thomas Aquinas, *The Summa Theologica*, Vol 2 (Fathers of the English Dominican Province tr, Encyclopaedia Britannica Inc 1952) 207.
[269] ibid.
[270] ibid 233.
[271] ibid 235.
[272] Giorgio Agamben, *State of Exception* (CUP 2008) 25.

fundamental human rights in constitutions and general international law should limit the types of obligations states undertake in investment treaties.[273]

A state is a juridical entity that acts only through agents or instrumentalities who have to be duly authorised by the state in the treaty-making process. However, the agents' treaty-making authority and competency are subject to structural limitations which relate to the political and legal framework within which the state functions in concluding treaties. Yelpaala argues that[274]

> [w]ithin this framework the State is generally limited by its constitution and structure of government. The competency of the State itself in treaty making is therefore subject to various limitations both under … municipal law and international law.
>
> Indeed, the treaty making process is subject to certain structural infirmities inherent in two forms of delegated authority: the one given to the State under its constitution and other legal instruments, and the other given by the State to its agents and instrumentalities. The first is necessarily subject to the principles of *delegatus non potest delegare* and *nemo dat quod non habet.* That is, the State itself is an instrument of its citizenry that is given certain functions and responsibilities which would tend to limit the powers of the State to delegate … It follows then that the efficacy of treaty obligations undertaken in … the name of investment protection is subject to these structural limitations and correspondingly to the competence of the State and its agents in concluding BITs.

It is imperative to consider whether a state can 'in the name of investment protection, undertake *any and every* obligation including those that pose significant risks to the health and safety of its citizens'.[275] The state's 'existence and powers are derived from its citizens who expect the State to exercise its powers for the general good of its citizens'.[276] The state 'has the *ultimate and indelible* responsibility of protecting its citizens from harm',[277] so it is 'doubtful whether the State can lawfully surrender these responsibilities and obligations and the corresponding rights and expectations of citizens in a treaty for private profit'.[278] When it comes to health and safety the state is constrained 'by both its international commitments and by its constitutional law obligations with respect to what treaty obligations it may undertake in its BITs practice'.[279]

[273] Yelpaala, 'Fundamentalism in Public Health Part II' (n 18).
[274] ibid 467–68.
[275] ibid 468.
[276] ibid.
[277] ibid.
[278] ibid.
[279] ibid 475.

The imperatives theory draws on Yelpaala's analysis and reasoning but uses specific constitutions and general international law obligations of Africa states involved as the subjects of its analysis. It emphasises that limitations on the exercise of the powers of governments are more compelling and exacting when those limitations are recognised under both a constitution and general international law. For this reason, a treaty that advances a constitutional purpose should trump one that does not.

Similarly, Evan Criddle and Evan Fox-Decent explain the peremptory status of *jus cogens* and their relationship with state sovereignty,[280] noting that *jus cogens* norms are constitutive of a state's authority to exercise powers as sovereign and to claim sovereign status as an international legal actor. In essence, the authors hold that[281]

> the state and its institutions are fiduciaries of the people subject to state power, and therefore a state's claim to sovereignty, properly understood, relies on its fulfillment of a multifaceted and overarching fiduciary obligation to respect the agency and dignity of the people subject to state power.

The fiduciary's power is 'purposive in that it is held or conferred for limited purposes, such as furthering exclusively the equitable interests of a trust's beneficiary'.[282] The fundamental fiduciary duty 'is to exercise the entrusted power exclusively for the … purposes for which it is held or conferred'.[283] Therefore, the '[e]xercises of state power that violate jus cogens are prohibited under international law precisely because they are inimical to the fiduciary principle that governs state-subject relations'.[284] Another implication of the fiduciary position of the state as agent of the people is that 'it cannot delegate or contract out essential fiduciary obligations of statehood (e.g., the state's duties to guarantee equal security and the rule of law) without providing adequate safeguards to those affected by the delegated powers'.[285]

The theory of the state as a fiduciary whose powers must be exercised for the benefit of the people for whom the state and its institutions are agents is appealing in the contexts of national constitutions in Africa such those studied in this book. The framework of government is established in these countries to secure for the people and posterity liberty, equality of opportunity and prosperity, the fact that sovereignty resides in the people, and the powers of government are to be exercised to promote the welfare of the people. The governments of these states, therefore,

280 Criddle and Fox-Decent, 'Theory of Jus Cogens' (n 58) 332.
281 ibid 347.
282 ibid 349.
283 ibid 350.
284 ibid 349.
285 ibid 384.

must not pursue an agenda that is contrary to the people's welfare by derogating from basic human rights (such as the right to a clean and safe environment and development) recognised under their constitutions or by entering into legal commitments that prevent the protection of basic rights or undermine the implementation of measures for the realisation or enjoyment of the rights.

Constitutions govern the making and coming into effect of investment treaties because they determine those who are endowed with the capacity to make treaties and define the conditions that must be followed for the treaties to come into force and the juridical consequences attendant to the conclusion of treaties.[286] Investment treaties are made and become valid and binding then because they are created in the manner determined not only by the law of treaties but also constitutions. These norms should determine the validity and effect of investment treaties.

2.5 The Foundations of the Imperatives Theory

2.5.1 Constitutional-General International Law Imperatives Defined

The foundations of the imperatives theory are constitutionalism, general international law, public interest, and the role of African states. The imperatives theory argues that the constitutions and general international law must inform the making and interpretation of investment treaties, given the primary duty of the states under these legal norms to protect the public interest. If states are to live up to these legal obligations, they must make investment treaties that are consistent with the norms that underlie and justify their duties and rights to regulate in the first place.

Both general international law and municipal law have important roles to play in the making of investment treaties and settlement of investment disputes. The obligations of states may also arise under both municipal law and general international law such as in the area of human rights protection. In such circumstances, it is time to shift from the principle that international law ranks higher than municipal law to examining the interrelationship between the two legal orders in terms of the common interests they protect and the role that such an interrelationship or bond should play in investment dispute resolution. Based on the imperatives theory, I argue that a state should not have the authority or competence to enter into treaties that expressly prevent it from acting to protect fundamental human rights. Such a limitation arises, for example, where an investment treaty prohibits performance requirements. Performance requirements relating to local content

[286] Constitution of Ghana (n 31) art 75 and VCLT (n 94) art 6.

for products, local jobs and training programmes for the local workforce, or to build the capacities of local suppliers of goods and services directly serve the public interest but they may be the subject of an investor–state suit.[287]

The constitutional-general international law imperatives refer to the various fundamental human rights, including the right to life, health, development, healthy environment, food, water, and cultural rights protected under a constitution and general international law and corresponding obligations of states. The concept also includes the remedial mechanisms adopted by states where those rights are violated, as well as the duties and obligations of states to ensure the realisation and enjoyment of these rights. These rights and duties are 'imperatives' because they emanate from the constitution and general international law and their existence and effective enjoyment are fundamental and essential for the dignity and well-being of human beings. The protection of these fundamental public rights of citizens is the main reason the powers to govern are entrusted to African states under discussion.

The constitutional-general international law imperatives are thus legal rights of human beings and the corresponding core duties of states. A foundational principle of constitutionalism is 'the protection and entrenchment of certain fundamental rights which cannot be derogated from, interfered with or otherwise compromised by the State and its organs without legal justification under established procedure'.[288] This is because 'the idea of government carries with it, the inherent conception of some modicum of respect for human dignity and welfare. Any system of government that rejects this is an aberration and does not have the legitimacy to continue to govern.'[289] These rights and obligations must therefore guide the making and interpretation of investment treaties. The fundamental human rights protected by the national constitutions in Africa and general international law should be the starting point for assessing the validity of treaties.

In African countries such as Cameroon, Egypt, Ghana, Kenya, Nigeria, and South Africa, fundamental human rights are part of national constitutions and other municipal laws. As members of the United Nations, these states also have obligation under Article 55(a) and (c) of the UN Charter to promote 'higher standards of living ... and conditions of economic and social progress and development' as well as 'universal respect for, and observance of, human rights and fundamental freedoms'.[290]The Charter provides in Article 103 that '[i]n the event of a conflict between the obligations of the Members of the United Nations under

[287] Suzy H Nikièma, *Performance Requirements in Investment Treaties* (IISD Best Practices Series—December 2014) at 2.

[288] Yelpaala, 'Fundamentalism in Public Health Part II' (n 18) 475.

[289] Kofi Quashigah, 'Trends in the Promotion and Protection of Human Rights in Ghana' in Kwame Boafo-Arthur (ed), *Ghana: One Decade of the Liberal State* (CORDESIA Books 2007) 21.

[290] Charter of the United Nations, signed in San Francisco, 26 June 1945 and entered into force 24 October 1945.

the present Charter and their obligations under any other international agreement, their obligations under the present Charter shall prevail'. The ICJ also held that the Charter prevails over conflicting treaty provisions.[291] The Court held in *Nicaragua v United States of America*[292] that 'all regional, bilateral, and even multilateral, arrangements ... must be made always subject to the provisions of Article 103 of the Charter'. The UN Charter in light of Article 103 'could be said to be of higher legal standing based on its source'[293] and the obligations 'under the UN Charter are cloaked with this higher legal standing'.[294] Article 103 'establishes the case of normative hierarchy by giving precedence to certain norms over others'.[295]

Most of the IETs, IHRTs and declarations African states are parties or signatory to make explicit reference to the UN Charter and its purposes. The preambles to the Universal Declaration of Human Rights, International Covenant on Civil and Political Rights, and International Covenant on Economic, Social and Cultural Rights show that these legal instruments were made and adopted by member states of the UN to provide further and more detailed legal bases for states to live up to their obligations under the UN Charter to promote universal respect for, and observance of, human rights and freedoms. Articles 55 and 103 of the UN Charter, interpreted together, emphasise the fundamental importance of human rights and the primary responsibility of states to secure the protection of these rights as against other treaty obligations. in The effect of Article 103 of the Charteris that governments' human rights and other public interest obligations under the Charter should trump investment treaties that compromise the full protection, realisation and enjoyment of fundamental human rights and societal values. This means that in the event of conflict, the Charter obligations must be complied with.

It is thus a constitutional-general international law imperative that states fulfil their usual functions pertaining to the protection of the public interest in the areas of development, human rights and the environment. The state as sovereign 'is formed entirely of the individuals who compose it, it has not, nor could it have, any interest contrary to theirs'.[296] Therefore, states must be free to regulate in the public interest. To be able to do this, African states must not make treaties that expressly and substantively require them to pay compensation for public interest regulation required by their constitutions and general international law without the need to pay such compensation. For, as Verdross has advised, if a state is burdened with

[291] *Bosnia v Serbia* (n 194) [99] and *Questions of Interpretation and Application of the 1971 Montreal Convention arising from the Aerial Incident at Lockerbie (Libyan Arab Jamahiriya v United Kingdom)*, Provisional Measures, Order of 14 April 1992, ICJ Reports 1992, 114, 126 [42].

[292] *Military and Paramilitary Activities in and against Nicaragua (Nicaragua v United States of America), Jurisdiction and Admissibility*, Judgment, ICJ Reports 1984, 392 at 440 para 107.

[293] Joost Pauwelyn, *Conflict of Norms in International Law: How WTO Law Relates to other Rules of International Law* (CUP 1999).

[294] ibid 338.

[295] Alexander Orakhelashvili, *Peremptory Norms in International Law* (OUP 2006) at 7.

[296] Jean-Jacques Rousseau, Maurice Cranston (tr) *The Social Contract* (Penguin Books Ltd 2004) at 18.

obligations (such as damages) making it impossible 'to fulfill the universally recognized tasks of a state ... no community would exist which would be able to care for ... human beings in an adequate way'.[297] This is particularly the case for Africa given its search for development, which makes it imperative that Africa should prioritise where and when its resources are expended.

Equally, as African states enter into the investment treaties so as to advance their development rather than protect foreign investment as an end in itself, any obligations they have assumed towards foreign investment must be interpreted consistently with the development objective and regulatory autonomy needed generally to further that objective.[298] Under the constitutional-general international law imperatives test, a state will assume investment treaty obligations that assure foreign investors that their covered investments will be accorded the necessary legal protection. However, those obligations must not be such that they can compromise the ability of current and future governments to exercise their inherent right to regulate in the interests of citizens through whom and for whom governments derive public power under their constitutions.

2.5.2 The Postulates of the Imperatives Theory

The following are the theoretical implications that arise from an analysis of the various African constitutions analysed and countries that have similar constitutional-general international law imperatives:

1. The state is formed of individuals who compose it and derives its powers and sovereignty from the people for the public good. The state does not have interests independent of those individuals of whom it is composed.
2. Under constitutions, governments are formed for the purpose of benefiting the governed and furthering the sovereign will of the people. The powers of governments derive from constitutions for the common good and must be exercised within the limits in constitutions.
3. Constitutions and general international law make provision for the protection of the public interest in the areas of fundamental human rights, essential security of the state, the environment, and the right to development and assign corresponding obligations in relation to these rights to the state. The duty to promote and protect these rights is the first and primary duty of the state as an agent and fiduciary of the people. Constitutions and general international law also recognise the protection of private property rights but

[297] Verdross, 'Forbidden Treaties' (n 19) 576.

[298] Dominic Dagbanja, 'The Development Objective as an Imperative in Interpretation of International Investment Agreements' (2018) 44(2) University of Western Australia Law Review 145

they place emphasis on the protection of the public interest as the primary role of the state, which makes it more compelling that the state does not encumber its public interest regulatory powers by investment treaties which focus solely on private investment interests, the public benefits of which are uncertain, unassured, or unrealisable. Most constitutions and municipal legislation would justify the making of investment treaties in developmental, public interest terms. Within this constitutional and general international law legal framework, the public interest must come first in international economic regulation.

4. States have capacity under their constitutions and general international law to make investment treaties. As the capacity to make investment treaties derives from constitutions and general international law, the investment treaties are subordinate to these norms and should be treated as invalid if they are made contrary to the process requirements of constitutions and general international law or if they conflict with substantive constitutional standards and *jus cogens*.
5. Since the primary duties of states are owed towards citizens under their constitutions, their capacity to make investment treaties must be qualified by a treaty's adverse effect upon their ability to fulfil those duties. Treaties that cannot be applied together with constitutional obligations towards citizens should be treated as invalid based on the obligations of states to prioritise the public interest and corresponding obligation of states.
6. Where governmental regulation has adversely affected the value of an investment and investment treaties do not expressly require the payment of compensation for the particular regulation, the presumption is that investment treaties are intended to comply with municipal law and general international law principles. In such a case, compensation should not be available to foreign investors if municipal law and general international law prohibit it.
7. The state has a legal obligation in general international law and municipal law to observe treaties that have been *validly made*. Treaties are validly made if they comply with the process and substantive requirements of the applicable constitution and general international law. Therefore, the state must respect and observe the terms of such investment treaties. A breach of enforceable investment treaties must give rise to the responsibility of the state to pay foreign investors damages arising directly out of the breach provided the investment treaty, which should have been capable of being entered into in the first place, expressly requires it.
8. As the state is an agent and fiduciary of the people, it cannot derogate from its obligations to protect fundamental human rights of citizens. Accordingly, investment tribunals must aim at interpreting investment treaties in a manner that accommodates the state's right to regulate in the

public interest. Much as investment interests must be protected, they cannot be protected at the expense of the public purpose for which the state has entered into the particular investment treaty and in disregard of the interests of the people whom governments represent. This requires tribunals to take into consideration the legal justification of the measure when making a decision on liability and damages. A 'balance' of rights cannot be said to exist in situations where the investor must always win.

9. Where a constitution assigns original, appellate, and *final* jurisdiction over legal disputes to local courts and institutions, irrespective of the subject matter and persons involved, the state lacks the capacity and must not agree to international arbitration allowing foreign investors to bypass local courts for foreign forums in disputes involving the state itself. An agreement to arbitrate in the face of such a constitutional assignment can only be effective where domestic remedies are unavailable or are proved to be ineffective in accordance with customary international law. In this regard, the appropriate forums for the resolution of investment disputes including those on the validity of investment treaties are national courts, state-to-state tribunals, and others recognised under customary international law and general international law agreed by the parties.
10. Foreign investors operate within national territories and rely on the regulatory support and institutional and individual goodwill of states to operate successfully. They take the benefit of domestic support and regulation. They must likewise be subject to domestic regulatory measures and adjudication that do not work in their favour provided those measures are not primarily and directly aimed at harming them.

The legal validity, binding effect, and interpretation of investment treaties should be linked to the competence of states to make the treaties. The question might arise whether a state's competence to enter into a treaty should not be distanced from the policy outcomes or material effects of that treaty. De-linking competence in investment treaty-making from the treaty's outcomes, it might be argued, is necessary to separate sovereignty from the material effects of the treaty. Such a position may be plausible but it does not correspond with the practice and reality in law-making and its implementation both at the municipal plane and international plane. It is axiomatic that laws are meant to have binding effect and be enforceable based on their material effects. Based on their material effects, laws may be valid and enforceable or invalid and unenforceable in light of the hierarchy of legal norms. Thus, the binding effect of legal norms or their material effects are always related to their legal and policy outcomes, which includes the extent to which the legal or policy outcomes conflict with existing legal norms. That is why while the *pacta sunt servanda* rule applies. Articles 7, 27, and 46 of the VCLT recognise, for example, that a state may be able to invoke a person's lack of capacity or the provisions of internal law as an excuse for non-compliance with a treaty. Articles 53 of the VCLT requiring the provisions of treaties to be void if they conflict with *jus cogens* relates intimately to the material effects or policy outcomes of the provisions against the demands of *jus cogens*.

The New York Convention in Article V(2)(b) empowers courts of an enforcing state to refuse the enforcement of an arbitral award on grounds of inconsistency with the public policy of the enforcing state.[299] Essentially these matters relate to the competence of a state to conclude treaties in light of existing legal forms or even prospective ones (eg in the case of new *jus cogens*). If a treaty could always be binding and enforceable irrespective of the policy outcomes, the objects of provisions such as 7, 27, 46, and 53 of the VCLT and others on the termination of treaties on grounds other than the expiry of the treaty would be defeated; in fact their inclusion in the VCLT would have been unnecessary. So the policy outcomes of a treaty can hardly be divorced from the competence to conclude it. If the policy outcomes of a treaty entered into by the state could always be distanced from the outcomes of the treaty, then a state could always enter into any treaty even if the treaty's coming into force meant an abandonment of the role of the state under a constitution and general international law.

2.6 Conclusion

In *Richardson v Mellish*,[300] Justice Burrough stated that once you get astride an unruly horse 'you never know where it will carry you'. There is a Ghanaian saying to similar effect, namely that *if you sit on a donkey and fail to direct it where it should send you, it will send you to the valley to eat grass*. It follows that if investment treaty standards are unqualified so as to provide absolute protection for foreign investment, they will achieve that objective by limiting the right to regulate. Similarly, if the reform of investment treaties merely ends at recognising or affirming the right to regulate in the investment treaties without concrete and enforceable obligations being imposed on foreign investors with respect to the public interest as appears to be the case with current reforms, then the right to regulate in the public interest cannot actually be retained or reclaimed in practice. Then the reforms would be otiose. Therefore, just as an unruly horse has to be tamed or restrained or a donkey has to be purposely directed to take its rider to where the rider wants to go, national constitutions and general international law (being the foundations for statehood, governance, public accountability, and the legal bases of states' defence of their

[299] Convention on the Recognition and Enforcement of Foreign Arbitral Awards, entered into force on 7 June 1959.

[300] *Richardson v Mellish*, [1824] 2 Bing 229, 130 ER 294 at 303.

right to regulate in the public interest) must substantively determine the type of investment treaty obligations African states can undertake.

States are the principal authors in the making and maintenance of the investment treaty regime which constrains their regulatory autonomy. To retain or reclaim their autonomy, states must act within the legal limits set by their constitutions and general international law (including CIL, IETs, and IHRTs) in order to preserve the public rights these norms protect. The norms and rights that matter for states and for which they need regulatory autonomy, and in the interest of which they enter into investment treaties, the constitutional-general international law imperatives must dictate the nature of the investment treaty obligations states can or cannot agree to in investment treaties. Securing absolute investment protection and thereby limiting regulation justified in the public interest without corresponding tangible and assured benefits as trade-off from investment protection puts investors and their investments first. This is inconsistent with African states' obligations under their constitutions and general international which require them to put the public interest first in all they do, including in foreign policy-making and international economic relations.

The legal validity of investment treaty terms based on an assessment of their limiting impact on the right to regulate should depend on the capacity of states to agree to the particular investment treaty term within the broader context of constitutional-general international law rights of citizens and corresponding non-derogable duties of African states, and indeed all states similarly situated. To the extent that the right and duty to regulate in the public derives from national constitutions and general international law to be exercised for the public good, it must supersede a conflicting investment treaty term in situations where that treaty term could not or ought not to have entered into in the first place. If the public interest is prioritised in investment treaty-making through enforceable exceptions for the right to regulate in investment treaties, regulatory autonomy can be reclaimed and sustainably retained.

3

The Legal Status and Limitations on Investor–State Arbitration in Africa

3.1 Introduction

The fulfilment of African states' constitutional and international law obligations towards the citizens as discussed in Chapters 1, 2, 4, and 5 is intimately linked to the functions of the courts as institutions responsible for the administration of justice through the resolution of all manner of legal disputes and the interpretation of national constitutions, domestic legislation, and applicable international conventions and norms. This chapter is concerned with the limitations investment treaty arbitration places on the exercise of judicial powers in Africa. The interest is particularly in how the powers of the domestic courts under national constitutions and customary international law might limit the competence of African states to agree to investment treaty arbitration and the implication of such limitation for the legal and juridical status of investment treaty arbitration.

Investor–state dispute settlement by arbitration (ISDS) has serious implications for the authority of municipal courts and the finality, efficacy, and enforcement of their decisions within domestic legal systems. As opined by Dame Sian Elias, the former Chief Justice of New Zealand, '[s]ome of the most intrusive impacts of international law on domestic legal systems are now arising in the context of investor–state Dispute Settlement processes'.[1] Underscoring that point, the former Chief Justice French of the Commonwealth of Australia questioned if this mechanism is 'a cut above the courts'.[2] Their concerns are appropriate because interim and final judgments of municipal courts under national constitutions have been ignored or vacated by investment tribunals as discussed in Section 3.4 later in this chapter. In this connection, an investor–state suit challenging the decision of a municipal court before an investment tribunal 'raises justifiable fears as to whether constitutional doctrines, such as separation of powers, and the exclusivity of control over matters within national jurisdiction, are not being left behind in the effort

[1] Sian Elias, *Barbarians at the Gate: Challenges of Globalization to the Rule of Law*, Address Given at the World Bar Association Conference (Heritage Hotel, Queenstown, Thursday 4 September 2014) at 3.

[2] RS French, *Investor-State Dispute Settlement—A Cut above the Courts?* (Supreme and Federal Courts Judges' Conference, Darwin, 9 July 2014)(hereafter, French, *Investor-State Dispute Settlement*).

The Investment Treaty Regime and Public Interest Regulation in Africa. Dominic Npoanlari Dagbanja, Oxford University Press.
 DOI: 10.1093/oso/9780192896179.003.0003

to create regimes for foreign investment'.[3] This chapter focuses on whether constitutional norms and customary international law prevent African states from agreeing to investment dispute resolution under ISDS or at least place some limitations on the use of the ISDS mechanism. It also addresses the related question of whether African national constitutions and customary international law require foreign investors to exhaust domestic remedies in Africa.

The question of the competence of a state to agree to ISDS is foundational in the search for regulatory autonomy in international investment law. Most existing legal scholarship relates to the flaws of ISDS. There is legal scholarship on arbitration and the exhaustion of local remedies,[4] the role of domestic courts in investment arbitration,[5] the impact of ISDS on domestic courts,[6] the necessity and virtues of ISDS,[7] and whether investor–state arbitration or municipal courts should settle investment disputes.[8] None has directly focused on the legitimacy of ISDS in terms of the constitutional and legal limitations on the competence of African states to agree to such constraints.

This chapter fills this lacuna by assessing the competence of African states such as Cameroon, Egypt, Ghana, Kenya, Nigeria, and South Africa to agree to a mechanism that permits foreign investors to bypass their domestic legal systems when challenging *state actions* and enables international tribunals to override the municipal courts whose jurisdiction under their constitutions is supreme, original, appellate, and final. The questions addressed include the following: can the public interest role of municipal courts and national institutions be constrained by ISDS? Since various African constitutions assign original, appellate, and final jurisdiction to municipal courts, do the states nevertheless have the competence to agree to investor–state arbitration that gives foreign investors direct access to investment tribunals to challenge state actions? Does customary international law limit the competence of African states to adopt an agreement that pre-commits the states to arbitrate? If an investor commences the settlement of an investment dispute in a domestic court, can it subsequently institute arbitral proceedings?

[3] Muthucumaraswamy Sornarajah, 'The Clash of Globalizations and the International Law on Foreign Investment' (2003) 10(2) Canadian Foreign Policy Journal 1, 10 (hereafter, Sornarajah, 'Clash of Globalizations').

[4] Stephen Schwebel and Gillis Wetter, 'Arbitration and the Exhaustion of Local Remedies' (1966) 60 American Journal International Law 484.

[5] Charles Brower II, 'Investor–State Disputes Under NAFTA: The Empire Strikes Back' (2001–2002) 40(1) Columbia Journal of Transnational Law 43; and George A Bermann, 'The "Gateway" Problem in International Commercial Arbitration' (2012) 37 Yale Journal of International Law 1.

[6] Gus Van Harten, *Investment Treaty Arbitration and Public Law* (OUP 2007) (hereafter, Harten *Arbitration and Public Law*); and Tom Ginsburg, 'International Substitutes for Domestic Institutions: Bilateral Investment Treaties and Governance' (2005) 25 International Review of Law and Economics 107.

[7] Stephan Schill, 'The Virtues of Investor–State Arbitration', <http://www.ejiltalk.org/the-virtues-of-investor-state-arbitration/> accessed 17 December 2021.

[8] Leon Trakman, 'Choosing Domestic Courts over Investor–State Arbitration: Australia's Repudiation of the Status Quo' (2012) 35(3) University of New South Wales Law Journal 979.

I argue that constitutions in Africa (eg that of Cameroon, Egypt, Ghana, Kenya, Nigeria, and South Africa) and customary international law limit the competence of the states in the conclusion of such an agreement. The ISDS mechanism can potentially shield foreign investors from being brought to justice in municipal courts for breaches of applicable laws and standards in Africa to the extent that any decision made by municipal courts can be challenged before investor–state tribunals. This can lead not only to damages that neutralise decisions arrived at by municipal courts but also to additional damages and costs that have a severe fiscal impact and a chilling effect on decisions of governments and judicial bodies, as shown in the cases analysed in Section 3.4. By the ISDS mechanism, investment tribunals can impugn judicial independence and the powers guaranteed to the courts under various constitutions in Africa.

From constitutional and public policy perspectives, giving investors the option of not having matters finally determined by the local courts is not a solution. Defending investor–state arbitral suits costs public money and resources. The process is secretive and lacks transparency, although efforts are being made to address some of these concerns as discussed in Section 3.6. Public participation may not be permitted and may be practically impossible given the foreign location of arbitral proceedings outside the African continent. Arbitral awards may not be published and the public may not know how much public resources states expend in particular arbitral proceedings. The secrecy and lack of transparency are reflected in deliberately hiding by redacting information on arbitral awards and the costs of arbitration as reflected in *Philip Morris Asia Ltd v Australia*.[9] Such secrecy and lack of transparency are inconsistent with constitutional principles on probity, accountability, and transparency in Africa.[10]

International arbitration also removes the accountability of governments from the courts and to the people, since disputes involving states and investors do not have to be resolved in national courts, through which African governments are accountable to the people. International arbitration undermines judicial authority and sovereignty in Africa because it does not respect the independence of the courts and the finality of their decisions which are fundamental principles under most African constitutions, as established in Section 3.4. This can undermine the ability of the courts to adjudicate effectively upon and protect constitutional issues and public rights that touch on and concern investment.

[9] *Philip Morris Asia Ltd v The Commonwealth of Australia* (PCA Case No 2012-12, Final Award Regarding Costs, 18 March 2017) [70], [72], [74–75], [77–79], [86–88], [93], [95], [103–105], and [108].

[10] Richard J Sweeney, 'Constitutional Transparency' in Jens Forssbæck and Lars Oxelheim (eds), *The Oxford Handbook of Economic and Institutional Transparency* (OUP 2014) 33; Carol Harlow, 'Accountability and Constitutional Law' in Mark Bovens, Robert Goodin, and Thomas Schillemans (eds), *The Oxford Handbook of Public Accountability* (OUP 2014) 195; and Nicholas Bamforth and Peter Leyland, *Accountability in the Contemporary Constitution* (OUP 2013).

I argue that these constitutional principles and norms and customary international law rules on exhaustion of local remedies do, or at least should, prevent African states from entering into ISDS or require African states to agree to ISDS mechanisms that respect constitutional norms and preserve their autonomy to regulate in the public interest. I argue also that where an investor has commenced an investment dispute settlement process in a local court, it is mandatory constitutionally and under the local remedies rule of customary international law to exhaust domestic remedies before any applicable international dispute resolution forum may be resorted to. In effect, the continued use of ISDS by arbitration must be informed by the constitutional position of each African state and relevant rules of customary international law.

The rest of the chapter is organised as follows.

Section 3.2 presents a review of the current criticisms of ISDS.

Section 3.3 shows that the courts in Africa have constitutional jurisdiction over all legal persons and legal disputes within national territorial boundaries and this includes jurisdiction over investment disputes and foreign investors. It examines the right of foreign investors under domestic law and investment treaties to access investor–state tribunals as an alternative to municipal courts in Africa.

Section 3.4 assesses conflict of jurisdiction between municipal courts and arbitral tribunals, showing how arbitral tribunals have used their powers to settle investment disputes to exert control over governmental decisions and final decisions reached by competent courts of jurisdiction in Africa. The exertion of such control leads to conflict between the jurisdiction of arbitral tribunals under investment treaties and the jurisdiction of municipal courts under municipal law in Africa. The exertion of such control by arbitral tribunals undermines constitutional principles of the rule of law, separation of powers, judicial independence, and the finality and efficacy of judicial decisions.

Section 3.5 challenges the constitutionality of ISDS and its compatibility with African states' obligations under customary international law. It proposes that African states must do away with ISDS on the ground that domestic courts have constitutional jurisdiction over all legal disputes and that they are competent to settle those disputes. The constitutional principles of accountability, probity, rule of law, separation of powers, and transparency and finality of judicial decisions dictate against African states being party to such a mechanism. The African states may only agree to ISDS mechanisms that preserve constitutional principles relating to the jurisdiction of municipal courts and the functions of government in the public interest.

Section 3.6 deals with developments in investor–state arbitration reforms in Africa at bilateral, regional, and continental levels, arguing that reforms need to be situated in relevant constitutional contexts.

Section 3.7 concludes the chapter by reiterating the need for constitutional principles to dictate the relations between foreign investors and their host states in Africa, including on the issue whether to use or not to use private tribunals to resolve investor–states' disputes.

3.2 The Legitimacy, and Efficacy of Investor–State Arbitration: A Global Resistance

The ISDS mechanism was designed to 'create a forum that would offer investors a fair hearing before an independent, neutral and qualified tribunal. It was seen as a mechanism for rendering final and enforceable decisions through a swift, cheap, and flexible process.'[11] The provision for ISDS in investment treaties demonstrates the importance states attach to this mechanism as a guarantee that disputes that arise between them and investors will be settled in a supposedly neutral and impartial forum. Such a guarantee, it is claimed, is necessary to attract foreign investment for development.[12] The supposed role of ISDS in investment attraction and depoliticisation of dispute settlement are also given as reasons giving rise to this mechanism.[13]

The actual functioning of ISDS reveals systemic and endemic deficiencies.[14] The issues with ISDS comprise 'a perceived deficit of legitimacy and transparency; contradictions between arbitral awards; difficulties in correcting erroneous arbitral decisions; questions about the independence and impartiality of arbitrators, and concerns relating to the costs and time of arbitral procedures'.[15] The International Centre for Settlement of Investment Dispute's (ICSID) reforms of the ICSID arbitral system seek to respond to some of these legitimacy and efficiency concerns.[16]

The legitimacy issues with ISDS have to do with its suitability to resolve disputes involving sensitive public policy issues,[17] given its ad hoc and private nature[18] and

[11] According to the United Nations Conference on Trade and Development (UNCTAD), *IIA Issues Note: Reform of Investor–State Dispute Settlement: in Search of a Roadmap* (No 2, United Nations, June 2013) 2 (hereafter, UNCTAD, *Reform of Investor–State Dispute Settlement*).

[12] Muthucumaraswamy Sornarajah, *The International Law on Foreign Investment* (3rd edn, CUP 2010) 48–49 (hereafter, Sornarajah, *Law on Foreign Investment*.

[13] Marc Bungenberg and August Reinisch, 'From Bilateral Arbitral Tribunals and Investment Courts to a Multilateral Investment Court: Options Regarding the Institutionalization of Investor–State Dispute Settlement' in Marc Bungenberg and August Reinisch (eds), *European Yearbook of International Law* (2nd edn, Springer International Publishing AG 2018) 13–22.

[14] UNCTAD, *Reform of Investor–State Dispute Settlement* (n 11) 2.

[15] ibid 1; and Leon Trakman, 'Investor State Arbitration or Local Courts: Will Australia Set a New Trend?' (2012) 46(1) Journal of World Trade 83, 100–08.

[16] Meg Kinnear and Paul Jean Le Cannu, 'Concluding Remarks: ICSID and African States Leading International Investment Law Reform' (2019) 34(2) ICSID Review—Foreign Investment Law Journal 542 (hereafter, Kinnear and Cannu, 'Concluding Remarks').

[17] David Schneiderman, 'Legitimacy and Reflexivity in International Investment Arbitration' (2011) 2(2) Journal of International Dispute Settlement 471 (hereafter, Schneiderman, 'Legitimacy and Reflexivity in International Investment Arbitration'); and Susan Frank, 'The Legitimacy Crisis in Investment Treaty Arbitration: Privatizing Public International Law through Inconsistent Decisions' (2005) 73(4) Fordham Law Review 1521.

[18] Gus Van Harten, 'The Public–Private Distinction in the International Arbitration of Individual Claims against the State' (2007) 56 International and Comparative Law Quarterly 371.

the secrecy and lack of transparency in arbitration proceedings.[19] The literature reveals 'divergent legal interpretations of identical or similar treaty provisions as well as differences in the assessment of the merits of cases involving the same facts'.[20] These inconsistencies are reflected in the cases analysed in Section 3.4. Inconsistent interpretations have led 'to uncertainty about the meaning of key treaty obligations and lack of predictability of how they will be applied in future cases'.[21] Arbitrators 'decide important questions of law without a possibility of effective review', and existing review mechanisms, namely the ICSID annulment process and national court review at the seat of arbitration, have a very narrow jurisdiction.[22] On the issue of cost and time-intensity of arbitration proceedings, 'practice has put into doubt the oft-quoted notion that arbitration represents a speedy and low-cost method of dispute resolution'.[23] The arbitral system is biased and its integrity is questionable in part because arbitrators tend to be sympathetic to the party appointing them and the security of their appointment is dependent on them asserting jurisdiction over claims.[24]

The ISDS mechanism has also become a very powerful tool that investors use to challenge measures adopted by states in the public interest. More than 70 per cent of the 2013 investor–state claims concerned investments in the services sector, where public interest regulation is important, such as the supply of electricity or gas, telecommunications, construction, tourism, banking, real estate services, water, media, and advertising.[25]

The growth in the number and severity of treaty-based disputes between host states and foreign investors may be attributed to the increase in foreign investment and in international investment agreements (IIAs). According to United Nations Conference on Trade and Development (UNCTAD),, the number of IIAs reached 3,360 by the end of 2020.[26] The ISDS claims brought by foreign investors

[19] Gary Born and Ethan Shenkman, 'Confidentiality and Transparency in Commercial and Investor–State International Arbitration' in Catherine Roger and Roger Alford (eds), *The Future of Investment Arbitration* (OUP 2009) 4 (hereafter, Born and Shenkman, 'Confidentiality and Transparency in Commercial and Investor–State International Arbitration').

[20] Campbell McLachlan, 'Investment Treaties and General International Law' (2008) 57 International and Comparative Law Quarterly 361; and Campbell McLachlan, 'The Principle of Systematic Integration and Article 31(3)(c) of the Vienna Convention' (2005) 54 International and Comparative Law Quarterly 279.

[21] Louis Wells, 'Backlash to Investment Arbitration: Three Causes' in Michael Waibel and others (eds), *The Backlash against Investment Arbitration: Perceptions and Reality* (Kluwer Law 2010) 341, 342 (hereafter Wiabel and others (eds), *Backlash against Investment Arbitration*).

[22] UNCTAD, *Reform of Investor–State Dispute Settlement* (n 11) 3.

[23] ibid 4.

[24] Gus Van Harten, 'Perceived Bias in Investment Treaty Arbitration' in Waibel and others (eds), *Backlash against Investment Arbitration* (n 21), 433; and Sam Luttrell, 'Bias Challenges in Investor–State Arbitration: Lessons from International Commercial Arbitration' in Chester Brown and Kate Miles (eds), *Evolution in Investment Treaty Law and Arbitration* (CUP 2011) 445.

[25] UNCTAD, *Reform of Investor–State Dispute Settlement* (n 11).

[26] UNCTAD, *World Investment Report 2021: Investing in Sustainable Recovery* (United Nations 2021) 122–23. See also UNCTAD, *World Investment Reports 2019: Special and Economic Zones* (United Nations 2019) 99.

against states reached 1,104 between 1987 and January 2021 involving 124 states as respondents.[27] By the end of 2020 about 740 ISDS proceedings had been concluded.[28] Between 1987 and 2020, 30 per cent of the resolved cases on the merits were decided in favour of the states, 29 per cent were decided in favour of foreign investors, 20 per cent were settled, and 12 per cent were discontinued.[29]

Investor–state arbitration has serious implications for the regulatory autonomy of states. Jeswald Salacuse argues:[30]

> The costs of investor-State disputes are placing growing financial and other hardships on individual countries, particularly on poor, developing countries. The potential costs of investor-State arbitration are basically threefold. First ... a host country faces the risk of having to pay awards that, in relation to its budget and financial resources, may prove extremely burdensome. Second, the host country must bear the substantial costs, both direct and indirect, of conducting the arbitration itself. Third, the 'policy cost' of investor-State arbitration is that a substantial award to the investor may require the host country to repeal or modify measures that were implemented for the public good.

These three factors raise 'questions as to whether means other than arbitration and litigation can be found to resolve treaty-based, investor-State disputes'.[31] Only investment tribunals that are capable of balancing competing interests should be made to resolve investor–state disputes.[32]

The challenges posed by the ISDS regime in terms of its efficiency, and ability to limit regulatory autonomy 'create momentum for its reform'.[33] Proposals to reform the ISDS regime include the promotion of alternative dispute resolution, tailoring the existing system through individual IIAs, limiting investor access to ISDS, introduction of an appeals facility, and the creation of a standing international investment court.[34] The pressure for reforms to ISDS also saw new UNCITRAL Rules on Transparency in Treaty-based Investor–State Arbitration coming into effect on 1 April 2014.[35]

[27] UNCTAD, *World Investment Reports 2019* (n 26) 103 and 104.

[28] UNCTAD, *World Investment Report 2021* (n 26).

[29] ibid 130.

[30] Jeswald Salacuse, 'Is There a Better Way? Alternative Methods of Treaty-Based, Investor–State Dispute Resolution' (2007) 31(1) Fordham International Law Journal 138, 145 (hereafter, Salacuse, 'Is there a Better Way').

[31] ibid, 139–40.

[32] Sornarajah, 'Clash of Globalization'(n 3) 9–10.

[33] UNCTAD, *Reform of Investor–State Dispute Settlement* (n 11) 1.

[34] ibid.

[35] United Nations Commission on International Trade Law (UNCITRAL), UNCITRAL Rules on Transparency in Treaty-based Investor–State Arbitration adopted by the UN General Assembly, 10 December 2014, entered into force 18 October 2017) (UNCITRAL, 'Rules on Transparency'). These rules resulted in the United Nations Convention on Transparency in Treaty-based Investor–State Arbitration, adopted by the UN General Assembly on 10 December 2014, to entered into force 19

States themselves have begun to question the wisdom and appropriateness of ISDS given the challenge it poses to regulatory autonomy and their opposition to the inclusion of ISDS in investment treaties has been growing. Bolivia, Ecuador, and Venezuela withdrew from ICSID in 2007, 2009, and 2012, respectively. Nicaragua and Venezuela no longer view ICSID as a preferred mechanism for resolving investor–state disputes.[36] Following a review of the actual value of investment treaties for investment inflows to South Africa and an assessment of the risk ISDS poses to the adoption of policies and domestic interventionist measures, South Africa terminated twelve of its fifty investment treaties.[37] The South African government also enacted the Protection of Investment Act 2015 to regulate the protection and promotion of investments domestically. The Act makes provision for the resolution of investment disputes by mediation, although an investor may also approach an independent tribunal or statutory body in South Africa for the resolution of a dispute. The South African government may consent to international arbitration subject to the exhaustion of domestic remedies.[38] Indonesia has terminated thirty-one of its seventy-three investment treaties.[39] India terminated seventy-four of its eighty-six investment treaties.[40] In 2015, the Union Cabinet of the government of India approved a revised Model Text for the Indian Bilateral Investment Treaty (BIT) to replace the 1993 India Model Investment Treaty.[41] Overall, there were 393 effective investment treaty terminations by the end of 2020.[42]

The European Union (EU) made efforts to reform substantially the investment protection and ISDS system. In 2014, the European Commission conducted a public consultation within the EU seeking feedback from individuals and organisations on whether the proposed EU approach to investment protection and arbitration would achieve the right balance between protecting investors and safeguarding the EU members' right to regulate in the public interest. That consultation revealed

January 2021 <https://uncitral.un.org/en/texts/arbitration/conventions/transparency/status> accessed 25 October 2021.

36 UNCTAD, IIA Issue Note: Denunciation of the ICSID Convention and BITs: Impact on Investor–State Claims (No 2, United Nations December 2010).

37 UNCTAD, International Investment Agreements Navigator: South Africa <https://investmentpolicy.unctad.org/international-investment-agreements/countries/195/south-africa> accessed 28 September 2020.

38 Protection of Investment Act 2015 (Act No 22) (Government Gazette Vol 606, No 39514, 15 December 2015) s 13 (hereafter, PIA).

39 UNCTAD, International Investment Agreements Navigator: Indonesia <https://investmentpolicy.unctad.org/international-investment-agreements/countries/97/indonesia> accessed 28 September 2020.

40 UNCTAD, International Investment Agreements Navigator: India <https://investmentpolicy.unctad.org/international-investment-agreements/countries/96/india> accessed 25 October 2021.

41 Model Text for the Indian Bilateral Investment Treaty <https://www.mygov.in/sites/default/files/master_image/Model%20Text%20for%20the%20Indian%20Bilateral%20Investment%20Treaty.pdf> accessed 28 September 2020.

42 UNCTAD, *World Investment Report 2021* (n 26) 123.

an opposition to investment protection and ISDS in the failed Transatlantic Trade and Investment Partnership Agreement (TTIP) between the United States and Europe.[43] Similar opposition had been expressed against the inclusion of ISDS in the Trans-Pacific Partnership.[44] In the United States (US), the National Centre for State Courts urged the US Trade Representative and Congress:[45]

> to only approve trade agreements provisions that recognize and support the sovereignty of state judicial systems and the enforcement and finality of state court judgments and to clarify that under existing trade agreements, foreign investors shall enjoy no greater substantive and procedural rights than US citizens and businesses.

In *Slowakische Republic (Slovak Republic) v Achmea AV*, decided on 8 March 2018, the Court of Justice of the European Union (CJEU) held that an arbitration agreement in an investment treaty between the Slovak Republic and the Kingdom of the Netherlands had an 'adverse effect on the autonomy' of EU law.[46] In the opinion of the CJEU, Articles 267 and 244 of the Treaty on the Functioning of the European Union[47] (TFEU)[48]

> must be interpreted as precluding a provision in an international agreement concluded between Member States, such as Article 8 of the BIT, under which an investor from one of those Member States may, in the event of a dispute concerning investments in the other Member State, bring proceedings against the latter Member State before an arbitral tribunal whose jurisdiction that Member State has undertaken to accept.

The CJEU reasoned that by concluding the investment treaty, the member parties to the treaty 'established a mechanism for settling disputes between an investor and a Member State which could prevent those disputes from being resolved in a manner that ensures the full effectiveness of EU law, even though they might

[43] European Commission, Report on Online Public Consultation on Investment Protection and Investor-to-state Dispute Settlement (ISDS) in the Transatlantic Trade and Investment Partnership Agreement (13 January 2015), <http://trade.ec.europa.eu/doclib/docs/2015/january/tradoc_153044.pdf> accessed 28 September 2020.

[44] Jane Kelsey and Lori Wallach, 'Investor–State Disputes in Trade Pacts Threaten Fundamental Principles of National Judicial Systems' <http://www.citizen.org/documents/isds-domestic-legal-process-background-brief.pdf> accessed 28 September 2020.

[45] National Centre for State Courts, Free Trade Agreements <http://www.ncsc.org/Services-and-Experts/Government-Relations/International/Free-Trade-Agreements.aspx>

[46] Case C-284/16 *Slowakische Republic (Slovak Republic) v Achmea AV* [2018] ECR I, [59]. (hereafter, *Slovak v Achmea*).

[47] Consolidated Version of the Treaty on the Functioning of the European Union (26.10.2012) OJ C 326/47 <https://eur-lex.europa.eu/legal-content/EN/TXT/PDF/?uri=CELEX:12012E/TXT&from=EN> accessed 28 September 2020.

[48] *Slovak v Achmea* (n 46) [60].

concern the interpretation or application of that law'.[49] The CJEU further reasoned that even though the disputes under the investment treaty fell within the jurisdiction of the arbitral tribunal related to the interpretation of the investment treaty and EU law, there was the possibility of those disputes being submitted 'to a body which is not part of the judicial system of the EU'.[50] The arbitral tribunal established under that investment treaty was thus not situated within the judicial system of the EU and it could not be regarded as a court or tribunal of a Member State within the meaning of Article 267 of TFEU.[51] In the opinion of the CJEU the 'consequence of a tribunal set up by Member States being situated within the EU judicial system is that its decisions are subject to mechanisms capable of ensuring the full effectiveness of the rules of the EU'.[52] The instant tribunal was not part of the judicial system of the Netherlands or Slovakia and therefore could not be classified under Article 267 of the TFEU as a court or tribunal of a Member State of the European Union (EU).[53] On 5 May 2020, twenty-three Member States of the European Union signed an agreement to terminate intra-EU BITs with a view to implementing the ruling in the *Achmea Case*. About 125 intra-EU BITs will be terminated when the agreement enters into force.[54]

In the European Union, concerns as to lack of transparency of ISDS, the lack of appellate process against investment tribunals' decisions, pro-investor bias of arbitral tribunals, and unqualified right to investors to challenge legitimate regulation in the public interest have necessitated initiatives within the European Union to establish a Permanent Investment Court.[55] The EU–Canada Comprehensive Economic and Trade Agreement (CETA) envisages the establishment of a multilateral investment tribunal and appellate mechanism to resolve investment disputes.[56] Thus, the resistance and retreat from ISDS is happening even among the European countries that championed and promoted this regime as the best mechanism for investment dispute settlement when they led and signed investment treaties with African and Asian countries and the developing world in general.

This analysis shows there is a substantial measure of dissatisfaction and disquiet with how ISDS operates. However, while the academic literature has questioned the wisdom, legitimacy, and efficacy of ISDS, a compelling issue that has not yet been addressed directly is ISDS' legal status in light of national constitutions and

[49] ibid [56].
[50] ibid [58].
[51] ibid [43].
[52] ibid.
[53] ibid [45]–[46].
[54] UNCTAD, 'World Investment Report 2020' (n 26) 108.
[55] August Reinisch, *The European Union and Investor–State Dispute Settlement: From Investor–State Arbitration to a Permanent Investment Court*, CIGI, Investor–State Arbitration Series Paper No 2—March 2016) 10 <https://www.cigionline.org/sites/default/files/isa_paper_series_no.2.pdf> accessed 28 September 2020.
[56] Comprehensive Economic and Trade Agreement between Canada, of the one part, and the European Union and its Member States, of the other part (signed 30 October 2016, provisionally entered into force 21 September 2017) (hereafter, CETA).

relevant principles of general international law. In this chapter this issue examined with particular reference to its impact on the jurisdiction of municipal courts in Africa.

3.3 The Jurisdiction of Domestic Courts and Investment Treaty Arbitration in Africa

The potential for conflict of jurisdiction domestic courts and arbitral tribunals over investment disputes and the interpretation of national constitutions cannot be adequately appreciated without analysing the jurisdiction of selected domestic courts under applicable constitutions in Africa. Accordingly, this Section studies the jurisdiction of domestic courts to provide a basis for analysing conflict of jurisdiction over investment disputes. It also analyses the right to investor–state arbitration in Africa

3.3.1 The Jurisdiction of Domestic Courts in Africa

Article 46 of the Constitution of Cameroon provides that the Constitutional Council 'shall have jurisdiction in matters pertaining to the Constitution. It shall rule on the constitutionality of laws'. Specifically, under Article 47, the Constitutional Council 'shall give a final ruling on the constitutionality of laws, treaties and international agreements'. Thus, even if investment disputes could be resolved by arbitral tribunals, when issues pertaining to the constitutionality of investment treaties and the interpretation of the Constitution of Cameroon come up in the course of arbitral proceedings, the state would naturally argue that those matters would not be capable of settlement by arbitration. An arbitral tribunal following the jurisprudential stance of the Ghanaian arbitral cases analysed in Section 3.4 would entertain jurisdiction over such constitutional issues and disregard any judicial pronouncements made by the Constitutional Council.

According to Article 50(1) of the Constitution of Cameroon, the rulings of the Constitutional Council 'shall not be subject to appeal'. In effect, the decision of the Constitutional Council is final and must have effect in accordance with Article 47. Yet, a dissatisfied investor can challenge the decision of the Constitutional Council under Cameroon's investment treaties providing for investor–state arbitration, thereby rendering the effect required to arise from the decision of the Constitutional Council otiose. The judicial branch, including the Supreme Court, Court of Appeal, and Tribunals have original and appellate jurisdictions and can issue final rulings.[57] How does Cameroon reconcile the original, appellate, and

[57] Constitution of the Republic of Cameroon 1972 (with Amendments through 2008) arts 37–41 (hereafter, Constitution of Cameroon).

final judicial powers of the Constitutional Council over the constitutionality of treaties with investor–state arbitration under investment treaties?

Article 192 of the Constitution of Egypt states that the Supreme Constitutional Court (SCC) 'is exclusively competent to decide on the constitutionality of laws and regulations, interpret legislative texts, and adjudicate in disputes pertaining to the affairs of its members'. In fact, Article 188 of the Constitution of Egypt provides that the judiciary 'adjudicates all disputes'. The assignment of exclusive jurisdiction to the SCC means that only this body has competence to decide on the specified matters. A legitimate question is can Egypt nevertheless agree to investor–state arbitration investment treaties directly or indirectly giving jurisdiction to arbitral tribunals over these matters? From a municipal constitutional law perspective, such an agreement would be unconstitutional. According to Article 151 of the Constitution of Egypt, '[i]n all cases, no treaty may be concluded which is contrary to the provisions of the Constitution'. Thus, to the extent that the SCC has exclusive jurisdiction over these subject matters, the exercise of arbitral jurisdiction over investment disputes under investment treaties will conflict with the constitutional functions of SCC, especially when a constitutional interpretation issue arises and the arbitral tribunal decides to interpret relevant constitutional issues arising in connection with the investment disputes as happened in the Ghanaian and South African cases analysed in Section 3.4. Moreover, with no constitutional qualification or proviso to the requirement that the judiciary shall adjudicate all disputes, it would seem Egypt cannot agree to a mechanism designed to exercise jurisdiction over disputes that are within the jurisdiction of one of the judicial bodies recognised under the Constitution, namely State Council, SCC, State Cases Authority, and Administrative Prosecution,[58] especially when those disputes involve the state as a disputant itself which must respect the independence and autonomy of its constitutionally established institutions.

By Article 126(1) of the Constitution of Ghana and the Courts Act 1993 (Act 459), the judiciary of Ghana consists of the Supreme Court, the Court of Appeal, Regional Tribunals, Circuit Court, and District Court. According to Article 125(1), justice 'emanates from the people and shall be administered in the name of the Republic by the Judiciary which shall be independent and subject only to this Constitution'. Consequently, Article 125(2) vests the judicial power of Ghana in the judiciary, which by Article 125(5) 'shall have jurisdiction in all matters civil and criminal'. The independence of the judiciary is clearly protected in Article 127(1) of the Constitution of Ghana which states that the judiciary 'is subject to only this Constitution and shall not be subject to the control or direction of any person or authority'. Arguably, 'any person' in Article 127(1) of the Constitution of Ghana includes international persons and institutions such as an arbitral tribunal.

[58] Constitution of the Arab Republic of Egypt 2014, arts 190–197 (hereafter, Constitution of Egypt).

Under Article 130(1) of the Constitution, the Supreme Court has 'exclusive original jurisdiction in ... all matters relating to the enforcement or interpretation' of the Constitution. The Court, by Article 129(1) of this Constitution, is also the 'final court of appeal.' The role of the courts in the administration of justice arises not only when the disputed matter involves private parties but also when the state is a party to a dispute.

The effect of these articles is that an arbitral tribunal or a state institution, for example, must not make a decision that takes away or varies the full effect of the decision of the Supreme Court when it has exercised its original or appellate powers and reached a *final* decision. Persons who are aggrieved by the Court's decision may only seek a review in accordance with Article 133 of the Constitution of Ghana. Thus, the decision of the Supreme Court can be reviewed only within the terms of the Constitution of Ghana and by the Court itself. There is a right of appeal from the decision of the Court of Appeal to the Supreme Court and from the decision of the High Court to the Court Appeal under Articles 131 and 137 of the Constitution of Ghana. These are the constitutionally recognised bases to challenge a judicial decision in Ghana.

Under Article 165(3)(a) of the Constitution of Kenya, the High Court has 'unlimited original jurisdiction in criminal and civil matters'. It also has jurisdiction over any question concerning the interpretation of the Constitution including the determination of the constitutionality of legislation and acts of government officials. According to Articles 164(3) and (4) of the Constitution of Kenya, appeals lie from the Court of Appeal to the Supreme Court and from the High Court and other courts to the Court of Appeal. Judicial power in Kenya has been effectively discussed elsewhere.[59] Given the 'unlimited original jurisdiction' of the High Court in civil matters, the Kenyan Parliament cannot remove the High Court from resolving investment disputes without an amendment of the Constitution of Kenya.

According to section 4(8) of the Constitution of Nigeria 'the exercise of legislative powers by the National Assembly or by a House of Assembly shall be subject to the jurisdiction of courts of law and of judicial tribunals established by law'. Accordingly, by this same provision, the National Assembly or a House of Assembly 'shall not enact any law that ousts or purports to oust the jurisdiction of a court of law or of a judicial tribunal established by law'. By this provision, the constitutionality of investment treaties and an agreement to arbitrate ratified by the National Assembly is subject to the jurisdiction of the courts, and the courts can therefore make a declaration of the constitutionality of investor–state arbitration and of investment treaties. Arguably, then investment treaties will be ousting the Nigerian courts from their jurisdiction if they make provision for a situation

[59] James T Gathii, *The Contested Empowerment of Kenya's Judiciary, 2010–2015: A Historical Institutional Analysis* (Sheria Publishing 2016); and Jackton B Ojwang, 'Constitutional Trends in Africa—The Kenya Case' (2000) 10(2) Transnational Law and Contemporary Problems 517, 533–35.

where courts may not substantively entertain the settlement of investment disputes involving Nigeria and a foreign investor.

Section 6(1) and (5) of the Constitution of Nigeria vests the judicial powers of the federation and the states in federal courts and state courts. This judicial power extends to 'all matters between persons, or between government or authority and to any persons in Nigeria, and to all actions and proceedings relating thereto, for the determination of any question as to the civil rights and obligations of that person'.[60] This jurisdiction is very wide and includes judicial settlement of investment disputes between Nigeria and foreign investors. The High Court in a state has jurisdiction where property of any person is compulsorily acquired on an application of the affected person.[61] Section 251(1) of the Constitution of Nigeria gives powers to the Federal High Court to 'exercise jurisdiction to the exclusion of any other court in civil causes and matters'.

The matters specifically under reference include:

1. the revenue of the government of the Federation in which the government or an organ of the government or a person 'suing or being sued on behalf of the said Government is a party'.[62]
2. the taxation of companies and other bodies established or carrying on business in Nigeria.[63]
3. customs and excise duties and export duties, including any claim by or against the Nigeria Customs Service.[64]
4. banking, banks, and other financial institutions, including any action by or against the Central Bank of Nigeria in the exercise of its regulatory functions.[65]
5. the operation of the Companies and Allied Matters Act 2020 and acts regulating the operation of companies incorporated under this Act.[66]
6. Federal enactments relating to 'copyright, patent, designs, trade marks and passing-off, industrial designs and merchandise marks, business names, commercial and industrial monopolies, combines and trusts, standards of goods and commodities and industrial standards'.[67]
7. admiralty jurisdiction.[68]
8. bankruptcy and insolvency.[69]

[60] Constitution of the Federal Republic of Nigeria 1999, s 6(6)(b) (emphasis added) (hereafter, Constitution of Nigeria).
[61] ibid ss 44 and 46.
[62] ibid s 251(1)(a).
[63] ibid s 251(1)(b).
[64] ibid s 251(1)(c).
[65] ibid s 251(1)(d).
[66] ibid s 251(1)(e).
[67] ibid s 251(1)(f).
[68] ibid s 251(1)(g).
[69] ibid s 251(1)(j).

9. aviation and safety of aircraft.[70]
10. mines and minerals.[71]
11. the operation and interpretation of the Constitution 'in so far as it affects the Federal Government or any of its agencies'.[72]

Each of these specific matters relates to business activities in which foreign investors can be involved. Disputes related to these matters would have to be resolved in the High Court as constitutionally stipulated. Therefore, a legitimate constitutional question arises whether in light of the specific assignment of these matters to the *exclusive* jurisdiction of the High Court the Nigerian government may nevertheless agree to ISDS that allows foreign investors to bypass the High Court. For example, an issue as to the constitutionality of an investment treaty or investor–state arbitration agreement involves and affects the federal government and by virtue of section 251(1)(q) of the *Constitution of Nigeria* must be subject to the exclusive jurisdiction of the High Court. Again, a claim against the federal government for compensation to be paid out of federal revenue would be subject to the exclusive jurisdiction of the High Court in accordance with section 251(1)(a) of the Constitution of Nigeria and arguably cannot be the subject of investor–state arbitration. Any such claim, being an investment dispute, has to be instituted through investor–state arbitration under Nigeria's investment treaties. Any of these claims under investment treaties would be inconsistent with the Constitution of Nigeria. The jurisdiction of arbitral tribunals over expropriation claims, for example, clearly conflicts with High Court's constitutional jurisdiction when the property of a person is compulsorily acquired.

Section 233 of the Constitution of Nigeria provides that an appeal from the Court of Appeal must go to the Supreme Court of Nigeria. An appeal from one court shall lie before another court established by the National Assembly under an Act, including matters relating to compulsory acquisition of property by Nigeria. In effect, when a decision is made by a Nigerian court, a decision shall lie before another Nigerian court until the case reaches the Supreme Court of Nigeria.[73] According to section 235 of the Constitution of Nigeria, '[w]ithout prejudice to the powers of the President or of the Governor of a state with respect to prerogative of mercy, no appeal shall lie to any other body or person from any determination of the Supreme Court'. In other words, the decision of the Supreme Court is final. No further appeal exists beyond the decision of the Supreme Court, yet an investor not satisfied with the Supreme Court's decision may use ISDS to challenge that decision. An investor–state arbitration is not an appeal *per se*. However, it does achieve

[70] ibid s 251(1)(k).
[71] ibid s 251(1)(n).
[72] ibid s 251(1)(q).
[73] ibid ss 233, 240, and 241.

the effect of an appeal because the institution of arbitral proceedings founded on a judicial decision is intended to secure a contrary decision to that reached by a court and thereby give the investors rights it could not secure in a court.

According to section167(3)(a)(b) and (c) of the Constitution of South Africa, the Constitutional Court 'is the highest court in all constitutional matters', may decide 'only constitutional matters', and make 'the final decision whether a matter is within its jurisdiction'. Section 168 provides for a Supreme Court of Appeal 'to decide appeals in any matter arising from the High Court of South Africa or a court of a status similar to the High Court of South Africa'.[74]

The constitutions of Cameroon, Egypt, Ghana, Kenya Nigeria, and South Africa give jurisdiction to the courts to resolve all sorts of disputes without exception and for the exhaustion of local remedies. Therefore, an investment dispute may be required not only to commence in a domestic court in any of these African countries but also once it is commenced the disputing party has an appellate right only as constitutionally established. It would be unconstitutional if an investor, having commenced a dispute in a domestic court, and a decision having been reached by that domestic court, to initiate fresh proceedings on the same dispute in relation to that judicial decision before anybody other than as constitutionally established or specified. The fact that the decisions of these supreme courts are *final* means that the decisions may not be challenged before any other body, unless relevant rules of constitutional law and customary international law on exhaustion of local remedies permit it. Being dissatisfied with a judicial outcome does not justify seeking remedy beyond a supreme court under customary international law unless it is shown that those remedies were not effective. These constitutional requirements together with the exhaustion of the local remedies rule would not permit abandoning the local courts in favour of investor–state arbitration without showing that remedies do not exist or are ineffectual and that resorting to them would not serve any useful purpose. It is questionable then whether a direct right to investor–state arbitration is consistent with these constitutions.

3.3.2 The Direct Right to Investor–State Arbitration in Africa

Domestic legislation on foreign investment and the investment treaties provides for ISDS in Africa. Under the investment treaty between Cameroon–Belgo–Luxembourg Economic Union (BLEU), if an investment dispute cannot be resolved amicably or by conciliation through diplomatic channels, the dispute at the

[74] Constitution of the Republic of South Africa 1996, s 168(3)(a) (hereafter, Constitution of South Africa).

request of the investor may be submitted to ICSID for conciliation or arbitration.[75] Under this BIT, each contracting party has given 'its irrevocable advance consent to the submission of any dispute to the Centre. Such consent implies a waiver of the requirement that internal administrative or judicial remedies first should have been exhausted.'[76] This provision has the telling effect of completely removing investment disputes from ever being entertained in Cameroonian courts. By Article 10(3) of the BIT, Cameroon cannot object to the jurisdiction of a tribunal even if the ground for the objection concerns an issue of constitutionality of an investment treaty even though the Constitution of Cameroon says such a matter must be decided by the Constitutional Council. The right to arbitration is also guaranteed under domestic law in Cameroon, namely Cameroon Investment Charter (2002), Articles 11–12.

The Egypt–Canada investment treaty also provides for investor–state arbitration which may be initiated by the investor.[77] Quite unlike other investment treaties, the right to arbitration is qualified. Thus, an investor may submit a dispute to arbitration only if the investor has consented in writing to arbitration, the investor has waived its right to initiate or continue any other proceedings before the courts or tribunals or in a dispute settlement procedure of any kind in the host state, a contracting party must have given its unconditional consent to the submission of a dispute to international arbitration if the dispute concerns taxation, or if the arbitration commenced within three years since the investor became aware or should have become aware of the breach and loss.[78] Investment law (Law No 72 of 2017) also provides for different mechanisms for resolving investment disputes, including investor–state arbitration.

The Ghana Investment Promotion Centre Act 2013 (Act 865) (GIPC Act) protects foreign investment in terms of investment incentives and dispute settlement. The GPIC Act provides in section 33(1) that mutual discussion should reach an amicable settlement where a dispute arises between a foreign investor and the government. Section 33(2) provides that a dispute which 'is not amicably settled through mutual discussion within six months may be submitted at the option of the aggrieved party to arbitration'. Under section 33(3), where there is no agreement to arbitrate for the settlement of investment disputes in a contract or investment agreement and the parties disagree on the mode of dispute resolution, the dispute is to be resolved through mediation under the Alternative Dispute

[75] Belgo–Luxembourg Economic Union and United Republic of Cameroon Convention concerning the reciprocal promotion and protection of investments (signed 27 March 1980, entered into force 1 November 1981) art 10(2).

[76] ibid.

[77] Agreement between the Government of Canada and the Government of the Arab Republic of Egypt for the Promotion and Protection of Investments (signed 13 November 1996, entered into force 3 November 1997) art XIII(1) and (2).

[78] ibid.

Resolution Act 2010 (Act 798) which establishes the legal and institutional framework for domestic resolution of disputes by methods other than court trial process.

Similarly, under Ghana's BITs investment disputes not resolved through mutual discussion within the specified times of written notification of a claim are to be settled by ISDS. The institutions specified include the Arbitration Institute of the Stockholm Chamber of Commerce, ICSID, UNCITRAL rules, or an international arbitrator or *ad hoc* arbitration tribunal appointed by a special agreement between the parties.[79]

There are variations between BITs. The Ghana–China investment treaty limits an investor–state dispute to '[a]ny dispute ... concerning the amount of compensation for expropriation',[80] while the Ghana–Malaysia, Ghana–Denmark, Ghana–Netherlands, and Ghana–United Kingdom investment treaties provide for arbitration in respect of disputes 'concerning *an obligation* ... in relation to an investment'.[81] The broad scope of the latter means, for example, that BIT disputes concerning the implementation of human rights norms that adversely affect the value of foreign investment still have to be settled through arbitration.

The GIPC Act and investment treaties thus provide for two ways to resolve investment disputes: mutual discussion for an amicable settlement and arbitration. The specification of these two modes of investment dispute settlement indicates that the courts are to have nothing to do with substantive investment dispute settlement. In the fact, the requirement in section 33(3) of GIPC Act that where there is no agreement to arbitrate a dispute is to be resolved through *mediation* under the Alternative Dispute Resolution Act removes investment disputes from the jurisdiction of the courts.

Kenya's Arbitration Act 1995 (Cap 49) provides in section 4(1) that arbitration agreement 'may be in the form of an arbitration clause in a contract or in the form of a separate agreement'. Nigeria's Arbitration and Conciliation Act 1988 (No 11) (ACA) also provides in section 1 that an agreement to arbitrational shall be writing. The faith in and respect for arbitration in Nigeria is reflected in section 2 of

[79] Agreement between the Government of the United Kingdom of Great Britain and Northern Ireland and the Government of the Republic of Ghana for the Promotion and Protection of Investments (signed 22 March 1989, entered into force 25 October 1991) art 10; Agreement on Encouragement and Reciprocal Protection of Investments between the Kingdom of the Netherlands and the Republic of Ghana (signed 31 March 1989, entered into force 1 July 1991) art 9; Agreement between the Kingdom of Denmark and the Government of the Republic of Ghana Concerning the Promotion and Protection of Investments (signed 13 January 1992, entered into force 6 January 1995) art 10(1)(3); Agreement between the Government of the Republic of Ghana and the Government of Malaysia for the Promotion and Protection of Investments (signed on 8 November 1996, entered into force 18 April 1997) art 7; and Agreement between the People's Republic of China and the Government of the Republic of Ghana Concerning the Encouragement and Reciprocal Protection of Investments (signed 12 October 1989, entered into force on 22 November 1991) art 10.

[80] Ghana–China Investment Treaty (n 79) art 10(1).

[81] Ghana–Malaysia Investment Treaty (n 79) art 7(1); Ghana–Denmark Investment Treaty (n 79) art 10(1); Ghana–Netherlands Investment Treaty (n 79) art 9(1); and Ghana–United Kingdom Investment Treaty (n 79) art 10(1).

the ACA wherein it is provided that an agreement to arbitrate shall terminate only by agreement of the parties or by the leave of the court. The investment treaties of Kenya,[82] Nigeria,[83] and South Africa[84] also provide for investor–state arbitration. These African countries, apart from South Africa, are also parties to the Convention for the Settlement of Investment Disputes between States and Nationals of Other States[85] (ICSID Convention) and the Convention on the Recognition and Enforcement of Foreign Arbitral Awards (New York Convention).[86] Article 20 of the Agreement Establishing African Continental Free Trade Area (AfCFTA) established a Dispute Settlement Mechanism which applies to the settlement of trade disputes arising between contracting parties.[87] The AfCFTA thus prefers state-to-state dispute settlement.

Given that domestic investment legislation and the investment treaties provide for ISDS, they have internationalised jurisdiction over investment disputes to international arbitral bodies located mostly outside of Africa.

3.4 A Case Study of Jurisdictional Conflict over Investment Disputes Settlement in Africa

Arbitral cases involving Ghana, South Africa, and Egypt provide typical practical examples to study this subject of conflict of jurisdiction between domestic courts and arbitral tribunals over investment and commercial disputes between African states and foreign investors and other business entities. The Ghanaian cases in particular are of unique importance and relevance because of the decisions of the Supreme Court of Ghana on constitutional matters have been at the centre of arbitration claims before private arbitrators. Most other African countries have not had such conflicting constitutional issues with international arbitration and the jurisdiction of the courts except to a limited extent Kenya[88] and South

[82] Agreement between the Government of Japan and the Government of the Republic of Kenya for the Promotion and Protection of Investment (signed 28 August 2016, entered into force 4 September 2017) art 15.

[83] Treaty between the Federal Republic of Germany and the Federal Republic of Nigeria Concerning the Encouragement and Reciprocal Protection of Investments, signed 28 March 2000, entered into force 20 September 2007) art 11.

[84] Agreement between the Government of the People's Republic of China and the Government of the Republic of South Africa concerning the Reciprocal Promotion and Protection of Investments (signed 03 November 1997, entered into force 1 April 1998) art 9.

[85] Convention on the Settlement of Investment Disputes between States and Nationals of Other States (opened for signature 18 March 1965, entered into force 14 October 1966) 8359 UNTS 575. On the list of Member States to the ICSID Convention see ICSID, Database of ICSID Member States <https://icsid.worldbank.org/en/Pages/about/Database-of-Member-States.aspx> accessed 04 February 2020.

[86] Convention on the Recognition and Enforcement of Foreign Arbitral Awards (adopted 10 June 1958, entered into force 7 June 1959).

[87] Agreement Establishing African Continental Free Trade Area (signed 21 March 2018, entered into force 30 May 2019).

[88] *Cortec Mining Kenya Limited v Republic of Kenya*, ICSID Case No ARB/15/29, Award, 22 October 2018 (analysed in Chapter 4).

Africa.[89] Given the similarities of constitutional requirements on the jurisdiction of the courts in Cameroon, Egypt, Ghana, Kenya, Nigeria, and South Africa as well as similarities in their investment treaties' terms, the analysis of these cases using the selected countries can reasonably be applied *mutatis mutandis* to other African countries.

Salacuse rightly warned that '[a]lthough investor–state arbitration has become increasing common, the uniqueness and power of this form of legal process should not be overlooked'.[90] The ISDS not only 'empowers foreign investors to bypass domestic courts and sue governments for cash damages in international tribunals', it also enables investment tribunals to exert influence over domestic courts and threaten fundamental principles of domestic legal systems.[91] Investment tribunals 'are far more willing than courts to assert control over a foreign court, and do so with increasing frequency'.[92] Investment tribunals are likely to exert power over domestic courts to protect their own jurisdiction, to prevent the intrusion of state courts into ISDS, to preserve the parties' rights through interim measures, or to do justice.[93]

Constitutional courts 'are ... fundamental to the ... stability of their respective nations because they are ... responsible for the social acceptance of the constitution and fundamental autochthonous norms and address the tensions between complex political structures and interests'.[94] If the decisions of such constitutional courts can be overturned and discarded by arbitral tribunals composed of disaggregated individuals who, overall are faithful to an investment treaty regime which favours absolute protection of foreign investment, the value and effect of those courts within the domestic context will be seriously eroded. International arbitration can have such an effect because it can affect and disrupt the operation of due process and the jurisdiction, independence, credibility, and effectiveness of the judiciary as constitutionally established.[95] The analysis in this chapter also shows that even when a tribunal accepts that a court has jurisdiction, the tribunal may nevertheless find reason to exercise its jurisdiction anyway and thereby taking away the court's jurisdiction. While investor rights need to be properly protected, and obvious injustices in national courts against foreign investors corrected, rights created by investment treaties must not displace citizens' rights and corresponding

[89] *Piero Foresti v The Republic of South Africa*, Case No ARB(AF)/07/1, Award, 4 August 2010 (hereafter, *Foresti v South Africa*).

[90] Salacuse, 'Is there a Better Way' (n 30) 144.

[91] Kelsey and Wallach 'Investor–State Disputes in Trade Pacts Threaten Fundamental Principles of National Judicial Systems' (n 38).

[92] Michael D Goldhaber, 'The Rise of Arbitral Power Over Domestic Courts' (2013) 2 Stanford Journal of Complex Litigation 373, 374 (hereafter Goldhaber, 'Rise of Arbitral Power').

[93] Ibid 374.

[94] Sergio Puig, 'Investor–State Tribunals and Constitutional Courts: The Mexican Sweetener Saga' (2013) 5(2) Mexican Law Review 199, 201.

[95] Ibid 238.

obligations of states under domestic law, the realisation of which depends, in part, on municipal courts.[96]

The limitations investment tribunals place over domestic courts[97] are well illustrated by the following arbitral cases challenging decisions reached by the courts in Africa. These cases demonstrate how investment tribunals can disregard the decisions of domestic courts and thereby render them ineffectual. While some of these disputes involved international agreements other than investment treaties, those agreements specified the same arbitral mechanism as do investment treaties for the resolution of disputes between foreign investors and the states. The difference between these agreements and investment treaties is that the latter provide for more sweeping rights for investors than the former. However, both kinds of agreements remove investors from the jurisdiction of municipal courts and assign the jurisdiction to foreign tribunals.[98]

3.4.1 Balkan Energy Ltd v Ghana

Balkan Energy Ltd (Ghana) (BELG) was a limited liability company incorporated under the laws of Ghana. Its sole shareholder was Balkan Energy Limited (incorporated in the United Kingdom), which was in turn wholly owned by Balkan Energy LLC of the United States. Balkan Energy Ltd entered into a power purchase agreement (PPA) with Ghana in 2007 for the refurbishment and commissioning of dual fired (diesel and gas) barge and associated facilities.

The PPA provided for the settlement of disputes by ISDS. Balkan Energy Ltd alleged that the state failed to (i) provide adequate site electricity and connection to the national grid through a proper transmission line; (ii) to comply with its obligation to facilitate the importation of equipment and the acquisition of all necessary permits, approvals, and visas; and (iii) owed it tolling fees totalling over USD50 million.[99] In December 2009, BELG instituted arbitration proceedings against the state seeking a declaration that Ghana had breached the PPA, and for an order that Ghana pay the tolling fees and damages for the breaches.[100] The Tribunal

[96] Goldhaber, 'Rise of Arbitral Power' (n 94) 395 and 399.

[97] See for example, *The Loewen Group, Inc v United States of America*, ICSID Case No ARB(AF)/98/4, Award, 26 June 2003; *The Loewen Group, Inc v United States of America*, ICSID Case No ARB AF/98/3, Decision on hearing of Respondent's Objection to Competence and Jurisdiction, 5 January 2001; *Chevron Corporation v Republic of Ecuador*, PCA Case No 2009-23, Fourth Interim Award on Interim Measures, 7 February 2013; *Ambiente Ufficio SpA v Argentine* ICSID Case No ARB/08/9, Decision on Jurisdiction and Admissibility, 8 February 2013.

[98] For the different between treaty claims and contract claims in arbitration see Muthucumaraswamy Sornarajah, *Resistance and Change in the International Law on Foreign Investment* (CUP 2015) 130ff; and Eric De Brabandere, *Investment Treaty Arbitration as Public International Law: Procedural Aspects and Implications* (CUP 2013) 31–48.

[99] *Balkan Energy (Ghana) Ltd v Ghana*, UNCITRAL, PCA Case No 2010-7, Interim Award, 22 December 2010, para 375 (hereafter, *BELG v Ghana*).

[100] ibid [6–7].

was constituted in April 2010. The terms of appointment specified the UNCITRAL Rules as the governing rules and the laws of Ghana as the governing law of the PPA.[101]

In June 2010 after the appointment of the Interim Tribunal, Ghana applied to the High Court of Ghana for an interlocutory injunction against the continuance of arbitral proceedings. In June 2010, the High Court issued an injunction restraining BELG from proceeding with arbitration pending the determination of the enforceability of the arbitration clause and the PPA under Article 181(5) of the Constitution of Ghana.[102] Ghana objected to the jurisdiction of the Interim Tribunal, arguing that both the PPA and the arbitration clause were void because the PPA did not receive Parliamentary approval as required by Article 181(5) of the Constitution.[103]

The Tribunal had to decide whether the arbitration agreement was valid and whether the High Court injunction affected the jurisdiction of the Tribunal.[104] Ghana maintained that both the PPA and the arbitration clause were an 'international business or economic transaction,' and were therefore void and unenforceable for lack of prior parliamentary approval.[105] Ghana argued that the determination of the validity of either the PPA or the arbitration clause involved questions of interpretation of the Constitution, and was, therefore, non-arbitrable. The state argued that even if the Tribunal found that it was competent to rule on the validity of the PPA and the arbitration clause, 'the proper and practical course would be for the Tribunal to exercise restraint and to await a definitive determination of the issues of Ghanaian Constitutional law by the Ghana Supreme Court, which is seized of those issues'.[106]

The state submitted that the PPA was governed by the laws of Ghana because there was a threshold constitutional law question as to whether the PPA was valid in the absence of parliamentary approval. According to Ghana, the Court had not yet clearly spoken as to whether Article 181(5) of the Constitution applied to transactions between the government and a local entity, but which has international elements.[107] The state argued that since the Court has exclusive original jurisdiction 'in all matters relating to the enforcement or interpretation' under Article 130(1)(a) of Constitution, questions relating to the interpretation of the Constitution were non-arbitrable. Ghana also cited the Alternative Dispute Resolution Act which states that issues of enforcement and interpretation of the Constitution cannot be subject to arbitration.[108] In the state's view, the Tribunal could have jurisdiction

[101] ibid [17].
[102] ibid [8 and 45].
[103] ibid [9].
[104] ibid [61].
[105] ibid [117–119].
[106] ibid [64].
[107] ibid [65].
[108] ibid [66].

to hear the dispute only if the arbitration clause was valid and binding. However, there were serious questions[109]

> as to whether the arbitration agreement itself is an international business or economic transaction, within the meaning of Article 181(5) of the … Constitution, and thus invalid for lack of Parliamentary approval. Thus, for the Tribunal to consider the validity of the arbitration agreement with a view to determining its jurisdiction would require it to engage in interpretation of a provision of the Ghanaian constitution, a function which Ghanaian law does not permit an arbitral tribunal to perform.

In the view of the state,[110]

> the conclusion that the Tribunal is not competent is particularly appropriate given the fundamentally public nature of the task of constitutional interpretation. Moreover … a pronouncement by this Tribunal that it is competent to decide the dispute between the Parties would have the 'untenable' consequence that the review of the Tribunal's interpretation of the Ghanaian Constitution could ultimately fall to foreign courts (for example, in enforcement proceedings outside Ghana).

Despite the High Court's interim injunction and the constitutional arguments advanced by the state, the Interim Tribunal proceeded with the hearing on its jurisdiction. The Tribunal held that it was competent to decide on the validity of the arbitration agreement and had jurisdiction to entertain the substantive suit under the competence-competence and separability principles in international arbitration which allow tribunals to determine questions concerning their jurisdiction and the substantive validity of the arbitration clause respectively.[111] According to the Tribunal, the arbitration clause was valid because all the formalities for its validity had been met.[112] The Tribunal held that the law applicable to the arbitration agreement was the law of the seat of arbitration, namely the Netherlands, thereby disregarding the parties' choice of Ghanaian law as the governing law.[113] It reasoned that the constitutional interpretation issue did 'not necessarily fall within the public policy restriction in The Netherlands, because, if it did, any arbitration agreement or contract which encounters an argument of constitutional nature in a foreign country would be excluded from the jurisdiction of an arbitration tribunal to decide upon.'[114]

[109] ibid [71].
[110] ibid.
[111] ibid [152–153], [167], and [99].
[112] ibid [147].
[113] ibid [152–153].
[114] ibid [144].

The Tribunal referred to the decision of Ghana's Supreme Court in *Attorney-General v Faroe Atlantic Co Ltd*[115] that principles of estoppel do not apply to and cannot render enforceable a contract that is unconstitutional. Despite that, the Tribunal held that[116]

> [w]hile there may be valid reasons for the Ghanaian Constitution to impose restrictions on the State's powers to enter into certain kinds of international transactions, there are circumstances where such a restriction cannot derogate from the effectiveness of the arbitration agreement to which the Parties are committed and which has been held out as valid by the competent Ghanaian officials. That is very much the case here. The very fact that the Respondent proposed the alternative of arbitration to settle the dispute indicates that the arbitration agreement was considered by it to be valid and in force, even if the Respondent ultimately decided not to pursue this line of action.

Under the Constitution of Ghana, it is the Supreme Court that has the final say on the issue of the constitutionality of governmental actions, including the constitutionality of legal advice given by government officials. Yet, the effect of the quoted passages is that once government officials have given legal advice to the government and private parties as to the constitutionality or legality of a matter, not even the courts can question the constitutionality of that advice. The effect of the passage is that even if a court declares such conduct or advice unconstitutional, the state would nevertheless be bound and liable. Such a position is contrary to practice in municipal law and general international law on the power of courts in relation to governmental actions.

On the effects of the High Court's injunction on the arbitral proceedings, the state had argued that the Tribunal 'should accord respect' to the injunction because it rested on sound legal grounds and accordingly suspend proceedings.[117] If the Tribunal continued with the arbitral proceedings, it risked subjecting the parties 'to conflicting decisions or to inconsistent judgments' and thereby placed them 'in the difficult position of having to choose between violating the Ghana High Court's injunction, or participating in the arbitral proceedings under protest'.[118] The state asserted that BELG's insistence that the Tribunal should proceed to determine the validity and enforceability of the PPA and the arbitration clause 'could constitute contempt of the Ghana High Court Order', since the intent and spirit of the injunction required that the state 'refrain from arguing the merits of the constitutional

115 *The Attorney-General v Faroe Atlantic Co Ltd* [2005–2006] SCGLR 271 (hereafter, *AG v FACL*).
116 *BELG v Ghana* (n 102) [163].
117 ibid [169] and [170].
118 ibid [172].

issue before this Tribunal' and 'to urge the Tribunal to defer further proceedings pending the outcome in the Ghana litigation'.[119]

Balkan Energy Ltd in turn argued that the injunction of the High Court contravened fundamental principles of international law and undermined international arbitration. The principles of international law relied on were the doctrines of competence-competence, party autonomy, judicial abstention until an award is rendered, and prohibitions in the New York Convention against domestic courts blocking arbitration.[120] These arguments ignored the fact that the order of the High Court was an interim injunction which did not have the effect of perpetually barring the arbitral tribunal from ever proceeding with arbitration and determining the case on the merits upon the expiry of the order. The BELG never argued that a stay of arbitral proceedings would cause it irreparable harm. In these circumstances, the investor's arguments were quite misplaced. The Tribunal claimed it had 'the highest respect for the courts of Ghana and its legal system as a whole'.[121] So at the minimum, it could have, out of that respect and comity, stayed proceedings pending the expiry of the injunction and the substantive decision of the court. Proceeding to determine both the validity of the agreement to arbitrate and the jurisdiction of the tribunal in disregard of the High Court's injunction is inconsistent the Tribunal's claim of respecting the courts.

The Tribunal held that the order of the High Court of Ghana for a stay of arbitral proceedings could not stop it from proceeding to determine substantively the dispute because Ghana had an obligation under the New York Convention to give effect to the arbitration agreement and recognise any award made pursuant to it. According to the Tribunal, a party to a treaty is bound to perform it in good faith and may not invoke the provisions of its internal law as justification for its failure to perform a treaty. Even though an injunction is only an interim relief, the Tribunal held that the issuance of an 'anti-arbitration' injunction that purported to 'block' an international arbitral remedy to which the state is committed was inconsistent with the New York Convention's purpose to ensure that agreements to arbitrate and the resultant awards are recognised and enforced.[122]

Ghana did not argue that by virtue of municipal law it did not have an obligation to give effect to the PPA and the arbitration agreement and it did not challenge the competence of the Tribunal to resolve the dispute itself either. Ghana simply argued that there was a constitutional issue to be resolved in relation to the investment dispute, that is, whether the PPA and the arbitration agreement were constitutional for which it argued for a stay of arbitral proceedings. Since the Constitution of Ghana was the sole and primary basis for determining the validity

[119] ibid [174].
[120] ibid [78].
[121] ibid [62].
[122] ibid [191].

of the PPA as part of the governing law chosen by the parties, the state was not invoking internal law to evade the performance of an international agreement as such. This case is different from a situation where an obligation under international law conflicts with an obligation under municipal law and a state seeks to evade the international obligation by citing municipal law in defence.

In fact, the Tribunal did not deny that the constitutionality of the PPA had to be decided under the Constitution and that the issue was within the jurisdiction of the Supreme Court. Indeed, the Tribunal ultimately resolved this issue based on an interpretation of the Constitution and not the investment treaties, the PPA, and arbitration agreement which the state had an obligation to observe in international law. It follows that the question of Ghana not wanting to observe these international agreements and seeking to invoke internal law in justification *simpliciter* did not strictly arise for the consideration of the Tribunal. Therefore, the Tribunal's reference to the obligation of the state to observe international agreements under the New York Convention and Article 27 of the Vienna Convention of the Law of Treaties (VCLT)[123] which prohibit the state from invoking internal law to excuse the non-observance of the PPA was unjustified and unnecessary.

In any case, under the New York Convention recognition and enforcement of an arbitral award may be refused if the subject matter of the legal dispute is not capable of settlement by arbitration under the law of that country, or recognition or enforcement of the award would be contrary to the public policy of the country. So, the argument by the state that the agreement to arbitrate and the PPA were invalid and the institution of proceedings in the competent municipal court to determine the validity of the agreements was not inconsistent with international law. On the contrary, allowing municipal courts to determine the validity of the agreements would have helped the Tribunal and the investor. After all, if the tribunal proceeded to make a final award in favour of the investor, recognition, and enforcement could be refused if the competent court in Ghana found the subject matter (in this case the PPA) to be incapable of arbitration or as contrary to public policy in Ghana.

Furthermore, an interim injunction cannot properly be described as 'anti-arbitration' in the sense that it was not against arbitration and did not purport to 'block' an arbitral remedy but merely to suspend or stop proceedings in the interim. The issue before the court was the arbitrability of the constitutional issue and so the procedural right to arbitration had not been taken away by the injunction and competence of the Tribunal to adjudicate upon the investor–state dispute itself had not been questioned either.

On the issue of the Tribunal's competence to engage in constitutional interpretation, the Tribunal stated:[124]

[123] Vienna Convention on the Law of Treaties (opened for signature 23 May 1969, entered into force 27 January 1980) 1155 UNTS 331 (hereafter, VCLT).

[124] *BELG v Ghana* (n 102) [143].

> Arbitration tribunals are not infrequently confronted with the need to interpret and apply constitutional provisions relevant to the resolution of disputes submitted to them, just as they are normally required to interpret and apply treaties that are relevant to the disputes. There is nothing abnormal in exercising a judicial function necessary for the proper administration of justice. Hence the Tribunal does not consider that, in asserting its competence to determine its jurisdiction in this case, it is disregarding or in any way contradicting the force of Article 130 of the Constitution of Ghana. In the view of the Tribunal, the purpose of that provision ... is to establish the judicial supremacy of the Supreme Court in the organization and allocation of powers in the domestic context of Ghana. When there is a case that transcends national borders because of an arbitration agreement or some other legal commitment, such a provision becomes qualified and not necessarily predominant. Otherwise ... any dispute involving some element of constitutional interpretation, or any dispute in which an objection is raised that there is such an element, which is not difficult to do, would automatically be excluded from international arbitration, in spite of the existence of a clear commitment by the Parties to subject the dispute to arbitration.

Arbitral tribunals may interpret and apply constitutional provisions relevant to the resolution of disputes submitted to them for the 'proper administration of justice'. However, I disagree with the Tribunal imposing on the state its views on what the position of domestic law is or should be when in fact the competent municipal courts have pronounced their position on what the law is in the particular circumstances. The international nature of the case does not justify such an arbitral imposition. In the case at instance, the issue was not whether the Tribunal could interpret certain constitutional provisions in its administration of justice but whether the Tribunal had the jurisdiction to determine the constitutionality of the PPA.

The investment treaty regime that gives the Tribunal the power to settle the dispute does not empower it to make such a determination or to perform judicial functions reserved for municipal courts. Even if it had the jurisdiction under investment treaties to make findings on the validity of these agreements, that could not have given it the power to engage in interpretation aimed at determining the *constitutionality* of the agreements as the Tribunal on the merit did. In the circumstances, the Tribunal ought to have deferred the issue of the constitutionality of the PPA to the Court. It disrespected the Court when, without finding that the Court erred in its judgment or denied the BELG certain rights, it arrived at an alternative interpretation of the constitutionality of the PPA in disregard of criteria specified by the Court. It is also not the case, as claimed by the Tribunal, that if an objection is raised in an investment dispute involving issues of constitutional interpretation that will lead to *automatic exclusion* of international arbitration. Any such objection will simply mean that the tribunal will have to stay proceedings to allow for the competent court to adjudicate upon the constitutional issue.

3.4.2 Balkan Energy Ltd v Ghana II

In the Interim Award on jurisdiction analysed in Subsection 3.4.1 above, the Tribunal left the question of the substantive validity of the PPA to be decided on the merits.[125] So in the Award on the Merits (*BELG v Ghana II*), the Tribunal, composed of the same panel as in the Interim Award, considered whether the PPA was valid and enforceable.[126] Before this issue, the Supreme Court had already heard arguments in *The Attorney-General v Balkan Energy Ltd (Ghana)*[127] (*AG v BELG*) on whether the same PPA and the agreement to arbitrate each constituted an international business or economic transaction within the meaning of Article 181(5) of the Constitution of Ghana.

The Supreme Court held that a business or economic transaction is international if it is 'major' with a 'significant' foreign element or the parties to the transaction have a foreign nationality or reside in different countries or, in the case of companies, the place of their central management and control is outside Ghana.[128] The Court held that an analysis of Article 181(5) should focus on the substance of the transaction over its form.[129] In relation to the PPA, the Court observed that the transaction for the refurbishment of the barge involved foreign investment by a US company in a power generation project for the supply of energy to Ghana that involved negotiations with the government of Ghana. Although BELG was incorporated under the laws of Ghana, it was wholly owned by a US company. The directors were foreign, and the control and central management of the company were in foreign hands. The PPA not only provided for arbitration but some of its clauses, such as the waiver of sovereign immunity, are usually contained in foreign investment transactions.[130]

Based on these findings, the Supreme Court held that the PPA constituted 'an international business transaction within the meaning of Article 181(5) of the Constitution'.[131] With respect to the arbitration clause in the PPA, the Court reasoned that such a clause in and of itself could not constitute an international business or economic transaction because arbitration is not an autonomous transaction, commercial in nature, which pertains to or impacts on the wealth and resources of a nation. Arbitration clause contained in or in relation to the main or underlying agreement which itself is an international business or economic transaction is equally an international business and economic transaction because the

[125] ibid [138].

[126] *Balkan Energy Limited (Ghana) v The Republic of Ghana*, UNCITRAL, PCA Case No 2010-7, Award on the Merits, 1 April 2014 (hereafter, *BELG v Ghana II*).

[127] *The Attorney-General v Balkan Energy Ltd (Ghana)*, Writ No J6/1/2012, Judgment, 16 May 2012 (hereafter, *AG v BELG*).

[128] ibid 34 and 37.

[129] ibid 31.

[130] ibid 38–39.

[131] ibid 40–41.

arbitration clause cannot be operate in a vacuum, that thus it cannot operate to protect substantive rights independently. An arbitration clause is a feature of the main agreement because it derives its life, existence, and meaningful operative effect from that agreement, whether embedded in it or drafted separately.

The Supreme Court had previously stated in *The Attorney-General v Faroe Atlantic Co Ltd*[132] (*AG v FACL*) that international business or economic transactions to which the government is a party require parliamentary approval, so that any such transaction that has not been approved 'cannot take effect'.[133] Because the PPA in question was an international business or economic transaction and it did not receive parliamentary approval, it was unconstitutional and the company could not make any claims for compensation founded on a constitutionally void agreement.[134]

Based on these Supreme Court precedents, the state argued that the tribunal in *BELG v Ghana II* must follow the Court's determination that the PPA was an international business transaction and declare it invalid because the decision of the Supreme Court was the final pronouncement on the issue of the invalidity of the PPA.[135] The state argued that 'the Tribunal is bound to follow the law of Ghana as applied by Ghana's highest court' and hold that the PPA was void *ab initio*.[136] In the opinion of the state, the Supreme Court 'has original and exclusive jurisdiction over all matters relating to the enforcement or interpretation of the Constitution, pursuant to Article 130(1)(a) of the Constitution' and arbitral tribunals 'do not have power to enforce or interpret national constitutions, except for considerations of transnational public policy inapplicable in this case'.[137]

The state also asserted that it was a 'fundamental principle of international law and arbitration that arbitral tribunals should recognize and defer to judgments ... with force of *res judicata*'.[138] The state maintained that the decision of the Court 'is not open to future determination'[139] and that in this case '[a] determination as to the validity of the PPA under the laws of Ghana has ... been made by the Supreme Court of Ghana'.[140] The decision of the Court on the validity of the PPA, the state maintained, was final given that BELG did not apply for review, a right it had under the Constitution and the Court's rules of procedure.[141]

The Tribunal disagreed with the state's arguments and with the decision and reasoning of the Supreme Court in *AG v BELG*. It held that BELG had reasonable

[132] *AG v FACL* (n 115) 104.
[133] ibid 305.
[134] ibid 297.
[135] *BELG v Ghana II* (n 126) [360] and [364–370].
[136] ibid [361]
[137] ibid [363].
[138] ibid [364].
[139] ibid [366].
[140] ibid [366].
[141] ibid [367].

expectation that Ghana had accepted the validity of the PPA and was, therefore, entitled to rely on it and to expect the state would fulfil its obligations thereunder.[142]

According to the Tribunal, the Court's interpretation of Article 181(5) 'was plausible but it is only one possible alternative'.[143] The Tribunal admitted that the Court had made an affirmative finding that the PPA constituted an international business transaction under Article 181(5).[144] It agreed with the reasoning of the Court that the PPA embodied the existence of significant foreign components and contained several international components, such as the nature of the business and the related investments made, and the waiver of sovereign immunity.[145] The Tribunal also admitted that the Court 'rightly considered the provisions' of paragraph 5 in the context of Article 181 as a whole, the main concern of which ... is that an agreement entered into by the Government for the granting of a loan out of public funds or public accounts must be authorized by Parliament'.[146]

Yet, when confronted with the issue whether the PPA constituted an international business transaction within the meaning of Article 181(5) of the Constitution of Ghana, the Tribunal determined that it was not. In *AG v BELG*, the Supreme Court had emphasised substance over form in determining whether a transaction was international and needed parliamentary approval. The Tribunal insisted on form over substance holding that although the PPA involved foreign components as found by the Court, it was entered into by a company registered in Ghana and which had its principal place of business in Ghana. It held further that the production envisaged under the PPA was to supply the domestic electrical market and payments were to be made in Ghana, which suggested that 'performance under the PPA was entirely a domestic business'.[147] Disregarding the criteria specified by the Supreme Court, the Tribunal upheld BELG's arguments that it 'was organized as a Ghanaian company in compliance with the applicable legislation' and thus 'the foreign ownership of the company or the foreign nationality of its executives should not necessarily be an obstacle to concluding' that it was not an international business transaction.[148]

According to the Tribunal, the identification of a number of internationally related components of the PPA made by the Attorney-General and accepted by the Supreme Court 'do not alter the fact that the company was incorporated in Ghana as required by the Ghanaian legislation and regulations'.[149] It distinguished the case from 'a situation in which a foreign company or an agency ... operates in a certain country without a proper legal registration therein'.[150]

142 ibid [397].
143 ibid [387].
144 ibid [376].
145 ibid [380].
146 ibid.
147 ibid [388].
148 ibid [380].
149 ibid [383].
150 ibid.

The Tribunal further reasoned that since the Attorney-General had advised on the constitutionality of the PPA before it was executed, Ghana could not be heard to argue the contrary.[151] Yet, the Supreme Court had held in *AG v BELG* that the certification of the Attorney-General as to whether a transaction constituted an international business or economic transaction 'cannot be conclusive', since such certification has to be made 'before a dispute has arisen between the Government and any party'.[152]

In rejecting the Court's view, the Tribunal reasoned that the constitutionality of a contractual agreement between a party and the government 'should not be subject to an after-the-event scrutiny when that agreement has been acknowledged and prosecuted by that very Government for years', especially so 'if any uncertainties are due to the Government's failure to seek any necessary Parliamentary approval and to clarify the application of the constitutional provisions in question'.[153] Ultimately, the Tribunal decided:[154]

> with due deference and respect, after having considered the Supreme Court's judgment in detail, the Tribunal must depart from the conclusion reached by that Court. The Tribunal is convinced by the Claimant's views on the need to apply a test taking into account the 'totality of the circumstances' as the guideline for determining whether a given agreement is subject to the Constitutional provisions discussed. It is not enough to identify the foreign components of the PPA, which as noted do exist, but also the fact that the PPA was entered into by a Ghanaian company registered in Ghana cannot be ignored.

The state was ordered to pay BELG USD12 million and interest thereon in consideration of works BELG commissioned at the power station, and USD50,000 in respect of the arrest of one of BELG's officers. The investor was ordered to pay the amount of USD300,000 for its own breach of contract. Each party was to pay half of the costs of arbitration which totalled USD1 million.[155]

3.4.3 Bankswitch Ghana Ltd v Ghana

The constitutionality of an international agreement between the state and a foreign investor also came up for consideration by the Permanent Court of Arbitration in 2014 in *Bankswitch Ghana Ltd (Ghana) v Ghana*[156] (*Bankswitch v Ghana*). The

[151] ibid [393].
[152] *AG v BELG* (n 130) 37.
[153] *BELG v Ghana II* (n 126) [391].
[154] ibid [388].
[155] ibid [642].
[156] *Bankswitch Ghana Ltd (Ghana) v The Republic of Ghana*, PCA 118294, UNCITRAL, Award Save as to Costs, 11 April 2014 (hereafter, *Bankswitch v Ghana*).

state and Bankswitch, whose shareholders were domiciled in Switzerland, entered into the Ghana Customs, Excise and Preventive Service Secure Document Management System Agreement in December 2007 (the Agreement).[157] Under the Agreement, Bankswitch was to provide the state with intelligent price-evaluation software to assist customs officers in the price-evaluation process and electronic data interchange system to enable a secure data interchange between customs, importers, and carriers.[158]

The Agreement provided in Clause 19 that the parties would endeavour to settle any and all disputes, differences, or disagreements through conciliation. In the event that they could not settle such disputes or differences in that manner, the aggrieved party could refer that matter for arbitration under UNCITRAL Arbitration Rules.[159] Clause 22 of the Agreement specified the laws of Ghana as the governing laws.[160] Bankswitch instituted arbitration proceedings against the state alleging breach of the Agreement, specifically for stopping monthly down payments without any official notification to Bankswitch.[161]

Among the legal issues considered by the Tribunal was whether the Agreement was valid and enforceable under the laws of Ghana, specifically whether the Agreement was an international business or economic agreement within the meaning of Article 181(5) of the Constitution. The state argued that pursuant to Article 181(1) and (2) of the Constitution, the Agreement could not come into operation unless and until it was approved by a resolution supported by the affirmative votes of a majority of all the Members of Parliament. As no such resolution was ever passed, the Agreement could not have come into operation, and was thus void and of no effect.[162] Bankswitch argued that the state officials had represented that the Agreement was valid and enforceable and that the state could not be heard to argue the contrary.[163] This is a fair and valid argument to the extent that Bankswitch did not have any other means of determining the validity of the Agreement. The investor's argument is necessary and reasonable because state officials must not enter into agreements in disregard of domestic legal norms and turn round to use their own non-compliance with the same norms to claim the unenforceability of agreements. However, the final decision on the constitutionality of acts of government officials resides in the courts so it cannot be right to argue that the constitutionality of such representation or non-compliance can never be raised simply because a government official had given advice on the constitutionality.

[157] ibid [2.1].
[158] ibid [6.1].
[159] UNCITRAL Arbitration Rules, GA Res 31/98, 1976 (as revised 2010).
[160] *Bankswitch v Ghana* (n 156) [2.5].
[161] ibid [6.83–6.84] and [7.2].
[162] ibid [9.11.6].
[163] ibid [9.5.6] and [9.5.11–9.5.12] and [11.56].

The Tribunal applied the Supreme Court's decision in *AG v FACL* and determined whether the Agreement fell under the ambit of an international business or economic transaction that required the approval of Parliament.[164] The Tribunal found that Bankswitch was significantly owned by foreign shareholders and the Agreement provided for the development of a national customs system dealing with imports to Ghana which had numerous international elements. Based on these factors which the Tribunal found were additional to those present in *BELG v Ghana II*, the Tribunal concluded that the Agreement was an international business or economic transaction under Article 181(5) of the Constitution as interpreted by the Supreme Court of Ghana in *AG* v *BELG*.[165] The Tribunal then considered whether Ghana was estopped from relying on this provision in defending its position.

The Tribunal observed that Ghanaian law adopts the doctrine of incorporation (dualism) and concluded that the principles of customary international law were part of the laws of Ghana.[166] Therefore, the government's conduct must be measured against international standards and principles of customary international law.[167] Accordingly:[168]

> To avoid its international legal obligations based on its domestic law ... would be inconsistent with public international law. The Government cannot rely on its own Constitution to avoid the customary international law rule that a host State must act in good faith and in a manner that is consistent with international law principles when dealing with a foreign investor.

In stating this position, the Tribunal relied on the *Treatment of Polish Nationals and Other Persons of Polish Origin or Speech in the Danzig Territory*[169] wherein the PCIJ stated that 'a State cannot adduce as against another State its own Constitution with a view to evading obligations incumbent upon it under international law or treaties in force'.[170] The Tribunal also relied on the *Case of Certain Norwegian Loans (France v Norway)*.[171] In this case, Judge Lauterpacht stated that the 'question of conformity of national legislation with international law, is a matter of international law. The notion that if a matter is governed by national law, it is for that reason at the same

164 ibid [11.27].
165 ibid [11.29–1134].
166 ibid [11.36–11.50] and [11.62–11.63].
167 ibid [11.57].
168 ibid [11.59].
169 *Treatment of Polish Nationals and Other Persons of Polish Origin or Speech in the Danzig Territory* (Advisory Opinion) 1932 [PCIJ] Series A/B No 44.
170 ibid 24.
171 *Case of Certain Norwegian Loans (France v Norway)* (Judgment of 6 July 1957) (Separate Opinion of Judge Lauterpacht) 1957) ICJ Reports 9, 34 (hereafter, *France v Norway*).

time outside the sphere of international law is both novel and, if accepted, subversive of international law.'[172]

The *Bankswitch v Ghana* Tribunal also found that the government of Ghana made various representations as to the validity of the Agreement, including payment of invoices, down payments, and express statements by the Attorney-General and Minister of Justice. These representations reasonably led Bankswitch to believe that the Agreement was valid and enforceable under Ghana law.[173] Moreover, it was for the government to submit the Agreement for parliamentary approval. Bankswitch reasonably relied on the representations to its detriment because it put significant investments into the project.[174] Under the *pacta sunt servanda* principle, the state must perform its obligations under the Agreement in good faith.[175]

The state was also found to have been estopped by 'international public policy' (whatever its content) from entering into an international agreement only to claim subsequently that the agreement was void for non-compliance with its internal law because a foreign entity had carried out substantial performance of its obligations.[176] Ghana could not be heard then to claim that the Agreement was void and unenforceable under Article 181(5) of the Constitution.[177] Ghana was consequently found to have breached the Agreement[178] and an amount of GHC197.4 million (about USD87.2 million) was awarded in favour of Bankswitch.[179]

The Tribunal's decision on whether internal law could be invoked to excuse the non-performance of a treaty was made *per incuriam* because it did not consider the current position of treaty law on the subject. The two cases the Tribunal relied on were decided in 1932 and 1957 respectively when the VCLT did not exist and had not come into force, although certain of the provisions of the VCLT might be said to be customary in nature and therefore preceded the VCLT. Article 46 of the VCLT permits a state to invoke the fact that its consent to be bound by a treaty was expressed 'in violation of a provision of its internal law regarding competence to conclude treaties as invalidating its consent' if the 'violation was manifest and concerned a rule of its internal law of fundamental importance' as fully discussed at Section 2.4.1.4 of Chapter 2. The International Court of Justice (ICJ) in 2002 in *Land and Maritime Boundary between Cameroon and Nigeria (Cameroon v Nigeria)* recognised a constitution as an 'internal law of fundamental importance' which a state may be able to invoke to excuse the performance of treaty obligations.[180]

172 ibid at 37.
173 *Bankswitch v Ghana* (n 156) [11.82–11.85].
174 ibid [11.92–11.93].
175 ibid [11.62–11.63].
176 ibid [11.72–11.81].
177 ibid [11.82].
178 ibid [12.1.2].
179 ibid [12.1.3].
180 *Land and Maritime Boundary between Cameroon and Nigeria (Cameroon v Nigeria)*, Judgment, (2002) ICJ Reports 303 [258–166].

According to Article 27 of the VCLT, the principle that a state may not invoke the provisions of internal law as an excuse to the non-performance of a treaty obligation is without prejudice to Article 46 of the VCLT.

Although the Tribunal agreed with the decision of the Supreme Court as to the elements of an international business or economic transaction, the Tribunal's position rendered otiose the decision of the Court in *AG v FACL* that estoppel could not override an unconstitutional contract or agreement and that damages could not flow from breach of such a contract or agreement.[181] For the Tribunal, while the law of Ghana 'may not allow for a party to plead estoppel to a constitutional question, there is no such prohibition in international law'.[182]

The issue in *Bankswitch v Ghana* was whether the Agreement constituted an international economic or business transaction within the meaning of Article 181 of the Constitution and was invalid for lack of parliamentary approval. That determination had to be made under municipal law (the Constitution) and not investment treaties or the Agreement itself or under any other principles of international law. Therefore, it is inaccurate for the Tribunal to hold that the arguments Ghana advanced about the invalidity of the Agreement under the Constitution were intended to enable Ghana to evade its international obligations under the Agreement based on domestic law. Indeed, like in *BEGL v Ghana II*, this Tribunal ultimately resolved the issue of whether the Agreement was an international economic or business transaction by relying on the decisions of the Supreme Court (which were made under the Constitution) and directly on the Constitution itself.

The issue was not one of conflict between an international obligation and municipal legal obligation for which the international obligation had to prevail over municipal legal obligation. No international law principle as against domestic law had to be relied on in finally determining the validity of the Agreement because there was no conflict between municipal law and international law on the validity or otherwise of the Agreement. As the Constitution was the only basis to determine the validity of the Agreement, it is not accurate to say that Ghana was invoking internal law to evade a treaty obligation. In the circumstances, Article 27 of the VCLT was inapplicable. Since the parties to the PPA and the Agreement chose the laws of Ghana as the governing law, the Tribunal had an obligation to follow that law which included judicial decisions.[183] There was no conflict between the law of Ghana and international law on the question of the validity of the Agreement. Therefore, the principle that international law trumps municipal law in the event of conflict was not applicable. It is only if the validity of the Agreement were not a

[181] *AG v FACL* (n 115) 299–98, 302, and 310.

[182] *Bankswitch v Ghana* (n 156) 11.75, 9.

[183] Constitution of the Republic of Ghana 1992 art 11(2) (hereafter, Constitution of Ghana); and Dominic Dagbanja, 'The Scope and Legal Effect of Choice of Law in International Arbitration' (2019) IV(1) Cambridge Law Review 59.

core in issue that Ghana could arguably not rely on internal law to excuse the non-performance of its obligation under the Agreement

3.4.4 Waterville Holdings Limited v Ghana

In 2006, the government of Ghana entered into contracts with Waterville Holdings (BVI) Ltd (Waterville) to construct stadia in Ghana at the contract price of EUR39,925597.69. The contracts were governed by Ghanaian law as agreed by the parties. The contracts contained agreements to arbitrate. Waterville carried out some works. The government repudiated the contracts upon commencement of work. These works were independently valued and the government agreed under a settlement agreement reached in October 2010 to pay EUR25,000,000 to Waterville. The sums were subsequently paid.[184]

In June 2012, Martin Amidu, a former Attorney-General and Minister for Justice, commenced an action in the Supreme Court of Ghana for a declaration that payments made to Waterville pursuant to the stadia contracts and settlement agreement were unlawful because these contracts and ensuing settlement agreement were international economic business transactions which had to be approved by Parliament in accordance with Article 181(5) of the Constitution of Ghana. Since these agreements were not approved they were invalid and could not give rise to the payment of the agreed sum to Waterville.[185] A year later in June 2013, the Supreme Court held that the stadia contracts and the settlement agreement were invalid for want of parliamentary approval in accordance with Article 181(5) of the Constitution of Ghana. The Court ordered Waterville to repay the amount it received from the government.[186] In July 2013, the Attorney-General commenced proceedings in the High Court (based on the Supreme Court's decision) to recover the sum of EUR47,365,624.40 paid to the Waterville.[187] The parties had disagreed on the amount paid to Waterville.[188] Waterville sought a stay of judicial proceedings, in the High Court to allow for arbitration.

In November 2013, the High Court dismissed the application for stay of proceedings reasoning that the contracts Waterville sought to rely on to stay court proceedings did not exist because the Supreme Court had found them null and void for their inconsistency with the Constitution of Ghana. The High Court reasoned that once the 'highest court of the land has pronounced on them and held them to be null and void, it is not open to any other court to determine them valid and

[184] *Waterville Holdings (BVI) Limited v The Republic of Ghana*, ICC Arbitration Case No 205.61/TO, Partial Award on Jurisdiction, 20 March 2017 [1–3].

[185] ibid [4–5].

[186] ibid [4] and [67–69].

[187] ibid [4].

[188] ibid [70].

accord either party the benefits of any of the said contracts'.[189] The High Court also held that the arbitration agreement was part and parcel of the main contract.[190] Waterville appealed to the Court of Appeal against the decision of the High Court. The Court of Appeal dismissed the appeal. By the analysis in Section 3.3.1 earlier in this chapter, Waterville should have appealed to the Supreme Court. It chose, however, to commence International Chambers of Commerce arbitration, seeking among other reliefs a declaration that that the stadia contracts and settlement agreements were valid.[191]

The government of Ghana opposed the arbitration proceedings. It argued that the governing law to the stadia contracts was Ghanaian law and that this same law governed the arbitration agreements. The arbitration agreements were not autonomous as it drew its life from the main contracts. Therefore, the arbitration agreements were not severable from the main contracts by virtue of Article 181 of the Constitution of Ghana.[192] The government argued that the issue as to the validity of the main contracts was exclusively within the jurisdiction of the Supreme Court, which had already decided on the matter. The Tribunal did not have appellate jurisdiction over decisions of the Supreme Court.[193] The government also argued that Waterville waived its right to arbitrate by participating in the proceedings before the Supreme Court without objecting to the jurisdiction of the Court and without requesting for a stay of proceedings to commence arbitration.[194] Waterville argued that the governing law was the closest law (namely, the law of the seat of arbitration) and that the arbitration agreements were severable based on the separability principle.[195]

Based on an application of English conflict of law rules, the law of the seat of arbitration (London), the Tribunal held that the arbitration agreements were governed by the law of Ghana.[196] Since the parties had not made an express choice of law to the arbitration agreements, it was 'reasonable to assume that the parties intended their entire relationship to be governed by the "same system of law". If they had intended otherwise, they could have easily provided so.'[197] The choice of the seat of arbitration does not overcome this presumption.[198] The Tribunal came to the conclusion that:[199]

[189] ibid [72].
[190] ibid.
[191] ibid [74].
[192] ibid [82–84].
[193] ibid [107].
[194] ibid [85].
[195] ibid [87–89].
[196] ibid [92–93].
[197] ibid [96].
[198] ibid [97].
[199] ibid [98] (emphasis added).

> while the arbitration proceedings are subject to the English Arbitration Act 1996 as the law of the seat (to the extent the provisions are mandatory), the law governing the Arbitration Agreements is the law of Ghana. This means that such matters as the validity and enforceability of the Arbitration Agreements, including whether a particular dispute is arbitrable, will fall to be determined by the relevant provisions of Ghan[a]ian law.

The Tribunal also held that the separability principle was part of Ghanaian common law and section 3 of the Alternative Dispute Resolution Act and section 7 of the English Arbitration Act 1996.[200] Based on this reasoning, the Tribunal came to the conclusion that the Arbitration Agreements were 'valid, binding and separable under the laws of Ghana and are not extinguished by the alleged invalidity of the Stadia Contracts or the Settlement Agreement'.[201] The Tribunal also reasoned that the Supreme Court of Ghana had not pronounced on the constitutionality of an agreement to arbitrate.[202]

The decision of the Tribunal to apply the separability principle is legally absurd. Since the Tribunal found that the law of Ghana governed the main contract and the arbitration agreements and 'determined ... the validity and enforceability of the Arbitration Agreements,'[203] it is not clear why the application of the separability principle was necessary to determine the validity of the same arbitration agreements. Even if the laws of Ghana governed the determination of the issue of whether the arbitration agreements were separable from the main contract, this same law was found to govern the 'validity and enforceability of the Arbitration Agreements'. Since the law governing the validity and enforceability of the arbitration agreements had already been determined by the Tribunal, it was no longer necessary for the same Tribunal to use the separability principle to determine which law determined the validity of the arbitration agreements in each of the main contracts, unless the object of doing so was to hold the arbitration agreements valid against the dictates and objects of the law found to govern the main contract.

Moreover, the common law and statute law which govern the separability principle are subject to the Constitution of Ghana as the supreme law of the land. An agreement to arbitrate contained in the main contract is term of that contract just like any other term of that contract. Therefore, the Supreme Court's decision that affects the validity of the entire contract affects an agreement to arbitrate contained in it. For example, if an agreement to arbitrate contained in the main contract sought to oust the Supreme Court of its jurisdiction over the interpretation and enforcement of the Constitution of Ghana, such an agreement would be found to be

[200] ibid [100].
[201] ibid [105].
[202] ibid [101].
[203] ibid [98].

inconsistent with Article 130 of the Constitution. It cannot be said such an agreement is constitutionally valid by virtue of the separability principle, and it would be unnecessarily duplicitous of a court's time and resources to have to hold separate proceedings to determine the validity of the main contract and an agreement to arbitrate contained in it merely because of the separability principle.

Constitutionally, therefore, any decision of the Supreme Court that effects the validity of the main contract affects or should affect the validity of the agreement to arbitrate embedded in it. If this were not so, arbitration agreements saved under the separability principle could be used to defeat the object of constitutional principles on which the main contract would have been declared constitutionally invalid when the merits and legitimacy of those constitutional principles may not be denied in relation to the main contract.

The Tribunal concluded that Waterville's right to commence the arbitration had not been extinguished by the settlement agreement because the settlement agreement did not revoke the agreements to arbitrate. The Tribunal said the arbitration dispute arose out of and in connection with the stadia contracts and a party could commence more than one dispute settlement procedure under the arbitration agreements.[204] The Tribunal held that Waterville's participation in proceedings before the Supreme Court did not waive its right to arbitrate because the Court's proceedings were not commenced by a party to the arbitration agreements and the issues before the Court were within the Court's exclusive jurisdiction.[205]

On the request of Waterville to the Tribunal to declare the stadia contracts and settlement agreement valid, the Tribunal held that it did not have jurisdiction to so declare because this was a public interest and interpretive issue that was within the exclusive jurisdiction of the Supreme Court pursuant to Articles 2 and 131 of the Constitution of Ghana. Therefore, Waterville had an obligation to repay as directed by the Court.[206] The Tribunal however said it had jurisdiction over the parties' disagreement as to the amount to be repaid.[207] The Tribunal reasoned that 'aspects of the Parties' disputes 'which do not involve an issue of interpretation of the Ghan[a]ian Constitution would be arbitrable'.[208]

The Tribunal's decision on its jurisdiction over the dispute on the quantum to be repaid is erroneous and problematic. As it decided it did not have jurisdiction on the validity of the main contracts and settlement agreement out of which the dispute over the quantum to be repaid arose, it is less clear how its jurisdiction over the amount to repay can be justified. The amount to repay was not independent of the validity of the underlying agreements over which the Tribunal rightly decided it did not have jurisdiction. Indeed, the amount paid to Waterville was the

204 ibid [103].
205 ibid [104].
206 ibid [110] and [112–115].
207 ibid [115].
208 ibid [110]

foundation and reason for the public interest litigation to recover this amount and any interest that accrued on it. It was the same Supreme Court, which the Tribunal found had *exclusive* jurisdiction over the dispute on the validity of the main contracts and settlement agreement, that decided on the amount to repay.

The amount to repay was a public interest issue, just as was the issue as to the constitutionality of the main contract and settlement agreement which gave rise to the determination of the amount to repay. So how could it be that the amount to repay which the Court had already determined and which the parties did not dispute could not be within the exclusive jurisdiction of the same Court? Such an issue fell within the jurisdiction of the Supreme Court and the investor had the constitutional right to seek a review of the decision in the Supreme Court over the amount if there was a genuine dispute. The Tribunal unjustifiably severed the exclusive jurisdiction of the Supreme Court over matters that were inseparable and thereby gave itself jurisdiction where that jurisdiction did not obviously exist considering its own finding on the exclusive jurisdiction of the Court. The Tribunal usurped the jurisdiction of the Supreme Court and, therefore, would impose on Waterville the obligation to repay an amount that would not have been in the contemplation of the Supreme Court if it exercised jurisdiction by itself.

These cases allow the point to be made that the international arbitration system is designed for states to be accountable to foreign investors irrespective of the public interest objectives and constitutional issues underlying states' actions. Constitutional systems in Africa do not envisage African states being accountable to private parties, whether domestic or foreign, at the expense of the citizens for and by whom governments are constituted. On the contrary, both public and private actors are supposed to ensure that their actions enure to the benefit of the public.

3.4.5 *Piero Foresti v South Africa* and Ensuing Legislative Reforms

In *Foresti v South Africa*, South Africa advanced its arguments in support of the role of municipal law and domestic law in the protection of investments and in the resolution of investment disputes. In this case, the investors alleged that South Africa breached South Africa–Italy BIT[209] and South Africa–Luxembourg[210] BIT provisions on expropriation. The measures that brought about the alleged expropriation were (i) the enactment and coming into effect of the Mineral and

[209] Agreement between the Government of the Republic of South Africa and the Government of the Italian Republic for the Promotion and Protection of Investments, signed in Rome on 9 June 1997.

[210] Agreement between the Republic of South Africa and the Belgo–Luxembourg Economic Union on the Reciprocal Promotion and Protection of Investments, signed in Pretoria on 14 August 1998.

Petroleum Resources Development Act 2002 (MPRDA) which extinguished their mineral rights, and (ii) the coming into effect of the Mining Charter 2004, which introduced compulsory equity divestiture requirements with respect to their shares in operating companies in South Africa.[211]

South Africa objected to the jurisdiction of the Tribunal on the basis that the BITs required 'a meaningful juridical entitlement over an asset, existing under domestic law'.[212] South Africa also argued that the definitions of 'investment' in both BITs made it clear that for jurisdiction to exist, the investors must show that the assets alleged to constitute investments were owned by the investors 'in a legally relevant sense under the law governing the common law mineral rights (*i.e.*, South African law),'[213] which the claimants could not do. According to South Africa its 'law did not grant the Claimants ownership or anything akin to it over the common law mineral rights. Instead . . . the relevant rights belonged to—or were vested in—the Operating Companies, or more commonly their lessors: they were investments of those companies, not the Claimants'.[214] The common law mineral rights could not constitute investments under the two BITs, and the Tribunal accordingly lacked jurisdiction with respect to claims based on the common law mineral rights.[215]

South Africa argued that it had met its obligation under the BITs to provide immediate or prompt compensation. First, its obligations as to the payment of compensation was to provide the investors with access to an effective mechanism for the determination whether compensation was due and the amount if it was due. Secondly, once that mechanism determined that compensation was due, it was to be paid within a short time after the amount had been fixed with appropriate interest. South African law complied with these compensation requirements because it provided for an effective mechanism for the determination whether compensation was due. However, the claimant companies 'failed to use the available domestic procedures and were therefore, the cause of the alleged loss claimed to have suffered'.[216]

On the question of the due process requirement for lawful expropriation, South Africa argued that the MPRDA and the Mining Charter complied with the due process requirements of both BITs. According to South Africa, through their operating companies, the claimants could make a claim for remedies for expropriation before both administrative and judicial bodies. They could also seek judicial review of the decision of the Department of Minerals and Energy as well as challenge the constitutionality of the MPRDA [217] South Africa submitted that access to these

[211] *Foresti v South Africa* (n 89) [54].
[212] ibid [46].
[213] ibid [48].
[214] ibid [49].
[215] ibid.
[216] ibid [71].
[217] ibid [73].

legal procedures was all that was required and that due process did not entitle the claimants to a substantive outcome of their preference. It was also argued that due process did not entitle the claimants individualised hearing before South Africa could adopt a statute that had an expropriatory effect.[218] The case was eventually settled.

The case illustrates the issues South Africa had with using investment treaties and investment arbitration. It suggests that South Africa preferred, as a matter of law and principle, that where investment treaties incorporate the role of municipal law and domestic courts for the protection of investments and the resolution of investment disputes, then municipal law and domestic courts must play the roles assigned to them. Investment treaty protections cannot and should not be available to investors if they choose not to avail themselves of the protections accorded them under domestic law.

This case tested South Africa in terms of whether it was able to pursue policies aimed addressing socio-economic disparities among historically disadvantaged groups in the country arising from apartheid. The case also illustrates the conflict between domestic courts and institutions on the one hand, and investment treaty tribunals on the other, in the resolution of investments disputes. The experience from this case, in part, informed the enactment of the Protection of Investment Act 2015 (Act 22)[219] (PIA herein) as revealed in its preamble.

Thus, in enacting the legislation, the South African government was 'conscious of the obligation to protect and promote the rights enshrined in the Constitution'.[220] Consideration was also given to the responsibility of the government to provide 'a sound legislative framework for the protection of all investments, including foreign investments, pursuant to constitutional obligations'.[221] Emphasis was placed on the 'the rights related to access to just administrative action' and 'access to justice'.[222] According to the preamble to the PIA, investment 'must be protected, in accordance with the law, administrative justice and access to information' and within the context of the government's 'commitment in respect of international law to ensure that human rights, fundamental freedoms and protection of peoples' resources are adequately protected'. The PIA was thus enacted in order for South Africa to assert some significant measure of control over the regulation of foreign investment, and this included giving a special role for domestic institutions, including the courts, in the resolution of investment disputes.

[218] ibid.

[219] Malebakeng Agnes Forere, 'The New South African Protection of Investment Act: Striking a Balance between Attraction of FDI and Redressing the Apartheid Legacies' in Fabio Morosini (ed), *Reconceptualizing International Investment Law from the Global South* (CUP 2017) 251.

[220] PIA (n 38) preamble. ibid s 13(2)(b).

[221] ibid.

[222] ibid.

The PIA provides for the resolution of investment disputes by mediation,[223] with the mediator 'appointed by agreement between the government and the foreign investor'.[224] However, '[s]ubject to applicable legislation', an investor, 'is not precluded from approaching any competent court, independent tribunal or statutory body within the Republic for the resolution of a dispute relating to an investment'.[225] The PIA now effectively does away with investor–state arbitration and gives preference to state-to-state arbitration upon the exhaustion of local remedies. Section 13(5) of the PIA provides as follows:

> The government may consent to international arbitration in respect of investments covered by this Act, subject to the exhaustion of domestic remedies. The consideration of a request for international arbitration will be subject to the administrative processes set out in section 6. Such arbitration will be conducted between the Republic and the home state of the applicable investor.

Section 6 of the PIA under reference in this passage requires, among other things, that the government 'ensure[s] administrative, legislative and judicial processes do not operate in a manner that is arbitrary or that denies administrative and procedural justice to investors in respect of their investments as provided for in the Constitution and applicable legislation'.[226] Section 6(2) of the PIA provides that '[a] dministrative decision-making processes must include the right to be given written reasons and administrative review of the decision consistent with section 33 of the Constitution and applicable legislation'. Section 6(3)of the PIA also provides for investors' right of 'access to government-held information in a timely fashion and consistent with section 32 of the Constitution and applicable legislation'. Subject to the right to approach any competent court in South Africa to resolve an investment dispute, investors, according to section 6(4) of the PIA,

> must, in respect of their investments, have the right to have any dispute that can be resolved by the application of law decided in a fair public hearing before a court or, where appropriate, another independent and impartial tribunal or forum consistent with section 34 of the Constitution and applicable legislation.

The PIA thus requires and gives preference to the settlement of investment disputes in South African courts with competent jurisdiction, especially given the requirement for exhaustion of local remedies in section 13(5). Under section 13(5) of the PIA, the government cannot legally give consent to arbitration unless local

[223] ibid s 13(1).
[224] ibid s 13(2)(b).
[225] ibid s 13(4).
[226] ibid s 6(1).

remedies have been exhausted. The legal effect of sections 13(5) and 6 of the PIA is that the decision on a request for international arbitration upon exhaustion of local remedies will be based on whether (i) whether government ensured impartiality in administrative, legislative, and judicial processes; (ii) the action or decision challenged was lawful, reasonable, and procedurally fair, and the investor was given written reasons for the action or decision; and (iii) government-held information was given to the investor in a timely fashion. Once all these conditions are met, refusal for a request for international arbitration will be lawful under the PIA.

The PIA helps restore the role of the South African courts and other institutions in the resolution of investment disputes in consonance with their jurisdiction under the Constitution of South Africa. In terms of reconciling standards of investment protection, including investor–state provisions, with constitutional and public interests demands, South Africa leads other African countries the legislation of which settled fully for investor–state arbitration with incidental and minimal involvement of domestic courts in investment disputes settlement.[227] Relatedly, Cameroon has affirmed 'its commitment to ensuring the establishment of alternative mechanisms for conflict resolution, including a national court of arbitration for the settlement of industrial and commercial disputes'.[228]

3.4.6 The Egyptian Cases

Jurisdictional conflicts or issues have also arisen between domestic courts in Egypt and investor–state tribunals in Egypt, although they did not involve constitutional issues. In *Middle East Cement Shipping and Handling Co SA v Egypt*,[229] Egypt argued that the investor had waived its right to contest the procedure and validity of the auctioning of a ship when it resorted to the Egyptian state courts to nullify the auction.[230] The Tribunal held that the investor could institute the investor–state suit. The Tribunal noted that Article 10.2 of the 1993 Egypt–Greece BIT[231] provided that an investor could submit an investment dispute either to the competent court of a contracting party, or to an international arbitration tribunal.[232]

The Tribunal reasoned that Article 10.1 of the BIT referred to disputes that concerned an obligation of a contracting state under the BIT. However, the case

[227] Cameroon: Law No 2002/004—Investment Charter 2002 art 11; Egypt: Investment Law 2017, arts 85–91; Ghana Investment Promotion Centre Act 2013 (Act 865) s 33; and Nigerian Investment Promotion Commission Act, ch N117 Laws of the Federation of Nigeria (Decree No 16 of 1995) s 26.

[228] Investment Charter (Law No 2002/004) art 12.

[229] *Middle East Cement Shipping and Handling Co SA v Arab Republic of Egypt*, ICSID Case No ARB/99/6, Award, 12 April 2002.

[230] ibid para 70.

[231] Agreement between the Hellenic Republic and the Arab Republic of Egypt for the Promotion and Reciprocal Protection of Investments (signed 16 July 1993, entered into force 6 April 1995).

[232] *Malicorp Limited v The Arab Republic of Egypt*, ICSID Case No ARB/08/18, Award, 7 February 2011 [71] (hereafter, *Malicorp v Egypt*).

brought by the investor before the Egyptian courts 'regarding the alleged nullity of the auction, was not and could not be "concerning" Egypt's obligations under the BIT, but could only be concerning the validity of the auction under national Egyptian law'.[233] Accordingly, the Tribunal concluded that Article 10.2 of the BIT did 'not exclude the admissibility of Claimant's objections to the auction of the ship'.[234]

Malicorp Limited v Egypt involved an arbitration claim against Egypt before the Cairo Regional Centre for International Commercial Arbitration (CRCICA). Egypt brought a claim for the arbitration clause to be ruled null and void by the Council of State Administrative Court of Cairo (CSACC). The CSACC held that the arbitration clause contained in the underlying contract was void. It then ordered the Tribunal to suspend the arbitration proceedings. The CRCICA Tribunal nevertheless went ahead with the proceedings claiming it was relying on Arbitration Law No 27/1994.

The Tribunal issued an arbitral award, holding that the arbitration agreement in the contract was binding on Egypt contrary to the decision of CSACC.[235] The Tribunal dismissed the claim for damages for the loss caused by the termination of the contract. The Tribunal reasoned that Egypt had been a victim of a fundamental error when it signed the contract in that 'it had wrongly believed that the capital registered and paid by Malicorp was 100 million pounds sterling and that for this reason the Contract was void'.[236] It nevertheless ordered Egypt to reimburse Malicorp for costs, invoices, and the salaries of its employees amounting to USD14,773,497 with interest.[237] The Paris Court of Appeal dismissed an application of Malicorp to attach the assets of Egypt in France to enforce the award.[238]

While CRCICA arbitration proceedings were pending, criminal proceedings were instituted against individuals directly or indirectly connected with Malicorp for various unlawful and fraudulent acts. These individuals included five shareholders of Malicorp who were charged with falsification of the Companies Register with respect to Malicorp.[239] The Cairo Court of Assizes found some of the civil servants guilty of forgery and fraud and sentenced them to imprisonment.[240] In the present claim before ICSID Arbitral Tribunal, Malicorp alleged that Egypt violated its obligations on expropriation under the 1975 Egypt–United Kingdom BIT.[241] Egypt argued that the contract was entered

[233] ibid.

[234] Agreement between the Government of the Hellenic Republic and the Government of the Republic of South Africa on the Promotion and Reciprocal Protection of Investments, signed 19 November 1998, entered into force 6 September 2001.

[235] *Malicorp v Egypt* (n 235) [53–57].

[236] ibid [58].

[237] ibid.

[238] ibid [66 and 70].

[239] ibid [71–73].

[240] ibid [73].

[241] ibid [74].

into as a result of fraud and that the Tribunal lacked jurisdiction because Egypt's consent to provide protections under the BIT did not extend to situations where there was fraud.[242] However, the Tribunal found that it had jurisdiction, reasoning that[243]

> defects undermining the validity of the substantive legal relationship, which is the subject of the dispute on the merits, do not automatically undermine the validity of the arbitration agreement. Thus, an arbitral tribunal is competent to decide on the merits even if the main contract was entered into as a result of misrepresentation or corruption. Only defects that go to the consent to arbitrate itself can deprive the tribunal of jurisdiction. In the present case, there is nothing to indicate that the consent to arbitrate, as distinct from the consent to the substantive guarantees in the bilateral Agreement, was obtained by misrepresentation or corruption or even by mistake.

The case was decided on the merit in favour of Egypt. The case points to how investors can use investment treaty law and arbitration to avoid the legal effect of judicial decisions made not only by the courts of the host state but also even those of the enforcing state. In this case, the Tribunal disregarded the decision of the court of Egypt, declaring the agreement to arbitrate invalid. In addition, the investor instituted fresh arbitral proceedings before a completely different tribunal based on its right to arbitration under the Egypt–United Kingdom BIT to avoid the decision of the Paris Court of Appeal which refused to allow enforcement because Egyptian law had been wrongly relied on. Thus, the investment treaty regime allows investors to use investor–state arbitration to make a mockery of municipal courts. This should not be so. As held in *Jan de Nul NV v Egypt*, '[i]t is not the role of a tribunal constituted on the basis of a BIT to act as a court of appeal for national courts'.[244] Similarly, *Helnan International Hotels A/S v Egypt*[245] held that the domestic courts' decision within their jurisdiction on matters of contractual law governed by domestic law must be respected by arbitral tribunals, and international tribunal would 'not act as an instance to review matters of domestic law in the manner of a court of higher instance'.[246] However, this is not the approach most tribunals have adopted as revealed by the cases analysed in this chapter.

[242] ibid [78].
[243] ibid [119(a)].
[244] *Jan de Nul NV and Dredging International NV v Arab Republic of Egypt*, ICSID Case No ARB/04/13, Award, 6 November 2008 [209].
[245] *Helnan International Hotels A/S v The Arab Republic of Egypt*, ICSID Case No 05/19, Award, 3 July 2008.
[246] ibid [106]. See also [105] and [125–126].

3.5 The Legal Obligation to Exhaust Local Remedies in Africa

3.5.1 The Local Remedies Rule in Customary International Law

Foreign investors must have recourse to and exhaust domestic remedies in municipal courts. Recourse to municipal courts is necessary to restore judicial sovereignty in Africa and ensure that both African governments and foreign investors do not run from their responsibility to abide by constitutional and municipal laws in Africa. Recourse to municipal courts and exhaustion of local remedies may be excused under customary international law on the basis that it would be futile to go to the courts in the first place. In such circumstances, international adjudicating bodies, including investment tribunals, must perform their functions in a manner that balances competing interests.

The exhaustion of local remedies requirement 'has long been established as a general principle of international law'.[247] In *Certain Norwegian Loans Case*, the ICJ held that the exhaustion of local remedies may only be excused where no effective remedy is available domestically.[248] The various constitutions analysed in this chapter make provision for the realisation of this principle by establishing mechanisms for domestic appeals.

Violations of rights that constitutions guarantee 'are less suitable for resolution by privately appointed arbitrators with no commitments to the relevant constitutional doctrine or culture'.[249] Indeed, arbitral tribunals have declined jurisdiction over issues involving human rights on the basis that it was not within their jurisdiction to settle disputes concerning human rights.[250] Moreover, the African investment treaties under study require compliance with constitutional and other municipal legal requirements before the treaties could come into force as a matter of municipal law.[251] As compliance with domestic law is required for the investments to be admitted, the substantive operation of investment treaties must not defeat the underlying objectives for which such compliance is required before admission.

The courts in Africa (eg in Ghana, Kenya, Nigeria, and South Africa) have final jurisdiction over all persons and legal disputes. The constitutional position on the jurisdiction of municipal courts does not make exception for the courts to be

[247] Jan Paulsson, *Denial of Justice in International Law* (CUP 2005) 102 ((hereafter, Paulsson, *Denial of Justice*).

[248] *France v Norway* (n 171) [34].

[249] Kojo Yelpaala, 'Fundamentalism in Public Health and Safety in Bilateral Investment Treaties Part II' (2008) 3(2) Asian Journal of WTO & International Health Law and Policy 465, 479.

[250] *Biloune and Marine Drive Complex Ltd v Ghana Investments Centre and the Government of Ghana*, Award on Jurisdiction and Liability, 29 October 1989.

[251] Ghana–China Investment Treaty (n 79) art 14; Kenya–Japan Investment Treaty (n 82) art 1; Nigeria–Germany Investment Treaty (n 83) art 1; and South Africa–China Investment Treaty (n 84) art 11;

bypassed, except perhaps in cases involving the state and another state in which the issue of which state's court will have jurisdiction will arise, thus calling for a neutral forum such as the ICJ. In cases involving a private party and the state and the use of public funds and resources over an issue that is justiciable and subject to the jurisdiction of the courts under the national constitutions, relevant constitutional principles on accountability and separation of powers prohibit the removal of the courts from exercising jurisdiction over investment disputes including when they relate to constitutional issues and the public policy and involve the state as a party.

Under Article 125(5) of the Constitution of Ghana, Parliament may determine the jurisdiction of the courts. This provision requires Parliament to confer further jurisdiction on the courts in addition to the criminal and civil jurisdiction. It does not empower Parliament to take away from the courts their existing jurisdiction, which includes jurisdiction over investment disputes involving the state as a party. So, the Executive and Parliament cannot take away the state itself from the jurisdiction of the courts in matters involving foreign investment because recourse to municipal courts and exhaustion of local remedies are mandatory under the Constitution. They are also mandatory customary international law except where a case of futility is established.

International arbitration undermines the credibility, dignity, effectiveness, and independence of the judiciary as guaranteed by the constitutions under study by allowing foreign investors to challenge the decision of the courts. By this mode of settling investment disputes, foreign investors are able to question the decisions of the courts before tribunals the decisions of which may render judicial decisions of no effect, contrary to the provisions of the various constitutions which vest original, appellate, review, and final judicial powers in the courts. Therefore, it is substantively unconstitutional to permit foreign investors to bypass the courts established under the constitutions. The constitutions do not recognise arbitral tribunals as having powers to hear appeals or entertain suits arising from the decisions of municipal courts. To the extent that an agreement to arbitrate ousts the courts of jurisdiction over investment disputes which are justiciable under the constitutions and denies the states the right to go to municipal courts over foreign investment disputes, it is substantively unconstitutional. The states cannot choose to protect foreign investment at no price to foreign investors when doing so is to be achieved at the expense of constitutional principles governing the exercise of the powers of governments in the public interest.

The foregoing analysis is not to say that foreign investors should be left at the mercy and pleasure of states. It is necessary to guarantee foreign investors reliable access to effective administration of justice in cases involving them. One of the foundational elements of the doctrine of denial of justice 'is prohibition against nationality-based discrimination in the administration of justice'.[252] It is said that

[252] Todd Weiler, *The Interpretation of International Investment Law: Equality, Discrimination and Minimum Standard of Treatment in Historical Context* (Martinus Nijhoff Publishers 2013) 296.

governments often denied foreigners adequate access to municipal courts.[253] Due process, which includes the right to be heard, is an important aspect of determining access to justice or denial of justice to foreigners, including foreign investors.[254] The enjoyment of 'access to unbiased and procedurally fair dispute settlement mechanisms remains a fundamental requirement of international investment law'.[255] The 'right of access to courts is fundamental and uncontroversial; its refusal the most obvious form of denial of justice. Legal rights would be illusory if there were no entitlement to a procedural mechanism to give them effect.'[256]

Foreign investors have the right of access to justice in Africa. Where this is not municipally available they can resort to international mechanisms to resolve their disputes with host states.[257] As held by the Inter-American Court of Human Rights in *Velasquez Rodriguez Case*, a 'remedy must ... be effective - that is, capable of producing the result for which it was designed'.[258] If a remedy 'is not adequate in a specific case, it obviously need not be exhausted'.[259] Foreign investors should be made to show that practically they do not have the right of access to justice within each municipal legal system before recourse to ISDS can be justified. Such a case could be made before a tribunal duly constituted by the state parties which is duly placed to decide on competing interests of private and public nature, and not under the current ISDS mechanism which is biased in favour of the private business entity.

Not requiring the exhaustion of local remedies, let alone complete removal of foreign investors from the jurisdiction of municipal courts without showing a lack of domestic remedies, cannot be justified in constitutional law and general international law. The idea that the local remedies rule 'is accepted as a customary rule of international law needs no proof today, as its basic existence and validity has not been questioned'.[260] In the *Interhandel Case*, the ICJ held that '[t]he rule that local remedies must be exhausted before international proceedings may be instituted is a well-established rule of customary international law ... *A fortiori* the rule must be observed when domestic proceedings are pending.'[261] In the *ELSI Case*,[262] the ICJ ruled on the need to exhaust local remedies unless remedies do not exist. Some arbitral cases have recognised the need for foreign investors to resort to local

[253] ibid 296.
[254] ibid 296–97.
[255] ibid 297.
[256] Paulsson, *Denial of Justice* (n 247) 134.
[257] Alfred von Verdross, 'Forbidden Treaties in International Law: Comments on Professor Garner's Report on The Law of Treaties' (1937) 31 American Journal of International Law 571, 574.
[258] *Velasquez Rodriguez Case*, Judgment (29 July 1988) Inter-AmCtHR (Ser C) No 4 (1988) [66] (hereafter, *Velasquez Rodriguez Case*).
[259] ibid [64].
[260] Chittharanjan Felix Amerasinghe, *Local Remedies in International Law* (2nd edn, CUP 2004) 3 (hereafter, Amerasinghe, *Local Remedies*).
[261] *Interhandel Case (Switzerland v United States of America)*, Judgment of 21 March 1959, ICJ Reports (I959) 6 at 27.
[262] *Elettronica Sicula SPA (ELSI)*, Judgment (1989) ICJ Reports 15 [55]–[56] and [59] (hereafter, *ELSI Case*).

remedies but did not require the investors to exhaust the remedies.[263] If local remedies are not resorted to at all or are resorted to but not exhausted then claims of denial of justice or ineffectiveness of the judiciary cannot be validly and legitimately made. The Tribunal in *Chevron Corporation v Ecuador* underscored this point when it stated that[264]

> in the consideration of whether the means provided by the State to assert claims and enforce rights are sufficiently 'effective' the Tribunal must consider whether a given claimant has done its part by properly using the means placed at its disposal. A failure to use these means may preclude recovery if it prevents a proper assessment of the 'effectiveness' of the system for asserting claims and enforcing rights.

A case is also made for recourse to and exhaustion of local remedies because African investment treaties provide for initial amicable settlement of investment disputes between the states and investors upon failure of which they may go to arbitration. The ICJ held in the *ELSI Case* that where there has in fact been resort to a local remedy of some sort, and there remain other avenues which have the power to resolve the dispute in question, a different forum cannot be used.[265] It has to be established by the litigant concerned that the remaining domestic remedies cannot guarantee the alien a fair and equitable solution to the dispute[266] or that there are 'circumstances which do not permit any hope of redress to be placed in the use of those remedies'[267] before direct resort to an international dispute foreign can be justified. The local remedies rule in customary international law 'is a recognition of the judicial sovereignty of the state over issues that fall within its jurisdiction. It should not be lightly disregarded'.[268] So, in customary international law, at the minimum, local remedies must be resorted to. Thus, while states and foreign investors have the autonomy to agree to ISDS by arbitration, they must do so only within the bounds of national constitutions and customary international law.

Ursula Kriebaum has argued that since ISDS 'was intended as an exclusive remedy for investment disputes between the investor and the host state,'[269] or to replace the vagaries of adjudication of investment claims against states by their own

263 *Generation Ukraine, Inc v Ukraine*, ICSID Case No ARB/00/9, Award, 16 September 2003, paras 20.30 and 20.33; and *Jan de Nul NV Dredging International NV v Egypt*, ICSID Case No ARB/04/13, Decision on Jurisdiction, 16 June 2006 para 121.

264 *Chevron Corporation v Ecuador*, UNCITRAL, Partial Award on the Merits, 30 March 2010 [324].

265 *ELSI Case* (n 262) 264 [63].

266 Amerasinghe, *Local Remedies* (n 260) 179.

267 *The Ambatielos Claim (Greece, United Kingdom of Great Britain and Northern Ireland)* Reports of International Arbitral Awards (Vol XII, 6 March 1956) 83, 119.

268 Sornarajah, *Law on Foreign Investment* (n 12) 220.

269 Ursula Kriebaum, 'Local Remedies and the Standards for the Protection of Foreign Investment' in Christina Binder and others (eds), *International Investment Law for the 21st Century: Essays in Honour of Christoph Schreuer* (OUP 2009) 417, 457.

courts, requiring the exhaustion of local remedies will make ISDS 'subsidiary' or an 'alternative' to national court jurisdiction.[270] According to her, '[t]o require a preliminary determination of the legality of the domestic act by domestic courts as a requirement for the existence of a breach of a protection standard runs counter to the concept of international arbitration as an alternative to domestic litigation and an exclusive remedy'.[271] Logically, this is an accurate argument. However, the historical origins of investment arbitration in post-colonialism[272] and the very fact that it has not been convincingly proven why municipal courts are capable of effectively adjudicating upon all disputes within national territories except foreign investment disputes render claims that national courts are not well placed to resolve investment disputes suspect and direct access to ISDS unjustified. Moreover, as the impartiality, efficiency, neutrality, and transparency of investment tribunals are subject to question,[273] they cannot claim better legitimacy over investment disputes than national courts. Further, investment tribunals are not better placed to interpret municipal laws which are equally relevant in the resolution of investment disputes.[274]

There is a presumption of interpretation that 'treaties are not intended to derogate from customary law'.[275] Such a presumption is plausible because treaties bind only the states parties to that treaty. Customary international law, however, binds all states irrespective of their explicit consent and subject matter.[276] In this regard, it is settled in both customary international law and municipal law that municipal courts have jurisdiction within the domestic context to adjudicate upon legal disputes including those touching upon fundamental rights of citizens.[277] If the courts do not perform this function or are inhibited from doing so effectively, people will have no remedy against abuses. The law and practice are that it is the function of the courts to protect fundamental rights of citizens. This constitutes the basis of territorial jurisdiction. The jurisdiction of municipal

[270] ibid.

[271] ibid 460.

[272] Antony Anghie, *Imperialism, Sovereignty and the Making of International Law* (CUP 2005); and Kate Miles, *The Origins of International Investment Law: Empire, Environment and the Safeguarding of Capital* (CUP 2013); Dominic N Dagbanja, 'The Limitation on Sovereign Regulatory Autonomy and Internationalisation of Investment Protection by Treaty: An African Perspective' (2015) 60(1) Journal of African Law 56.

[273] Schneiderman, 'Legitimacy and Reflexivity in International Investment Arbitration' (n 17); Harten, *Arbitration and Public Law* (n 6); Born and Shenkman, 'Confidentiality and Transparency in Commercial and Investor–State International Arbitration' (n 19) 4.

[274] Hernando Diaz-Candia, 'The Role of Municipal Laws in Investment Arbitration' in Andrea Bjorklund (ed), *Yearbook on International Investment Law and Policy 2012–2013* (OUP 2014) 517.

[275] Michael Akehurst, 'The Hierarchy of the Sources of International Law' (1975) 47(1) British Yearbook of International Law 273, 275.

[276] Ralf Michaels and Joost Pauwelyn, 'Conflict of Norms or Conflict of Laws?: Different Techniques in the Fragmentation of Public International Law' (2011–2012) 22 Duke Journal of Comparative and International Law 349, 63.

[277] Malcolm Shaw, *International Law* (6th edn, CUP 2008) 652–64 (hereafter, Shaw, *International Law*).

courts over issues such as human rights and environment should be treated as a peremptory norm which states cannot contract out of or impair by the agreements they reach with other states or parties. A treaty that abolishes or impairs the jurisdiction of the courts with respect to the protection of fundamental rights of citizens conflicts with a peremptory norm of general international law on jurisdiction and is inconsistent with Article 53 of the VCLT. General international law should prohibit states from reaching agreements that seek to abolish the jurisdiction of the courts or subject that jurisdiction to requirements that in effect render the jurisdiction of no use.

3.5.2 The Competence of African States to Agree to Investor–State Arbitration

Certain constitutional principles counsel against the inclusion of investor–state arbitration in international agreements and contracts in Africa. In *Apaloo* v *Electoral Commission*, Justice Bamford-Addo stated that '[t]he people' of Ghana 'promulgated for themselves a constitution, which vested sovereign power in the people and provided a democratic system of government based on certain fundamental principles'.[278] These fundamental principles include the supremacy of the constitution,[279] the fiduciary nature of the state and its agents and organs in relation to the people,[280] probity and accountability,[281] equality before law and freedom non-discrimination,[282] rule of law,[283] separation of powers,[284] independency of the judiciary,[285] finality of judicial decisions,[286] and open and transparent administration of justice.[287] Under Article 10(2) of the Constitution of Kenya,

> national values and principles of governance include—(a) patriotism, national unity, sharing and devolution of power, the rule of law, democracy and participation of the people; (b) human dignity, equity, social justice, inclusiveness, equality, human rights, non-discrimination and protection of the marginalised; (c) good governance, integrity, transparency and accountability; and (d) sustainable development.

278 *Apaloo* v *Electoral Commission*, [2001–2002] SCGLR 1 at 9–10.
279 Constitution of Ghana (n 183) art 1(1).
280 ibid art 1(1).
281 ibid preamble.
282 ibid art 17.
283 ibid preamble and arts 23 and 296.
284 ibid arts 57–92, 93–124, and 125–161.
285 ibid art 127.
286 ibid art 129.
287 ibid art 126(3).

According to Article 10(1) of the Constitution of Kenya, these values shall be followed in the application and interpretation of the Constitution, in the enactment, application, and interpretation of other legislation and in the making and implementation of public policy. These principles weigh heavily in favour of the public interest than private interests.

African governments are accountable to the people through municipal courts in which acts of governments can be challenged. This is not the case with ISDS, which can facilitate the governments avoiding accountability since arbitral tribunals do not have jurisdiction over political and public policy issues and their processes promote secrecy and 'fail to meet basic principles of transparency, consistency and due process common to [domestic] legal systems',[288] which can conceal governments' misfeasance. These factors prevent the African states from agreeing to investor–state arbitration in relation to matters that pertain to the interpretation and enforcement of their constitutions, the jurisdiction of the courts on matters of public importance, and public interest regulation. Further, constitutional principles on the rule of law and accountability and effective administration of justice by municipal courts can be impaired if foreign investment disputes and foreign investors are allowed to bypass the jurisdiction of the courts, especially because foreign investment disputes always involve a state and public resources.

A number of constitutional arguments therefore weigh heavily against arbitral tribunals entertaining investor–state claims that challenge judicial decisions in Africa. First, arbitral tribunals do not have the jurisdiction to interpret the constitutionality of acts of government officials. The interpretation and enforcement of the African constitution are the exclusive preserve of the relevant courts in each jurisdiction.

Secondly, arbitral tribunals do not have appellate or review powers under both the African constitutions and the investment treaties to entertain cases that the courts as the final appellate courts on which they have definitely and finally pronounced. The jurisdiction of arbitral tribunals under investment treaties to resolve investment disputes does not empower them to adjudicate upon constitutional and public policy issues constitutionally reserved for municipal courts. There is nothing in investment treaties in substance and procedure that permits arbitral tribunals to hear and review final judicial decisions. It cannot be reasonably and necessarily implied from the power of investment tribunals to resolve investment disputes that they have the power to hear cases in which domestic courts have made final decisions. If foreign investors submit to the jurisdiction of the domestic courts, then they are bound by the decisions of the courts and may only appeal against those decisions where there is an explicit right of appeal. There does not

[288] Elizabeth Evatt and others, *An Open Letter from Lawyers to the Negotiators of the Trans-Pacific Partnership Urging the Rejection of Investor–State Dispute Settlement* (8 May 2012) <https://tpplegal.wordpress.com/open-letter/> accessed 28 September 2020.

exist a right of appeal in favour of foreign investors under the constitutions and the investment treaties to foreign arbitral tribunals. The right to challenge a decision of a municipal court before an arbitral tribunal has to be shown to exist in substance and procedure. It cannot simply derive from the power of an arbitral tribunal to settle investment disputes.

Foreign investors and states are both subject to and affected by the decisions of domestic courts. Moreover, the decision of a domestic court involving a foreign investor is not the same thing as the measure giving rise to the dispute. Therefore, such a court decision cannot amount to a measure under investment treaties and may be a subject of arbitration under customary international law on the basis that justice has not been done. Consequently, under existing investment treaties investment tribunals cannot entertain suits challenging the decisions of municipal courts without the exception under customary international law for recourse to an international adjudicating body having been established.

Thirdly, while private parties may choose to have their legal disputes resolved by other methods of dispute resolution, whether municipal or international, other than by the courts, the African states which derive their powers from their constitutions cannot do so. The mandate of the judiciaries in Africa to administer justice in the name of the people and constitutional values on probity and accountability cannot work to their purposes if the states themselves as fiduciaries of the people can choose to say their own courts cannot entertain disputes involving them and private profit-seeking organisations. If the states can choose to exclude the courts from entertaining such disputes, citizens can hardly hold governments to account, without consequences under investment treaties and investor–state arbitration. Under Article 2 of the Constitution of Ghana citizens can go to court to challenge the constitutionality of acts or omissions of the government. This right can be weakened by ISDS. This is because if a citizen challenges a decision of a government in relation to foreign investment and a court finds in favour of the citizen, such a finding can be subjected to investor–state arbitration if a foreign investor perceives that the value of its investment would be affected by a decision of the court or if the investor is dissatisfied with the decision.

The ISDS' 'long-term implications for national judicial systems as an aspect of wider concerns about democratic governance should be considered when decisions are being made on whether to include any and if so what kinds of ISDS arbitral provisions in BITs'.[289] African states must never include investor–state arbitration in future investment treaties and other international contracts and agreements if they are to reassert the authority of municipal courts and the integrity and finality of their decisions in matters involving foreign investors. The sovereignty of African states and exclusive jurisdiction of the courts over legal disputes arising in

[289] French, *Investor–State Dispute Settlement* (n 2) 3.

the applicable African states justify reliance on municipal courts. Foreign investors like everybody else must be subject to the jurisdiction of the courts of host country in which they operate. There is no justifiable reason for a prior exemption of foreign investors from the jurisdiction of municipal courts without irrefutable evidence that the courts whose jurisdiction the investors are running away from are just incapable of resolving investment disputes. The historical reasons behind ISDS and general theories that claim foreign investment leads to development can no longer be the justification for the investment treaty regime in light of the practical inefficiencies from the operation of arbitral tribunals which were seen as credible and neutral alternatives to the courts. A case could be made for ISDS if it were in a position to take into consideration the protection of social and community interests, as well to provide protection for foreign investors. However, the system as it exists now focuses on absolute protection of foreign investment sometimes, if not always, at the expense of communal interests. Muthucumaraswamy Sornarajah argues that[290]

> [w]hen coupled with wide concepts of taking, the compulsory unilateral right of recourse to arbitration that has been created by treaty regimes work to the detriment of social interests. There is, however, a need for machinery to settle purely contractual disputes. For an acceptable balance to be struck, it has to be conceded that certain types of disputes are inherently incapable of being settled through consensual processes such as arbitration. Tribunals such as ICSID and NAFTA tribunals are undemocratic tribunals, incapable of assessing the competing social and ethical interests. As commercial arbitral tribunals are wont to do, they pay attention only to the commercial considerations that are involved in the dispute. Their concern for the values of the international community is weaker than their concern for contractual sanctity and the securing of their next appointment to a tribunal on the basis of their display of commercial probity and their loyalty to the values of multinational business. There is a need to evolve a doctrine that requires consideration of environmental and human rights issues and ensures that this consideration is not enmeshed with doctrines that assert contractual concerns ... The issues raised here involve the interests not of the parties alone but of the society of the host states in which the foreign investment takes place and those of the wider international community. International tribunals, which can balance these issues adequately, should settle such issues.

The need to resort to the courts or other credible alternatives to ISDS cannot, therefore, be overemphasised. Such an alternative exists in Africa and could be adapted. For example, the Alternative Dispute Resolution Act of Ghana by section

[290] Sornarajah, 'Clash of Globalizations' (n 3) 9–10.

1 exempts disputes touching on the national or public interest, the environment, and the enforcement and interpretation of the Constitution of Ghana from being settled by alternative dispute resolution methods, including arbitration. This Act applies to domestic alternative dispute resolution and will be applicable to investment disputes only when the parties have not agreed to ISDS and are subsequently unable to agree on a mode of dispute resolution.[291] If African states want to continue with ISDS, then to ensure that investment disputes that touch on public interest regulation are not arbitrable, explicit provision should be made in future investment treaties to that effect. It must also be specified that disputes arising from general regulation (ie regulation not specifically aimed at regulating the activities of foreign investors expropriating their property rights) and constitutional issues are not arbitrable. In any case, only pure commercial disputes may be the subject of arbitration. Future African investment treaties must also be clear that decisions of the courts on public interest regulation and the interpretation and enforcement of the various constitutions are not arbitrable.

Pure investment disputes, disputes arising from non-public interest direct governmental regulation of investors' activities, may be resolved either in the courts or by domestic investment arbitration. An appeal from the decision of a domestic arbitral body could be made to ISDS suitably adapted to handle issues involving public policy. In light of the above arguments on the customary international law position on recourse to municipal courts and exhaustion of local remedies and the constitutionality of ISDS, the right to arbitrate under existing investment treaties accrues only when a case has been made that domestic remedies are not available or ineffective prior to resort to ISDS. Then a case can be justified to have recourse international arbitration which in resolving disputes must take competing interests into consideration. Malcolm Shaw argues that[292]

> [j]urisdiction concerns the power of the state under international Law to regulate or otherwise impact upon people, property and circumstances and reflects the basic principles of state sovereignty, equality of states and non-interference in domestic affairs. Jurisdiction is a vital and indeed central feature of state sovereignty, for it is an exercise of authority which may alter or create or terminate legal relationships and obligations.

The ISDS mechanism defeats these basic attributes of jurisdiction because it removes foreign investors from the jurisdiction of municipal courts of the very host country in which the investors operate. This can undermine the ability of African states to regulate the activities of foreign investors and to hold them accountable under municipal law. To assess what can be done with ISDS and its implications for

[291] Ghana Investment Promotion Centre Act 2013, s 33(3).
[292] Shaw, *International Law* (n 277) 645.

the jurisdiction of municipal courts, it is important to consider whether states can or should be agreeing to this mechanism.

The principle that a treaty is binding on a party and the party may not invoke internal law to excuse the non-performance of a treaty obligation is premised on the idea of such international agreements having been validly made. Where international agreements are not validly made, then the principles on their binding effect and the need to comply with them have no application. The prohibition in Article 27 of the VCLT against invoking the provisions of internal law as justification for a state's failure to perform a treaty is, therefore, not absolute.

I argue that without a prior showing of lack of remedy within the domestic courts, direct access to ISDS violates constitutional principles and customary international law criteria for bypassing municipal courts. An agreement to arbitrate contrary to customary international law cannot bind states in accordance Article 53 of the VCLT. Thus, the right of foreign investors under existing investment treaties to ISDS must be interpreted as requiring recourse to and exhaustion of local remedies in municipal courts unless a case is established under customary international law for direct access to international tribunals.

The Inter-American Court of Human Rights held in the *Velasquez Rodriguez Case* that every norm 'is meant to have an effect and should not be interpreted in such a way as to negate its effect or lead to a result that is manifestly absurd or unreasonable'.[293] The jurisdiction of the courts over all persons and matters will be defeated if foreign investors can be sued in municipal courts only at the risk of damages being awarded against states if the decision of a municipal court is challenged in ISDS on matters that involve the public interest.

3.6 Investor–State Arbitration Reforms in Africa

Recent literature has discussed Africa and the reform of investment treaty law and arbitration extensively.[294] African countries are parties to over 900 investment

[293] *Velasquez Rodriguez Case* (n 258) [64].

[294] Hamed El-Kady and Mustaqeem De Gama 'The Reform of the International Investment Regime: An African Perspective' (2019) 34(2) ICSID Review—Foreign Investment Law Journal 482 (hereafter, El-Kady and Gama, 'Reform of II Regime'); Makane Moïse Mbengue, 'Africa's Voice in the Formation, Shaping and Redesign of International Investment Law' (2019) 34(2) ICSID Review –Foreign Investment Law Journal 455 (hereafter, Mbengue, Africa's Voice'); Antonio R Parra, 'The Participation of African States in the Making of the ICSID Convention' (2019) 34(2) ICSID Review—Foreign Investment Law Journal 270; Won Kidane, 'The Culture of Investment Arbitration: An African Perspective' (2019) 34(2) ICSID Review—Foreign Investment Law Journal 411; Kinnear and Cannu, 'Concluding Remarks' (n 16); 'Makane Moïse Mbengue, Africa and the Reform of the International Investment Regime' (2017) 18 Journal of World Investment and Trade 371; and Okechukwu Ejims, 'The 2016 Morocco–Nigeria Bilateral Investment Treaty: More Practical Reality in Providing a Balanced Investment Treaty?' (2019) 34(1) ICSID Review—Foreign Investment Law Journal 62.

treaties that contain provisions for ISDS arbitration.[295] Africa has received its share of investment treaty arbitration claims. Of the over 1,104 investment treaty claims against states, about 100 investor–state suits have been brought against African countries. In these claims, foreign investors sought at least US$40 billion against African states. Various forms of economic sectors have been involved in these cases including construction projects, mining and quarrying, and manufacturing.[296] Nevertheless, based on the perception that ISDS can enhance the attractiveness of their economies to foreign investors, the 'majority of African States still foresee this method of dispute resolution as an attractive alternative to domestic courts across the continent'.[297]

The participation or non-participation of African countries in the use of investment treaty arbitration to resolve investment disputes must be informed by the dictates of national constitutions, which are the fundamental legal basis of the right to regulate. Investment treaties and investment arbitration must not be agreed to in disregard of the role that national constitutions assign to domestic courts to resolve legal disputes, including investment disputes. The right to regulate cannot be retained or reclaimed in situations where African states subordinate their duties to protect citizens and the public interest under national constitutions to the interests of foreign investors.

The African continent needs to be involved in going reforms of investment treaty arbitration, including by ICSID,[298] to ensure African states' right to regulate are not unreasonably restrained by the decisions of arbitral tribunals if the continent needs to continue to participate in the system at all. In this regard, African countries have taken various actions at the national, regional, continental, and bilateral levels to reform investment treaty arbitration substantively and procedurally.[299]

3.6.1 Regional and Bilateral Investor–State Arbitration Reforms

At the regional level, Article 2 of the Uniform Act on Arbitration 2017[300] of the *Organisation Pour L'harmonisation En Afrique Du Droit Des Affaires* or Organisation for the Harmonisation of Business Law in Africa (OHADA)[301]

295 Mbengu, Africa's Voice' (n 294) 473.
296 ibid; El-Kady and Gama, 'Reform of II Regime' (n 294) 489 and 493–95.
297 Mbengu, Africa's Voice' (n 294) 473.
298 Kinnear and Cannu, 'Concluding Remarks' (n 16).
299 Mbengu, 'Africa's Voice' (n 294) 473–78.
300 Uniform Act on Arbitration, adopted 23 November 2017 entered into force, 15 March 2018, 2 <https://www.ohada.org/attachments/article/2490/Acte-uniforme-Arbitrage-English.pdf> accessed 28 September 2020 (hereafter, 'Uniform Act').
301 According to article 1 of the Treaty on the Harmonization in Africa of Business Law, signed on Port Louis on 17 October 1993, as Revised in Quebec on 17 October 2008: <https://www.ohada.org/index.php/en/component/content/article?id=7:ohada-treaty-reviewed> accessed 28 September 2020. The purpose of this Treaty is to harmonize business laws in States Parties by developing and adopting

entitles a natural or legal person the right 'to resort to arbitration with respect to any rights on which she has the free disposal'. While states, public territorial bodies and entities, and any other legal person under public law may be a party to an arbitration, they are not allowed 'to invoke their own laws to object to the arbitrability of the dispute, to their capacity to submit to arbitration or to the validity of the arbitration agreement'.[302] This is to secure consistency in investment protection among the member states in line with the harmonisation objectives of OHADA.

However, the Uniform Act on Arbitration provides for the role of competent courts of Member States (i) when there is a challenge of an arbitrator's appointment, with the right to appeal to Common Court of Justice and Arbitration (CCJA),[303] (ii) when the arbitration agreement 'is manifestly null or manifestly inapplicable to the case', and (iii) in the 'event of a recognized and reasoned emergency, to order provisional or conservatory measure'.[304] While the arbitral tribunal retains jurisdiction to determine its jurisdiction,[305] the validity of the arbitration agreement, and the merits of the case, the competent court of jurisdiction in a Member State has jurisdiction over conservatory seizures[306] and annulment proceedings.[307] If the competent court of a Member State does not render a decision within three months of its seizure, it is discharged of the case. The action may then be brought before the CCJA.[308] When exercising its power over annulment proceedings, the competent court in the member state can rule on a provisional enforcement dispute.[309] The decision on an annulment action may 'only be appealed on points of law before'[310] the CCJA.

The approach adopted by Member States of OHADA is novel: allowing arbitral tribunals to decide on their jurisdiction, the validity of the arbitration agreement, and the merit of the case; the competent court in the Member State has jurisdiction over annulment and provisional or conservatory measures applications; and the CCJA has appellate jurisdiction on annulment decisions. The Uniform Act on Arbitration does not define the criteria for annulment except the reference to a situation where a tribunal 'ruled without an arbitration agreement or on a void or expired one'.[311] This means an annulment of an award could be made on other grounds. Therefore, the exercise by a competent court in the Member State of

simple, modern, and common rules adapted to their economies, setting up appropriate judicial procedures, and encouraging recourse to arbitration for settlement of contractual disputes.

302 Uniform Act (n 300) art 2.
303 ibid art 8.
304 ibid art 13.
305 ibid arts 11 and 13.
306 ibid art 14.
307 ibid art 27.
308 ibid.
309 ibid art 28.
310 ibid art 25.
311 ibid art 29.

jurisdiction over annulment proceedings could ensure that arbitral awards made contrary to the public policy, the public interest, and the constitution of a Member State is annulled. Through the annulment process, the Member State could preserve its right to regulate and preserve its constitutional and public policy values.

It could be argued that the annulment requirement before domestic courts could be used to defeat the very purpose of the arbitration. However, the right to appeal against an annulment decision to the CCJA could serve to ensure that the competent court in the Member State exercises its annulment jurisdiction and decision fairly, reasonably, and in accordance with the law and due process. Thus, the OHADA approach to arbitration has a strong potential to ensure a more objective, reasonable, and measured basis for protection of the rights of investors and the state.

The Southern African Development Community (SADC) Model BIT provides for the conditions for submission of a claim to arbitration that are unique in their terms, and a claim may not be entertained unless these conditions are met. First, an arbitration claim must be submitted after the lapse of six months since the filing of notice of intent to arbitrate.[312] Second, a claim must have been submitted before the host state's domestic courts to pursue local remedies. A claim before domestic courts must be preceded by the exhaustion of available administrative remedies. To proceed to arbitration upon the submission of a dispute before a local court, the investors must establish failure to reach a resolution 'within a reasonable period of time from its submission to a local court'.[313] Alternatively, it must be established that 'there are no reasonably available legal remedies capable of providing effective remedies of the dispute concerning the underlying measure, or the legal remedies provide no reasonable possibility of such remedies in a reasonable period of time'.[314]

Third, the investor must waive the right to pursue and/or to continue to pursue any claim relating to the measures underlying the claim before local courts in host state or in any other dispute settlement forum.[315] In other words, other dispute settlement rights relating to the treaty claim must be waived. Fourth, the claim must not be more than three years from the date on which the investor first acquired, or should have first acquired, knowledge of the breach, or one year from the conclusion of the request for local remedies initiated in the domestic courts.[316] Fifth, the investor must consent in writing to arbitration.[317] Sixth, and finally, in the event of conflict, the provisions in the Model BIT relating to arbitration procedures prevails over those in the arbitration rules selected to govern the arbitration.[318]

312 SADC Model Bilateral Investment Treaty Template with Commentary (July 2012) art 29.4(a).
313 ibid art 29.4(b)(i).
314 ibid art 29.4(b)(ii).
315 ibid art 29.4(c).
316 ibid art 29.4(d).
317 ibid art 29.4(e).
318 ibid art 29.4(f).

These requirements reserve space for the role of the courts in investment dispute settlement. Arguably, investors are looking for remedies not the forum where the dispute is resolved *per se*. If the courts prove effective in resolving investment disputes to the satisfaction of investors, they may not be interested pursuing remedies independently of or beyond the courts. Therefore, requiring investors to exhaust local remedies or to show that those remedies do not exist at all or are ineffectual before an investor can go to arbitration does not disadvantage investors in any anyway. On the contrary, these requirements place the burden on host states and their local courts to ensure effective administration of justice in the settlement of investment disputes. Most investment treaties do not contain these conditions to have recourse to arbitration. Specifying that the Model BIT's provisions on arbitration procedures shall prevail over conflicting applicable rules of arbitration avoids doubt as to the applicable rules in case of actual of conflict.

To ensure corporate accountability and observance of domestic laws, the SADC Model BIT states that investors and investments 'must comply with all laws, regulations, administrative guidelines and policies of the Host State concerning the establishment, acquisition, management, operation and disposition of investments'.[319] The host state, its institutions, and officials, and even private persons and organisations may initiate a civil action in domestic courts against an investor or investment for damages arising from an alleged breach of the obligations set out in the SADC Model BIT.[320] Similar action may be initiated in the domestic courts of the home state against the investor.[321] These provisions are crucial to ensure investor accountability. Investment treaties often do not contain provisions directly allowing a host state to sue the investor. These provisions fill that gap. The SADC Model BIT goes far to ensure the protection of the interests of both the investor and the host state.

The Economic Community of West African States (ECOWAS) Common Investment Code also requires exhaustion of 'all local remedies including the ECOWAS Court of Justice or national dispute settlement systems before resorting to the international mechanisms' except where an investment contract provides for the use of international arbitration mechanisms.[322] The ECOWAS approach is less entailing compared to the OHADA and SADC approaches.

The Investment Agreement for the Common Market for Eastern and Southern Africa (COMESA) Common Investment Area provides for the resolution of investment disputes by arbitration if the dispute has failed resolution through the good faith effort of the parties. The investor may choose to have the matter resolved by *arbitration* through the competent court of the host state, to the COMESA

[319] ibid art 11.
[320] ibid art 19.3.
[321] ibid art 19.4.
[322] (ECOWAS) Common Investment Code July 2018 art 54(4).

Court of Justice or to international arbitration.[323] An election to submit a claim at one of these fora is 'definitive and the investor may not thereafter submit a claim relating to the same subject matter or underlying measure to other fora'.[324]

The COMESA approached is similar to the bilateral approach as reflected in Cameroon–Korea BIT.[325] The Cameroon–Canada BIT makes it mandatory for the parties to 'hold consultations in an attempt to settle a claim amicably before an investor may submit a claim to arbitration',[326] provides for a limitation period of three years for commencement of an investor–state suit and for a waiver of the right to commence action before another forum, such as a court or administrative body, once the investor proceeds to arbitration as the mode of dispute settlement.[327]

3.6.2 Continental Investor–State Arbitration Reforms

In 2016, the African Union prepared a Draft Pan-African Investment Code (PAfIC) for African countries to use as a guiding instrument to bring about national and continental coherence in investment policy-making.[328] The PAfIC provides for the role of national courts and domestic law in the resolution of investment disputes, which are not found in most investment treaties African countries entered into in the 1960s and the early 2000s. Therefore, it is a useful guide for how to make investment treaties that accommodate the right to regulate. First, it draws attention to the need for Member States to agree to utilize the investor–state dispute settlement mechanism in line with domestic policies.[329] Second, disputes may be resolved through arbitration subject to either applicable laws of the host state or the mutual agreement of the disputing parties or to both. Arbitration may also be resorted to 'subject to exhaustion of local remedies'.[330]

Third, the PAfIC encourages Member States to conduct arbitration using any established African public or African private alternative dispute resolution centre.[331] The requirement for exhaustion of domestic remedies ensures that domestic laws and institutions fulfil their purposes, and this may work out well in the mutual

323 Investment Agreement for the Common Market for Eastern and Southern Africa (COMESA) Common Investment Area (signed 23 May 2007) art 28(1).

324 ibid art 28(3).

325 Agreement between the Government of the Republic of Korea and the Government of the Republic of Cameroon for the Promotion and Protection of Investments (signed 24 December 2013, entered into force 13 April 2018).

326 Agreement between Canada and the Republic of Cameroon for the Promotion and Protection of Investments (signed 03 March 2014, entered into force 16 December 2016) art 21(1).

327 ibid art 21(2)(e)(i) and (f).

328 African Union Commission, Draft Pan-African Investment Code (December 2016) <preamblehttps://au.int/sites/default/files/documents/32844-doc-draft_pan-african_investment_code_december_2016_en.pdf> accessed 28 September 2020.

329 ibid art 42(1).

330 ibid art 42(1)(c).

331 ibid art 42(1)(d).

interests of the parties. It is also in line with customary international law as analysed in Section 3.5 earlier in this chapter. Fourth, the choice of one dispute resolution forum excludes the others and the decision of the chosen forum is final.[332] The issue remains whether the gains of requiring exhaustion of domestic remedies would not be eroded by resorting to investor–state arbitration upon exhaustion of local remedies given, arguably, the investment tribunal's lack of neutrality because of affiliation bias[333] and questions around its legitimacy to adjudicate upon public policy and public interest issues.[334]

The AfCFTA[335] establishes a Dispute Settlement Mechanism and Protocol on Rules and Procedures on the Settlement of Disputes for its administration. The Protocol on Rules and Procedures on the Settlement of Disputes provides for the establishment of the Dispute Settlement Body (DSB) composed of representatives of member states of AfCFTA. This Body is responsible for establishing Dispute Settlement Panels and Appellate Bodies,[336] which are responsible for original and appellate hearing of cases and preparing reports to the DSB. These are applicable to state-to-state disputes in the context of promoting trade.[337] Therefore, the Agreement establishing AfCFTA does not seem to be directly relevant for investment dispute settlement in its present focus on trade. However, the adoption of state-to-state dispute settlement raises the question as to why this mode of dispute settlement will not be appropriate for investor–state disputes.

Drawing from AfCFTA and the trade regimes generally, future investment treaties could require state-to-state dispute resolution by assigning investment tribunals, duties similar to those performed by Dispute Settlement Panels and Appellate Bodies, which hear and determine cases and develop reports to assist state parties through the DSB in the resolution of trade disputes. Alternatively, the state-to-state dispute resolution mechanism could resolve both trade and

[332] ibid art 42(2).

[333] Sergio Puig and Anton Strezhnev, 'Affiliation Bias in Arbitration: An Experimental Approach' (2017) 46(1) Journal of Legal Studies 371; and Loretta Malintoppi, 'Independence, Impartiality, and Duty of Disclosure of Arbitrators' in Peter Muchlinski, Federico Ortino, and Christoph Schreuer (eds), *The Oxford Handbook of International Investment Law* (OUP 2008) 789.

[334] Susan D Franck, 'The Legitimacy Crisis in Investment Treaty Arbitration: Privatizing Public International Law Through Inconsistent Decisions Public International Law Through Inconsistent Decisions' (2005) 73(4) Fordham Law Review 1521; Lisa Diependaele, Ferdi De Ville, and Sigrid Sterckx, 'Assessing the Normative Legitimacy of Investment Arbitration: The EU's Investment Court System' (2019) 24(1) New Political Economy 37 (hereafter, Diependaele, Ville, and Sterckx, 'Normative Legitimacy'); Jean d'Aspremont and Eric De Brabandere, 'The Complementary Faces of Legitimacy in International Law: The Legitimacy of Origin and the Legitimacy of Exercise' (2011) 34 Fordham International Law Journal 190; and Thomas Dietz, Marius Dotzauer, and Edward S Cohen, The Legitimacy Crisis of Investor–State Arbitration and the New EU Investment Court System (2019) 26(4) Review of International Political Economy 749 (hereafter, Dietz, Dotzauer, and Cohen, 'Legitimacy Crisis').

[335] Agreement Establishing the African Continental Free Trade Area (signed 21 March 2018, entered into force 30 May 2019).

[336] ibid. Protocol on Rules and Procedures on the Settlement of Disputes art 5.

[337] ibid art 20 and AfCFTA: Protocol on Rules and Procedures on the Settlement of Disputes, art 3.

investment disputes, to avoid overlapping litigation between investor–state arbitration and trade dispute settlement mechanisms. Apart from foreign investment being long-term commitments, investors are arguably not in a unique position when compared to other business entities engaged in trade and other forms of commerce. The same business entity may be engaged in trade and investment in the same host state yet would be subject to different disciplines for dispute resolution: state-to-state for trade disputes and investor–state for investment disputes. Two different foreign business entities, one engaged in trade and the other in investment in the host state, may be making the same or different but equally significant contributions to the national economy of the host state as both pursue the same business motive of making profit. Given the convergence and interconnection between trade and investment, the maintenance of different modes of dispute resolution based on whether the business activity is trade or investment is unnecessary.

The separation between international investment law and international trade law 'is increasingly neither necessary nor desirable'.[338] Both trade treaties and investment treaties are creatures of states. States agree to the mechanisms for the settlement for trade disputes and investment disputes under these treaties.

On the similarities or convergences of international trade law and international investment law, Jürgen Kurtz argues that[339]

> [b]oth systems share common and important legal terrain. Indeed, the usual assumption … of hermitic separation breaks down under careful observation. Consider the manner in which foreign investment in the services sector is regulated extensively within the WTO [World Trade Organization] against the vital role of that sector as a proportion of foreign direct investment (FDI) flows. There are four modes of service supply defined in the WTO General Agreement on Trade in Services (GATS), with the third encompassing provision of services through 'commercial presence' of a foreign supplier. The common coverage of foreign investment issues extend[s] far beyond FDI in the GATS. Performance requirements are disciplined both under many BITs as well as in the WTO Agreement on Trade-Related Investment Measures (TRIMs). These are conditions imposed on foreign investors (often linked to the grant of an incentive by the host state) that may be explicitly trade distorting, such as local content obligations (mandating that products produced by the investor in the host state contain local materials), or export performance requirements (requiring a certain proportion of the investor's output to be exported). Many BITs also include intellectual property within the scope of assets protected by substantive treaty provisions. In direct parallel, the WTO Agreement on Trade-Related Intellectual Property

338 Jürgen Kurtz, *The WTO and International Investment Law: Converging Systems* (CUP 2016) 10.
339 ibid 10–11 and 13.

> Rights (TRIPs) requires WTO members to protect various types of intellectual property as a form of investment in their domestic jurisdictions.
>
> Across this common subject matter, both systems have always encompassed a respectable number of shared micro norms. This includes, most notably, restrictions against state discrimination in the form of both national and most-favoured-nation treatment. These important disciplines operate as a first-order guarantee of equality of competitive opportunity between foreign and domestic goods, services and investors.
>
> As a second converging factor, the exact same measure can fall within jurisdictional reach of both systems, invoke a common legal norm and may even be adjudicated simultaneously. This visible entanglement between the two systems was strikingly embedded in the long-standing softwood lumber dispute between Canada and the United States, which had triggered claims both in the WTO and in NAFTA [North American Free Trade Agreement].

In these circumstances, maintaining two completely different systems of dispute resolution merely because the subject matter of the business activity is an investment or trade would seem impolitic and superfluous. The AfCFTA provides opportunity for Africa to consider a state-to-state dispute resolution mechanism for both trade disputes and investment disputes, rather than have two separate ones.

3.6.3 Investor–State Arbitration Reforms Beyond Africa

Beyond the African continent, various proposals have been made for the reform of investor–state arbitration. The UNCITRAL has not only developed rules on transparency[340] but has also proposed various ways in which investor–state arbitration could be reformed.[341]

The European Union and its partners' inclusion of investment dispute provisions in CETA[342] and TTIP[343] received significant public opposition. This led the European Union to propose changes to investment dispute settlement procedures and proposals for the creation of an Investment Court System (ICS).[344] The EU model for investment dispute settlement works towards a permanent court with judges appointed by state parties and paid a fixed salary by the parties as well as an appellate body.[345] This evidences a rejection of investor–state arbitration.

340 UNCITRAL, 'Rules on Transparency' (n 35).
341 UNCTAD, *Reform of Investor–State Dispute Settlement* (n 11).
342 CETA (n 56).
343 The Transatlantic Trade and Investment Partnership negotiations were launched in 2013. Negotiations ended without definite agreement at the end of 2016. See Council of the European Union, Council Decision 6052/19, April 2019. <https://www.consilium.europa.eu/media/39180/st06052-en19.pdf> accessed 28 September 2020.
344 Diependaele, Ville, and Sterckx, 'Normative Legitimacy' (n 334).
345 Dietz, Dotzauer, and Cohen, 'Legitimacy Crisis' (n 334).

The new system (i) does away with case-by-case tribunals under investor–state arbitration and creates a system of permanent investment courts that has jurisdiction over specific investment treaties, (ii) requires the contracting parties to appoint the judges rather than the disputing parties, (iii) fixes the wages of judges, and (iv) develops more restrictive rules on the selection and working of the members of investment courts and how they operate (eg requirements relating to qualifications and expertise and code of conduct).[346] The CETA's Article 8.29 envisages such a court system when it provides that the parties 'shall pursue with other trading partners the establishment of a multilateral investment tribunal and appellate mechanism for the resolution of investment disputes'. The existing investment dispute resolution under CETA has comprehensive rules and procedures to ensure efficiency of investor–state arbitration including the establishment of an Appellate Tribunal under article 8.28 to review awards rendered by original Tribunal.

3.6.4 Reflection on Investor–State Arbitration Reform Options for Africa

In summary, the reform of ISDS has taken various forms. These include (i) fixing existing ISDS mechanisms, for example adding new elements such as requiring local litigation as a precondition for ISDS; (ii) adding new elements to existing ISDS mechanisms such as alternative dispute resolution and appellate mechanisms; and (iii) replacing existing ISDS mechanisms (eg creating an international investment court, requiring state-to-state dispute settlement, and replacing ISDS with domestic dispute resolution).[347]

What should be the way forward for African countries? As Thomas Dietz, Marius Dotzauer, and Edward Cohen argue:[348]

> When the contested institution is widely detached from prevailing normative expectations resulting in a perception of illegitimacy of the institution, states must either change the focal institution radically or create a new institution that better meets the prevailing generalized standards of appropriateness.

The legitimacy and efficacy of investor–state arbitration and the case for change or reform has already considered in Section 3.2 of this chapter and elsewhere.[349] The key issue with existing investment dispute settlement institutions is that they

[346] ibid 762–63.

[347] UNCTAD, *Reforming Investment Dispute Settlement: A Stocktaking* (IIA Note, Issue 1, March 2019) at 5.

[348] Dietz, Dotzauer, and Cohen, 'Legitimacy Crisis' (n 334) 755.

[349] ibid 756–61; and Robert Howse and others, *The Legitimacy of International Trade Courts and Tribunals* (CUP 2018) (hereafter, Howse and others, *Legitimacy of Trade Courts*).

were 'not designed to address complex issues of public policy that now routinely come into play in investor–state disputes.'[350] Dietz, Dotzauer, and Cohen have summarised the critique of ISDS thus:[351]

> [A] more fundamental critique of the regime asks whether it is necessary in the first place. In this view, ISDS provides private investors with a privileged legal status that exempts their claims from the judicial structures of host states. By creating a unique dispute resolution system just for private investors, ISDS in this view undermines the ability of political communities—and especially democracies—to collectively determine the rules by which society and economy will be structured. While such a system may be justified in situations where the rights of foreign investors are unlikely to be protected in domestic law (a question on which critics are divided), it seems particularly inappropriate in the context of democratic states with independent legal and judicial orders.

investor–state arbitration and the investment treaty regime must not privilege and comfort foreign investors by securing them absolute standards of investment protection at the expense of citizens for and by whom governments are constituted or at the expense of the public interests that lead states to enter into investment treaties. The investment dispute settlement system must ensure that investors are subject to the same standards of rule of law as every foreign individual or business entity in a host state that is contributing to the development of the host state in its own way. The investment dispute settlement must be one that ensures that the legitimate interests of the disputing parties and all concerned are accorded the protections they deserve. It cannot be said it takes only investment tribunals to do so. Therefore, all options should be open to states so long as they are consistent with national constitutions.

Investment treaty tribunals are created by states. Their effectiveness depends on national implementation and the goodwill of these same states.[352] Thus, the very states that invest public money, effort, and time in making and sustaining the investment treaty arbitration they complain about must reconsider the role of their own institutions in the resolution of investment disputes, including domestic courts and other state-to-state mechanisms. They should not limit themselves to investor–state arbitration.

Investor–state arbitration does not have or come with any inherent, unique, automatic, or ready-made qualities and advantages that make it or should make

[350] Department of Trade and Industry, 'Bilateral Investment Treaty Policy Framework Review' (Government Position Paper 0001, June 2009) 45 <http://pmg-assets.s3-website-eu-west-1.amazonaws.com/docs/090626trade-bi-lateralpolicy.pdf> accessed 28 September 2020 (hereafter, DTI, 'BIT Policy Framework Review').

[351] Dietz, Dotzauer, and Cohen, 'Legitimacy Crisis' (n 334) 758.

[352] Robert Howse 'Conclusion' in Howse and others, *Legitimacy of Trade Courts* (n 349) 503, 508.

it the most preferred mode of investment dispute settlement such that it must always be chosen and stuck to without the option of alternatives whatsoever as the insistency on its reform would seem to suggest. States must invest their public resources in a system that works for all. Investor–state arbitration must not enjoy an automatic and unquestionable right of preference. Public institutions must have that preference and must be the starting, if not final, point because investors operate within host states with the support of host state institutions, which they rely on to operate to make profit. Investors cannot rely on state institutions only when all works well for them but then disown and disdain the same institutions when it comes to dispute settlement.

In consonance with their constitutions which constitute the fundamental legal frameworks for governance and the protection of the public interests, African states must lead the way in making a case for the return to domestic courts and institutions for the settlement of investment disputes, at least for investors operating within the continent. The South African Department of Trade and Industry rightly argued that[353]

> [c]entral to any developing country agenda on investment is a requirement to ensure that the approach to dispute settlement is fully revisited. There is no compelling reason why review of an investor's claims against a state cannot be undertaken by the institutions of the state in question—provided these are independent of the public authority that is in dispute and they discharge their duties in accordance with basic principles of good governance, including an independent judiciary. Unfortunately, there is little indication in the texts of BITs that negotiators have acted with prudence to promote better domestic dispute settlement in the host state.

Africa and the developing world in general have long defended their sovereign right to regulate the activities of multinational businesses entities within their jurisdiction and to control the exploration, development, and disposition of their natural resources and wealth with the support of the United Nations. This is reflected in the Declaration on the Establishment of a New International Economic Order,[354] the Charter of Economic Rights and Duties of States,[355] and the Declaration on Permanent Sovereignty over Natural Resources.[356] The values embodying these norms include respect for sovereignty over natural wealth and resources,[357] the

[353] DTI, 'BIT Policy Framework Review' (n 350) 45.

[354] Declaration on the Establishment of a New International Economic Order, General Assembly of the United Nations A/RES/3201(S-VI), adopted 1 May 1974 (hereafter, 'NIEO').

[355] Charter of Economic Rights and Duties of States, General Assembly of the United Nations Resolution 3281 (XXIX), adopted 12 December 1974 (hereafter, 'Charter of Economic Rights and Duties of States').

[356] Permanent Sovereignty over Natural Resources, General Assembly of the United Nations Resolution 1803 (XVII, adopted 14 December 1962).

[357] ibid [1] and[8]

need to respect domestic law and exhaust local remedies,[358] and the sovereign right to regulate and exercise authority over foreign investment and the activities of investors and other multinational business entities.[359] These are the values and principles that underly current global reforms of investment treaties and investment arbitration led by developed countries, albeit indirectly. There is the need to revisit these earlier debates and norms with the lead taken by Africa and developing countries.

In line with the goal of continental integration, the African continent should be open to a Multilateral Trade and Investment Court, a state-to-state dispute resolution mechanism. This body will have jurisdiction over not only investment and trade disputes but all sorts of transborder business disputes in situations where local remedies are non-existent or prove futile. South Africa has led the way by removing investor–state arbitration and replacing it with state-to-state arbitration. Africa can do the same as a continent. An effective continental business dispute resolution mechanism will ensure that such disputes are resolved in Africa and minimise the costs of having to settle them outside the continent at huge public expenditure.

3.7 Conclusion

African countries' experiences with ISDS provides justification for African states to reject it in future investment treaties unless ISDS can accommodate the public interest and effectively protect it. The fundamental principles of African legal systems in which the courts have original, appellate, and final jurisdiction over all legal disputes and persons and in which the principles of probity, separation of powers, rule of law, accountability, and transparency are entrenched and paramount prohibit African states being party to the ISDS mechanism that, from the start and in practice, is pro-investor.

Customary international law also does not grant foreign investors an automatic right of direct recourse to ISDS. It is a principle of customary international law that to access an international dispute settlement forum a foreign investor needs to show that it will be futile to have recourse to domestic remedies or to seek to exhaust them. The investment treaty regime itself does not expressly entitle foreign investors the right to appeal against decisions made by municipal courts. The jurisdiction of arbitral tribunals to settle disputes under investment treaties and domestic legislation does not give them the substantive and procedural right to entertain disputes between African states and foreign investors that have been finally

[358] ibid [2] and [4]

[359] ibid; and 'Charter of Economic Rights and Duties of States' (n 355) art 2(1)(a); and 'NIEO' (n 354) [4(g)].

adjudicated upon by municipal courts. Thus, there does not exist a legal basis under the investment treaties themselves for the decisions of municipal courts to be challenged by foreign investors and to be heard by investment tribunals. Moreover, the decision of a domestic court involving a foreign investor is not the same thing as the measure giving rise to the dispute because foreign investors and states are both affected by the decisions of the courts. Therefore, such a court decision cannot amount to a measure under the investment treaties and may be a subject of arbitration before an appropriate body under customary international law on the basis that justice has not been done.

The ISDS regime promotes the idea that foreign investors can use domestic institutions and the good faith support of those institutions in Africa, or anywhere for that matter, to carry on their business but then when it comes to dispute settlement, these domestic institutions in the form of the courts do not work and are said to be incapable of effectively and efficiently resolving investment disputes. The assumption that the courts, whether in Africa or elsewhere, simply lack the capacity to resolve disputes efficiently and effectively only when it comes to foreign investors lacks empirical support and cannot legitimately justify investor–state arbitration. Unless it is admitted that constitutional governance, including separation of powers, the rule of law, judicial independence, and the actual operation of the courts in Africa or host states generally do not work to protect them or work to their detriment in practice, singling out foreign investors from the jurisdiction of domestic courts by giving foreign investors direct access to investor–state arbitration lacks principle and merit.

The failings of the ISDS mechanism which have necessitated the reforms of the regime evidences the fact that the ISDS mechanism too is not infallible. It is less clear then why the ISDS mechanism should automatically enjoy a prior status when it comes to investment disputes settlement. Therefore, if the reform of the ISDS mechanism is necessary then the very states that are leading the reforms of the regime should revisit the role and reform of their domestic courts too since the ISDS does not come with automatic operative advantages over domestic courts. The rule of law, accountability, fair play, and good faith are central in the resolution of disputes and these values are not inherent attributes of investor–state arbitration. Therefore there is the need for an introspective rethink of the role of domestic courts in the settlement of investment disputes in the context of constitutional governance and the rule of law for all, citizens and non-citizens. Future investment treaties will need to be very clear as to areas of public interest regulation that cannot be subject to ISDS if a case is made for African states to continue to agree to ISDS.

4

The Environment, Human Rights, and the Investment Treaty Regime in Africa

4.1 Introduction

There are two central themes to this chapter. The first and primary theme is the extent to which fundamental environmental rights and human rights and corresponding obligations of African states might limit African states' competence in the execution of investment treaties. The second theme, which is the foundation to the first, is the potential effects of investment treaties and investor–state arbitration on environmental and human rights protection in Africa.

These themes are informed by the fact that human beings 'have evolved within, depend on and are part of the world of nature',[1] and the need to protect the environment thereof. In the *Legality of the Threat of Use of Nuclear Weapons Case*, the International Court of Justice (ICJ) stated that 'the environment is not an abstraction but represents the living space, the quality of life and the very health of human beings, including generations unborn'.[2] Melisa Thorme expressed a similar view when she stated:[3]

> Human life and the human environment are inseparable. To survive, humans must have air to breathe, water to drink, food to eat, and a place in which to live and sleep. If these elements become polluted, contaminated, or are eliminated or destroyed, life will cease to exist. To protect human life . . . environmental life support system must be maintained and protected.

The importance of the environment for human health, livelihood, and sustainable development has also been well articulated in international environmental treaties (IETs) and instruments, including the Rio Declaration on Environment and Development (Rio Declaration).[4] The Rio Declaration states that human beings

[1] Martin Holdgate, *From Care to Action: Making a Sustainable Future* (Earthscan 1996) 1quoted in Duncan French, *International Law and Policy of Sustainable Development* (Manchester University Press 2005) 10.

[2] *Legality of the Threat of Use of Nuclear Weapons Case*, ICJ Reports 1996, 226 para 29.

[3] Melissa Thorme, 'Establishing Environment as a Human Right' (1990–1991) 19 Denver Journal of International Law and Policy 301.

[4] United Nations Conference on Environment and Development, *Report of the United Nations Conference on Environment and Development* Vol I *Resolutions Adopted by the Conference* (United

The Investment Treaty Regime and Public Interest Regulation in Africa. Dominic Npoanlari Dagbanja, Oxford University Press.
 DOI: 10.1093/oso/9780192896179.003.0004

should be at the centre of sustainable development, which means they should be entitled to a healthy and productive life in harmony with nature.[5] The right to development must be fulfilled in a manner that equitably meets developmental and environmental needs of present and future generations[6] and states must enact environmental legislation on liability and compensation for those who suffer from pollution and other environmental damage.[7] The *Transforming Our World: The 2030 Agenda for Sustainable Development* bears a similar message.[8]

At the regional level in Africa, Article 36(9) of the Constitution of Ghana says the state 'shall take appropriate measures needed to protect and safeguard the national environment for posterity; and shall seek co-operation with other states and bodies for purposes of protecting the wider international environment for mankind'. This duty to protect the environment for posterity is a constitutional recognition of a customary land law principle in Africa that 'land belongs to a vast family of whom many are dead, a few are living and countless host are still unborn.'[9] Legally, this duty is fulfilled through the enactment and enforcement of environmental laws and regulations. Many African countries including Ghana, Kenya, Nigeria, and South Africa are parties to a number of investment treaties which are intended to provide the legal protection for foreign investment analysed in Chapter 1. These countries must live up to their duties to protect the environment and human rights and at the same time fulfil investment treaty obligations. However, as the Commission for Environmental Cooperation of North America (CECNA) has argued, environmental regulations may run afoul of investment treaties.[10]

Municipal laws, international environmental law, and international human rights law depend for their effectiveness on domestic implementation. However, one of the challenges facing environmental law is the difficulty of enforcement, particularly where environmental protection objectives come into conflict with economic interests.[11] Business activities can have harmful effects on the environment and human health which may call for state intervention, particularly in Africa where large foreign investments go into the extractive industries. Obsolete and hazardous technology exported for investment purposes can have harmful

Nations publication, Sales No E.93.I.8 and corrigendum, 12 August 1992) <https://www.un.org/esa/dsd/agenda21/Agenda%2021.pdf> . accessed 27 December 2020

[5] ibid Principle 1.
[6] ibid Principle 3.
[7] ibid Principles 11 and 13.
[8] *Transforming Our World: The 2030 Agenda for Sustainable Development* (Resolution adopted by the General Assembly on 25 September 2015).
[9] Nii Amaa Ollenu, *Principles of Customary Land Law in Ghana* (Sweet and Maxwell 1962) 4.
[10] Commission for Environmental Cooperation of North America, *Free Trade and the Environment: The Picture Becomes Clearer* (2002) at v, <http://www3.cec.org/islandora/en/item/1871-free-trade-and-environment-picture-becomes-clearer-en.pdf> accessed 27 December 2020.
[11] Philippe Sands and others, *Principles of International Environmental Law* (3rd edn, CUP 2012) 15 (hereafter, Sands and others, *Principles of IEL*).

effects on the environment and life.[12] The World Commission on Environment and Development (WCED) suggested as far back as 1987 that 'economics and ecology can interact destructively and trip into disaster'.[13] The disputes in the Ogoni region in Nigeria provide an excellent example of how the people of a host state have to bear environmental degradation caused largely by foreign oil exploration and exploitation companies while the profits go to the foreign business community.[14] Thus, while economic ideas and tools can contribute to the achievement of environmental and human rights protection and safety goals, there can equally be tension between environmental and human rights protection goals and business operations.[15]

Conflict with investment treaties is one of the reasons both municipal law and international environmental law rules suffer from inadequate domestic implementation.[16] Writing on the potential for international investment law to limit environmental regulation, the United States (US) Trade Representative stated:[17]

> In the Trade Act, Congress recognized that securing a stable investment climate and a level playing field for U.S. investment abroad is an important objective of U.S. trade policy. By fostering economic growth and job creation, investment can bring important benefits, including potential benefits to the environment: as wealth grows and poverty decreases, more resources become available for environmental protection, with potential benefits for developing countries, particularly as they develop constituencies in favor of increased environmental protection. Congress, however, also gave weight to concerns that arbitral claims brought by investors against governments (through 'investor–State' arbitration) could be used inappropriately to challenge U.S. domestic laws and regulations, including those concerning the environment.

I explore the issue of foreign investment and environmental and human rights protection in Africa and the potential effects of Africa's investment treaties on

[12] Muthucumaraswamy Sornarajah, *The International Law on Foreign Investment* (3rd edn, CUP 2010) 57, 109, and 110 (hereafter, Sornarajah, *Law on Foreign Investment*).

[13] World Commission on Environment and Development, *Report of the World Commission on Environment and Development: Our Common Future* (United Nations, August 1987) ch 1, [18]–[19] <file://uniwa.uwa.edu.au/userhome/staff5/00092945/Downloads/our_common_futurebrundtlandreport1987%20(1).pdf> accessed 8 February 2022. .

[14] Sornarajah, *Law on Foreign Investment* (n 12) 79.

[15] James May and J Patrick Kelly, 'The Environment and International Society: Issues, Concepts, and Context' in Shawkat Alam and others (eds), *Routledge Handbook of International Environmental Law* (Routledge 2013) 13, 18 (hereafter, May and Kelly, 'Environment and International Society').

[16] Sands and others, *Principles of IEL* (n 11) 15–16.

[17] United States Trade Representative, *Final Environmental Review of the Dominican Republic—Central America—United States Free Trade Agreement* (United States Trade Representative February 2005) 29 <https://ustr.gov/archive/assets/Trade_Agreements/Regional/CAFTA/Transmittal/asset_upload_file804_7819.pdf> accessed 8 February 2022. .

environmental and human rights regulation.[18] The core questions addressed are is it the case that investment treaties could impair the ability or narrow the regulatory autonomy of African governments to take measures to protect the environment? Do the constitutional and general international law duties of African states to protect the environment and human rights limit the investment treaty obligations the states can or should undertake? How should conflict between the legal duties to protect the environment and human rights and compliance with investment treaty obligations be addressed?

The potential limitations of investment treaties on environmental and human rights regulation are particularly important for Africa. Environmental degradation occasioned by the activities of businesses, especially in the mining and extractive industries, calls for environmental regulation by African states which may result in conflict with investment treaty obligations if an investment is adversely affected by such regulation. Most of Africa's investment treaties, especially those that came into force in the 2000s do not make exceptions for public interest regulation, such as environmental and human rights protection. They require the payment of compensation to foreign investors where the adverse effects of governmental regulation of an investment are considered an expropriation, whether directly or indirectly, and even if regulation is for a public purpose.[19]

I focus specifically on the potential for investment treaties to limit the adoption of environmental and human rights protection measures, such as the enactment and enforcement of legislation. I argue that key aspects of the legal regimes for environmental protection in Africa, such as the cancellation and termination of environmental permits and regulation of environmental hazardous substances for purposes of human rights protection, could be challenged by foreign investors as breaching investment treaties.

The protection of human rights and the environment has been constitutionalised in Africa. Human rights and environment are protected under national constitutions, domestic law, IETs, and international human rights treaties (IHRTs). Therefore, the protection of the environment and human rights is not limited to domestic constitutional law only; it is also required under IETs and IHRTs. Indeed, most of the constitutions analysed in this chapter not only require African governments to enact and implement domestic environmental and human rights

[18] See Abba Kolo and Thomas Waelde, 'Environmental Regulation, Investment Protection and 'Regulatory Taking' in International Law' (2001) 50(4) International and Comparative Law Quarterly 811 (hereafter, Kolo and Waelde, 'Investment Protection and Regulatory Taking').

[19] These include investment treaties include Treaty of Friendship and of Commerce between the Swiss Confederation and the Republic of Liberia, Treaty of Friendship and of Commerce between the Swiss Confederation and the Republic of Liberia, signed 23 July 1963, entered into force 22 July1964; Treaty between the Federal Republic of Germany and the Republic of Liberia for the Promotion and Reciprocal Protection of Investments, signed 12 December 1961 and entered into force 22 October1967; and Agreement between the Government of the Cameroon United Kingdom of Great Britain and Northern Ireland and the Government of the United Republic of Cameroon for the Promotion and Protection of Investments, signed 4 June 1982, entered into force 7 June 1985.

legislation but also to observe human rights and environmental treaty obligations. Thus, it is a *constitutional-general international law imperative* for African countries to respect and uphold their human rights and environmental law obligations.

I argue that because investment treaties could compromise the constitutional and general international law duties in Africa to protect the environment for present and future generations, those duties, given they derive their source from national constitutions and general international law and considering their public interest orientation, place legal limitations on the investment treaty obligations African countries can assume. Given their primary obligations to protect human rights and the environment, African states do not have the competence to conclude investment treaties that explicitly and directly prevent them from adopting environmental protection measures. Thus, African countries must not agree to the payment of compensation under investment treaties in situations where their constitutions and municipal environmental laws require the adoption of the environmental measures in question and prohibit the payment of compensation to affected individuals.

The rest of chapter is organised as follows. Section 4.2 deals with the state of the environment and the relationship between foreign investment and environmental degradation in Africa. It shows that the human health and economic importance of the environment and the level of environmental damage in Africa (occasioned in part by the activities of both local and foreign mining companies) justify African states' active role in the protection of the environment and human rights.

Section 4.3 addresses the right to a safe and healthy environment and shows that constitutions, domestic legislation, and IETs impose legal duties on African states to protect the environment.

Section 4.4 focuses on the legal duties to protect human rights in Africa. It establishes that the protection of human rights is a matter of constitutional law and general international law in Africa as various constitutions not only provide for the protection of human rights but also require African states to observe their IHT obligations.

Section 4.5 reviews and interprets arbitral case law to assess the legal effects of investment treaties on environmental and human rights protection in Africa. It focuses on how the standards of investment protection by treaty, such as national treatment, expropriation, fair and equitable treatment, and full protection and security contained in African investment treaties, could limit the adoption and enforcement of environmental and human rights legislation and other measures. It argues that standards of investment can restrain African states from adopting measures to protect the environment.

Section 4.6 assesses the efficacy of exception provisions in investment treaties for environmental and human rights protection in Africa. It argues that most of the exceptions do not really preserve the right to regulate to protect the environment and human rights, given that they merely affirm the right to regulate coupled with provisos that limit their scope and operative effect

Section 4.7 assesses the constitutional and general international law duties to protect the environment and human rights and its implications for the making of investment treaties in Africa. It argues that the duties of African states under their constitutions and general international law with respect to environmental protection and human rights must guide the states in the making of investment treaties. It points to the need for Africa to put its obligations to protect the environment and human rights first in its international economic relations with other nations and foreign businesses. To this extent, it proposes that African states must include the most-favourable home and third-states clause in investment treaties requiring foreign investors to carry out their operations in the host country in accordance with the most favourable environmental, human rights, and labour standards in the home state or third state.

Section 4.8 concludes the chapter, reiterating the need for standards of investment protection under both domestic laws and investment treaties to be reconciled with African states' constitutional and general international law obligations to protect the environment and human rights.

4.2 Foreign Direct Investment, Environment, and Human Rights in Africa

Environmental protection is important for Africa because its ecosystems support human livelihoods and the economy generally. Natural resources such as the soils, water, minerals, forests, and wildlife are essential for the productive sectors of the economies of Africa. The majority of Africa's working population depends on farming activities for their livelihoods; about 70 per cent of Africa's population is dependent on agriculture.[20] Millions of smallholder farms provide livelihoods for over 2 billion people. In sub-Saharan Africa and Asia smallholder farms also produce up to 80 per cent of food.[21] Agriculture contributes to food security, provides raw materials for local industries, generates foreign exchange, and provides employment and incomes for most of the population, especially those living in the rural areas. For example, around 11 million of Ghana's 30 million people live in forest areas, and about two-thirds of Ghanaians are supported by forest-related activities.[22]

[20] Alliance for a Green Revolution in Africa (AGRA), *Africa Agriculture Status Report: The Business of Smallholder Agriculture in Sub-Saharan Africa* (Issue 5, 2017) vi; Ghana Statistical Service, *2010 Population & Housing Census National Analytical Report* (May 2013) 287 and 400.

[21] Kanayo Nwanze, 'Foreword' to Alliance for a Green Revolution in Africa, *Africa Agriculture Status Report: The Business of Smallholder Agriculture in Sub-Saharan Africa* (Issue 5, 2017) iv.

[22] Government of Ghana, *Growth and Poverty Reduction Strategy (GPRS II) (2006–2009)* (National Development Planning Commission, November 2005) 31 (hereafter, 'GPRS II').

Most African countries have suffered from excessive exploitation of their natural resources (especially in the extractive industries) to the detriment of ordinary people who should benefit from the natural resources in the very environments in which they are born, bred, and lead their lives.[23] Investment in Africa's mining industry is largely held by foreign investors.[24] Environmental degradation, defined as deleterious and undesirable change or disturbance to the environment,[25] is a major impediment to increased productivity and sustainability in Africa's agriculture sector.[26] Environmental degradation affects people's health through impacts on physical and social environments. The economic costs of those impacts, including malnutrition, are also large.[27] Over 1,000 deaths in about 1 million people occur in Ghana due to environmental causes.[28] Many other studies depict a similar picture of the state of the environment in Ghana.[29] In Nigeria, mineral exploration, with particular reference to the oil industry, has led to adverse effects on land, water, air quality, and environmental quality generally.[30] A 2015 study on the Niger Delta region of Nigeria suggest 'consistent flow of industrial waste, oil spills, gas flares, fire disaster, acid rain, flooding erosion, etc., which has led to the pollution of farmlands and fishponds'.[31] Kenya,[32] South Africa,[33] and many other African countries share similar experiences with the extractive industry.[34]

[23] International Union for the Conservation of Nature, *An Introduction to African Convention on Conservation of Nature and Natural Resources* (IUCN Environmental Policy and Law Paper No 56, 2004).

[24] See, for example, Joseph Ayee and others, 'Political Economy of the Mining Sector in Ghana' (World Bank Policy Research Working Paper 5730, July 2011).

[25] DL Ambrose Johnson and others, 'Meanings of Environmental Terms' (1997) 26(3) Journal of Environmental Quality 581, 584.

[26] GPRS II (n 22) 33.

[27] United Nations Development Programme, *Human Development Report 2011* (Palgrave Macmillan 2011) 51.

[28] ibid.

[29] Environmental Protection Agency, *Ghana Environment Sector Study* (February, 2007) 4; Government of Ghana, *The Coordinated Programme of Economic and Social Development Policies, 2010–2016: An Agenda for Shared Growth and Accelerated Development for a Better Ghana* (National Development Planning Commission December 2010) 21; World Bank, *Ghana: Country Environmental Analysis* (Report No 36985-GH, 2 November 2007) [13] (hereafter, World Bank, *Environmental Analysis*); World Bank, *The Republic of Ghana: Selected Policy Issues* (Report No 69622-GH, June 30, 2012) [72] (hereafter, World Bank, *Ghana: Selected Policy Issues*).

[30] IO Akinwumi, TO Oyebisi, and AT Salami, 'Environmental degradation in Nigeria: Implications and Policy Issues—A Viewpoint' (2001) 58(5) International Journal of Environmental Studies 585, 586.

[31] Paul Peters Ugboma, 'Environmental Degradation in Oil Producing Areas of Niger Delta Region, Nigeria: The Need for Sustainable Development' (2015) 4(2) International Journal of Science and Technology 75

[32] Eunice Omanga and others, 'Industrial Air Pollution in Rural Kenya: Community Awareness, Risk Perception and Associations between Risk Variables' (2014) 14 BMC Public Health 377

[33] South African Human Rights Commission (SAHRC), *National Hearing on the Underlying Socio-economic Challenges of Mining-affected Communities in South Africa* (2016) 9 <https://www.sahrc.org.za/home/21/files/SAHRC%20Mining%20communities%20report%20FINAL.pdf> accessed 27 December 2020 (hereafter SAHRC, *Socio-Economic Challenges of Mining*).

[34] See for example United Nations Economic Commission for Africa and African Union, *Minerals and Africa's Development: The International Study Group Report on Africa's Mineral Regimes* (United Nations Economic Commission for Africa 2011) 50–66 hereafter, UNECA and AU, *Minerals and Africa's Development*).

The negative environmental impacts are of particular significance to note given the mining companies are largely owned and run by foreign investors.[35] The adoption of internal policies on environmental protection by foreign firms is very low.[36] A study conducted by Ghana's Commission on Human Rights and Administrative Justice (CHRAJ) into mining communities in 2008 evidences environmental degradation from mining operations.[37] The mining community of Anyinam alleged that air was polluted with dust, chemicals, and smoke and that a pungent smelly effluent was discharged into the community from an ore treatment plant. Residents further claimed that toxic chemicals from a sulphur treatment plant affected the health of community members.[38] Skin diseases were attributed to the release of poisonous gas into the atmosphere from a ventilation shaft located in the middle of the community. The community accused AngloGold Ashanti Ltd (AngloGold), an extractive industry giant, of entrenching poverty, since the chemicals the company used for mining resulted in infertile and contaminated land and the destruction of crops due to surface mining.[39] The affected communities received 'highly inadequate compensation from the company for destroyed farms and crops'.[40]

The effect of mining on the environment has negative consequences for human rights in Ghana. In that country, 'there has been widespread pollution of communities' water sources'.[41] Rivers and streams which previously served as sources of water for the communities dried up having 'been polluted, destroyed due to mining activities or diverted for company use'.[42] Tests of water samples from twenty-two out of twenty-eight mining communities showed that at least two water-quality parameters with health implications were present, in concentrations significantly higher than the World Health Organization maximum allowable limits for drinking water.[43] Mining companies provided alternative sources of water, such as pipes, boreholes, and hand-dug wells for the affected communities. However, those alternatives were left to be maintained or replaced by communities who lack the technology, know-how, and financial resources to do so. The alternatives sources of water were malfunctioning with some of the facilities unsafe for drinking.[44]

Serious health, social, and economic consequences of mining activities needed to be addressed 'with legislative reforms'.[45] Thus there is the need for the

[35] UNCTAD, *Investment Policy Review: Ghana* (United Nations, June 2003), 7.

[36] Uchenna Efobi and others, 'Environmental Pollution Policy of Small Businesses in Nigeria and Ghana: Extent and Impact' (2019) 26 Environmental Science and Pollution Research 2882.

[37] Commission on Human Rights and Administrative Justice, *The State of Human Rights in Mining Communities in Ghana* (DPI Print Ltd 2008) (hereafter CHRAJ, *Human Rights in Mining Communities*).

[38] ibid 35.

[39] ibid 38.

[40] ibid 37.

[41] ibid 172.

[42] ibid 174.

[43] ibid 174–75.

[44] ibid 174.

[45] ibid 193–94.

government of Ghana to review the Minerals and Mining Act 2006 (Act 703) to give better protection to people living in mining areas. Given the 'widespread poverty in the mining communities and the changing economy of food crop production ... the Government should not grant or renew any mineral rights until a cost benefit analysis of the mining industry has been done'.[46] These findings on mining and human rights support an earlier study conducted by the World Bank in 2007 which recommended strengthening the capacity of the regulatory institutions to efficiently manage contracts with the private operators and to improve the monitoring of the quality of water provision by secondary providers across the distribution chain.[47]

According to the Environmental Protection Agency of Ghana (EPA), a significant number of major environmental problems, including environmental degradation, pollution of water bodies, deforestation, poor waste management, and risks from chemical use, result from the activities of mining companies.[48] The EPA environmental rating of mining companies for 2012 shows that the emissions and effluents of AngloGold exceeded the environmental quality standards for discharging toxics into the environment and that onsite hazardous waste management practices caused serious risk to physical and human environments.[49] Other companies such as Ghana Bauxite Company Ltd and Prestea Sankofa Gold Ltd failed to comply with legal requirements on environmental permitting by not having a valid permit or a certificate as required by the Environmental Assessment Regulations 1999 (LI 1652).[50]

The EPA also found that a large number of companies had poor environmental performance in terms of waste management, toxic releases, and monitoring and reporting. Of the sixteen mining companies rated on environmental performance, only two were in full compliance with environmental standards, applied best practices, and were responsive to public complaints. Five of the sixteen were rated as unsatisfactory, that is, not in compliance with environmental standards. Six were rated as posing serious risks to environmental quality.[51] The EPA further found a majority of companies (foreign and domestic) in the manufacturing industry, including timber and chemicals, did not comply with best practices on environmental protection. Most of them operated without the requisite environmental permits.[52]

[46] ibid 194.

[47] World Bank, *Environmental Analysis* (n 29) 68–69.

[48] Environmental Protection Agency, *Ghana: State of Environment Report 2004* (Environmental Protection Agency April 2005) 3

[49] Environmental Protection Agency, *AKOBEN Environmental Rating and Disclosure Programme*, <http://www.epa.gov.gh/epa/projects/akoben> accessed 27 December 2020.

[50] ibid.

[51] ibid. See also Serwaa Akoto Bawua and Richmond Owusu, 'Analyzing the Effect of Akoben Programme on the Environmental Performance of Mining in Ghana: A Case Study of a Gold Mining Company' (2018) 17 Journal of Sustainable Mining 11.

[52] Environmental Protection Agency, *Ghana AKOBEN Programme* <http://www.epa.gov.gh/epa/projects/akoben> accessed 27 December 2020.

It follows that most mining companies operated largely without complying with environmental quality laws, regulations, and guidelines. Non-compliance may be due to lack of or poor enforcement of environmental and human rights regulation.

These environmental issues and their serious implications for communities' health and livelihoods require governmental intervention in making and implementing environmental laws, policies, and guidelines. In 2012, the World Bank suggested that Ghana 'urgently' needed 'to use the presence of the mining industry to induce growth and sustainable benefits, while minimizing environmental impacts'.[53] The World Bank called on the government to carry out a comprehensive cost–benefit analysis of the sector, including fiscal benefits and non-fiscal benefits, and potential social and environmental costs.[54] A meaningful right to a healthy environment in mining communities requires substantive environmental standards to regulate the activities of companies undertaking large-scale surface mining that causes pollution and environmental degradation.[55] Mining companies must pay fully for the environmental costs of their operations. Penalties for failure to pay compensation to communities and individuals adversely affected by bad environmental practices by mining companies should be introduced and strictly enforced.[56]

The South African Human Rights Commission (SAHRC) similarly found in relation to mining that 'the right to water is vulnerable to grievous violation where inadequate safeguards and remediation measures are in place'.[57] On the impact of mining on the environment, the SAHRC found that 'the most crucial factors raised with respect to environmental impact were increased levels of dust, safety concerns over blasting activities, and the impact of these factors on food security, health, and overall conditions of well-being'.[58] Similar findings on the impact of mining on environment and human rights have been made in the case of Cameroon.[59]

In effect, the environmental burden of mining is retained in Africa. This effect also reduces the benefits received from Africa' minerals.[60] The exploitation of minerals in Africa 'has been associated with the violation of human rights, and it is one of the most prominent issues raised by mining-affected communities and civil society organizations working on mining issues'.[61]

A failure of regulation to protect the environment and human rights would require capital resources to be expended in the future to redress losses arising from

[53] World Bank, *Ghana: Selected Policy Issues* (n 29) [104].
[54] ibid [110].
[55] CHRAJ, *Human Rights in Mining Communities in Ghana* (n 37) 178–79.
[56] ibid 178–79.
[57] South Africa Human Rights Commission (SAHRC), *Socio-economic Challenges of Mining* (n 33) 8.
[58] ibid 42.
[59] Ministry of Justice, *Report of the Ministry of Justice on Human Rights in Cameroon in 2017* (12 February 2019) <https://www.spm.gov.cm/site/sites/default/files/Report%20of%20the%20Ministry%20of%20Justice%202017%20ANGL_0.pdf> accessed 27 December 2020.
[60] UNECA and AU, *Minerals and Africa's Development* (n 34) 46.
[61] ibid 59.

environmental damage. Environmental and human rights protection is thus necessary to avoid or obviate the social and economic costs of environmental damage. Environmental regulation and liability rules should specify the grounds and procedures for the grant or revocation of environmental permits or certificates, requirements for environmental impact assessment, and the imposition of fines to remedy environmental damage.[62] Environmental and human rights protection by legislation makes the state, not the market, the arbiter and protector of the public interest.[63] This is consistent with various African constitutions and IETs to which African countries are parties.

4.3 Environmental Rights and Corresponding Duties of African States

4.3.1 Constitutional Environmental Rights

Environmental rights are broadly divided into two categories:[64] substantive environmental rights, which relate to the right to a healthy environment, and procedural environmental rights, which include the right to information, public participation, and access to environmental justice.[65] Domestic constitutions express environmental goals in a number of ways, including as a policy directive, a procedural right, an explicit substantive right, or as an implicit substantive right derived from another enumerated right.[66]

African constitutions not only provide for the substantive and procedural right to a healthy and clean environment, they also impose corresponding obligations on states with regards to the fulfilment of this right. Among the principles affirmed in the preamble to the Constitution of Cameroon is one that states that 'every person shall have a right to a healthy environment. The protection of the environment shall be the duty of every citizen. The state shall ensure the protection and improvement of the environment'. The Constitution of Egypt provides in Article 46:

> Every individual has the right to live in a healthy, sound and balanced environment. Its protection is a national duty. The state is committed to taking the necessary measures to preserve it, avoid harming it, rationally use its natural resources

[62] Sands and others, *Principles of IEL* (n 11) 700.

[63] John Kenneth Galbraith, *Economics and the Public Purpose* (Deutsch 1974) 289.

[64] Stephen Turner, *A Global Environmental Right* (Routledge 2014) 24–28 (hereafter, Turner, *A Global Environmental Right*).

[65] Riccardo Pavoni, 'Environmental Rights, Sustainable Development, and Investor–State Case Law: A Critical Appraisal' in Pierre-Marie Dupuy, Ernst-Ulrich Petersmann, and Francesco Francioni (eds), *Human Rights in International Investment Law and Arbitration* (OUP 2009) 255, 256–57.

[66] James R May and Erin Daly, 'Global Constitutional Environmental Rights' in Alam and others (eds), *Routledge Handbook of International Environmental Law* (n 15) 603, 604.

to ensure that sustainable development is achieved, and guarantee the rights of future generations thereto.

Under Article 1(2) of the Constitution of Ghana, citizens have the procedural right to enforce the Constitution by going to the Supreme Court to ensure state institutions and individuals act in accordance with the Constitution. There is a substantive duty on the state of Ghana in Article 36(9) to protect and safeguard the environment. Citizens also have a duty under Article 40(k) to protect and safeguard the environment. Article 257(6) of the Constitution vests minerals in the President and Article 269(1) requires the Fishery Commission, Forestry Commission and Minerals Commission to regulate and manage the utilisation of natural resources such as fisheries, forestry, and minerals. The EPA is the primary institution responsible for environmental protection in Ghana.

The duty to protect the environment by 'appropriate measures' in Article 36(9) of the Constitution of Ghana implies a recognition of the right to a clean and safe environment in Ghana or, at least, the importance of the environment for some other purposes, such as for farming and health. A measure is 'appropriate' if it effectively meets environmental protection objectives. The right to life, property, work under 'satisfactory and healthy conditions', and the right to health recognised in Articles 13, 18, 24, and 30 of the Constitution of Ghana reinforce the substantive human right to a safe and healthy environment in Ghana.

Article 295(1) of the Constitution of Ghana defines the public interest as 'any right or advantage which enures or is intended to enure to the benefit generally of the whole of the people of Ghana'. In *Dey v The Republic*, Justice Forster decided that the public interest 'connotes those rights or advantages in things that are public *juris* and therefore considered as vested in the public, the entire State or community and not restricted to the dominion of a particular private person'.[67] Justice Forster conceived of such public interest as consisting of 'a clean environment, the unfettered right to enjoy the beaches and the greenery' and concluded that various offences including 'dumping of toxic matter' were 'clearly offences committed against the public interest'.[68] This reasoning applies to the activities of mining companies that have caused environmental damage in Ghana.

The Constitution of Kenya provides for the substantive and procedural right to a clean and healthy environment and access to environmental justice by giving the right to all persons to enforce this right.[69] According to Article 42 of the Constitution '[e]very person has the right to a clean and healthy environment, which includes the right to have the environment protected for the benefit of

[67] *Dey v The Republic* [1997–1998] 2 GLR 919 at 927.

[68] ibid.

[69] Brian YK Sang, 'Tending Towards Greater Eco-Protection in Kenya: Public Interest Environmental Litigation and Its Prospects Within the New Constitutional Order' (2013) 57(1) Journal of African Law 29.

present and future generations through legislative and other measures'. Article 69 of this Constitution of Kenya imposes a duty on Kenya to 'ensure sustainable exploitation, utilisation, management and conservation of the environment and natural resources, and ensure the equitable sharing of the accruing benefits', to 'protect genetic resources and biological diversity'; to 'eliminate processes and activities that are likely to endanger the environment', and to 'utilise the environment and natural resources for the benefit of the people of Kenya'. The state has authority by virtue of Article 66(1) of the Constitution to 'regulate the use of any land, or any interest in or right over any land, in the interest of defence, public safety, public order, public morality, public health, or land use planning'.

In *Waweru v Republic of Kenya*,[70] the applicants and other interested parties were charged with discharging raw sewage into a public water source and the environment (which was nuisance) and failure to comply with statutory notice from the public health authority contrary to the Public Health Act (Chapter 242, Laws of Kenya). The owners of plots of land connected underground pipes to their septic tanks which served as overflow outlets leading to the discharge of liquid waste waters into the open environment and flowing downstream into the Kiserian river.[71] The applicant challenged the charges against them alleging fundamental rights and freedoms had been violated contrary to the Constitution of Kenya then in force. The High Court found that due process had not been followed in laying the charges and quashed the charges against the twenty-three applicants.[72] The Court then made various rulings on the environmental issues which formed the basis for the charges.

According to the High Court of Kenya, 'sustainable development has a cost element which must be met by the developers' of the lands.[73] The Court said time limitations on bringing the charges did not apply in this case 'because nuisance can by its very nature have a silent continuing effect—say with effluent percolating slowly into the water table and polluting the same without being detected and also because it has repetitive nature'.[74] Moreover, 'as regards environmental offences the task of restoration could take the same period which the degradation took or more'.[75] '

The Court stated that in resolving this matter, it 'cannot escape from touching on the law of sustainable development,' in light of the constitutional provision on the right to life and the statutory requirement in the Environment Management and Coordination Act 1999 (EMCA), that 'courts take into account certain universal

[70] *Peter K Waweru v Republic of Kenya*, High Court of Kenya at Nairobi, Miscellaneous Civil Application 118 of 2004 2 March 2006.
[71] ibid [8].
[72] ibid [12]–[17].
[73] ibid [19].
[74] ibid [20].
[75] ibid [21].

principles' in determining environmental cases.[76] The EMCA provided in section 3(1) that every person in Kenya was entitled 'to a clean and healthy environment and has the duty to safeguard and enhance the environment'. The EMCA section 3(3) also provides for the standing and right of access to the High Court to seek redress with regards to environmental matters. It further provides in section 3(5) that in exercising its jurisdiction, the High Court shall be guided by principles of sustainable development including on public participation in the development of policies, plans, and processes for the management of the environment; international cooperation in the management of environmental resources; intergenerational equity; the polluter pays principle; and the precautionary principle.

In the case at instance, the Court found sustainable development, precautionary principle, polluter pays, and public trust as directly relevant for the resolution of the dispute.[77] The Court stated that the 'essence of the public trust is that the state, as trustee, is under a fiduciary duty to deal with the trust property, being the common natural resources, in a manner that is in the interests of the general public'.[78] The right to life under section 71 of the Constitution of Kenya all

> is not just a matter of keeping body and soul together because in this modern age that right could be threatened by many things including the environment. The right to a clean environment is primary to all creatures including man, it is inherent from the act of creation, the recent restatement in the statutes and the Constitutions of the world.[79]

The Court further stated that '[w]hereas the literal meaning of life under section 71 means absence of physical elimination, the dictionary covers the activity of living. That activity takes place in some environment and therefore the denial of wholesome environment is a deprivation of life.'[80] Thus, 'a development that threatens life is not sustainable and ought to be halted. In environmental law, life must have this expanded meaning as a matter of necessity'.[81] The Court made reference to various international instruments and declarations including the African Charter on Human and Peoples' Rights[82] and stated that '[i]t is quite evident from perusing the most important international instruments on the environment that the word life and the environment are inseparable and the word life means much more than keeping body and soul together'.[83] The government of Kenya, according to the Court, has obligation under the law 'to approve sustainable development and

[76] ibid [26].
[77] ibid [25]–[30].
[78] ibid [31].
[79] ibid [26].
[80] ibid [35].
[81] ibid [37].
[82] ibid [38]–[40].
[83] ibid [40].

nothing more, which is development that meets the needs of the present generation without compromising the ability of future generations to meet their needs'.[84]

The Constitution of Nigeria provides in section 20 that the state 'shall protect and improve the environment and safeguard the water, air and land, forest and wild life'. In fact, section 17(2)(d) of this Constitution states that in furtherance of a social order founded on the ideals of freedom, justice, and equality, the 'exploitation of human or natural resources in any form whatsoever for reasons, other than the good of the community, shall be prevented'. The provisions empower the Nigerian government to regulate activities of businesses engaged in natural resources extraction to operate in a manner that brings public good. These constitutional[85]

> provisions imply that the government of Nigeria should always take necessary steps and precautions to protect the rights of the people in all policies formulated to exploit the natural and human resources of the State. Naturally, such steps should inter-alia include taking positive measures against environmental hazards capable of destroying life and property as well as the provision of relief materials and compensation for victims of environmental degradation due to exploitation of natural resources by the government.

Section 33(1) of the Constitution of Nigeria, which is justiciable, provides that '[e]very person has a right to life, and no one shall be deprived intentionally of his life, save in execution of the sentence of a court in respect of a criminal offence of which he has been found guilty in Nigeria'. Although this 'provision has no direct relationship with environmental protection, it can be argued that allowing a person to live in an unprotected or unhealthy environment could amount to a deprivation of the person's right to life since a poor and unhealthy environment could put a person's life in danger'.[86]

The Constitution of South Africa is also explicit on environmental rights: It provides:

> [section] 24. Everyone has the right—(a) to an environment that is not harmful to their health or wellbeing; and (b) to have the environment protected, for the benefit of present and future generations, through reasonable legislative and other measures that—(i) prevent pollution and ecological degradation; (ii) promote conservation; and (iii) secure ecologically sustainable development and use of natural resources while promoting justifiable economic and social development.

[84] ibid [43]

[85] Olu Awolowo, 'Environmental Rights and Sustainable Development in Nigeria' (2017) 10(6) OIDA International Journal of Sustainable Development 17, 20. Awolowo argues that sections 17 and 20 of the Constitution are not justiciable, citing the case of *Morebishe v Lagos State House of Assembly* (2000) 3 WRN 134; and *Okogie v A.G. of Lagos State* (1980) FNR 445/(1981) 1 NCLR 218.

[86] Awolowo, 'Environmental Rights and Sustainable Development in Nigeria' (n 85) 20.

In *HTF Developers (Pty) Ltd v The Minister of Environmental Affairs and Tourism*, the Supreme Court of Appeal of South Africa stated that the 'primary purpose of section 31A' of the Environment Conservation Act 73 of 1989[87]

> is to promote the right to an environment that is not harmful to the wellbeing and health of the people. It also imposes an obligation on the respondents [Minister of Environmental Affairs and Tourism] to maintain a clean and healthy environment. In cases of damage they are required to direct the person responsible for the damage to remedy it as soon as possible. In the event of such person failing to do so, the respondents must take remedial steps themselves and recover costs incurred in the process from that person. However, the respondents cannot undertake remedial steps without first calling upon the offending party to do so because s 31A(3) requires the offending party's failure before they themselves could act.

According to the Supreme Court of Appeal, the 'nature and extent of the powers' in section 31A of the ECA[88]

> are extraordinary. They were clearly intended to deal with extra-ordinary situations. The lawmaker must have been aware that some situations may call for drastic urgent action in order to achieve the objective of the Act which is the effective protection of the environment. In the current constitutional dispensation the right to a clean environment must enjoy recognition equal to that which is accorded to other rights.

The same Court held in *Director: Mineral Development, Gauteng Region v Save the Vaal Environment* that the Constitution of South Africa,[89]

> by including environmental rights as fundamental, justiciable human rights, by necessary implication requires that environmental considerations be accorded appropriate recognition and respect in the administrative process in our country. Together with the change in the ideological climate must also come a change in our legal and administrative approach to environmental concerns.

[87] *HTF Developers (Pty) Ltd v The Minister of Environmental Affairs and Tourism* [2007] SCA 37 RSA [21].

[88] ibid [25].

[89] *Director: Mineral Development, Gauteng Region and Another v Save the Vaal Environment and Others* 1999 (2) SA 709 (SCA) at 719C-D. See also *Fuel Retailers Association of Southern Africa v Director-General Environmental Management, Department of Agriculture, Conservation and Environment, Mpumalanga Province* [2007] ZACC 13.

The SAHRC has ably interpreted this provision, connecting to human rights and environmental rights in the mining industry:[90]

> This constitutional right recognises the close links between sustainable development and 'justifiable' social and economic development ... [P]overty is linked to unsustainable environmental protection and ... the State's environmental responsibility is linked to the responsibility to respect, protect and fulfil socio-economic rights. Furthermore, environmental degradation, and the failure to conserve biodiversity, prejudice the realisation of numerous other human rights, particularly the right to equality, but also the rights of access to sufficient food and water, health, housing, land and ultimately, the right to live with dignity. Thus, a key objective of environmental legislation is the protection of the basic needs of vulnerable groups, as it is these groups that unfairly bear the negative impacts of mining.

Therefore, the protection of environmental rights has been constitutionalised in Africa. This shows the fundamental importance African countries attach to environmental rights. These environmental rights are contained not just in domestic constitutions alone[91] but also derive from IETs.

4.3.2 International Environmental Treaty Rights

Human rights have emerged as an important area of discourse in international environmental law in Africa. Fundamental human rights, such as the right to life, health, food, water, and indeed property, cannot be achieved without adequate environmental conditions of clean water, air, and land.[92] In this regard, nation states within and outside Africa have agreed to various international agreements and have made declarations aimed at protecting the environment. The environment is essential to human 'well-being and to the enjoyment of basic human rights—even the right to life itself'.[93] There is a fundamental right of human beings 'to freedom, equality and adequate conditions of life, in an environment of a quality that permits a life of dignity and well-being'.[94] For this reason, humankind bears 'a solemn

[90] SAHRC, *Socio-economic Challenges of Mining* (n 33). See also Anél du Plessis, 'South Africa's Constitutional Environmental Right (Generously) Interpreted: What is in it for Poverty' (2011) 27(2), South African Journal on Human Rights 279.

[91] On constitutional environmental rights see: Tim Hayward, *Constitutional Environmental Rights* (OUP 2004); James R May and Erin Daly, 'Global Constitutional Environmental Rights' in Alam and others (eds), *Routledge Handbook of International Environmental Law* (n 15) 603; Carl Bruch, *Environmental Law: Giving Force to Fundamental Principles in Africa* (Environmental Law Institute 2000); and Loretta Feris, 'Constitutional Environmental Rights: An Under-Utilised Resource' (2008) 24(1) South African Journal on Human Rights 29.

[92] May and Kelly, 'Environment and International Society' (n 15) 21; and Turner, *A Global Environmental Right* (n 64) 18–22.

[93] United Nations Environmental Programme, *Declaration of the United Nations Conference on the Human Environment* (United Nations 16 June 1972) <https://legal.un.org/avl/pdf/ha/dunche/dunche_e.pdf accessed (8 February 2022) preamble [1].

[94] ibid Principle 1.

responsibility to protect and improve the environment for present and future generations'.[95]

African countries are parties to a large number of ITEs and IHRTs which strengthen constitutional environmental rights. One of such treaties is the African Charter on Human and Peoples' Rights,[96] which states in Article 24 that '[a]ll peoples shall have the right to a general satisfactory environment favourable to their development'.

In *Social and Economic Rights Action Centre v Nigeria*,[97] the African Commission on Human and Peoples' Rights (African Commission) interpreted Article 24 of the African Charter. In this case, the complainants alleged that the government of Nigeria had been directly involved in oil production through a state oil company, which was the majority shareholder in a consortium with Shell Petroleum Development Corporation. The complainants argued that the oil operations caused environmental degradation and health problems resulting from the contamination of the environment among the people of Ogoni. The oil consortium, the complainants argued, exploited oil reserves in Ogoniland with no regard for the health and environment of the local communities. Toxic wastes were discharged into the environment and local waterways in violation of ITEs and applicable international environmental standards. The consortium did not maintain its facilities which led to spills in the proximity of villages. The resulting contamination of water, soil, and air had health impacts, including skin infections, gastrointestinal and respiratory ailments, increased risk of cancers, and neurological and reproductive problems. The complainants alleged that the Nigerian government violated their right to health and a healthy environment by failing to fulfil the minimum duties under Articles 16 and 24 of the African Charter.[98]

The African Commission held that the government of Nigeria did not comply with Articles 16 and 24 of the Charter because it failed to undertake appropriate monitoring and to provide both information to communities exposed to hazardous activities and opportunities for them to be heard and participate in decisions affecting them.[99] Performing these duties would have protected the rights of the victims of the violations.[100] The African Commission, per Commissioner Emmanuel Dankwa , held that[101]

> [t]he right to a general satisfactory environment, as guaranteed under Article 24 of the African Charter … imposes clear obligations upon a government. It

[95] ibid.

[96] African Charter on Human and Peoples' Rights adopted 27 June 1981, entry into force 21 1986.

[97] *Social and Economic Rights Action Centre v Nigeria*, African Commission on Human and Peoples' Rights, Comm. No 155/96 (2001).

[98] ibid [1]–[2] and [50].

[99] ibid [53].

[100] ibid [54].

[101] ibid [51]–[53] and [68].

> requires the State to take reasonable and other measures to prevent pollution and ecological degradation, to promote conservation, and to secure an ecologically sustainable development and use of natural resources. Article 12 of the International Covenant on Economic, Social and Cultural Rights … requires governments to take necessary steps for the improvement of all aspects of environmental and industrial hygiene. The right to enjoy the best attainable state of physical and mental health enunciated in Article 16(1) of the African Charter and the right to a general satisfactory environment favourable to development … obligate governments to desist from directly threatening the health and environment of their citizens.
>
> Government compliance with the spirit of Articles 16 and 24 of the African Charter must also include ordering or at least permitting independent scientific monitoring of threatened environments, requiring and publicising environmental and social impact studies prior to any major industrial development, undertaking appropriate monitoring and providing information to those communities exposed to hazardous materials and activities and providing meaningful opportunities for individuals to be heard and to participate in the development decisions affecting their communities.
>
> International law and human rights must be responsive to African circumstances. Clearly, collective rights, environmental rights, and economic and social rights are essential elements of human rights in Africa.

The complainants also alleged violations of Article 21 of the African Charter, which guarantees all Africans the right to dispose freely of their wealth and natural resources, and imposes a corresponding duty on African states to 'eliminate all forms of foreign exploitation particularly that practised by international monopolies so as to enable their peoples to fully benefit from the advantages derived from their national resources'. The complainants alleged that the government of Nigeria failed to monitor or regulate the operations of the oil companies, which paved the way for the oil consortiums to exploit oil reserves in Ogoniland, and it did not involve the Ogoni communities in the decisions that affected the development of Ogoniland.[102] The Commission held that despite its obligation to protect persons against interferences in the enjoyment of their rights, the Nigerian government facilitated the destruction of the Ogoniland by giving 'the green light to private actors, and the oil companies in particular, to devastatingly affect the well-being of the Ogonis'.[103] Such conduct violated Article 21 of the African Charter. Dankwa reasoned that[104]

[102] ibid [55].
[103] ibid [58].
[104] ibid [57].

> [g]overnments have a duty to protect their citizens, not only through appropriate legislation and effective enforcement but also by protecting them from damaging acts that may be perpetrated by private parties. This duty calls for positive action on part of governments in fulfilling their obligation under human rights instruments. The practice before other tribunals also enhances this requirement as is evidenced in the case *Velàsquez Rodríguez v. Honduras.* In this landmark judgment, the Inter-American Court of Human Rights held that when a State allows private persons or groups to act freely and with impunity to the detriment of the rights recognised, it would be in clear violation of its obligations to protect the human rights of its citizens. Similarly, this obligation of the State is further emphasised in the practice of the European Court of Human Rights, in *X and Y v. Netherlands.* In that case, the Court pronounced that there was an obligation on authorities to take steps to make sure that the enjoyment of the rights is not interfered with by any other private person.

Other international instruments create similar rights and obligations to the African Charter. The states parties to the International Covenant on Economic, Social and Cultural Rights[105] (ICESCR), including Cameroon, Egypt, Ghana, Kenya, Nigeria, and South Africa, 'recognize the right of everyone to the enjoyment of the highest attainable standard of physical and mental health'.[106] To achieve the full realisation of this right, the parties shall take steps necessary for the 'improvement of all aspects of environmental and industrial hygiene'.[107] The objectives of the African Convention on Conservation of Nature and Natural Resources are 'to enhance environmental protection; to foster the conservation and sustainable use of natural resources; and to harmonize and coordinate policies in these fields with a view to achieving ecologically rational, economically sound and socially acceptable development policies and programmes'.[108] Article III recognises the right of Africans to an environment favourable to their development and a corresponding duty of states to protect the environment. Parties have a 'fundamental obligation' under Article IV of the Convention which requires that they

> shall adopt and implement all measures necessary to achieve the objectives of this Convention, in particular through preventive measures and the application of the precautionary principle, and with due regard to ethical and traditional values as well as scientific knowledge in the interest of present and future generations.

[105] *International Covenant on Economic, Social and Cultural Rights*, 16 December 1966, 993 UNTS 3, entered into force 3 January 1976

[106] Constitution of the Republic of Ghana 1992, art 12(1).

[107] ibid art 12(2)(b).

[108] African Convention on the Conservation of Nature and Natural Resources, 15 September 1968, CAB/LEG/24.1, 1001 UNTS 3, entered into force 16 June 1969), art II.

The UN resolution on Permanent Sovereignty over Natural Resources states that foreign investment agreements freely entered into by states 'shall be observed in good faith' but it equally makes clear that states and international organisations 'shall strictly and conscientiously respect the sovereignty of peoples and nations over their natural wealth and resources'.[109] *Agenda 2063: The Africa We Want* manifests Africa's aspiration for 'a healthy, valued and protected' natural endowments, environment and ecosystem by the year 2063.[110] This aspiration is reflected in the *2030 Agenda for Sustainable Development* by which Member States of the United Nations 'are determined to address decisively the threat posed by climate change and environmental degradation' and to 'decouple economic growth from environmental degradation'.[111]

These ITEs, IHRTs, and instruments have been *constitutionalised* in Africa in the sense that various African constitutions require African states to observe such international treaties they have entered into so that the obligation to observe is not just a matter of international law, it is also a constitutional obligation. In *Abacha v Fawehinmi*, heard in the Supreme Court of Nigeria, Justice Michael Ekundayo Ogundare expressly admitted the constitutionalisation of the African Charter thus:[112]

> [the] treaty is enacted into law by the National Assembly, as was the case with the African Charter which is incorporated into ... municipal (i.e. domestic) law by the African Charter on Human and Peoples' Rights (Ratification and Enforcement) Act Cap. 10 Laws of the Federation of Nigeria 1990 (... Cap. 10), it becomes binding and our Courts must give effect to it like all other laws falling within the Judicial power of the Courts. By Cap. 10 the African Charter is now part of the laws of Nigeria and like all other laws the Courts must uphold it. The Charter gives to citizens of member states ... rights and obligations, which rights and obligations are to be enforced by our Courts, if they must have any meaning. *It is interesting to note that the rights and obligations contained in the Charter are not new to Nigeria as most of these rights and obligations are already enshrined in our Constitution.*

The Constitution of Cameroon requires respect for international treaties and agreements[113] and goes so far as to say that '[d]uly approved or ratified treaties

[109] Permanent Sovereignty over Natural Resources, GA Res 1803 (XVII), 17 UN GAOR Supp (No17) 15 UN Doc A/5217 (1962) [8].

[110] African Union, *Agenda 2063: The Africa We Want* (African Union Commission, September 2015) at 3.

[111] *Transforming Our World: The 2030 Agenda for Sustainable Development*, Resolution adopted by the General Assembly on 25 September 2015 [31] and Goal 8.4

[112] *General Sanni Abacha v Chief Gani Fawehinmi* (SC 45/1997) [2000] NGSC 17 (28 April 2000) (SC 45/1997) [1960] NGSC 1 (27 April 2000) (emphasis added) 6 <https://nigerialii.org/ng/judgment/supreme-court/2000/17>.

[113] Constitution of the Republic of Cameroon 1972 (with Amendments through 2008), art 5(2).

and international agreements shall, following their publication, override national laws, provided the other party implements the said treaty or agreement'.[114] The preamble to the Constitution of Egypt affirms this Constitution's consistency with the Universal Declaration of Human Rights. Article 93 also manifests Egypt's constitutional commitment 'to the agreements, covenants, and international conventions of human rights that were ratified by Egypt'. Articles 40(c) and 73 of the Constitution of Ghana require the government of Ghana to promote respect for international law and treaty obligations. Under Article 2(6), of the Constitution of Kenya, ratified treaties form part of the laws of Kenya. Section 19(d) of the Constitution of Nigeria requires respect for international law and treaty obligations. By Section 231(2) of the Constitution of South Africa, international agreements approved by resolution in both the National Assembly and the National Council of Provinces bind South Africa. Moreover, the principles of free consent, good faith, and the *pacta sunt servanda* rule in general international law bind every treaty in force upon the parties to it.[115]

A breach of a treaty obligation is an internationally wrongful act and gives rise to the international responsibility of the state concerned.[116] States that are responsible for the fulfilment of international obligations concerning the conservation and utilisation of natural resources and protection of the environment generally are therefore subject to liability in accordance with general international law.[117] International environmental treaty obligations require states to prevent particular environmental harm and refrain from carrying out or permitting activities that could lead to environmental damage.[118]

In *Pulp Mills on the River Uruguay (Argentina* v *Uruguay)*,[119] the ICJ elaborated on states' duty to protect the environment. Argentina brought an action against Uruguay under the Statute of the River Uruguay,[120] claiming that by allowing the discharge of nutrients into a river that suffered from reverse flow and stagnation, Uruguay violated the obligation to prevent pollution and failed to comply with applicable IETs.

The ICJ held that a duty to preserve the aquatic environment and prevent pollution by prescribing appropriate rules and measures under an IET entails the adoption of appropriate rules and measures, vigilance in their enforcement, and the

[114] ibid art 45.

[115] Vienna Convention on the Law of Treaties, 23 May 1969, 1155 UNTS 331, entered into force 27 January 1980 (VCLT), preamble at para 4 and art 26.

[116] International Law Commission (ILC), Draft Articles on Responsibility of States for Internationally Wrongful Acts, adopted by the ILC at its fifty-third session, November 2001, Supplement No 10 (A/56/10), arts 1 and 2.

[117] International Law Commission, *Draft Principles of Conduct for the Guidance of States in the Conservation and Harmonious Exploitation of Natural Resources Shared by Two Or More States* (Nairobi, 9 May 1978).

[118] Sands et al, *Principles of International Environmental Law* (n 11) 704.

[119] *Pulp Mills on the River Uruguay (Argentina v Uruguay)* ICJ Reports 2010, 14.

[120] Statute of the River Uruguay, entered into between Argentina and Uruguay on 26 February 1975.

exercise of administrative control, including monitoring activities undertaken by public and private operators. A failure to do so diligently would engage the state party's responsibilities under an IET if the failure leads to adverse effects on citizens within or outside the state.[121] In other words, international environmental treaty obligations require the adoption of rules and measures that give effect to the treaty objective to protect the environment.

The right to environmental safety which derives from national constitutions and IETs is central to the realisation of the right to health and livelihood. The provisions in these constitutions for environmental rights reflect the public interest (as against limited private interests) orientation of these constitutions and similarly placed ones in Africa. Therefore, it is a *constitutional-general international law imperative* and must be treated as taking precedence over an investment treaty obligation which seeks to prevent or limit the adoption of measures required for the realisation of this environmental right.

4.4 Human Rights and Corresponding Duties of African States

4.4.1 Constitutional and International Human Rights in Africa

The idea of human rights and corresponding duties is as old as or even pre-dates the concept of the state itself.[122] However, it was only in seventeenth and the eighteenth centuries that serious efforts aimed at having written guarantees of human freedom were made.[123] The concept of 'human rights' came into everyday parlance in its international form and content only after the Second World War and the founding of the United Nations.[124] Today there is widespread acceptance of the concept of human rights as reflected in national and international legal norms, although this wide acceptance does not mean that there is complete agreement on the nature and scope of such rights.[125]

Human rights are rights 'held by individuals simply because they are part of the human species. They are rights shared equally by everyone regardless of sex, race,

[121] ibid [197].

[122] John Lock, *Two Treaties of Civil Government* (JM Dent & Sons Ltd 1962); Michelle R Ishay, *The History of Human Rights: From Ancient Times to the Global Era* (University of California Press 2004) (hereafter, Ishay, *History of Human Rights*); and Jack Mahoney, *The Challenge of Human Rights: Origin, Development, and Significance* (Blackwell Publishing 2007).

[123] Abdulrahim P Vijapur, 'The Concept of Human Rights: National and International Perspectives' (2009) 2(IV) International Politics 1, 11

[124] Burns Weston, 'Human Rights' in *New Encyclopaedia Britannica* Vol 20 (15th edn, Encyclopaedia Britannica, 1992) reproduced in Henry J Steiner, Philip Alston, and Ryan Goodman, *International Human Rights in Context: Law, Politics and Morals* (3rd edn, OUP 2008) 476.

[125] ibid 478; Peter Cane and Joanne Conaghan (eds), *The New Oxford Companion to Law* (OUP 2008) 553.

nationality, and economic background.'[126] Human rights, as Judge Tanaka of the ICJ stated in the *South West Africa Case*,[127] are 'derived from the concept of man as a *person* and his relationship with society which cannot be separated from universal human nature ... Human rights have always existed with the human being. They existed independently of, and before, the State.'[128] However, human rights are made concrete by legal enactments and their enjoyment and realisation depend on their protection by the state. In that sense, human rights are creatures of the state as much as they can be described as inherent in human being nature. In this regard, human rights are legal rights.[129] The concern of this section is human rights as derived from or as guaranteed by constitutions and IHRTs in Africa.

Various constitutions in Africa provide for the protection of what they describe as fundamental (human) rights. The preamble to the Constitution of Cameroon affirms the people of Cameroon's 'attachment to fundamental freedoms enshrined in the Universal Declaration of Human Rights, the Charter of the United Nations, the African Charter on Human and Peoples' Rights and all duly ratified International Conventions'. Article 55(2) of the Constitution of Cameroon provides that the councils of regional and local authorities have a duty 'to promote the economic, social, health, educational, cultural and sports development'. The political system in Egypt shall be based on respect for human rights and freedoms as set out in the Constitution of Egypt and in international conventions of human rights.[130] The human rights protected under the Constitution of Egypt include workers' rights,[131] the right 'to health and to comprehensive health care with quality criteria',[132] and the 'right to live in a healthy, sound and balanced environment'.[133]

In Ghana, human rights have always been guaranteed, recognised, and protected under customary law and the various constitutions from 1957 to the current Constitution of Ghana.[134] Chapter Five of the Constitution is specifically devoted to the protection of *fundamental human rights and freedoms*. These rights include the right to life; the right to personal liberty; the right to human dignity, including freedom from any condition that detracts or is likely to detract from a person's dignity and worth as a human being; and freedom from slavery or forced labour.[135]

[126] Ishay, *History of Human Rights* (n 122) at 3.

[127] *South West Africa* case *(Ethiopia v South Africa; Liberia v South Africa)* Second Phase, Judgment [1966] ICJ Rep 6 Dissenting Opinion of Judge Tanaka 250.

[128] ibid 297.

[129] Melissa Thorme, 'Establishing Environment as a Human Right' (1990–1991) 19 Denver Journal of International Law and Policy 301, 302.

[130] Constitution of the Arab Republic of Egypt 2014 arts 5 and 93.

[131] ibid art 13.

[132] ibid art 18.

[133] ibid art 46.

[134] Nana KA Busia, Jr 'Ghana: Competing Visions of Liberal Democracy and Socialism' in Abdullahi Ahmed An-Na'im (ed), *Human Rights under African Constitutions: Realizing the Promise for Ourselves* (University of Pennsylvania Press 2003) 52, 53–64.

[135] Constitution of Ghana (n 106) arts 13–16.

The Constitution of Ghana also recognises and guarantees equality before the law and freedom from discrimination, the right to privacy,[136] the right to property, the right to information, social and educational rights, cultural rights, and the right of the sick to seek medical treatment.[137] There is also the 'right to work under satisfactory, safe and healthy condition',[138] the right to equal pay for equal work,[139] and the right to form and join a trade union.[140] Every person in Ghana is entitled to these fundamental human rights and freedoms 'subject to respect for the rights and freedoms of others and for the public interest'.[141]

The scope of human rights and corresponding obligations in Ghana are not limited to those specifically provided for in the Constitution of Ghana. The Constitution provides in Article 33(5) that the fundamental human rights and freedoms and corresponding duties specifically stated do not exclude others not specifically stated therein but which 'are considered to be inherent in a democracy and intended to secure the freedom and dignity of man'. By this provision and Article 11(2) of the Constitution, customary international law principles on human rights will be applicable in Ghana to the extent that they are consistent with the Constitution.[142]

In *New Patriotic Party v Inspector General of Police*,[143] the Supreme Court of Ghana held that fundamental human rights are inalienable and can neither be derogated from nor taken away by anyone or any authority whatsoever. The Supreme Court held that the courts have a constitutional obligation to see to it that human rights are respected and enforced.[144] According to the Supreme Court, 'fundamental human and civil rights ... have become the bulwark of the Constitution'.[145] Therefore, they 'cannot be derogated'[146] from and 'are to be enjoyed freely without any impediments or preconditions',[147] except with regard to 'the rights of others and for the public interest'.[148] Thus, 'any law which seeks to abridge these freedoms and rights must be struck down as unconstitutional'.[149] Kofi Quashigah argues that '[r]espect for human rights is one of the fundamental

[136] Dominic N Dagbanja, 'Privacy in Context: The Right to Privacy, and Freedom and Independence of the Media under the Constitution of Ghana' (2014) 22(1) African Journal of International and Comparative Law 40.
[137] Constitution of Ghana (n 106) arts 13–18, 21(1)(f), 25–26, and 30.
[138] ibid art 24(1).
[139] ibid art 24(1).
[140] ibid art 24(3).
[141] ibid art 12(1).
[142] See *The Republic of Ghana v High Court, Ex Parte the Attorney-General; NML Capital & the Republic of Argentina*, Case No J5/10/2013, Judgment of 20 June 2013, 2.
[143] *New Patriotic Party v Inspect General of Police* [1993–94] 2 GLR 457.
[144] ibid 482.
[145] ibid 491.
[146] ibid 483.
[147] ibid.
[148] ibid.
[149] ibid 502 (emphasis added).

principles on which the Constitution is built, as for instance is clearly announced in the preamble to the Constitution and in the Directive Principles of State Policy which prescribe the general philosophical principles according to which governance should be ordered'.[150]

The position in Ghana on human rights is like that in Kenya, Nigeria, and South Africa. In making the Constitution of Kenya, Kenyans aspired 'for a government based on the essential values of human rights, equality, freedom, democracy, social justice and the rule of law'.[151] Under Article 10(2)(b) of this Constitution, the 'national values and principles of governance include human dignity, equity, social justice, inclusiveness, equality, human rights, non-discrimination and protection of the marginalised'. There is the right to own property subject to the possibility of compulsory acquisition by law and the payment of compensation for such acquisition.[152]

The right to life, equality, and freedom from discrimination are guaranteed.[153] The Constitution of Kenya guarantees the right to the highest attainable standard of health and healthcare services and the right to clean and safe water in adequate quantities.[154] Article 46 provides for the right to (i) goods or services of reasonable quality and associated information; (ii) the protection of health, safety, and economic interests in relation to goods or services supplied or provided; and (iii) compensation for loss or injury arising from defects in goods or services. The legal protection for these rights empowers Kenya to enact laws and to implement them to bring about their realisation. Thus in terms of the corresponding obligation of Kenya to bring about the realisation of these fundamental human rights, Article 21(1) states that '[i]t is a fundamental duty of the State and every State organ to observe, respect, protect, promote and fulfil the rights and fundamental freedoms in the Bill of Rights.' The state 'shall enact and implement legislation to fulfil its international obligations in respect of human rights and fundamental freedoms'.[155] It is further provided that '[t]he purpose of recognising and protecting human rights and fundamental freedoms is to preserve the dignity of individuals and communities and to promote social justice and the realisation of the potential of all human beings'.[156] Based on these constitutional rights and corresponding obligations, Kenya can regulate the activities of mining companies, for example, to address human rights abuses arises from their operations.

The Constitution of Nigeria provides for similar *fundamental rights* in Chapter IV, Articles 33–46 as under the constitutions of Ghana and Kenya. These rights

[150] Kofi Quashigah, 'Trends in the Promotion and Protection of Human Rights in Ghana' in Kwame Boafo-Arthur (ed), *Ghana: One Decade of the Liberal State* (CORDESIA Books 2007) 21.
[151] Constitution of the Republic of Kenya 2010, preamble.
[152] ibid art 40.
[153] ibid arts 26–27.
[154] ibid art 43(1)(a) and (d).
[155] ibid 21(4).
[156] ibid art 19(2).

include the right to own property and compensation for compulsory acquisition by law of the said property.[157] The state shall 'control the national economy in such manner as to secure the maximum welfare, freedom and happiness of every citizen'.[158] The state also has an obligation to 'direct its policy towards ensuring that the economic system is not operated in such a manner as to permit the concentration of wealth or the means of production and exchange in the hands of few individuals or of a group'.[159] These provisions give primacy to the public interest of citizens and empower the state to regulate the activities of businesses, whether local or foreign, to advance the common good of Nigerians.

Human dignity, the achievement of equality, and advancement of fundamental human rights are founding values of the Constitution of South Africa.[160] Fundamental human rights are specifically addressed in Sections 7–39 of the Constitution and include the right to choose and practise a trade subject to regulation,[161] a healthy environment,[162] compensation for compulsory acquisition of property, healthcare services, and sufficient food and water.[163] Legislative and other measures must be taken to achieve the progressive realisation of the right of access to healthcare services, food, and water.[164]

Constitutional fundamental rights are primarily about citizens, not private businesses whose activities do not come with any tangible public benefits. These states may, therefore, treat non-citizens differently in terms of the exercise and enjoyment any of these rights. In fact, in some cases these constitutions explicitly place limitations on the activities of non-citizens and require them to be subject to special regulation. The Constitution of Ghana does not impose a similar duty on the state when it comes to promoting and protecting foreign investment as it does in the case of fundamental human rights. On the contrary, the Constitution requires in Articles 36(4) and 17(4)(c) that foreign investment shall be promoted and protected subject to existing domestic laws governing investment protection and they empower the state to impose restrictions on the economic activities of non-citizens. There is specific limitation on landholding by non-citizens under the Constitution of Kenya. Thus a 'person who is not a citizen may hold land on the basis of leasehold tenure only, and any such lease, however granted, shall not exceed ninety-nine years'.[165] For this purpose, a body corporate is taken to be a citizen of Kenya only if it is wholly owned by a citizen or citizens.[166] Property held

[157] Constitution of the Federal Republic of Nigeria 1999, ss 43 and 44.
[158] ibid s 16(1)(b).
[159] ibid 16(2)(c).
[160] Constitution of the Republic of South Africa 1996, ss 1(a) and 7.
[161] ibid s 22.
[162] ibid s 24.
[163] ibid s 27(1).
[164] ibid s 27(2).
[165] Constitution of Kenya (n 151) art 65(1).
[166] ibid art 65(3)(a).

in trust for such a body corporate is treated as 'being held by a citizen only if all of the beneficial interest of the trust is held by persons who are citizens'.[167] These are compelling legal reasons for the constitutional duty to promote and protect human rights to override or prevail over or void the investment treaty duty to promote and protect foreign investment in the event of conflict between the two.

These African countries are also parties to a number of IHRTs which further strengthen the position of citizens with regards to human rights protection. These conventions and international instruments include the Universal Declaration of Human Rights,[168] the International Covenant on Economic Social and Cultural Rights,[169] the International Covenant on Civil and Political Rights[170] and its two Optional Protocols,[171] and the African Charter on Human and People's Rights.[172] International human rights law has become an important source of law for domestic jurisprudence in Africa.[173] Therefore, there are constitutional and general international law duties on each of these African states to put in place measures that will ensure the realisation of these various human rights including policy and legislation on corporate conduct and corporate social responsibility.[174]

4.4.2 Investment Treaties and Human Rights Measures in Africa

As established in Subsection 4.4.1, it is settled as a matter of municipal law and general international law that '[s]tates have the primary responsibility to promote, secure the fulfilment of, respect, ensure respect of and protect human rights'.[175]

[167] ibid art 65(3)(b).

[168] Adopted by General Assembly Resolution 217 A (III) of 10 December 1948.

[169] Universal Declaration of Human Rights, adopted 16 December 1966, entered into force 3 January 1976.

[170] International Covenant on Economic Social and Cultural Rights, the International Covenant on Civil and Political Rights, adopted 16 December 1966, entered into force 23 March 1976. Ghana ratified this Covenant and Covenant on Economic Social and Cultural Rights on 7 September 2009. Ministry of Justice, *Republic of Ghana Treaty Manual* (Republic of Ghana 2009)<http://ir.parliament.gh/bitstream/handle/123456789/572/GhanaTreatyManual2009.pdf?sequence=1&isAllowed=y> accessed 8 February 2022, 15–16.

[171] First Optional Protocol to the International Covenant on Civil and Political Rights adopted by UN General Assembly on 16 December 1966 and entry into force 23 March 1976. This protocol established an individual complaint mechanism for the International Covenant on Civil and Political Rights. Ghana ratified this protocol on 7 September 2000. *Republic of Ghana Treaty Manual* (n 169) 16.

[172] African Charter on Human and Peoples' Rights, adopted 27 June 1981, entry into force 21 October 1986.

[173] Magnus Killander (ed), *International Law and Domestic Human Rights Litigation in Africa* (Pretoria University Law Press 2010); and Magnus Killander, 'The Role of International Law in Human Rights Litigation in Africa' in Emmanuel Quansah and William Binchy (eds), *The Judicial Protection of Human Rights in Africa* (Clarus Press 2009) 7.

[174] Dominic Dagbanja, 'Human Rights, Mineral Rights and Corporate Social Responsibility in Ghana: Legal and Policy Analyses' (2012) 13 Ghana Mining Journal 6, 69 (hereafter, Dagbanja, 'Human Rights, Mineral Rights and CSR').

[175] Norms on the Responsibilities of Transnational Corporations and Other Business Enterprises with Regard to Human Rights, UN Doc E/CN.4/Sub.2/2003/12/Rev.2 (2003) Preamble [3], available at http://www1.umn.edu/humanrts/links/norms-Aug2003.html accessed 30 July 2014. A useful reading

The issue as to the implications of business for human rights has long since engaged the attention of international investment law scholars, states and human rights advocacy groups.[176] The Organisation for Economic Cooperation and Development's (OECD) attempt to draft a Multilateral Agreement on Investment (MAI) in 1995 failed due, in part, to criticisms by a coalition of human rights activists. The critics were of the view that the MAI emphasised the protection of investment at the expense of the need to protect human rights from abuse by multinational business entities.[177] The criticisms and opposition to MAI, suggests that both developed and developing countries share the view that foreign investment promotion and protection by treaty operates in a manner that undermines the adoption of measures aimed at promoting and protecting human rights.[178] The United Nations Commission on Human Rights argues that[179]

> [e]conomic agreements concluded by States, either with other States or with business enterprises—such as bilateral investment treaties, free trade agreements or contracts for investment projects—create economic opportunities for States. But they can also affect the domestic policy space of Governments ...

on the intersection of human rights and investment treaties in Africa is Fola Adeleke, *International Law and Policy in Africa: Exploring a Human Rights Based Approach to Investment Regulation and Dispute Settlement* (Routledge 2018).

[176] Christoph Schreuer and Ursula Kriebaum 'From Individual to Community Interest in International Investment Law' in Ulrich Fastenrath and others (eds), *From Bilateralism to Community Interest: Essays in Honour of Judge Bruno Simma* (OUP 2011) 1079); Freya Baetebs (ed) *Investment Law within International Law: Integrationist Perspectives* (CUP 2013chs 1–5; Kristina Nadavukaren Schefer (ed), *Poverty and the International Economic Legal System: Duties to the World's Poor* (CUP 2013); Commission on Human Rights, *Guiding Principles on Business and Human Rights: Implementing the United Nations 'Protect, Respect and Remedy' Framework* (United Nations 2011); Human Rights Council, *Report of the Special Representative of the Secretary-General on the Issue of Human Rights and Transnational Corporations and Other Business Enterprises, John Ruggie: Guiding Principles on Business and Human Rights: Implementing the United Nations 'Protect, Respect and Remedy' Framework* (A/HRC/17/31, 21 March 2011); Howard Mann, *International Investment Agreements, Business and Human Rights: Key Issues and Opportunities* (IISD Publication Centre 2008); Dupuy, Francioni, and Petersmann (eds), *Human Rights in International Investment Law and Arbitration* (n 65: Ernst-Ulrich Petersmann, 'Human Rights and International Economic Law in the 21st Centre: The Need to Clarify Their Interrelationships' (2001) 4 Journal of international Economic Law 3; Bruno Simma 'Foreign Investment Arbitration: A Place for Human Rights?' (2011) 60 International and Comparative Law Quarterly 57; Olivier De Schutter (ed), *Transnational Corporations and Human Rights* (Hart Publishing 2006); Kojo Yelpaala, 'Fundamentalism in Public Health and Safety in Bilateral Investment Treaties [Part II]' (2008) 3(2) Asian Journal of WTO & International Health Law and Policy 465; Kojo Yelpaala 'Fundamentalism in Public Health and Safety in Bilateral Investment Treaties [Part I]' (2008) 3(2) Asian Journal of WTO & International Health Law and Policy 235; CHRAJ, *Human Rights in Mining Communities* (n 37)); and Dagbanja, 'Human Rights, Mineral Rights and CSR' (n 174).

[177] Sornarajah, *Law on Foreign Investment* (n 12) 3, 27, 54, 143.

[178] ibid 4.

[179] Commission on Human Rights, Guiding Principles on Business and Human Rights: Implementing the United Nations 'Protect, Respect and Remedy' Framework (United Nations, 2011) Commentary to Principle 9 at 12. See also Smita Narula, 'International Financial Institutions, Transnational Corporations and Duties of States' in Malcolm Langford and others, *Global Justice, State Duties: The Extra-Territorial Scope of Economic, Social and Cultural Rights in International Law* (CUP 2013) 114.

> [T]he terms of international investment agreements may constrain States from fully implementing new human rights legislation, or put them at risk of binding international arbitration if they do so.

A state's human rights obligations may come into play in international investment law and arbitration in a number of ways. First, a state may regulate the market, including foreign investment activities and operations, to further human rights obligations. For example, a state may regulate the number of people a foreign business should employ as required by municipal labour laws.[180] This may trigger potential breaches of a state's investment treaty obligation towards foreign investors such as prohibition against performance requirements.[181]

Secondly, the activities of foreign investors may harm the human rights of the people in a host country. Foreign investment in certain industries presents risks that 'are characteristic of or unique to them'[182] that pose a challenge to the protection of human rights. Investments in the mining sector involving the extraction of precious metals such as gold and diamonds are linked directly to occupational health diseases such as tuberculosis and silicosis,[183] exemplified in the case of Ghana, Nigeria, and South Africa in Section 4.2 of this chapter. Investments in the chemical industry also involve hazardous and ultra-hazardous activities. Commercial industrial accidents from this industry can lead to horrendous and irreparable casualties on human life.[184] For example, in 1984 a gas leak from a facility owned by Union Carbide India Limited in Bhopal, India, led to the deaths of 4,000 human beings between 1984 and 1992. Between 30,000 and 40,000 people were maimed and about 200,000 people were estimated to have been affected by the disaster.[185] The industrial chemical production company was 51 per cent owned by Union Carbide Corporation of the United States. Many of the people affected by the disaster have not been compensated.[186] Such health risks naturally invite state intervention through the use of local human rights norms and enforcement institutions which might adversely affect foreign investment and lead to foreign investors challenging any such regulatory intervention as breaching standards of investment protection such as expropriation, fair and equitable treatment, and full protection and security.

Thirdly, human rights obligations of states may arise in relation to foreign investment and arbitration when states simply seek to introduce or implement

[180] Bruno Simma and Theodore Kill, 'Harmonizing Investment Protection and International Human Rights: First Steps Towards a Methodology' in Christina Binder and others (eds), *International Investment Law for the 21st Century: Essays in Honour of Christoph Schreuer* (OUP 2009) 678.

[181] UNCTAD, *Selected Developments in IIA Arbitration and Human Rights* (United Nations 2009) at 2.

[182] ibid 254, 74.

[183] ibid.

[184] ibid 256.

[185] ibid.

[186] Sornarajah, *Law on Foreign Investment* (n 12) 147.

constitutional human rights obligations or broader public policy objectives such as on health and the right to water,[187] as shown in Subsection 4.5.2 later in this chapter. In any of these instances, it is often the investor that will initiate investor–state arbitration.

Human rights can be protected primarily by means of legislative and enforcement mechanisms by state institutions, including local courts which prevent or redress the abuse of human rights by others and ensure compliance with applicable human rights standards. It is the performance of these functions that can lead to conflict between states' legal duties to protect human rights and their investment treaty obligations. States may be afraid to take legislative and enforcement actions in relation to foreign investment to protect human rights because[188]

> [k]nowing that damages awarded by arbitral tribunals can amount to millions, just the prospect of such a challenge could deter host states from implementing ambitious human rights policies, at least when they are under applicable international investment disciplines.
>
> [G]iven the many protections afforded to investors with regard to host state measures detrimental to them, states may be reluctant to bring an action or to adopt a sanction against the investor under domestic law. For the same reason, host states may even be precluded from passing the very domestic legislation which would allow them to do so.

Investment treaties have developed principally as instruments for the promotion and protection of foreign investment. The protection of the public interest including human rights is not a primary objective of these treaties.[189] Given their primary focus on investment protection, investment tribunals lack jurisdiction to entertain human rights claims and defences.[190] In any case, it is states that have the primary duty to promote and protect human rights. These facts make it imperative that local human rights courts and institutions retain their autonomy to enforce human rights norms. This autonomy can be compromised by investor–state

[187] Emma Trustwell, 'Thirst for Profit: Water Privatisation, Investment Law and a Human Right to Water' in Chester Brown and Kate Miles (eds), *Evolution in Investment Treaty Law and Arbitration* (CUP 2011) 570; and Audrey Gaughran, 'Business and Human Rights and the Right to Water' (2012) 106 Proceedings of the Annual Meeting of American Society of International Law 52.

[188] Jan Wouters and Nicolas Hachez, 'When Rules and Values Collide: How Can a Balanced Application of Investor Protection Provisions and Human Rights Be Ensured?' (2009) 3(2) Human Rights and International Legal Discourse 301, 309–10 and 311.

[189] Schreuer and Kriebaum (n 177) 1079; and Dominic Dagbanja, 'The Limitation of Sovereign Regulatory Autonomy and the Internationalization of Investment Protection by Treaty: An African Perspective' (2014) Journal of African Law 1.

[190] *Biloune and Marine Drive Complex Ltd. v Ghana Investments Centre and the Government of Ghana*, Award on Jurisdiction and Liability, 29 October 1989 (1990) 95 ILR 184 (hereafter, *Biloune v Ghana*).

arbitration because decisions of local courts can be challenged before private arbitrators as violating standards of investment protection.

In Section 4.5, the use of investment treaties to challenge environmental and human rights legislation and other policies is considered.

4.5 The Limitations Investment Treaties Place on Environmental and Human Rights Regulation in Africa

4.5.1 Investor–State Arbitration and Environmental Regulation in Africa

This section analyses how investment treaties pose a challenge to environmental regulatory autonomy in Africa.[191] A state discharges its legal duty to protect the environment by the enactment and enforcement of environmental laws and regulations. The ability and willingness of investor–state tribunals to accommodate or take account of environmental duties of host states to protect the environment is determined by examining a number of arbitral decisions that have been made when foreign investors challenged the performance of these duties.

The cases I analysed in this chapter were selected because they involve disputes over environmental measures of the kinds specifically required under the environmental laws and regulations in Africa. The cases involved alleged breaches of similar investment protections to those recognised under investment treaties to which African countries are parties: full and *adequate* protection or full protection and *security*,[192] fair and equitable treatment,[193] and expropriation,[194]

[191] On this subject see Sornarajah, *Law on Foreign Investment* (n 12), ch 10; Martin Wagner, 'International Investment, Expropriation and Environmental Protection' (1999) 29 Golden Gate University Law Review 465; and Jorge Viñuales, *Foreign Investment and the Environment in International Law* (CUP 2012 (hereafter, Wagner, 'Investment and Expropriation').

[192] Agreement between the Government of the Republic of Ghana and the Government of Malaysia for the Promotion and Protection of Investments, signed on 8 November 1996, entered into force18 April 1997, art 2(2); Agreement between the Government of Japan and the Government of the Republic of Kenya for the Promotion and Protection of Investment, signed 28 August 2016, entered into force 14 September 2017, art 5(1); Treaty between the Federal Republic of Germany and the Federal Republic of Nigeria Concerning the Reciprocal Promotion and Protection of Investment, signed 28 March 2000, entered into force 20 September 2007, arts 3(2) and 5(2).

[193] Agreement between the Kingdom of Denmark and the Government of the Republic of Ghana Concerning the Promotion and Protection of Investments, signed 13 January 1992, entered into force 6 January 1995, art 3(1); Kenya–Japan Investment Treaty (n 192) art 5(1); Nigeria–Germany Investment Treaty (n 192) arts 3(2) and 5(2); and Agreement Between the Government of the People's Republic of China and the Government of the Republic of South Africa concerning the Reciprocal Promotion and Protection of Investments, signed 30 December 1997, entered into force1 April 1998, arts 4; and 3(2).

[194] Agreement between the People's Republic of China and the Government of the Republic of Ghana Concerning the Encouragement and Reciprocal Protection of Investments, signed 12 October 1989, entered into force on 22 November 1991, art 10; Kenya–Japan Investment Treaty (n 192) art 10; Nigeria–Germany Investment Treaty (n 192) art 5(2); and South Africa–China Investment Treaty, art 3(1).

and provision for international arbitration of investment disputes,[195] fully discussed in Chapter 1.

Some of the investment treaties under which these cases were brought, such as North American Free Trade Agreement (NAFTA),[196] recognise the right of each treaty partner to establish its own levels of environmental protection and ensure that its laws and policies provide for and encourage high levels of protection. Yet, foreign investors have challenged environmental measures adopted by the contracting states and, in most cases, host states have been found to have breached the applicable standards of investment protection.

Most African investment treaties do not define the substantive standards of investment protection and with very limited exception for environmental regulation. This situation worsens Africa's position in relying on the investment treaties to defend environmental measures. In light of the similarities of disputed measures and standards of investment protection, conclusions can be drawn from these cases about the potential of investment treaties to narrow the capacity for environmental policy implementation and regulatory autonomy in Africa.

4.5.1.1 Fundamental Legal Requirements for Environmental Protection in Africa

To assess how investment treaties might limit environmental regulation in Africa it is important to review the legal duties on African governments to protect the environment. Ghana's Environmental Protection Agency (EPA) was established under the Environmental Protection Agency Act 1994 (Act 490) (EPA Act) for the protection and improvement of the environment in Ghana. Its functions are to enforce environmental policy and legislation, prescribe standards and guidelines, and inspect and regulate business operations relating to the environment. A number of its specific functions have the potential to conflict with the standards of investment protection as interpreted by investment tribunals. Section 2 of the EPA Act requires the Agency to:

1. issue environmental permits and pollution abatement notices for controlling sources of pollutants and substances which are hazardous or potentially dangerous to the quality of the environment;
2. issue notices in the form of directives, procedures, or warnings to persons for the purpose of controlling the volume, intensity, and quality of noise in the environment;

[195] Ghana–China Investment Treaty (n 194) art 4; Kenya–Japan Investment Treaty (n 192) art 15; Nigeria–Germany Investment Treaty (n 192) art 11; and South Africa–China Investment Treaty (n 193) art 9.

[196] North American Free Trade Agreement, entered into force 1 January 1994; The 2018 renegotiated NAFTA, now called the Agreement between the United States of America, the United Mexican States, and Canada, signed 30 November 2018, entered into force, 1 July 2020 <https://ustr.gov/trade-agreements/free-trade-agreements/united-states-mexico-canada-agreement/agreement-between> accessed 27 December 2020.

3. prescribe standards and guidelines relating to the pollution of air, water, land, and any other forms of environmental pollution;
4. ensure compliance with prescribed environmental impact assessment procedures in the planning and execution of development projects;
5. impose and collect environmental protection levies; and
6. regulate the import, export, manufacture, distribution, sale, and use of pesticides.

The EPA Act and its accompanying regulations, Environmental Assessment Regulations 1999 (LI 1652), mandate the EPA to require a person responsible for an undertaking which has, or is likely to have, an adverse effect on the environment to submit an environmental impact assessment within the period specified in the notice.[197] Where the EPA considers that the activities of an undertaking pose a serious threat to the environment, it may serve an enforcement notice on the person requiring them to take steps to prevent or stop the activities.[198] A failure to comply with an enforcement notice is an offence for which the offender is liable on summary conviction to a fine and in default to a term of imprisonment not exceeding one year or both.[199] The EPA Act even permits the use of force necessary to ensure compliance with an enforcement notice.[200] Any amount of money reasonably incurred to prevent or stop an offending activity may be recovered as a civil debt from the person responsible.[201]

The EPA has the power to suspend or cancel a licence if it has reasonable grounds to believe the licensee failed or refused to comply with environmental laws and regulations or any other conditions for the licence.[202] It may also suspend or cancel a licence if that is necessary to prevent or remove a hazard to human beings, crops, animals, or the environment.[203] A licensee aggrieved by a suspension or cancellation of the licence may appeal to the Minister of the Environment, and to the High Court if not satisfied with the Minister's decision.[204] The EPA has the power to suspend, cancel, or revoke an environmental permit where the holder of the permit fails to obtain any authorisation required by law, breaches enactments relating to environmental assessment, fails to make any payments required on the due date, or acts in breach of the conditions of the permit.[205]

The importation, exportation, manufacture, distribution, advertisement, sale, or use of unregistered pesticides is an offence.[206] A court has the power to direct

[197] Environmental Protection Agency Act, s 12(1) (EPA Act).
[198] ibid s 13(1).
[199] ibid s 13(3).
[200] ibid s 14(2).
[201] ibid s 14(4).
[202] ibid s 45(a)
[203] ibid s 45(b).
[204] ibid s 46.
[205] Environmental Assessment Regulations 1999 (LI1562) r 26.
[206] EPA Act, s 28(1) and 57(1).

the forfeiture of the equipment, pesticide, or appliance used in the commission of an environmental offence to the state, or to order the suspension or cancellation of a licence that may have been granted to the person concerned.[207] Under section 6 of the Forests Protection Act 1974 (NRCD 243) a court which convicts a person of an offence, such as the felling or damaging of forest trees, has the power to order the forfeiture of the forest produce, instruments, vehicles, and any other articles in respect, or by means, of which the offence was committed. Anything forfeited to the state may be sold or otherwise disposed of and the proceeds applied for forest rehabilitation.

The Minerals and Mining Act 2006 (Act 703) of Ghana requires in section 18(1) that before undertaking an activity or operation under a mineral right, the right-holder shall obtain the necessary approvals and permits from the Forestry Commission and the EPA for the protection of natural resources, public health, and the environment. Section 18(2) of Act 703 requires a holder of a mineral right to 'comply with the applicable Regulations ... for the protection of the environment in so far as it relates to exploitation of minerals'. By sections 65, 68–69, and 87 of the Act, the Minister responsible for mining has the power to suspend, cancel, or revoke mineral rights, licenses, and permits for non-compliance with the law or where it is in the public interest to do so.

These statutory provisions contain a number of key legal requirements for environmental protection in Ghana that might lead to investor–state arbitration under investment treaties. They include:

1. the grant, suspension, cancellation, or termination of environmental permits;
2. shifting the cost of environmental remediation onto persons whose activities cause environmental damage;
3. forfeiture of the assets of an offending person to the state to meet the cost of restoring the environment to its desirable state;
4. imposition of environmental fines and levies for non-compliance with environmental laws and regulations;
5. using local institutions, including the courts, to enforce environmental norms;
6. requiring those whose activities displace or affect owners or lawful occupiers of land to pay them compensation;
7. conviction and imprisonment of environmental offenders;
8. using force to ensure compliance with environmental notice;
9. no payment of compensation for general environmental regulation that affects property rights; and

[207] ibid s 60.

10. banning the export and import or restricting the use of chemicals and pesticides on environmental protection grounds.

Environment laws and regulations in Cameroon,[208] Egypt,[209] Kenya,[210] Nigeria,[211] and South Africa[212] provide for similar requirements, standards, offences, and penalties for the regulation of all forms of transactions and activities which have the potential to cause damage and harm to the environment and health.

The nature of the challenge that investment treaty rules and arbitration might pose to the adoption or enforcement of some of these environmental protection measures in Africa is assessed with case studies in Subsections 4.5.1.2 and 5.4.1.3.

4.5.1.2 The Cancellation, Suspension, and Termination of Environmental Permits

Permits and licences are very important for business activities, which cannot commence without them or continue if the permit is withdrawn. The revocation of a licence can affect the viability of a business concern even though the physical assets of the business are not directly expropriated. At the same time, a state can enforce its environmental laws and policies through denial, suspension, cancellation, or termination of environmental permits. Under domestic environmental laws in Africa, a state has the power not to approve or not to renew the permits of mining companies whose operations lead to environmental damage and human rights abuses so as to protect the environment and human health. Thus, limitations on how the state exercises its right to regulate through issuing permits can compromise its ability to regulate effectively the activities of enterprises that affect basic rights of citizens.[213]

The Supreme Court of Ghana in *New Patriotic Party v Inspector General of Police*[214] stated that '[w]hoever has power to grant a permit or licence has power to refuse it'.[215] In fact, '[t]here is general acceptance that a state has a right to cancel agreements or investment projects which cause significant environmental harm'[216] because this 'flows not only from the sovereignty of the state which permits the state to protect its territory from environmental harm but also from the fact that,

[208] Cameroon Mining Code Law No 2016/017 of 14 December 2016; and aw No 96/12 of August 5, 1996, on the Framework Law on the Environmental Management.

[209] Law Number 4 of 1994 Promulgating the Environmental Law as mended by Law No 9 for 2009; and Prime Minister's Decree No 338 of 1995 Issuing the Executive Regulations of the Environment Law promulgated by Law No 4 of 1994

[210] Environmental Management and Coordination Act No 8 OF 1999 (Cap 141) ss 9, 76, 74, 108–109, 11, 114, and 137–146. See also Environment and Land Court Act No 19 OF 2011 (Cap 12A).

[211] Environmental Impact Assessment Act 1992 (No 86) ss 13–53.

[212] Environment Conversation Act 1989 (No 73) ss 29–30 and 31A.

[213] Sornarajah, *Law on Foreign Investment* (n 12) at 16.

[214] *New Patriotic Party v Inspect General of Police* [1993–94] 2 GLR 457 at 473.

[215] ibid 473.

[216] Sornarajah, *Law on Foreign Investment* (n 12) 110.

in modern international law, a state is a repository of the right to safeguard the environment in the interests of humankind'.[217] Regulations 'are usually implemented through licensing systems, and the sanction is withdrawal of the licence'.[218] A state which seeks to terminate the foreign investment of a multinational business entity that it considers is causing unnecessary environmental harm will be told that such termination violates the foreign investment agreement and results in liability to pay compensation.[219]

The enforcement of environmental protection standards by revoking environmental permits or requiring foreign investors to comply with environmental regulations in Africa could lead to investor-initiated arbitration alleging breaches of standards of investment protection. Arbitral cases help illustrate how investment treaties and investor–state arbitration can significantly impact on environmental regulation in Africa drawing from the experiences of other countries with investor–state arbitration.

A case in point is *Clayton v Government of Canada*.[220] The investors and their company, Bilcon of Delaware, were engaged in supplying building materials, including concrete, in Canada. The business required a substantial supply of aggregate concrete for its projects, and proposed to establish and operate a quarry and marine terminal in Nova Scotia to extract and ship large quantities of basalt (used in the production of concrete and asphalt) by bulk tanker to the investor's New Jersey manufacturing site.[221] The proposed terminal underwent a lengthy environmental assessment by Nova Scotia government and the Canadian Federal government as required by state and federal environmental and fishery legislation. At the end of 2007, both governments decided not to approve the permit on environmental grounds in line with the recommendations of a Joint Review Panel (JRP).

The environmental assessment was conducted by experts in oceanography, planning, and resource and environmental studies. It involved extensive public hearings and led the JRP to recommend rejecting the proposed quarry for environmental and social reasons. It concluded that the 'imposition of a major long-term industrial site would introduce a significant and irreversible change to Digby Neck and Islands, resulting in sufficiently important changes to that community's core values to warrant the Panel assessing them as a Significant Adverse Environmental Effect that cannot be mitigated'.[222] Canada emphasised the importance and unique

[217] ibid 110.

[218] ibid 77.

[219] Muthucumaraswamy Sornarajah, 'The Clash of Globalizations and the International Law on Foreign Investment' (2003) 10(2) Canadian Foreign Policy Journal 1, 10.

[220] *Clayton v Government of Canada*, PCA Case No 2009-04, Award on Jurisdiction and Liability, 17 March 2015.

[221] International Arbitration Reports, 'Canada Sets Out Arguments in NAFTA Claim Arising out of Environmental Assessment of Quarry and Shipping Project' (19 September 2009), <http://www.iareporter.com/articles/20091008_14> accessed 27 December 2020.

[222] *Clayton v Canada* (n 221) [20].

nature of the biophysical and human environment in the proposed site at Digby Neck and the adjacent Bay of Fundy, which was the habitat of many endangered species. The economy of the local area was based on the region's ecological assets, including the fishing and ecotourism industries.[223]

Bilcon complained that Canada breached its NAFTA obligations: the minimum standard of treatment, national treatment, and most-favoured-nation (MFN) treatment. It argued that Canada acted in an unfair and unreasonable manner toward the investors by imposing biased, needless, and unfair procedures and obligations.[224] The investors also argued that Canada failed to accord them full protection and security by 'not taking steps to protect them from discriminatory and arbitrary treatment in the environmental regulatory process; not following its own laws with respect to governmental regulatory authority over the proposed quarry; and failing to accord the investors a fair hearing and reasonable decision'.[225] Bilcon claimed that its legitimate expectations, based on the extensive encouragement of Nova Scotia officials to invest in a quarry in the area, were frustrated by the rejection of the application.[226] The investor sought USD300 million in damages.

In a split decision, the Tribunal held that Canada breached the minimum standard of treatment, reasoning that the investors[227]

> understood that they would only obtain environmental permission if the project satisfied the requirements of the laws of federal Canada and Nova Scotia. They expected, however, that absent any change in the federal or provincial law, the project site was not effectively zoned against development, and that their project would be assessed on the merits of its environmental soundness in accordance with the same legal standards applied to applicants generally.

The majority held that the investor reasonably relied on specific encouragements, at the political and technical levels, to pursue the project not only in Nova Scotia but in the specific site the investors chose. They considered that encouragements by the government contributed to the investors' decision to proceed with their business plans and invest very substantive corporate resources and millions of dollars in good faith to obtain an Environmental Impact Statement. The JRP had acknowledged it adopted an unprecedented approach that was inimical to the proponents having any real chance of success based on an assessment of their individual project on its merits in accordance with the laws in force at the time.[228]

[223] ibid [130].
[224] ibid [352].
[225] ibid [366].
[226] ibid [394].
[227] ibid [447]–[453].
[228] ibid [449]–[459].

The majority concluded that the JRP had not carried out its mandate as required of it by the Canadian Environmental Assessment Act to apply its analysis of 'likely significant effects after mitigation' to the whole range of potential project effects when arriving at its conclusions.[229] As a result, the ultimate decision-makers in the governments of Canada and Nova Scotia were not provided with all the information that could have created a proper foundation to arrive at their own final conclusions.[230]

In the opinion of the Tribunal, states are entitled to regulate for purposes of environmental protection and general public interest but they still have to respect obligations they have entered into to protect foreign investment. Where states fail to do so, they can hardly escape liability. The Tribunal stated:[231]

> Modern regulatory and social welfare states tackle complex problems. Not all situations can be addressed in advance by the laws that are enacted. Room must be left for judgment to be used to interpret legal standards and apply them to the facts … State authorities are faced with competing demands on their administrative resources and there can be delays or limited time, attention and expertise brought to bear in dealing with issues. The imprudent exercise of discretion or even outright mistakes do not, as a rule, lead to a breach of the international minimum standard.
>
> At the same time, the international minimum standard exists and has evolved in the direction of increased investor protection precisely because sovereign states—the same ones constrained by the standard—have chosen to accept it. States have concluded that the standard protects their own nationals in other countries and encourages the inflow of visitors and investment.

The Tribunal also held that Canada breached the national treatment standard, reasoning the standard focuses on the way the investor or investment is treated, 'rather than confining concerns over discrimination to comparisons between similar articles of trade'.[232] Noting that a number of Canadian companies' operations of the quarry and marine terminal projects had the potential to affect the local community,[233] the Tribunal said the 'assessments in these cases were carried out in accordance with the usual 'likely significant adverse effects after mitigation' analysis'.[234] Therefore, these other investors received more favourable treatment than Bilcon, in like circumstances.[235]

229 ibid [452].
230 ibid [453].
231 ibid [437]–[438].
232 ibid [692].
233 ibid [696].
234 ibid.
235 ibid.

In a dissenting opinion Donald McRae explicitly warned the ruling would have a chilling effect on environmental protection. He held that the Clayton Group had no basis to claim a breach of national treatment or MFN treatment because it was treated in accordance with Canadian law, which all investors were entitled to expect.[236] The majority decision is 'a remarkable step backwards in environmental protection'[237] because it added a further control over environmental review panels. A failure of a review panel to comply with Canadian law now 'becomes the basis for a NAFTA claim allowing a claimant to bypass the domestic remedy provided for such a departure from Canadian law'.[238] McRae describes this as 'a significant intrusion into domestic jurisdiction [that] will create a chill on the operation of environmental review Panel'.[239] In the past, if environmental review panels made an error, for example by exceeding their jurisdiction or failing to comply with the law, the government would have ignored their recommendations or they would have been overturned on review by a federal court.[240]

The majority's finding that failure to comply in full with Canadian environmental law breached the minimum standard of treatment could place the proper application of Canadian law by an environmental review panel in the hands of a NAFTA Chapter 11 tribunal, 'importing a damages remedy that is not available under Canadian law'.[241] The majority's decision is especially 'troubling for the ability of a state to apply its environmental law'[242] because the state could end up liable for damages to an investor where a review panel 'put great weight on the effect of a project on the human environment and took account of the community's own expression of its interests and values'.[243] The majority's approach is a 'subjugation of human environment concerns to the scientific and technical feasibility of a project' and an intrusion into both the way an environmental review process is to be conducted and the environmental public policy of the state.[244] The effect of such intrusion is that 'a chill will be imposed on environmental review panels which will be concerned not to give too much weight to socio-economic considerations or other considerations of the human environment in case the result is a claim for damages'.[245]

For African states, this case means that decisions of their EPAs to enforce commissioned environmental reports and regulations on environmental permits stand the risk of being challenged by foreign investors. Threats of an investor–state suit

[236] *Clayton v Government of Canada*, PCA Case No 2009-04, Dissenting Opinion of Professor Donald McRae, 10 March 2017, para 53.
[237] ibid [51].
[238] ibid [48].
[239] ibid.
[240] ibid.
[241] ibid.
[242] ibid [49].
[243] ibid.
[244] ibid.
[245] ibid [51].

could have a chilling effect and result in the EPAs not giving considerable attention to environmental and social considerations when the interests of foreign investors are involved.

A related case is *Chemtura Corporation v Canada*[246] which involved Canada's termination of a pesticide (lindane) registration and ban on its use on public health and environmental grounds. Under the Canadian Pest Control Products Act 1997 and the Pest Control Products Regulations 1997, the sale or import into Canada of controlled products such as lindane was prohibited, unless the product was registered and conformed to prescribed standards. The Pest Management Regulatory Agency (PMRA), which was responsible for the regulation of pest control products in Canada, had the primary objective of preventing unacceptable risks to people and the environment from the use of pest control products.[247]

Following a risk assessment, the PMRA decided there was a need for regulatory action by suspending or terminating registration of lindane in light of significant concerns regarding the exposure of workers to health risks.[248] Chemtura Corporation's registration of lindane was terminated on grounds of environmental safety and health risks.[249] Chemtura argued that Canada breached the minimum standard of treatment, saying the review of its lindane registration was flawed because notice was unspecific and failure to complete the review in a timely way thwarted the investor's attempts to have the review re-evaluated in accordance with law. A further claim of breach of the minimum standard of treatment was Canada's prohibition on planting lindane-treated seed, contrary to previous assurances it had given.[250] The investor also alleged that the review of lindane use was conducted as a result of a trade irritant and not for health and environmental considerations.[251] It claimed damages of USD78.5 million.[252] Canada counterargued that the PMRA's conduct was a valid exercise of police powers,[253] and that the minimum standard of treatment under NAFTA did not 'limit the discretion of regulators to take steps in compliance with their duty to protect public health and the environment'.[254]

The investor's claim was dismissed. The Tribunal noted that lindane had raised serious concerns internationally and was listed among the chemicals designated for elimination under the Stockholm Convention on Persistent Organic Pollutants.[255] Canada succeeded in establishing that lindane raised increasingly serious concerns

[246] *Chemtura Corporation v Canada*, NAFTA/UNCITRAL, Award, 2 August 2010.
[247] ibid [10].
[248] ibid [29]–[30].
[249] ibid [32]–[34].
[250] ibid [93].
[251] ibid [133].
[252] ibid [95]–[96].
[253] ibid 97.
[254] ibid [183].
[255] ibid [135]–[136].

about its health and environmental implications and that the evidence on record did not show bad faith or disingenuous conduct on the part of Canada.[256] On the contrary, it showed the review was undertaken in pursuance of the Agency's mandate and as a result of Canada's international obligations.[257] Moreover, the investor was made aware of the importance of the exposure risks and was asked to provide information on the matter, but it failed to take advantage of these opportunities.[258] The investor was also afforded the same treatment as all other registrants of controlled products.[259] The PMRA took the measures within its mandate, in compliance with its standard regulatory practice, in a non-discriminatory manner, motivated by the increasing awareness of the dangers presented by lindane for human health and the environment. Therefore, the investor could not claim unfair treatment, bad faith, or breach of due process.[260]

Some tribunals thus recognise actions for environmental protection purposes under municipal law and general international law as legitimate. The review of lindane use and the cancellation of registration that followed arose 'out of legitimate regulatory concerns and in accordance with Canada's international commitments'.[261] In assessing whether treatment afforded to an investment accords with the minimum standard of treatment, a tribunal 'must take account of all circumstances, including the fact that certain agencies manage highly specialized domains involving scientific and public policy domains'.[262]

In assessing claims of bad faith, both procedure (eg adequacy of notice) and substance (Canada's legal commitments under municipal law and general international law) were considered.[263] It is not clear from the decision, if the procedural claims as to 'bad faith' had been established, Canada would have been found liable in spite of the legitimacy of the measure under law. It is likely that if bad faith (procedurally) and lack of transparency had been established, Canada would have been found liable.

The Tribunal also noted wide international recognition of the harmful environmental and health effects of lindane and the ban of lindane use in a number of other countries.[264] This leaves doubt as to what would have been the decision had the harmful effects of lindane not yet been widely recognised and prior to PMRA's taking of precautionary measures pending more information.

The cumulative effect of the decision is to protect environmental regulatory autonomy under both domestic environmental law and international environmental

[256] ibid [135] and [138].
[257] ibid [138] and [184].
[258] ibid [150].
[259] ibid [192] and [236].
[260] ibid [152] and [162].
[261] ibid [147].
[262] ibid [123].
[263] ibid [148]–[653].
[264] ibid [184].

law. Such a decision provides some regulatory comfort for African countries whose duties to protect the environment are founded under their constitutions and IETs, mindful that arbitral tribunals do not follow strict precedent.

Tecnicas Medioambientales Tecmed SA v Mexico[265] arose out of Tecmed's (a Spanish investor in Mexico) application to renew a licence to operate a landfill facility for hazardous industrial waste. The application was rejected and the company asked to institute a programme to close the landfill. The investor lodged a claim under the investment treaty between Spain and Mexico, which prohibited expropriation without the payment of compensation in similar terms to investment treaties with African countries.

Tecmed argued that the refusal to renew the environmental permit to operate the landfill constituted an expropriation of its investment.[266] Mexico argued in turn that the Resolution pursuant to which the permit was denied 'was a regulatory measure issued in compliance with the State's police power within the highly regulated and extremely sensitive framework of environmental protection and public health'.[267] Further, the site of the landfill did not comply with applicable regulations in terms of its location and characteristics.[268]

The Tribunal found that community opposition to the landfill 'was widespread and aggressive, as evidenced by several events at different times',[269] but that that was not the reason Mexico decided not to renew the licence and required the project to relocate. It found there were political motives (such as election and change of administration in the municipality) behind the Resolution and that the decision had not been made and applied transparently and predictably.[270] The Resolution had not suggested that the violations relating to hazardous waste compromised public health or impaired ecological balance or protection of the environment.[271]

The Tribunal reasoned that the investors would not have acquired the assets without access to the authorisations and permits to use them for a hazardous waste landfill.[272] It found the municipal regulatory agency undertook to keep current the existing licenses and authorisations for the operation of the landfill, including federal ones granted to the state company in which Tecmed invested, until Tecmed could obtain its own permits.[273] Access to those licenses, authorisations, or permits was a central part of the tender and acquisition of assets relating to the landfill and of Tecmed's expectations when it decided to invest.[274] Moreover, the Mexican

[265] *Tecnicas Medioambientales Tecmed SA v Mexico*, Case No ARB (AF)/00/2, Award, 23 May 2003 (hereafter, *Tecmed v Mexico*).
[266] ibid [95]–[96].
[267] ibid [97].
[268] ibid [105].
[269] ibid [108].
[270] ibid [127], [129]–[130], [132], [157], and [153]–[166].
[271] ibid [124].
[272] ibid [90].
[273] ibid [89].
[274] ibid [90].

officials and institutions involved had indicated on various occasions that the operation of the landfill complied with domestic legal provisions on environmental protection and public health preservation.[275] Mexico was found to have expropriated the investments because the company had to bear the financial cost of the relocation.[276] The Tribunal ordered Mexico to pay Tecmed USD5.3 million, plus compound interest at an annual rate of 6 per cent.[277]

The Tribunal admitted that a state's exercise of its sovereignty within the framework of its police powers 'may cause economic damage to those subject to its powers without entitling them to any compensation whatsoever is undisputable'.[278] It nevertheless emphasised the effect of governmental measures on investment[279] and held that its own function was to examine whether the Resolution in question violated the investment treaty and international law. It was not its function to 'review the grounds or motives of the Resolution in order to determine whether it could be or was legally issued,' and it would not do so.[280] There was no principle stating that regulatory actions *per se* did not give rise to liability under the applicable investment treaties 'even if they are beneficial to society as a whole—such as environmental protection—particularly if the negative economic impact of such actions on the financial position of the investor is sufficient'.[281] In view of these propositions, it is not clear in what circumstances a state will not be required to pay compensation for causing economic damage to those subject to its powers.

The Tribunal acknowledged that due deference is owed to a state when it defines issues that affect public policy or the interests of society as a whole, and in relation to actions that will be implemented to protect such values. However, this does not prevent an arbitral tribunal from examining the actions of the state to determine whether such measures are reasonable with respect to their goals (quite apart from their legitimacy), the deprivation of economic rights, and the legitimate expectations of those who suffer such deprivation.[282] The Tribunal thus placed primacy on the effect of a measure on an investment.

When assessing whether a measure was equivalent to an expropriation, the Tribunal looked at whether the measure radically deprived the investor of the economic use and enjoyment of its investments, or the assets involved had lost their value or economic use for their holder.[283] That determination is important because it is one of the main elements when distinguishing between a regulatory measure, which is an ordinary expression of the exercise of the state's police power that

[275] ibid [124].
[276] ibid [151], [157], [159], and [166].
[277] ibid [201].
[278] ibid [119].
[279] ibid [111] and [115]–[116].
[280] ibid [120].
[281] ibid [121].
[282] ibid [122].
[283] ibid [115].

entails a decrease in assets or rights, and a *de facto* expropriation.[284] The effects of the actions or behaviour under analysis were therefore relevant.[285]

The nub of the decision is that the Resolution terminating the environmental permit did not state environmental protection as its objective and the processes for granting and terminating the permit lacked transparency and consistency.[286] There is, however, nothing in the case to suggest that a decision would have been made in favour of the state if the purpose of the Resolution had been stated and the regulatory institutions acted transparently and consistently. As it is, the decision does not show in clear terms whether or not legitimate environmental regulation that adversely affects investment will not give rise to state liability. On the contrary, the Tribunal's emphasis on the effect on the investment suggests the state would most likely have been found liable even if it had linked its decision to an environmental protection objective and acted transparently and consistently.

These three cases illustrate the point that legislative enactments or amendments and imposition of conditions on environmental permits in Africa that could adversely affect foreign investors and their investments are capable of being the subject of arbitration. This can lead to tension between investor rights and environmental regulation in Africa. The threat of investor–state arbitration could lead to African countries rolling back on an intended environmental protection measure.[287] A conclusion can also be drawn from the cases that acting in compliance with due process, transparency, and good faith requirements is necessary to minimise the risk of being found in breach of standards of investment protection in Africa.

4.5.1.3 Export Ban of Environmentally Hazardous Substances

A state may exercise its powers to protect the environment by regulating the export, import, or use of chemicals and pesticides that have implications for environmental quality. For example, in Ghana using unregistered pesticides is an offence.[288] Under section 2(r) of the EPA Act, the EPA has the mandate 'to regulate the import, export, manufacture, distribution, sale and use of pesticides'. The Hazardous Chemicals Committee must monitor the use of hazardous chemicals by collecting information on those activities.[289] Commercial dealings with pesticides are permitted only in accordance with a licence issued under the EPA Act,[290] which may only be issued if the applicant will comply with its conditions.[291] The EPA may refuse a licence if it has reasonable grounds to believe the applicant will

284 ibid.
285 ibid.
286 ibid [127], [129]–[130], [132], [157], and [153]–[166].
287 Wagner, 'Investment and Expropriation' (n 191) 67.
288 Environmental Protection Agency Act 1994 (Act 490) (Ghana) s 28(1) and 57(1).
289 ibid s 10(2)(a).
290 ibid s 40(1).
291 ibid s 43.

not comply with the conditions of the licence or revoke the licence if the conditions are breached. Conducting those activities with pesticides which have not been registered or without a licence is an offence that attracts a fine or imprisonment to a term not exceeding two years or both.[292]

Several cases under NAFTA show environmental laws and regulations could come under attack. For example, Canada banned the export of a synthetic chemical compound known as polychlorinated biphenyl (PCB) into the United States. The goal of the ban was to ensure that Canadian PCB wastes were managed in an environmentally sound manner to prevent any possible significant danger to the environment and human health.[293] The ban was also to enable Canada to conform to its obligations under the Basel Convention.[294] In *SD Myers Incorporated v Canada*[295] the ban was found to be in breach of the national treatment standard under NAFTA.[296] Canada had argued that ban was consistent with Canadian Environmental Protection Act. The Tribunal held that Canada violated the national treatment standard[297] because its policy was intended 'to protect and promote the market share of enterprises that would carry out the destruction of PCBs in Canada and that were owned by Canadian nationals'.[298]

The decision of the Tribunal on the scope of application of the minimum standard of treatment seems to suggest that the purpose of governmental regulation is a viable defence in investment treaty arbitration and that investment tribunals will respect the decision of states to make governance and regulatory decisions as they deem fit.[299] The Tribunal held that breach of fair and equitable treatment and full protection and security[300]

> occurs only when it is shown that an investor has been treated in such an unjust or arbitrary manner that the treatment rises to the level that is unacceptable from the international perspective. That determination must be made in the light of the high measure of deference that international law generally extends to the right of domestic authorities to regulate matters within their own borders. The determination must also take into account any specific rules of international law that are applicable to the case.

However, the Tribunal also held that the fact that a host party has breached a rule of international law that is specifically designed to protect investors will tend to weigh

292 ibid s 7(1)(a) and (b).
293 *Tecmed SA v Mexico* (n 266) [106].
294 ibid [106]–[107] and [153].
295 SD *Myers Incorporated v Canada*, NAFTA, Partial Award, 13 November 2000.
296 ibid [130]–[137].
297 ibid [256].
298 ibid [162].
299 ibid [250], [261], and [263]–[264].
300 ibid [263].

heavily in favour of finding a breach of the fair and equitable treatment and full protection and security.[301] I argue that if foreign investors always have to prevail against states over the adoption of environmental measures because investment treaties are specifically designed to protect foreign investment, the freedom and duty to regulate and the purpose of governmental regulation will be subordinate considerations, and states may not want to adopt measures to protect the environment for fear of investor–state arbitration.[302]

Whereas *Myers v Canada* emphasised the effect of the challenged measure on investment, *Methanex Corporation v United States of America*[303] gave its support for environmental regulation. Methanex, a Canadian investor, initiated arbitration against the United States under Chapter 11 of NAFTA claiming that a Californian law and regulations banning the use of use of methyl tertiary-butyl ether (MTBE), a gasoline additive, on environmental and health grounds was intended to create a local ethanol industry where no significant industry had previously existed and to discriminate against and harm Methanex and all other foreign methanol producers contrary to the national treatment standard.[304] It also argued that the ban amounted to an expropriation of its investments. It sought almost USD1 billion in compensation from the United States.

The Tribunal dismissed the claim, reasoning that there was neither evidence nor ground to infer that the policy was legally connected with a desire to harm methanol producers or benefit domestic ethanol producers.[305] It was satisfied that no malign pretext underlay California's conduct and measures.[306] The Tribunal's focus on the purpose of the regulations shows that some investment tribunals are willing to accept environmental measures grounded on domestic environmental law as a valid defence in investor–state arbitration.

Methanex v United States, like *Chemtura v Canada*, provides some relief to states desirous of protecting the environment because the Tribunal considered the intent and purpose of the challenged measures and whether they were expressly connected to the investor. The requirement of 'a legally significant connection between the measure and the investor or the investment'[307] places practical limitations on investors' ability to challenge any and every measure that might adversely affect the value of an investment even if the measure was not expressly directed at the investment. A narrow reading of the phrase 'legally significant connection' 'is especially

301 ibid [264].

302 Todd Weiler, 'A First Look at the Interim Merits Award in S.D. Myers, Inc. V. Canada: It Possible to Balance Legitimate Environmental Concerns with Investment Protection' (2001) 24 Hastings International and Comparative Law Review 173.

303 *Methanex Corporation v United States of America*, NAFTA/UNCITRAL, Final Award, 7 August 2005.

304 ibid Pt IV—ch B, para 12; Pt II—ch D, paras 25 and 26.

305 *Methanex v United States: Final Award* Pt IV—ch E, para 22.

306 ibid; Pt IV—ch E [20].

307 ibid [22].

comforting to governments that are considering environmental regulation, which almost invariably imposes economic costs, and sometimes even direct business losses, on a variety of private parties'.[308] Environmental regulation of the use of environmentally hazardous substances under the various environmental legislation in Africa might lead to states being sued by foreign investors for money damages, and the legal outcome would be uncertain.

4.5.2 Investor–State Arbitration and Human Rights Protection in Africa

African countries need to be particularly concerned about the legal effects of investor–state arbitration for the autonomy of local courts and institutions to protect human rights because certain industries which are dominated by foreign investors have direct negative impacts on human rights. Mining and oil exploration and production, for example, have impacted negatively on the right to water in Ghana, Nigeria, and South Africa and many other African countries, which calls for a strengthened role of the courts and human rights institutions in the enforcement of human rights norms in Africa. Investment in the mining industry in Africa is largely held by foreign investors.[309]

The enforcement of regulatory sanctions such as termination of licences, summary conviction, or imposition of a fine based on national constitutions and domestic legislation[310] could lead to claims of breach of standards of investment protection by treaty. Regulatory measures, particularly changes in or implementation of laws and policies governing foreign investment to ensure efficient delivery of water, have been challenged before investment tribunals by virtue of ISDS by arbitration.[311]

[308] Sanford E Gaines, 'Methanex Corp. v. United States' (2006) 100(3) American Journal of International Law 683, 687. For further scholarship on this case and others analysed in this chapter see: Alessandra Asteriti, 'Regulatory Expropriation Claims in International Investment Arbitrations: A Bridge Too Far?' in Andrea K Bjorklund (ed) *Yearbook on International Investment Law and Policy: 2012–2013* (OUP 2016) 451; Jonathan Bonnitcha, *Substantive Protection under Investment Treaties: A Legal and Economics Analysis* (CUP 2014) ch 5 (hereafter, Bonnitcha, *Substantive Protection under Investment Treaties*); and Kate Miles, *The Origins of International Investment Law: Empire, Environment and the Safeguarding of Capital* (CUP 2013).

[309] Joseph Ayee and others, *Political Economy of the Mining Sector in Ghana* (World Bank Policy Research Working Paper 5730, July 2011) <http://elibrary.worldbank.org/doi/pdf/10.1596/1813-9450-5730> accessed 27 December 2020.

[310] Such as Cameroon's Law No 96/06 of 18 January 1993 on water, Egypt's Law No 4 of 1994, and Law No 48 of1982 Protection of the Nile River from Pollution, the Water Resources Commission Act 1996 (Act 522) of Ghana, the Public Utilities Regulatory Commission Act 1997 (Act 538) of Ghana, Kenya's Water Act 2016 (No 46), Nigeria's Water Use Act 1993 (No 101), and South Africa's National Water Act 1998 (No 36),

[311] See for example, *LG &E Energy Corporation v Argentina*, Decision on Liability, ICSID Case No ARB 02/1, 3 October 2006; *Azurix Corp v Argentina*, ICSID Case No ARB/01/12, Award, 14 July 2006; *Compañía de Aguas del Aconquija SA V Argentina* (ICSID Case No ARB/97/3) Award of 20 August 2007; *Suez, Sociedad General de Aguas de Barcelona SA v The Argentine Republic*, ICSID Case No ARB/

Under the Public Utilities Regulatory Commission Act 1997 (Act 538) of Ghana, a failure to meet regulatory and quality standards in the provision of utilities is offence which may lead to a summary conviction or a fine. In default of payment of the fine, the principal officer or the secretary of the public utility provider is liable to a term of imprisonment not exceeding two years.[312] An arrest, prosecution, or conviction of a manger of a multinational business entity under the Public Utilities Regulatory Commission Act could lead to ISDS on the basis that it amounts to unreasonable interference with the management of the business entity.

In *Balkan Energy (Ghana) Ltd v Ghana*, the General Manager of Balkan Energy Ltd was arrested by the Bureau of National Investigation on suspicion that he was removing or about to remove certain equipment from a power station.[313] The Tribunal held that the arrests 'took place at all and in conditions that do not appear to have duly taken into account the rights of the accused or their dignity'.[314] In awarding USD50,000 against Ghana for the arrest, the Tribunal stated that 'when the normal conduct of business is affected by such an arrest the question is no longer one that involves a personal claim by the person concerned. It is the business as a whole that suffers the consequences.'[315] In *Biloune v Ghana*,[316] an imprisonment and deportation of an investor was held to be expropriatory as it denied the investor the opportunity to manage the investment. By these decisions, if the manager of a multinational business entity is arrested for violations of human rights and the 'normal conduct of business is affected by such an arrest', it could form a basis of investor–state arbitration. In this respect, investor–state arbitration can be become a drawback to local institutional protection of human rights. Although a foreign investor who is unlawfully arrested may have remedies before local courts, because of ISDS he or she may choose to complain only before an investor–state tribunal and claim investment treaty arbitration.

The issue of access to safe and clean water has been raised in a number of investment disputes involving millions of US dollars. Countries such as Argentina and Tanzania granted concessions to foreign investors to ensure clean water distribution and to provide sewerage services for their citizens. They often grant these concessions because governments are barely able to provide such services satisfactorily.[317] These water concessions are often governed by investment protection

03/17, Decision on Liability, 30 July 2010; *Biwater Gauff (Tanzania) Ltd v Tanzania*, ICSID CASE No ARB/05/22, Award, 24 July 2008.

[312] Public Utilities Regulatory Commission Act 1997 (Act 538) (Ghana) s 13.

[313] *Balkan Energy Limited (Ghana) v The Republic of Ghana*, UNCITRAL, PCA Case No 2010-7, Award on the Merits, 1 April 2014[49].

[314] ibid [52].

[315] ibid [53].

[316] *Biloune v Ghana* (n 191).

[317] Jorge E Vinuales, Access to Water in Foreign Investment Disputes (2008–2009) 21 Georgetown International Environmental Law Review 733.

schemes including mechanisms for tariff setting and adjustment and investment treaties that guarantee fair and equitable treatment and full protection and security.[318] The right to water includes the rights to maintain access to existing water supplies and to 'be free from contamination of water supplies. Where the water system on which people rely is contaminated, the government must act to ensure that an alternative source of clean water is provided.'[319] Yet, various measures, particularly changes in laws or implementation of laws and policies governing foreign investment, to ensure efficient delivery of water have been challenged under investment treaties.

Arbitral disputes against Argentina, Bolivia, and Tanzania demonstrate the problem. The economic and financial crisis in Argentina in the early 2000s gave rise to the abrogation or amendments of laws and policies in the water industry that impacted on the realisation of human rights in Argentina. The crisis led to high unemployment and a gradual increase in poverty and indigence rates, poor healthcare, and lack of access to food and water and other basic social services.[320] In most of the cases in which measures adopted in response to these crises were challenged by foreign investors, Argentina was found to have breached both the full protection and security and fair and equitable standards. The tribunals held that these investment treatment standards require a stable legal environment for business.

In *Azurix Corporation v Argentina*,[321] Azurix claimed that Argentina violated obligations owed to it under the Argentina–United States investment treaty in respect of its investment in a utility company which distributed drinking water and treated and disposed of sewerage. The investor alleged that the regulatory institutions made orders for the non-payment of tariffs by consumers for each day in which water supply quality was not as agreed, until the quality was deemed acceptable to users. Argentina argued that conflict between investment treaties and IHRTs 'must be resolved in favor of human rights because the consumers' public interest must prevail over the private interest of service provider'.[322]

The Tribunal held that the calls by government officials for the non-payment of bills by customers verged on bad faith in breach of fair and equitable treatment.[323] It held that bad faith or malicious intention is not a necessary element in the fair and equitable treatment, but 'such intention and bad faith can aggravate the situation'.[324] However, 'frustration of expectations that the investor may

318 ibid.

319 Audrey Gaughran, 'Business and Human Rights and the Right to Water' (2012) 106 Proceedings of the Annual Meeting of American Society of International Law 52, 53.

320 *LG &E Energy Corporation v Argentina*, Decision on Liability, ICSID Case No ARB 02/1, 3 October 2006 para 234.

321 *Azurix Corp v Argentina*, ICSID Case No ARB/01/12, Award, 14 July 2006.

322 ibid [254].

323 ibid [376]–[377].

324 ibid [372].

have legitimately taken into account when it made the investment'[325] is a necessary element of the fair and equitable treatment. The Tribunal also found an interrelationship between the standards of fair and equitable treatment and full protection and security,[326] and concluded that Argentina breached both standards.[327] Finally, the Tribunal held that the public purpose of a measure was not sufficient to exonerate a state from liability under an investment treaty.[328]

In *Suez, Sociedad General de Aguas de Barcelona SA v Argentina*,[329] the investors made investments in a concession for water distribution and wastewater treatment in Argentina. Subsequently, Argentina either amended or repealed privatisation laws or policies which were in place at the time the investments were made. The investors alleged that Argentina's enactment of emergency law abolishing previously agreed adjustments to the tariff calculation and adjustment mechanisms resulted in losses to them in breach of fair and equitable treatment and full protection and security provisions of the investment treaties between Argentina and France and between Argentina and Spain. The investors argued that they were encouraged to make investments in sewage systems in Argentina and that important elements of that inducement were the various commitments that Argentina made to them in the legal framework governing the investment. Therefore, unilateral and fundamental alterations in that legal framework frustrated their legitimate expectations and breached the fair and equitable treatment standard.[330] The investors also argued that the unilateral termination of the water concession violated Argentina's promise to them of fair and equitable treatment.[331]

The Tribunal agreed with the investors and held that where investments were made based on laws, regulations, and policies adopted by the host country which created in the investor certain expectations about the nature of the treatment that it may anticipate from the host state, a sudden change in those laws, regulations, and policies which impairs investment would lead to a determination that the host country did not accord protected investments fair and equitable treatment.[332] The concession contract and the legal framework set down the conditions offered by Argentina at the time the investors made their investments. The investors' expectation that Argentina would respect the concession contract throughout the thirty-year life of the concession was legitimate, reasonable, and justified.[333] Argentina had the right to regulate the activities of the concession concerning a broad range

[325] ibid [372].
[326] ibid [408].
[327] ibid.
[328] ibid [311].
[329] *Suez, Sociedad General de Aguas de Barcelona SA v The Argentine Republic*, ICSID Case No ARB/03/17, Decision on Liability, 30 July 2010.
[330] ibid [183] and [185].
[331] ibid [188].
[332] ibid [203], [204], and [207].
[333] ibid [212].

of matters, including the tariff structure, investment standards, and performance. However, the Tribunal insisted that the investors had the legitimate expectation that the Argentine authorities 'would exercise that regulatory authority and discretion within the rules of the detailed legal framework ... established for the Concession.'[334]

Argentina's defence included a human rights argument that[335]

> [b]ecause of its importance to the life and health of the population ... water cannot be treated as an ordinary commodity. Because of the fundamental role of water in sustaining life and health and the consequent human right to water ... in judging the conformity of governmental actions with treaty obligations this Tribunal must grant Argentina a broader margin of discretion ... than in cases involving other commodities and services.

The Tribunal rejected the full protection and security claims but found that Argentina breached the fair and equitable treatment standard[336] because 'the stability of the business environment and legal security are more characteristic of the standard of fair and equitable treatment.'[337] Not only did the Tribunal admit that the concept was vague and flexible,[338] it also stated that 'the obligation of a host State to accord fair and equitable treatment to foreign investors is the *Grundnorm* or basic norm of international investment law.'[339] It was held that a finding by a tribunal that a state has breached the full protection and security and fair and equitable treatment standards means that the state has 'exceeded its reasonable right to regulate' so that a further finding on the issue whether the state has exceeded its legitimate police powers was circumlocutory and unnecessary.[340]

A similar case in which Argentina was found to have breached the fair and equitable treatment and full protection and security standards is *Compañía v Argentina*.[341] Argentina was accused of using its regulatory powers to impose unilaterally modified tariffs and for inciting customers not to pay water bills for undrinkable and potentially unhealthy water.[342] Argentina argued that investment treaties had never been deemed to provide investors 'with an insurance policy against the due exercise of the State's regulatory activity ... more so ... when the service provided is as vital as the provision of water and sewage services.'[343]

334 ibid [217].
335 ibid [232].
336 ibid [248].
337 ibid [167].
338 ibid [180] and [182].
339 ibid [181].
340 ibid [148].
341 *Compañía de Aguas del Aconquija SA V Argentina*, ICSID Case No ARB/97/3, Award of 20 August 2007.
342 ibid [3.3.2].
343 ibid [3.3.3].

Argentina similarly argued that it 'had the right and the responsibility to take the requisite steps to ensure the availability of safe drinking water for its population on an affordable and accessible basis'.[344] Argentina was found to have breached the fair and equitable treatment and full protection and security standards. The Tribunal reasoned that the isolated incidents of water turbidity in the water system did not pose any health risk to the people, whereas the complained of regulatory actions frustrated the concession agreement.[345]

Biwater Gauff (Tanzania) Ltd v Tanzania[346] arose out of a dispute over a concession to operate water and sewerage services awarded by Tanzania to a British company. The government of Tanzania found that the company failed to meet performance requirements under the contract and cancelled the contract. The investor brought an action under a United Kingdom–Tanzania investment treaty claiming breach of the fair and equitable treatment and full protection and security standards. Tanzania argued that '[w]ater and sanitation services are vitally important, and the Republic has more than a right to protect such services'.[347] The operating company's 'non-performance was already threatening the success of a USD165 million project to upgrade water and sanitation services'[348] and 'had created a real threat to public health and welfare'.[349]

The Tribunal held that Tanzania violated the applicable investment treaty in various ways. These included the issuance of a press release on the termination of the concession, withdrawal of value added tax exemption and failure to put in place an independent and 'impartial' regulator. However, none of Tanzania's violations caused the loss and damage for which compensation was complained and each of the claims for damages was accordingly dismissed.[350] Each party bore its own costs and the costs of arbitration were to be borne by each party in equal share.[351] Similar issues as in the above cases came up in *Aguas del Tunari v Bolivia*.[352]

It follows that where states have made specific administrative, legislative, and regulatory guarantees and protections to foreign investors and their covered investments, they may not subsequently change those guarantees and protections when the change has significant negative impacts upon investments. International investment law prefers regulatory stability to secure investment protection as against the human rights purpose for which regulatory change may be needed. The emphasis on regulatory stability can have a serious regulatory chilling effect on measures intended for the protection of human rights. Investment treaty terms

344 ibid [3.3.5].
345 ibid [4.12.4] and [7.4.18].
346 *Biwater Gauff (Tanzania) Ltd v Tanzania*, ICSID Case No ARB/05/22, Award, 24 July 2008.
347 ibid [434].
348 ibid [434].
349 ibid [436].
350 ibid [807].
351 ibid [813].
352 *Aguas del Tunari SA v Republic of Bolivia*, ICSID Case No ARB/02/3.

can abridge the regulatory freedom of African states to protect the right to water. The African governments might back off from pursuing certain water resources and health related measures if they think that by so doing the measures can be challenged before investment tribunals and lead to the award of huge damages. If the governments do not back off from pursuing such measures, they might incur extra cost if the measures are implemented and challenged under the investment treaties.

The prospects of investor–state dispute settlement by arbitration and possible award of damages against a state may lead to a situation where a state may not be able to arrest and prosecute a foreign investor for human rights violations or if it does arrest and prosecute the person, it may do so at the risk damages being awarded against it in favour of the affected investor. The redress that citizens have before local courts and water regulatory institutions is jeopardised by investor–state arbitration to the extent that it allows foreign investors to challenge before investment tribunals decisions that local courts may make.

4.6 Environmental Policy and Human Rights Protection Objectives in Investment Treaty Reforms in Africa

4.6.1 The Environment and Human Rights in Bilateral Investment Treaty Reforms in Africa

Environmental and human rights measures have been challenged in investor–state arbitration and will continue to be challenged so long those measures concern and adversely affect foreign investment protected under the applicable treaty. The challenge of those environmental and human rights measures has been made easy for foreign investors by the lack of substantive protection of the right to regulate for environmental and human rights protection purposes in investment treaties. The absence of environmental and human rights protection provisions is particularly revealed in investment treaties concluded from the late 1950s through to the early 2000s. This section is concerned with analysing provisions on investment, environment, and human rights and their efficacy in preserving the right to regulate to protect the environment.

Like all other investment treaties, most investment treaties to which African countries are parties do not contain provisions preserving the right to regulate for environmental and human rights protection purposes. For example, of the twenty-eight investment treaties Ghana signed between 1989 and 2016, only two refer to regulation to protect the environment and human rights. The most recent of Ghana's investment treaties signed in 2003 and 2016 contain provisions on the environment and human rights. Three of the most recent English texts of Cameroon's eighteen investment treaties concluded between 1962 and 2018 make reference to the environment and human rights. Three of Egypt's 115 investment treaties concluded between 1966 and 2014 (some of them terminated) refer to environment and human rights in the preamble. Three of Nigeria's thirty-one signed investment treaties between 1990 and 2016 refer to the environment and human rights. Kenya has the most of investment treaties (seven of them) containing references to or provisions on environment protections among the countries of study. It has twenty investment treaties signed between 1970 and 2018. Only one of South Africa's fifty investment treaties signed between 1994 and 2010 (twelve of which are terminated) contains a provision on environment and human rights.

A significant majority of investment treaties concluded by these African countries do not address environmental and human rights concerns individually and collectively. Most of the investment treaties addressing environmental and human rights concerns were concluded in the mid-2000s, the majority of which were concluded after 2010. The issue addressed is whether the few provisions on the environment and human rights truly preserve the contracting states' right to regulate in furtherance of human rights.

In the Ghana–Turkey investment treaty,[353] the parties expressed the view in the preamble that fair and equitable· treatment of investments was desirable for the maintenance of a stable framework for investment which would 'contribute to maximizing effective utilization of economic resources and improve living standards'. The parties also recognised the importance of 'providing effective means of asserting claims and enforcing rights with respect to investment'. The state parties were '[c]onvinced that these objectives can be achieved without relaxing health, safety and environmental measures of general application as well as internationally recognized labor rights'. The investment treaty contains a substantive provision on environment protection. Article 7(1)(a) and (b) of this investment treaty states that nothing in the agreement is to be construed 'to prevent' a contracting party from 'adopting, maintaining, or enforcing any non-discriminatory legal measures designed and applied for the protection' of health and the environment or 'related to the conservation of living or non-living exhaustible natural resources'.[354]

The Ghana–Botswana investment treaty[355] also recognised the right of the parties to establish their own levels of domestic environmental protection and environmental development policies and priorities, and to adopt or modify their

[353] Agreement between the Government of the Republic of Turkey and the Government of the Republic of Ghana for the Reciprocal Promotion and Protection of Investments, signed 1 March 2016.

[354] See also Agreement between the Government of the Republic of Turkey and the Government of the Republic of Cameroon Concerning the Reciprocal Promotion and Protection of Investments, signed 24 April 2012 preamble and art 5(1). See also art 4(1) of Agreement between the Government of the Republic of Kenya and the Government of the Republic of Turkey Concerning the Reciprocal Promotion and Protection of Investments, signed 8 April 2014; and art XVII(2) and (3) of Agreement between the Government of the Republic of South Africa and the Government of Canada for the Promotion and Protection of Investments, signed 27 November 1995.

[355] Agreement between the Government of the Republic of Botswana and the Government of the Republic of Ghana for the Promotion and Protection of Investments, signed 4 July 2003.

environmental laws. According to Article 5(3) of the Ghana–Botswana investment treaty, its provisions, 'shall not in any way limit the right' of a party to make laws and apply prohibitions or restrictions of any kind or take any other action which is directed to' the protection of health and the environment. The Ghana Model BIT 2008 states that except 'in rare circumstances', non-discriminatory measures intended to protect the environment do not constitute indirect expropriation.[356]

The Cameroon–Canada investment treaty prohibits performance requirements in connection with the establishment, acquisition, expansion, management, conduct, or operation of investments with regard to specified subject matters including those relating to transfer of technology, a production process, or other proprietary knowledge.[357] However, 'a measure that requires an investment to use a technology to meet generally applicable health, safety or environmental requirements is not inconsistent with' the prohibition of performance requirement relating to transfer and use of technology by an investor.[358] Measures designed and applied to protect legitimate public welfare objectives, including the health and environment, do not constitute indirect expropriation. Such measures may constitute indirect expropriation in 'rare circumstances, such as when a measure or series of measures is so severe in the light of their purpose that they cannot be reasonably viewed as having been adopted in good faith, non-discriminatory measures'.[359] The Kenya–Turkey investment treaty does not contain this qualification.[360]

The Cameroon–Canada investment treaty also says 'it is inappropriate to encourage investment by relaxing domestic health, safety or environmental measures' and therefore a party should not waive or derogate from those measures to encourage the establishment and maintenance of an investment of an investor.[361] A party may consult with the other party if such waiver or derogation is made. The parties should encourage enterprises 'to voluntarily' incorporate recognised international standards of corporate social responsibility including on labour, the environment, and human rights.[362]

The Cameroon–Canada investment treaty also makes provision for a tribunal to appoint an expert to report to the tribunal factual issues concerning, among others, any environmental matter raised by a disputing party.[363] This provision is

[356] Ghana Model BIT 2008, art 7(6).

[357] Agreement Between Canada and the Republic of Cameroon for the Promotion and Protection of Investments, signed 3 March 2014, entered into force, 16 December 2016, art 9(1)(f).

[358] ibid art 9(2).

[359] ibid art 9(6)(c).

[360] Kenya–Turkey Investment Treaty (n 354), art 5(2) 2. 'Non-discriminatory legal measures designed and applied to protect legitimate public welfare objectives, such as health, safety and environment, do not constitute indirect expropriation.'

[361] ibid art 15(1). Article 4(4) of Protocol to the Agreement on the Promotion and Protection of Investments between the Government of the Republic of Korea and the Government of the Republic of Kenya, signed 08 July 2014, entered into force 3 May 2017.

[362] Cameroon–Canada Investment Treaty (n 357), art 15(2). Article 22 of Kenya–Japan Investment Treat (n 192).

[363] Cameroon–Canada Investment Treaty (n 357), art 33.

significant for environmental protection since it allows for scientific opinions on environmental matters to inform the decision of a tribunal when environmental issues are raised in a dispute between an investor and the host state.

The Cameroon–Republic of Korea investment treaty's preamble indicates that the parties desire to achieve investment protection in a manner that is consistent with environmental protection goals. However, the treaty does not contain a substantive provision on environmental regulation. The Annex indicates that environmental and health measures do not constitute indirect expropriation if they are non-discriminatory and not extremely severe or disproportionate in light of their purpose. The Egypt–Finland investment treaty, Egypt–Mauritius investment treaty, and Egypt–Switzerland investment treaty make reference to the environment only in their preambles.[364] The Kenya–United Arab Emirates investment treaty says once established, investments may only be subjected to additional performance requirements only if they 'are deemed vital for reasons of public order, public health or environmental concerns and are enforced by law of general application'.[365]

Perhaps because of its experience of environmental degradation arising from the oil industry, Nigeria's investment treaties contain much more concrete provisions on the environmental protection since some of them are legally enforceable. The Nigeria–Morocco investment treaty[366] recognises the right of the parties to regulate including on environmental measures.[367] Significantly, Article 14 states:

1. Investors or the investment shall comply with environmental assessment screening and assessment processes applicable to their proposed investments prior to their establishment, as required by the laws of the host state for such an investment or the laws of the home state for such an investment, whichever is more rigorous in relation to the investment in question.
2. Investors or the investment shall conduct a social impact assessment of the potential investment. The Parties shall adopt standards for this purpose at the meeting of the Joint Committee.

[364] Agreement between the Government of the Republic of Finland and the Government of the Arab Republic of Egypt on the Promotion and Protection of Investments, signed 3 March 2004, entered into force 5 February 2005; Agreement between the Government of the Republic of Mauritius and the Government of the Arab Republic of Egypt on the Reciprocal Promotion and Protection of Investments, signed 25 June 2014, entered into force, 17 October 2014; and Agreement between the Swiss Confederation and the Arab Republic of Egypt on the Promotion and Reciprocal Protection of Investments, signed 07 June 2010, entered into force 15 May 2012.

[365] Agreement between the Government of The Republic of Kenya and the Government of the United Arab Emirates on the Promotion and Protection of Investments, signed 23 November 2013, entered into force 5 June 2017, art 3(4).

[366] Reciprocal Investment Promotion and Protection Agreement between The Government of the Kingdom of Morocco and the Government of the Federal Republic of Nigeria, signed 3 December 2016.

[367] ibid art 13.

3. Investors, their investment, and host state authorities shall apply the precautionary principle to their environmental impact assessment and to decisions taken in relation to a proposed investment, including any necessary mitigation or alternative approaches of the precautionary principle by investors and investments shall be described in the environmental impact assessment they undertake.

Article 18 of Nigeria–Morocco investment treaty establishes post-establishment obligations of investors and investments, stating:

1. Investments shall, in keeping with good practice requirements relating to the size and nature of the investment, maintain an environmental management system. Companies in areas of resource exploitation and high-risk industrial enterprises shall maintain a current certification to ISO 14001 or an equivalent environmental management standard.
2. Investors and investments shall uphold human rights in the host state.
3. Investors and investments shall act in accordance with core labour standards as required by the ILO Declaration on Fundamental Principles and Rights of Work, 1998.
4. Investors and investments shall not manage or operate the investments in a manner that circumvents international environmental, labour, and human rights obligations to which the host state and/or home state are Parties.

Similar positive obligations are imposed on foreign investors when it comes to corporate governance and practices in Article 19 of the Nigeria–Morocco investment treaty thus.

1. In accordance with the size and nature of an investment, a) Investments shall meet or exceed national and internationally accepted standards of corporate governance for the sector involved, in particular for transparency and accounting practices. b) Investments shall establish and maintain, where appropriate, local community liaison processes, in accordance with internationally accepted standards when available. c) Where relevant internationally accepted standards of the type described in this Article are not available or have been developed without the participation of developing countries, the Joint Committees may establish such standards.

Most of the provisions in the investment treaties do not do much in terms of preserving the right to regulate. The fact that a contracting party is not prevented from adopting environmental and human rights measures does not mean that if the measure is challenged a state would be able successfully to defend the right to regulate on the basis of provisions in the investment treaties to the effect that nothing in the treaty shall prevent the state from adopting the measure concerned.

The provisions do not say how a conflict between the right to adopt an environmental and human rights measures and the obligations to protect foreign investment is to be resolved.

The qualifications that the environmental and human rights measures must be non-discriminatory also serves to limit the potency of these exceptions. The phrase 'in rare circumstances' in the exceptions also makes room for environmental and human rights measures to be challenged as constituting indirect expropriation. A much more concrete provision on environmental protection is contained in Article 12(1) of the Ghana Model BIT which states that foreign investors 'shall be bound by the laws and regulations in force in the host State, including its laws and regulations on labour, health and the environment'. If foreign investors are by bound the laws and regulations, it means states can take action to enforce them. This type of provisions needs to be contained in investment treaties ultimately concluded by states and not just left in model BITs.

4.6.2 The Environment and Human Rights in Continental and Regional Investment Treaty Reforms in Africa

The Agreement Establishing the African Continental Free Trade Area (AfCFTA) addresses environmental concerns in the preamble wherein the parties reaffirmed their 'right to regulate within their territories and the State Parties' flexibility to achieve legitimate policy objectives' such as public health, safety, and the environment. The preamble to the Protocol on Trade in Services also recognises the 'the right of State Parties to regulate in pursuit of national policy objectives, and to introduce new regulations, on the supply of services, within their territories ... without compromising consumer protection, environmental protection and overall sustainable development'.

It is only in these preambles that environmental and human rights objectives are addressed in this Agreement. It follows that the Agreement does not substantively address how these objectives on regulating in furtherance of environmental objectives are to be achieved. In the absence of such substantive provisions on the environment state parties would lack a legal basis under the Agreement itself to regulate the operations and activities of businesses that adversely affect the environment and human rights unless state parties exercise their powers under national environmental laws and international environmental treaties.[368] Legally, this means that if environmental measures affect trade in goods and services and traders challenge them, the state parties would have nothing under the Agreement

[368] On environmental treaties in Africa Dominic Dagbanja, 'Africa and International Environmental Law' in Erika Techera and others (eds), *Routledge Handbook of International Environmental Law* (2nd edn, Routledge 2021) 279.

Establishing AfCFTA to defend those measures. However, given that treaties must be interpreted in accordance with their object and context as analysed in Chapter 2, states could argue that state parties' desire to promote and protect trade in a manner that is consistent with the right to regulate to protect the environment and human rights as stated in the preambles ought to guide the Dispute Settlement Body in resolving disputes under the Agreement that implicate human rights and environmental concerns.

The Pan-African Investment Code 2016 (PAfIC), a soft instrument for investment treaty negotiation, specifically addresses the environment in Article 37. It imposes a duty on Member States to 'ensure that their laws and regulations provide for environmental protection'[369] and that the Member States must 'not encourage investment by relaxing or waiving compliance with domestic environmental legislation'.[370] It also imposes a positive duty on investors to protect the environment where their activities cause damage to the environment by taking reasonable steps to restore the environment[371] and requires investors and states to carry out an environmental impact assessment.[372]

The PAfIC seeks to limit the scope of both the MFN and national treatment standard to accommodate environmental protection objectives. Thus, according to Articles 7(3) and 9(3) the concept of 'in like circumstances', used to compare national investors and foreign investors when establishing MFN and national treatment, requires an overall examination of all the circumstances of an investment, including 'its effects on the local, regional or national environment, the health of the populations, or on the global commons'. Relatedly, Articles 8(2) and 10(3) state that regulatory measures to 'protect or enhance legitimate public welfare objectives, such as public health, safety and the environment' do not constitute a breach of the MFN and national treatment principles. These are important qualifications to the MFN and national treatment that could help limit the scope of application of these standards for purposes of reserving the policy space to regulate to protect environment and human rights. However, these provisions are hardly taken into account in the actual conclusion of investment treaties. The goals behind them can hardly be achieved if they are not incorporated into concluded investment treaties.

The approach taken by Articles 8(2) and 10(3)of the PAfIC to limit the MFN and national treatment standards for purposes of environmental and human rights protection essentially reproduced Article 17(2)(b) and (a) of the 2007 Investment Agreement for the Common Market for Southern and Eastern Africa (COMESA) Common Investment Area.[373] On environment and human rights, the COMESA Investment Agreement states in Article 20(8):

369 Pan-African Investment Code 2016, art 37(1).
370 ibid art 37(2).
371 ibid art 37(3).
372 ibid art 37(4).
373 Investment Agreement for the COMESA Common Investment Area signed 23 May 2007.

> Consistent with the right of states to regulate and the customary international law principles on police powers, bona fide regulatory measures taken by a Member State that are designed and applied to protect or enhance legitimate public welfare objectives, such as public health, safety and the environment, shall not constitute an indirect expropriation.

The COMESA Investment Agreement also contains a general exception for the right to regulate to protect the environment and health with the proviso that such a measure must not be applied in a 'manner which would constitute a means of arbitrary or unjustifiable discrimination between investor where like conditions prevail, or a disguised restriction on investment flows'.[374] The Agreement also requires the appointment of an expert to report to a tribunal on environmental issues that come up in the course of arbitration, and thereby ties environmental protection objectives and investment dispute settlement.[375]

The Economic and Monetary Community of Central Africa Investment Convention[376] and the Economic Community of Western African States (ECOWAS) Supplementary Act[377] on Investments do not make a single reference to the environment and human rights. Under Article 5(3)(c) of the Treaty Establishing the East African Community,[378] the Community has a duty to ensure 'the promotion of sustainable utilisation of the natural resources of the Partner States and the taking of measures that would effectively protect the natural environment of the Partner States'. Articles 111–114 and 116 of this Treaty are devoted to environmental protection and management and wildlife issues. Under Article 51((1)(b) of the Treaty Establishing the Economic Community of Central African States,[379] states shall 'ensure the proper application of science and technology to the conservation of the environment' in the context of economic activities. Central and east African states which enter into investment treaties without reserving the right to regulate to protect the environment may well be in violation of their respective regional body founding treaty, if investment treaty standards now stand in the way of the states their duties to protect the environment and human rights.

African states have constitutional and general international law duties to protect the environment and human rights in the interests of their citizens. Therefore, they must put the environment and human rights first when they enter into investment

[374] ibid art 22(1)(b).

[375] ibid art 10.

[376] Convention on Investments in the States of the Customs and Economic Union of Central Africa, signed 14 December 1965, entered into force 1 April 1966.

[377] Supplementary Act A/SA.3/12/08 Adopting Community Rules on Investment and the Modalities for Their Implementation with ECOWAS, signed 19 December 2008, entered into force 19 January 2009.

[378] Treaty Establishing the East African Community, signed 30 November 1999, entered into force 7 July 2000.

[379] Treaty Establishing the Economic Community of Central African States, signed 18 October 1983, entered into force 18 December 1984.

treaties. Bilateral, regional, and continental legal frameworks on investment that provide for enforceable legal obligations against foreign investors in relation to the protection of the environment and human rights are consistent with the environmental and human rights protection obligations of African states.

Investment treaties pay lip service to environmental and human rights interests by merely *affirming* or *recognising* the right regulate. It is settled in domestic law and customary international law that states are endowed with the right to regulate. Therefore, a mere affirmation or recognition of the right to regulate in investment treaties does not serve any useful purpose in terms of enabling states to reclaim the right to regulate. To serve their intended purpose of preserving the right to regulate, provisions making exceptions for human rights and environmental protection must impose positive and negative obligations on foreign investors which must be enforceable against the investors. The substantive standards of investment protection guarantee foreign investors enforceable rights. So too must the obligations of foreign investors arising from their activities and operations be legally enforceable. A 'balance' of protection between the rights of foreign investors and states, if such a balance need be struck, cannot be achieved in situations where foreign investors have enforceable rights under investment treaties but states do not have enforceable rights against foreign investors under the same treaties.

4.7 Reconciling Investment Treatment Standards with Environmental and Human Rights Regulation in Africa

4.7.1 Environmental and Human Rights Protection Obligations, and Capacity of African States to Execute Investment Treaties

How is the conflict between investment treaty norms and African states' constitutional and general international law duties with respect to environment and human rights protection to be resolved? This question has to be addressed in terms of the limits to investment treaty-making powers of African states and in terms of treaty interpretation. Human rights and the right to environment must be put first to investment rights.

The African constitutions require governments to exercise their powers in a manner that advances the welfare of the people, including the protection of the environment and human rights. Various international, regional, and national efforts by various states aimed at protecting the environment and environment point to the existence of consensus on this subject.[380] So the obligations of African states to

[380] United Nations Education, Science, and Culture Organization (UNESCO), *Final Report: Intergovernmental Conference of Experts on Scientific Bases for Rational Use and Conservation of the Resources of the Biosphere* (4–13 September 1968), <http://unesdoc.unesco.org/images/0001/000172/017269eb.pdf>; GA Res 2542, UN Doc A/7833, A/L 583 (1969); *Permanent Sovereignty over*

protect the environment and human rights are not matters limited to constitutions in the continent, they are matters under IETs, IHRTs, and declarations as well. The various constitutions studied require their governments to cooperate with other states for purposes of protecting the environment and human rights. This is fulfilled by African states being parties to conventions such as the African Convention on Conservation of Nature and Natural Resources and African Charter on Human and Peoples Rights. Therefore, there is a link between African states' constitutional duties on fundamental environmental and human rights and their duties under IETs and IHRTs. This link creates what I have called *constitutional-general international law imperatives* on the matters of human rights and environmental protection.

The constitutions do not place a similar obligation on the states when it comes to foreign investment. So, the duty to protect foreign investment cannot be placed on the same footing as the duties to protect the environment and human rights, merely because foreign investment is governed by a treaty. The VCLT states in Article 27 that a 'party may not invoke the provisions of its internal law as justification for its failure to perform a treaty'. That prohibition is without prejudice to the right of a state to say a treaty is not binding on it because its consent to the treaty was expressed in manifest violation of internal law of fundamental importance under Article 46 of the VCLT. However, the issue is not even about African states' being able to excuse the performance of an investment treaty obligation on the basis of internal law. The issue is that since the duties to protect the environment and human rights derive from constitutions and IETs and IHRTs, these duties should be superior to investment treaty obligations.

The International Law Commission observed in 1981 that 'safeguarding the ecological balance has come to be considered an 'essential interest' of all States'.[381] In the *Case Concerning Gabcíkovo-Nagymaros Project (Hungary/Slovakia*,[382] the ICJ acknowledged and gave judicial backing to the duty of states to protect the environment when it stated that 'in the field of environmental protection, vigilance and prevention are required on account of the often irreversible character of damage to the environment and of the limitations inherent in the very mechanism of reparation of this type of damage'.[383]

In his separate opinion, Judge Weeramantry stated that ' there is always the need to weigh considerations of development against environmental considerations, as their underlying juristic bases—the right to development and the right

Natural Resources, GA Res 1803 (XVII), (1962); and *Report of the UN Conference on the Human Environment Stockholm*, UN Doc A/CONF.48/14/Rev 1 (1974) 4.

381 International Law Commission, *Yearbook of the International Law Commission 1980*, Vol II, Pt Two) (United Nations 1981) at 39.

382 *Case Concerning Gabcíkovo-Nagymaros Project (Hungary/Slovakia*, Judgment, ICJ Rep1997, 78.

383 ibid [140].

to environmental protection—are important principles of current international law'.[384] The protection of the environment

> is likewise a vital part of contemporary human rights doctrine, for it is a *sine qua non* for numerous human rights such as the right to health and the right to life itself. It is scarcely necessary to elaborate on this, as damage to the environment can impair and undermine all the human rights spoken of in the Universal Declaration and other human rights instruments.[385]

In the *Legality of the Threat or Use of Nuclear Weapon Case*,[386] the ICJ held that '[r]espect for the environment is one of the elements that go to assessing whether an action is in conformity with the principles of necessity and proportionality'.[387] It can be argued then that while IETs do not expressly prohibit states from entering investment treaties, they do limit the investment treaty obligations the states can assume in view of the duties they impose on the states to protect and safeguard the environment for the public good, including for foreign investors.

Thus, in view of African's states' constitutional and general international law obligations on the environment and human rights, there is a limit to the type of legal duties they can sign on to in investment treaties. Because IETs and IHRTs promote the protection of the environment and human rights in the same manner as do the various constitutions, they must be treated superior to investment treaties which seek to promote foreign investment through restriction of public interest regulation. Environmental rights, human rights, and corresponding duties must dictate the standards of investment protection the states can undertake.

In summary, I argue that combined legal force of constitutions, IETs, and IHRTs limit the competence of African states in investment treaty-making. As the primary duty of these states is to protect their citizens' fundamental human rights, the states cannot enter into investment treaty obligations that seek directly or indirectly to shield certain persons, including foreign investors, from being brought to effective justice before local courts and institutions for violations of human rights and environmental rights.[388] The ISDS mechanism shields foreign investors from being punished in local courts for violating human rights to the extent that any decision made by local courts can be challenged before investor–state tribunals. Therefore, ISDS by arbitration can constrain courts and regulatory institutions

[384] *Gabcikovo-Nagymaros Project (Hungary v Slovakia) (Separate Opinion of Vice-President Weeramantry)* [1997] ICJ Rep 7, 89.

[385] ibid [88–89].

[386] *Legality of the Threat or Use of Nuclear Weapon Case*, Advisory Opinion, ICJ Reports 1996, 226.

[387] ibid [30].

[388] A very useful reading on how human rights constraints what the State can or cannot do with public power is Evan Fox-Decent, *Sovereignty's Promise: The State as Fiduciary* (OUP 2011) ch IX.

from effectively adjudicating upon human rights and environmental issues in which foreign investors are involved.

The interpretation of investment treaties by investment tribunals or other investment dispute resolution bodies must take into consideration the legal justification for the adoption of an environmental protection measure giving rise to the dispute. Where measures are adopted in furtherance of municipal environmental law, and IETs' objectives, the link between municipal law and international environmental law must add legal significance to the legitimacy of the measure. In the words of Jorge Viñuales:[389]

> one important question that has sometimes been inadequately handled by investment tribunals is that of the legal effects attached to the justification of the measure. In an environmental context, this justification should be allowed to play a role at two levels. First, the legal basis of the measure is important. A measure adopted to comply with an international environmental obligation cannot be treated on the same footing as a purely domestic measure. The legal framework applicable to the assessment of the legality of a 'multilateral' measure is indeed different from that applicable to a 'unilateral' measure, at least as far as the applicable 'conflict rules' (the rules used to determine the priority of one norm over another) are concerned. Second, even for purely domestic measures, the interpretation of investment disciplines must leave sufficient room to accommodate environmental considerations.

Viñuales argues further that[390]

> the recognition of the link between a domestic measure and an environmental treaty would place the measure challenged at the same level as investment disciplines, thus excluding the application of the rule giving priority to international (investment) law over domestic (environmental) law.

Muthucumaraswamy Sornarajah raised the question of[391]

> whether matters of international concern relating to the environment or human rights are *ius cogens* principles which trump the rights of foreign investors under investment treaties unilaterally to institute arbitral proceedings. The argument can credibly be made that there are some values in international environmental law and human rights law that are so fundamental that the propositions of

[389] Jorge Viñuales 'The Environmental Regulation of Foreign Investment Schemes under International Law' in Pierre-Marie Dupuy and Jorge E Viñuales (eds), *Harnessing Foreign Investment to Promote Environmental Protection: Incentives and Safeguards* (CUP 2013) 273, 277.

[390] ibid at 286.

[391] Sornarajah, *Law on Foreign Investment* (n 12) 232.

investment treaties which are designed to protect large multinational corporations should give way to them.

I adopt Sornarajah's view that[392]

> [t]he progressive evolution of the right to a clean environment as a human right and as a norm incorporating higher values may lead to an inflexible right for the state to interfere in order to protect the environment and to regard this interference as not amounting to a taking which is not compensable. But, the right must be exercised on objective grounds.

Where an environmental measure is sanctioned by both municipal environmental law and international environmental law, the interpretive approach should either give rise to no liability at all or the award of damages must take into consideration both the merits of the measure and the fact that it derives its justification from both legal norms. Where the measure derives its source from municipal environmental law alone, its merits must be taken into consideration in deciding on liability and damages, if any.

The proposed interpretive approach is necessary to ensure that investment treaties, as international legal norms, do not become instruments for the flagrant disregard of established fundamental rights of citizens whether under domestic law, general international law, or both. Therefore, there is the need for a 'retreat from the perception that investment protection is the only purpose of the investment treaty' to the recognition of defences in the interpretation of investment treaties 'on the basis of the relevance of the international law generally and of the international law on human rights and the environment in particular'.[393] The interpretation of investment treaties and the award of damages against the host state cannot continue to ignore the fact that 'a state has the right to intervene in an investment that poses a danger to the environment or involves an abuse of human rights'.[394]

4.7.2 Protecting Legitimate Investment within Justified Limits

The argument that investment treaties must not undermine people's right to live in a clean and safe environment and enjoy their other human rights is not intended to say that the environment must be protected at the expense of foreign investment made within the host state. Thomas Waelde and Abba Kolo argue that:[395]

[392] ibid 110.
[393] ibid xvi.
[394] ibid 78.
[395] Kolo and Waelde, 'Investment Protection and Regulatory Taking' (n 18) 819–20.

> The major concern of the foreign investor is not with environmental regulation per se but rather it is with the uncertainty and surprise aspect of environmental regulation in particular and regulatory changes generally which upset the fiscal and regulatory regime under which the investment was made . . . Investment protection rather turns around the issue of unexpected change with an excessive detrimental impact on the foreign investor's prior calculation.
>
> If a company decides to invest, then it expects that the legal and fiscal conditions will remain relatively stable for some time. This is especially so for the natural resources, energy and infrastructure projects where investment is long-term, high risk, capital intensive and highly dependent on the exercise of government's regulatory powers. Stability of key investment conditions and protection against abuse or excess of regulatory powers is then of essence to the foreign investor . . . This is the more so if the investment was made based on promises given by the host State in an agreement with the investor or contained in the country's investment laws.

Legally unjustified discriminatory disguised and camouflaged in the name of environmental and human rights protection, in the sense of manifestly having nothing at all to do with environmental and human protection objectives, cannot be accepted in the face of legal commitments to protect foreign investment under investment treaties made within the legal limits of states. States must respect express promises they may make to foreign investors to refrain from certain forms of regulatory changes if those promises have been legally made under national constitutions and general international law. The idea then is not that states must not be accountable for the adverse impact of their decisions on investors and investments whatsoever or that investors must take risks and losses deliberately inflicted on them by states for no justifiable reason. However, the case for stability and predictability of the legal environment for investment cannot be taken in absolute terms. National and international environmental law 'are typically open-ended and very responsive to public opinion pressure'.[396] This may occasion the need to change these laws. Moreover, laws generally are made subject to being repealed, changed, or amended when the need arises. This is an inherent part of law-making and law implementation. The reason for doing so is often unexpected.

Therefore, investors should not claim too much surprise (if they can claim surprise at all) when the law is changed or repealed. If investments are long term and the economic and social conditions in which the investments were made change, this in turn may demand changes in the legal framework governing the investment or changes in law generally. In such circumstances, it can hardly be reasonably and legitimately expected that laws and regulations, whether they affect foreign

[396] ibid 820.

investment or not, should remain stable and unchangeable.[397] Foreign direct investment by its nature is carried out for a long duration. It is reasonable and legitimate then to expect change in laws and regulations depending on changed circumstances over the life span of foreign direct investment. Therefore, it is quite a contradiction to say foreign investors have *legitimate* expectation for laws and regulations to remain *stable* as they were when the investment was admitted. On the contrary, it is rather states that should have legitimate expectation to change their laws depending on the circumstances.

Thus, if an enactment, amendment, or repeal of laws is manifestly needed, an investment tribunal's analysis of its adverse impact on investment should focus as well on the merits of the amendment and not just on its unexpectedness and impact on investment alone. Requiring compensation for every (significant) diminution in the value of an investment caused by legally justified environmental and human rights regulation will unduly restrain legitimate policymaking and undermine the rule of law because claims for compensation can cripple governments economically. Environmental and human rights regulation is required and should not be treated as expropriatory if the primary motive for such regulation which interferes with investment rights was protection of the environment and human rights and not to expropriate as such.[398]

While the entry of foreign investment has beneficial effects,[399] it could also have negative effects. Jonathan Bonnitcha argues that 'the effectiveness of measures to protect the environment is a function of their achievement of non-economic conservation objectives. The economic interests of foreign investment may occasionally coincide with these objectives, but they are not representative of them'.[400] In view of this, an investment treaty that is premised on the notion that all foreign investment is uniformly, always, and definitely beneficial so that all forms of regulation must be frozen in the interest of the investment is misleading and dangerous to the national interest.[401]

Therefore, there is the need for exception to liability for interference with foreign investment on environmental and human rights grounds in existing investment treaties in Africa. As the duties of the states to protect the environment and human rights derive from municipal law, IETs and IHRTs, that duty must not be

397 For changed circumstances and investment protection see Christina Binder, 'Changed Circumstances in Investment Law: Interfaces between the Law of Treaties and the Law of State Responsibility with Special Focus on the Argentine Crisis' in Binder and others (eds) *International Investment Law for the 21st Century* (n 180) 608; and Asif Quresh, 'The Economic Emergency Defence in Bilateral Investment Treaties: Development Perspective' in Binder and others, ibid 631.

398 Sornarajah, *Law on Foreign Investment* (n 12) 111.

399 Amokura Kawharu, 'International Law's Protection of Foreign-Owned Property against Uncompensated Expropriation: Preserving Host State Regulatory Freedom' in David Grinlinton and Prue Taylor (eds), *Property Rights and Sustainability: The Evolution of Property Rights to Meet Ecological Challenges* (Brill 2011) 343.

400 Bonnitcha, *Substantive Protection under Investment Treaties* (n 308) 132.

401 Sornarajah, *Law on Foreign Investment* (n 12) 230.

subordinated to investment treaty obligations. For future investment treaties, provisions on expropriation must provide for effective safeguards that will ensure the adoption and use of environmental protection measures.[402] Future investment treaties will also need to consider the suitability of investment tribunals to resolve issues of law, policy, and business. There is room[403]

> for the further proposition that these issues should not be dealt with by arbitral tribunals that are created under investment treaties which have only a narrow mandate to decide issues that arise from the foreign investment. Instead, tribunals that reflect the interests of the international community as a whole should deal with such disputes. There must be a doctrine of arbitrability created which ensures that issues that concern the international community as a whole should not be disposed of by arbitral tribunals which draw their jurisdiction from the will of only the parties to the dispute before them.

Conversely, allowing the state to regulate in disregard of commitments it undertakes in relation to foreign investment and without any attention to compensation would result in over-regulation uninhibited by the economic costs attendant to the state's actions.[404] The normative value of interests of the state and foreign investors at stake must be taken into consideration and not just the value of an investment and the effect of a governmental action has on it. This is the only way both unbridled and extensive investment protection and excessive and unjustified regulation can be checked.

4.7.3 The Most-Favoured-Home and Third-States Clause in African Investment Treaties

African countries must begin to include a *Most-Favoured-Home-Third States Clause* (MFHT Clause) in investment treaties they sign with other countries, and between and among African themselves. The MFHT Clause will establish the operating and performance standards and obligations (OPSOs) for foreign investors with reference to their home states and the third states, aligned with or independently of national treatment and MFN treatment. The core of the MFHT Clause is that it imposes the home state and third state best environmental, human rights, labour, industry, and other OPSOs on foreign investors when they carry on their business in the host state. The MFHT Clause will impose the most favourable OPSOs in the home state and third state on foreign investors. The OPSOs are the

[402] ibid 272.
[403] ibid 232.
[404] Kolo and Waelde, 'Investment Protection and Regulatory Taking' (n 18) 839.

most favourable to the host state and its citizens when compared to similar ones in the host state.

This means that foreign investors have obligations to operate at the highest and most favourable levels of environmental, human rights, labour, and industry standards as applicable or obtains in their home states or in third states in comparison with standards in the host state. The *most favourable* (not the worst favourable or less/least favourable) OPSOs in the home state and third state must follow the investor to the host state. An MFHT Clause will impose obligations on foreign investors to operate in the host state at no less favourable OPSOs than they would do had they been operating in home states or in third states. The host state's OPSOs are the default standards. However, if among all the standards required in the host state, home state, and third state, the OPSOs in the home state or the third state prove most favourable, either or both shall apply, and the investor's liability or otherwise will be determined accordingly.

As foreign investors take the benefits of investment treatment standards such as national treatment (NT) and MFN treatment, there is the need for the host state to derive equivalent benefits directly from the home state and third state arising from the activities of foreign investors in the host state. The MFHT Clause ensures *reciprocity of benefit* (ROB) and *reciprocity of obligation* (ROO); the investor enjoys NT and MFN based on its investment in the host state and the host state in turn enjoys the benefit of the most rigorous OPSOs in the home state and third state that would be required of foreign investors if they carried on business there. The enjoyment of these benefits comes with corresponding obligations. These benefits and obligations derive from and would not be available but for the relationship between the investors and the host state under the applicable investment treaty. With the MFHT Clause, a host state is able, through the applicable investment treaty, to import appropriate and acceptable human rights, environmental, labour, industry, and other operating and performance standards from the home state of the foreign investor or from a third state to be observed by foreign investors in the host state.

The burden will be on the host state to prove the most favourable applicable operating and performance standards just as it is on foreign investors to prove NT or MFN. Thus, NT, MFN, and MFHT clauses come with their respective burdens on the investor or host state as the case may be. The most favourable OPSOs may be imposed independently of the availability of MFN and national treatment standards. This is *fair and equitable* exchange and it ensures *equal protection and security* for both the investor and the host state.

4.8 Conclusion

The duties to protect the environment and human rights in Africa are statutory and constitutional. They are also founded on customary international law, IETs, and IHRTs. Various African constitutions considered in this book require African governments to conduct their international affairs, including the making of investment treaties in consonance with principles of public international law and in a manner that is consistent with their national interests. Environmental and human rights protection are about public interest. It is in the national interests of African states that the environment should be protected because of the importance of the environment for human right to health and livelihood. Investment treaties cannot be said to be in the public interest if their provisions impair or prevent African states from discharging their constitutional and general international law duties to protect the environment and human rights. For this reason, the constitutional and general international law duties to protect the environment and human rights must place limitations on the investment treaty obligations African states can assume.

The consistency of investment treaties with environmental rights and human rights and corresponding obligations of African states must be at the forefront of any negotiation and the ultimate conclusion of investment treaties. Merely affirming or recognising the right to regulate in investment treaties does not bring about that consistency. There is the need for enforceable obligations to be imposed on foreign investors in investment treaties and states must have the standing to enforce those obligations against foreign investors just as foreign investors have enforceable rights against states. Foreign investors must also take risks inherent in governmental regulation and must not seek to operate absolutely free from and untouched by the challenges, difficulties, realities, and consequences (financial or otherwise) associated with undertaking business in a foreign country.

5

The Right to Development, Development Policy-making and the Investment Treaty Regime in Africa

5.1 Introduction

The right to development goes with a corresponding duty of the state to make development policies 'of its choice' and to implement them for the realisation of this right.[1] How might the investment treaty regime stand in the way of African states' right to pursue development policies of their choice? This chapter is aimed at ascertaining whether African constitutions recognise and protect the right to development, and if so whether the duties and obligations of African governments to adopt measures to bring about the realisation of this right limit the competence of African countries in the execution of international investment agreements (IIAs) or investment treaties. This analysis is premised on a consideration of the actual and potential limitations or effects of investment treaties and investor–state arbitration on development policy-making and implementation in Africa.

As discussed in Chapter 1, the prevailing orthodoxy is that there is a link between foreign investment and development.[2] There 'is an enduring belief that all foreign investments should be protected because they are beneficial to the development goals of the host states'.[3] Based on this premise, most countries in Africa and other parts of the world have liberalised or strengthened their legal regimes for the

[1] Sonia Rolland, *Development at the World Trade Organization* (OUP 2012) 26 (Rolland, *Development at WTO*).

[2] Stephan Schill, 'International Investment Law as International Development Law' in Andrea K Bjorklund (ed), *Yearbook on International Investment Law and Policy 2012–2013* (OUP 2014) 327, 329–30 (hereafter, Schill, 'IIL as International Development Law'); Organisation for Economic Cooperation and Development, *Foreign Direct Investment for Development: Maximising Benefits, Minimising Costs* (OECD Publishing 2002) 7 (hereafter, Organisation for Economic Cooperation and Development, *FDI for Development*); and UNCTAD, *Midrand Declaration and A Partnership for Growth and Development* (TD/377, 24 May 1996) 14, para 36. For contested literature about the role of foreign investment treaties in the attraction of foreign investment and their benefits see generally Karl Sauvant and Lisa Sachs (eds), *The Effects of Foreign Direct Investment: Bilateral Investment Treaties, Double Taxation Treaties, and Investment Flows* (OUP 2009); and Dominic Dagbanja, 'Can African Countries Attract Investments without Bilateral Investment Treaties? Example from Ghana' (2019) 40(2) The Australasian Review of African Studies 71.

[3] Muthucumaraswamy Sornarajah, *The International Law on Foreign Investment* (3rd edn, CUP 2010) 51 (hereafter, Sornarajah, *Law on Foreign Investment*).

The Investment Treaty Regime and Public Interest Regulation in Africa. Dominic Npoanlari Dagbanja, Oxford University Press.
 DOI: 10.1093/oso/9780192896179.003.0005

promotion and protection of foreign investment, and international law on foreign investment has been preoccupied with the treatment to be accorded to foreign investment and associated private property rights.[4]

Yet, the benefits of foreign investment are neither assured nor do they accrue automatically.[5] Muthucumaraswamy Sornarajah states that '[w]ithin economics itself, the idea that there is a single explanation of the effects of foreign investment on development or that there is only a single and uniform means of achieving economic development is heavily contested'.[6] The effects of foreign investment on development depend on the conditions prevailing in the host country, the value of the investment to the national economy, the activities and strategies of foreign investors, and the host government's policies.

As foreign investment is not the sole means through which states can develop, I argue that African governments must not surrender their general regulatory autonomy in order to attract investment. Taxation, capital account regulation, industrial and targeted social and economic policies also matter for the realisation of development, and it is the role of African governments to make and implement such policies. The adoption of such measures may adversely affect foreign investments and lead to investor–state arbitration as demonstrated in Subsection 5.4.1.1. For example, African states may prohibit the marketing of a particular type of product, restrict the manner in which an investment may be used, or impose compliance costs on foreign investors. They may also adopt measures in response to the conduct of foreign investors' activities, such as those in mining that negatively impact on their populations. African governments must be concerned that foreign investors have challenged a range of development-related measures as breaching investment treaty obligations.[7]

I go further than defending the space and autonomy to regulate for development and I argue that the right to development and corresponding duties of African states to make and implement development policies limits the type of investment treaty obligations they can assume.

Three important points about the relationship between investment treaties and development need to be highlighted. The first is that capital investment, whether at home or abroad, is motivated primarily by profit-making and does not necessarily lead to development. Kwame Nkrumah, first President of Ghana, argued that[8]

[4] Shyami Fernando Puvimanasinghe, *Foreign Investment, Human Rights and the Environment: A Perspective from South Asia on the Role of Public International Law for Development* (Martinus Nijhoff Publishers 2007) xi.

[5] Organisation for Economic Cooperation and Development, *FDI for Development* (n 2) 7; and United Nations Conference on Trade and Development (UNCTAD), *Economic Development in Africa: Rethinking the Role of Foreign Direct Investment* (United Nations 2005) 64–65.

[6] Sornarajah, *Law on Foreign Investment* (n 3) 52.

[7] Caroline Henckels, 'Balancing Investment Protection and Sustainable Development: The Role of Deference in Bjorklund, *Yearbook on Investment Law and Policy* in Andrea K. Bjorklund (ed), *Yearbook on International Investment Law and Policy 2012–2013* (OUP 2014) 305, 306 (hereafter, Henkles, 'Balancing Investment Protection and Sustainable Development').

[8] Kwame Nkrumah, *Revolutionary Path* (Panaf Books 2001), 415, 416.

> [t]he basic principle of capitalism and . . . private enterprise (which in Africa generally means foreign private enterprise) is that an industrial or commercial project shall depend for its initiation or continuance . . . on how much profit it makes for the individual or group of individuals, such as shareholders. Capitalists or private entrepreneurs always seek projects which provide them with the greatest profit for the least investment in the shortest time. This is the principle on which they operate.
>
> It means in Ghana they are only going to support or introduce such projects as will show them the maximum possible profits for the smallest effort in the shortest time, and in the most convenient place to fulfil these conditions.
>
> They are not going to do something in Ghana if they can do it more cheaply and with greater profit somewhere else. Nor are they going to do it in Ghana if it is in competition with some similar project they already have somewhere else.
>
> National development is impossible under this system. How can we develop Ghana as a whole if the test of every project is its attractiveness to foreign investors and its rapid profitability? Which foreign investor is going to develop the Northern Region of Ghana, for example, when the quickest source of profit is in the Southern Region?

The second point is that even if investment treaties enhance investment promotion and protection objectives, they also impose constraints that[9]

> could take many forms: they could limit options for developing countries in the formulation of development strategies that might call for differential treatment of investors, e.g. industrial policies; or they could hinder policymaking in general, including for sustainable development objectives, if investors perceive new measures as unfavourable to their interests and resort to IIA-defined dispute settlement procedures outside the normal domestic legal process.

Third, although states sign investment treaties to attract foreign investment for their development, most arbitral tribunals do not regard an investment's contribution to development as a central element in the definition of investment. Consequently, a state may not be entitled to a successful claim that an investment should not be protected under an investment treaty because of its lack of contribution to the state's development. Hence, measures adopted by states to promote their development may give rise to investment treaty liability if the measures adversely

[9] UNCTAD, *World Investment Report 2012: Towards a New Generation of Investment Policies* (United Nations 2012) 133.

affect an investment, even if the investment does not contribute to national development. Diane Desierto highlights this problematic, observing that[10]

> the concept of development figures in two highly polemical questions that have become a staple in contemporary investment arbitral disputes. The first question asks whether development should be treated as an essential element or criterion (rather than simply a descriptive feature) to establish the existence of an 'investment' to which the international investment agreement ... would apply.... The second question inquires if the state's regulatory prerogative to pursue development objectives forms part of [the] subject matter that can be deemed excluded from the applicability of an IIA ... [T]hese questions speak to a much broader *problématique* about the extent of applicability of an IIA to an Investor–state dispute when the host state has to contend with challenging adverse development situations arising during the life of an investment.

Development policy space is about the autonomy of states to adopt and implement measures they consider appropriate for the realisation of development. It is about the sovereign freedom and legal responsibilities to make and implement development policies. On the one hand, investment treaties seek to create attractive and favourable conditions for investors through liberalisation. On the other hand, investment treaties by their very nature tend to limit states' measures that might be required and necessary for the realisation of development. The question then is how can African states fulfil investment treaty obligations to protect foreign investment and at the same time retain regulatory autonomy for development policy-making and implementation according to their judgment, needs, and conditions?[11]

I explore the relationship between standards of investment protection by treaty and development policy-making and implementation obligations under various constitutions and general international law in Africa with particular reference to Cameroon, Egypt, Ghana, Kenya, Nigeria, and South Africa. The constitutions of these countries require the respective governments to manage the economies in a manner that maximises development, to provide for adequate means of livelihood and sustainable employment, and to aim at a democracy that secures the necessities of life. The states are also parties to a number of international environmental treaties (IETs) and international human rights treaties (IHRTs) and that provide for the right to development and corresponding duties of the states. To ensure that these states live up to their obligations to take measures that assure the realisation of development, the standards of investment protection the states assume or agree

[10] Diane Desierto, 'Deciding International Investment Agreement Applicability: The Development Argument in Investment' in Freya Baetebs (ed), *Investment Law within International Law: Integrationist Perspectives* (CUP 2013) 240, 240–41 (Desierto, *Investment Agreement Applicability*).

[11] UNCTAD, *International Investment Agreements: Key Issues*, Vol I (UNCTAD/ITE/IIT/2004/10. United Nations 2004) 55.

to must in the first place respect and be consistent with those obligations to regulate in furtherance of development.

The rest of the chapter is structured as follows. Section 5.2 examines development as a right and corresponding duties of states in Africa. It argues that the duties to make and implement development policies are specifically assigned to governments, which must not have the authority to make treaties that directly or indirectly prohibit the performance of these duties.

Section 5.3 shows that development is an objective of African investment treaties. Yet that objective has not been influential in investment arbitration when it comes to defining the concept of investment and whether an investment is entitled to protection. This trivialises and undermines the development objectives contained in the preambles of most investment treaties.

Section 5.4 deals with the relationship between standards of investment protection and development policy-making in Africa, using two examples. The first examines the tension between selected standards of investment protection and constitutional powers and duties relating to targeted development policies that are designed to assist domestic businesses and citizens. The second example relates to transfer of investment capital and associated funds and foreign exchange regulation.

Section 5.5 addresses the implications of African states' development obligations for the status of existing investment treaties and the adoption of future ones.

Section 5.6 analyses investment treaty reforms in Africa supposedly aimed at accommodating the right to regulate in the public interest, including for development It proposes that investment treaty reforms must be informed by the dictates of the terms of specific national constitutions.

Section 5.7 concludes that the right to development and corresponding duties of African states must shape and define the investment treatment standards to which African countries agree.

5.2 The Right to Development and Corresponding Duties of African States

5.2.1 The Concept of Development and Its Relationship with Neoliberalism

5.2.1.1 The Concept of Development

The concept of 'development' does not have a universally accepted definition because development theory is not value-free.[12] It 'is necessarily normative in that it must

[12] Ann Willcox Seidman, *Ghana's Development Experience 1951–1965* (PhD thesis, Submitted in Partial Fulfilment of the Requirements for the Degree of Doctor of Philosophy to the Graduate School

contain – explicitly or implicitly—value judgments as to what "ought" to happen in the development process, what goals development 'ought' to achieve'.[13] For this reason, the definition of development, like beauty, 'usually lies in the eye of the beholder'.[14]

Development theorists have formulated a variety of goals which each considers as critical elements of development. One approach equates development with economic growth where, for example, the rate of development may be measured by increase in per capita income.[15] For example, William Barber argues that the development condition is 'satisfied when two conditions have been met: the . . . economy expands in real terms; and the per capita real income . . . also improves through time'.[16] However, defining development in terms of economic growth is fundamentally problematic because economic growth can be attained without addressing real problems like poverty, and social deprivation.[17]

It is, in part, because of the limitation of the economic approach to development that the United Nations Development Programme (UNDP) developed the Human Development Index (HDI) in 1990 as an alternative measure of development.[18] The HDI combines the indicators of life expectancy, educational attainment, and income. Human development is defined as 'a process of enlarging people's choices. The most critical ones are to lead a long and healthy life, to be educated and to enjoy a decent standard of living.'[19] This approach to development is also reflected in the *UN's Millennium Development Goals* (MDGs). The MDGs set the standards aimed at eradicating extreme poverty and hunger; achieving universal primary education; promoting gender equality and empowerment of women; reducing child mortality; improving mental health; combating HIV/AIDS, malaria, and other diseases; and ensuring environmental sustainability.[20] The *2030 Agenda for*

of the University of Wisconsin at the University of Wisconsin, 1968) 9 (hereafter, Seidman, *Ghana's Development Experience*).

[13] ibid 10.

[14] Rumu Sarkar, *International Development Law: Rule of Law, Human Rights, and Global Finance* (OUP 2009) 37.

ibid 38.

[15] Seidman, *Ghana's Development Experience* (n 12) 10.

[16] William J Barber, *The Economy of British Central Africa: A Case Study of Economic Development in a Dualistic Society* (Stanford University Press 1961) 8.

[17] Richard Peet and Elaine Hartwick, *Theories of Development: Contentions, Arguments and Alternatives* (Guildford Press 2009) 2 (hereafter, Peet and Hartwick, *Theories of Development*).

[18] United Nations Development Programme, *Human Development Report 1990: Concept and Measurement of Human Development* (OUP 1990).

[19] ibid 10.

[20] See for example Government of Ghana and United Nations Development Programme, *West Gonja Human Development Report 2007: Vulnerability and the Attainment of the MDGs at the Local Level* (United Nations Development Programme 2007) at 4 <https://hdr.undp.org/sites/default/files/undp westgonjareport2007.pdf> accessed 8 February 2022; ; United Nations, *The Millennium Development Goals Report 2013* (United Nations 2013); World Commission on Environment and Development, *Report of the World Commission on Environment and Development: Our Common Future* (United Nations 1987) [27] <file://uniwa.uwa.edu.au/userhome/staff5/00092945/Downloads/our_common_futurebrundtlandreport1987%20(1).pdf> accessed 8 February 2022.. See also United Nations,

Sustainable Development retains this human-centred focus as reflected in its seventeen goals.[21]

Arthur Lewis posited an alternative to economic growth approach, the 'people's test' which is centred on 'what is happening to food, clothes, education, health services, housing and employment'.[22] According to Lewis, a development plan is unsatisfactory if it makes output its goal rather than consumption or if it gives excessive weight to future consumption at the expense of current needs.[23] In similar vein, Amartya Sen describes development as 'a process of *expanding* the real freedom that people enjoy'.[24] Development 'requires *the removal* of major sources of . . . poverty as well as tyranny, poor economic opportunities as well as systemic social deprivation, neglect of public facilities ...'.[25]

A basic needs approach recognised under the constitutions of Cameroon, Egypt, Ghana, Kenya, Nigeria, and South Africa emphasises the need to enlarge people's choices in life. The basic needs approach to development provides a conceptual framework for analysing and explaining development normatively, based on national and international human rights standards. Development then is both an individual and state right with a corresponding duty to be performed by the state.[26] From a human development perspective, a state's duty in relation to development requires the integration of legal norms protecting basic rights of citizens into the plans, policies, and processes of development.[27]

Following the basic needs approach, I conceive of development as those basic and essential entitlements, things and values that are fundamental to human life. These entitlements and values include the right to food, water, housing and health. Development must focus on human beings and must be inclusive, which means making life better for everyone: sufficient food, a safe and healthy place in which to live, and affordable social and economic services to everyone.[28] This social and human approach to development is reflected in the various development frameworks in Africa[29] as reflected in the constitutions analysed in Subsection 5.2.2 later

Transforming Our World: The 2030 Agenda for Sustainable Development (A/RES/70/1, adopted by the General Assembly 25 September 2015) (hereafter, '2030 Agenda for Sustainable Development').

21 United Nations, '2030 Agenda for Sustainable Development' (n 20).

22 W Arthur Lewis, *Development Planning: The Essentials of Economic Policy* (Harper and Row 1966) 96.

23 ibid.

24 Amartya Sen, *Development as Freedom* (Anchor Books 1999) 4 (emphasis added).

25 ibid.

26 Brigitte Hamm, 'A Human Rights Approach to Development' (2001) 23(4) Human Rights Quarterly 1005.

27 World Health Organisation, *Right to Water* (Health and Human Rights Publication Series No 3, February 2003) 9–10.

28 Peet and Hartwick, *Theories of Development* (n 17) 1.

29 See for example in the case of Ghana Office of the Planning Commission, *Seven-Year Plan for National Reconstruction and Development. Financial Years 1963/1964—1969/1970* (Government Printer 1964); Government of Ghana, *Ghana Poverty Reduction Strategy 2003–2005: Agenda for Growth*

in this chapter. For example, by Articles 1(1) and 36(2)(e) of the Constitution of Ghana, the powers of government shall be exercised to promote the 'welfare' and 'basic necessities of life' of the people of Ghana. In this sense, the duties to make and implement development policies must determine what the states can do or cannot do with their powers, taking into consideration the implications of the particular exercise of the powers for the realisation of the right to development.

5.2.1.2 Development and Neoliberalism

James Gathii describes neoliberal economic policies as 'mainly preoccupied with displacing statist regulatory interventions in the market place while integrating national economies into the international market economy with little or no constraints on the flow of international capital'.[30] The reliance on the concept of development and the role of the state in relation to it in this chapter as justification for a limitation to be placed on the capacity of African states in investment treaty-making does not ignore the fact that development is not an unproblematic concept or that it has been used to justify neoliberalism. I do not present development as an inherently stable and positive standard against which the legal validity and effect of an investment treaty can be determined. Indeed, there are scholars who might question whether the right to development and corresponding duties of states should be used as a framework for determining the extent of the capacity to execute investment treaties given that development is used as justification for liberal legal and regulatory framework for foreign investment protection as discussed in Section 1.1 of Chapter 1, Sections 2.1 and 2.2 of Chapter 2, and Section 5.1 of this chapter.

and Prosperity (National Development Planning Commission 19 February 2003) <https://www.ircwash.org/sites/default/files/GPRS-2003-Agenda.pdf> accessed 7 February 2022; Government of Ghana, *Growth and Poverty Reduction Strategy (GPRS II) (2006–2009)* (National Development Planning Commission November 2005); Government of Ghana, *The Coordinated Programme of Economic and Social Development Policies, 2010–2016: An Agenda for Shared Growth and Accelerated Development for a Better Ghana* (National Development Planning Commission December 2010) <https://www.cabri-sbo.org/uploads/bia/ghana_2010_planning_external_national_plan_author_region_english__1.pdf> accessed 07 February 2022 (hereafter, *Economic and Social Development Policies*); Nana Addo Dankwa Akufo-Addo, *The Coordinated Programme of Economic and Social Development Policies (2017–2024): An Agenda for Jobs: Creating Prosperity and Equal Opportunity for All* (Republic of Ghana October 2017) <http://www.mop.gov.gh/wp-content/uploads/2018/04/Coordinated-Programme-Of-Economic-And-Social-Development-Policies.pdf> accessed 07 February 2022, Government of Ghana, Medium-Term National Development Policy Framework: *Ghana Shared Growth and Development Agenda (GSGDA), 2010–2013*, Vol I (National Development Planning Commission December 2010); and Government of Ghana, *Medium-Term National Development Policy Framework National Medium-Term Development Policy Framework* 2022–2025 (National Development Planning Commission December 2021) <file://uniwa.uwa.edu.au/userhome/staff5/00092945/Downloads/MTNDPF_2022-2025_Dec-2021.pdf> accessed 07 February 2022.

[30] James Thuo Gathii, 'Good Governance as a Counter Insurgency Agenda to Oppositional and Transformative Social Projects in International Law' (1999) 5 Buffalo Human Rights Law Review 107, 108 (hereafter, Gathii, 'Good Governance as Counter Insurgency Agenda').

Antony Anghie not only shows that colonialism was central in the development of international law but he also shows how the concept of development which was presented to satisfy neoliberal ideals has contributed to the construction of international legal regime for private foreign investment promotion and protection. With the attainment of independence, the new states were concerned with providing their populations with a decent standard of living that could be achieved through development. The West and the new states alike 'understood that private actors, MNCs [multinational corporations], played a vital role in achieving development'.[31] The legal framework appropriate for the regulation of these new entities could be provided by 'transnational law', which comprised a combination of domestic law, private international law, and public international law. Specifically, the increasing engagement of MNCs in the economic affairs of the 'Third World' led to the emergence of the international law of foreign investment.[32] The distinction between the 'developed' and the 'developing' became central to the operation of the Bretton Woods institutions which were to formulate new techniques to bridge the difference between the 'advanced' and the 'backward' countries.[33] The neoliberal logic about the role of foreign investment in development that justifies the limitations the investment treaty regime places on regulatory autonomy has also been questioned by Sornarajah who argues that the innate nature of arbitration enables pro-business arbitrators to articulate and shape investment treaties in a manner that entrenches and expands neoliberal principles in international investment law. The expansionist ideals are achieved through nebulous standards of investment protection.[34]

Sundhyia Pahuja analyses how the concept of development has been used to make the rule of law and international law universal.[35] She argues that[36]

> [o]nce the rule of law was cast as being relevant to the legitimacy of a state and a certain model of democracy was put forward as universal, the concept of development was engaged implicitly to underwrite that universalisation. In other words, in universalizing a particular model of democracy and its attendant rule

[31] Antony Anghie, *Imperialism, Sovereignty and the Making of International Law* (CUP 2005) 203–04.

[32] ibid 223–26.

[33] This is reflected for example in the Convention on the Settlement of Investment Disputes between States and Nationals of Other States (opened for signature, 18 March 1965, entered into force 14 October 1966) 4 ILM 524 (hereafter, 'ICSID Convention') which established the International Centre for Settlement of Investment Disputes (hereafter, 'ICSID'); Convention Establishing the Multilateral Investment Guarantee Agency (adopted 11 October 1985, entered into force 12 April 1988); World Bank, *World Investment Report 1997: The State in a Changing World* (OUP 1997); and World Bank, *World Development Report 2000/2001: Attacking Poverty* (OUP 2001).

[34] Muthucumaraswamy Sornarajah, 'The Retreat of Neo-Liberalism in Investment Treaty Arbitration' in Catherine A Rogers and Roger P Alford (eds), *The Future of Investment Arbitration* (OUP 2009) 273, 276–81.

[35] Sundhya Pahuja, *Decolonising International Law: Development, Economic Growth and the Politics of Universality* (CUP 2011) 172–85

[36] ibid 185.

> of law … styles of liberal evangelism were relevant on a development narrative. Once the concept of development was engaged implicitly in defining the rule of law, it was a short step for the rule of law to become the explicit concern of international economic institutions. The embrace by international economic institutions proved to be a powerful engine in the universalization of a particular model of the rule of law on both a conceptual and practical level. This is because of the mutually sustaining nature of the relationship between development and the concept of law as understood by those institutions.

Jennifer Beard similarly points out that the market in liberal capitalism is central to an 'understanding of how rule of law development programmes operate at the metaphysical level'.[37] According to Beard, the[38]

> rule of law development reforms are a technique for the constitution of legal subjectivity at both the national and individual level. Legal subjectivity at the national level is being shaped by the restructuring of the nation's institutions and legal system structures … Legal subjectivity at the individual level is regulated through the construction and universalisation of individual rights, freedoms and desires. The objective of all of these reforms is to create legal subjects willing obedience to a universal rule of law.
>
> Just as the early Christian was trained to confess his sins to the clergy, contemporary underdeveloped peoples are trained within development practices to speak of their economic and cultural practices in terms of their 'willingness to reform' to the rule of law instituted and structured by various development agencies. These agencies, in turn, claim to be able to mediate and transform these peoples into a truer, more developed form of subject.

Beard is 'particularly dubious about a discourse that is packed predominantly with the historical and cultural effects of a small minority of "Western" peoples—market-driven growth, open, rule-based multilateral trade, capital investment, technology, capital financing, democracy, human rights and fundamental freedoms, liberal governance and a "civil" society'.[39] For this reason, Beard proposes that the definition of development (insofar as it leads to distinctness and delineation) 'ought to be opened to the point that it can no longer be identified—to the extent that the West ought no longer to call itself "developed" '.[40]

[37] Jenny Beard, 'The Confessional Framework of Rule of Law Development: How to Offer Salvation to Willing Legal Subjects' (2006) 75 Nordic Journal of International Law 409, 410.

[38] ibid 412.

[39] Jenny Beard, 'Representations of the Liberal State in the Art of Development' (2001) 10 Griffith Law Review 6, 9 (hereafter, Beard, 'Representations of the Liberal State').

[40] Jennifer Beard, 'The Political Economy of Desire: International Law, Development and the Nation State' (23 March 2009), University of Melbourne Legal Studies Research Paper No 380, <http://ssrn.com/abstract=1367439 or http://dx.doi.org/10> accessed 29 September 2020 (hereafter, 'The Political

Development has become a basis for the universalisation of Western values relating to law, human welfare, and human rights and calls for the strengthening of the rule of law in developing countries.[41] As Tom Ginsburg argues:[42]

> The new wave of law and development activity corresponds with a shift toward market-oriented economic policies in the developing world. Reform of legal institutions is now seen as one pillar of a tripartite package of reforms that also includes democracy and economic liberalization. The relationships between law and politics on one hand and law and economy on the other are not well understood, but they are usually seen to be mutually reinforcing. In both the political and economic spheres the task of law is to constrain the state and empower private economic actors. Thus, liberal notions of autonomous law are at the core of the new law and development activity.

Gathii similarly argues that 'good governance serves as the World Bank's short hand for measuring which parts of the human rights agenda are compatible or consistent with its financial and economic mandate'.[43] This requirement, he argues, 'severely constrains the possibilities within the good governance agenda that prior development policies offered human rights advocates and activists'.[44]

Whatever may be the benefits that derive from the concept of development as a right, there is the risk of it being used to justify neoliberal ideas that underlie the investment treaty regime and liberal economic theories such those on structural adjustments in Africa.[45] The concept of development 'is used as a convenient name for a particular socio-economic status'[46] which, like the concepts of the Global North and the First World, is 'closely associated with particular social and economic divisions in and of the world' whereby 'it is the developed world that claims for itself that space, which exists only as transcendence'.[47] Development discourse in that sense 'represents a very real and effective form of imperial power that is concerned with the maintenance of a particular (western) version of subjectivity

Economy of Desire'). See also Jennifer Beard, *The Political Economy of Desire: International Law, Development and the Nation State* (Routledge-Cavendish 2006).

41 Tom Ginsburg, 'Review: Does Law Matter for Economic Development? Evidence from East Asia' (2000) 34(3) Law and Society Review 829 (hereafter, Ginsburg, 'Does Law Matter for Economic Development?').

42 ibid at 831.

43 Gathii, 'Good Governance as Counter Insurgency Agenda' (n 30) 108.

44 ibid.

45 Kwadwo Konadu-Agyemang (ed), *IMF and World Bank Sponsored Structural Adjustment Programs in Africa: Ghana's Experience, 1983–199* (Ashgate 2001); International Monetary Fund, *Ghana: Enhanced Structural Adjustment Facility Economic and Financial Policy Framework Paper, 1998–2000* <http://www.imf.org/external/np/pfp/ghana/ghana0.htm> accessed 29 September 2020; and Kwabena Donkor, *Structural Adjustment and Mass Poverty in Ghana* (Ashgate 1997).

46 Beard, 'The Political Economy of Desire' (n 40) 6.

47 ibid.

through its appropriation of history' to the extent that development cannot be understood 'without the binary of underdevelopment'.[48] There is also tension between the centrality of law in theories of development and existing evidence from Asia.[49]

The appropriateness of the definition and use of the concept of development is thus questionable. Those questions are legitimate and important for two reasons. First, they point to the fact that international economic relations have a history of actual or potential exploitation and abuse in the name of protecting 'vulnerable' states that are 'poor' and lack the capacity to govern themselves to prosperity without adopting the paths followed by the 'developed' world.[50] Critical scholarship helps address the question of whether investment treaties are really intended to attract foreign investment for development and if so, why their terms largely do not explicitly make room for the protection of development measures against legal suits by foreign investors.[51] Such critical analysis helps lift the veil of the investment treaty regime to see what is really behind them. By such analysis, the conclusion can be drawn that the historical origins of investment treaties and international relations generally have influenced the terms of these treaties and the terms in turn define the way the treaties are interpreted and enforced.[52]

Second, the critical approaches to the concept of development reflected in the works of Pahuja, Anghie, and Beard are important given that there does not exist one path to development, and development itself is not and should not be treated as a value-free concept. Thus, I adopt Maxwell Chibundus' view that 'the relevance of law for development must be grounded in the experiences of the society under study and in ways giving form and meaning to those experiences by their institutionalization, not through internationalizing the societies, nor through a universalist or global conception of procedural mechanisms or substantive rights and duties'.[53]

However, general international law and socio-economic development 'both rest on the belief that individuals, and more belatedly, peoples, are meant to live in circumstances that grant them certain rights and freedoms fundamental to their humanity. To this end, international law seeks to provide peace and security, mechanisms of good governance.'[54] General international law, development, and

[48] ibid 5.

[49] Ginsburg, 'Does Law Matter for Economic Development?' (n 41) 830.

[50] Dominic Dagbanja, 'The Limitation on Sovereign Regulatory Autonomy and Internationalization of Investment Protection by Treaty: An African Perspective' (2015) 60(1) Journal of African Law 1, 22 (hereafter, Dagbanja, 'The Limitation on Sovereign Regulatory Autonomy').

[51] ibid 20.

[52] ibid 22.

[53] Maxwell O Chibundu, 'Law in Development: on Tapping, Gourding, and Serving Palm-Wine' (1997) 29 Case Western Reserve Journal of International Law 167, 171.

[54] Beard, 'The Political Economy of Desire' (n 40) 1.

the nation state 'may be understood as instrumental to the *process* of improving human life'.[55] This is reflected in IETs and IHRTs African states are parties to, especially as analysed in this chapter and Chapter 1, 2, and 4 of this book. Thus, while the development discourse 'opens up the possibility of international organisations such as the World Bank' and may exclude different ways of understanding who human beings in their differing geographical and cultural settings are and what the state is, it may equally open the possibility of various forms of legitimate government in different polities.[56]

Especially, if the concept of development has to do with the basic needs of citizens and the state has a role in the realisation of those needs, as I argue it is, then development can be used as framework for determining the capacity of the state to conclude investment treaties and how those treaties should be interpreted, depending on the nature of the terms of those treaties for the state in the performance of that role. This approach is particularly justified in the context of African states the constitutions of which place the welfare of the people at the centre of the exercise of the powers of governments and require the governments in their dealings with other nations to act in accordance with accepted principles of public international law and in the national interest.[57] In any case, the fact that development is presented as justification of the legal regime for private foreign investment promotion and protection supports the need to place development centre stage in the making of investment treaties. Any argument that advocates for a peripheral place for development in international investment law is inconsistent with the very neo-liberal ethos that underlies the investment treaty regime, namely that the regime is *sine qua non* for investment attraction *for development*.[58]

The choice of development then as a framework for the analysis in this chapter is informed and justified by the public importance constitutions and IHRTs in Africa attach to this concept as a right for citizens, and in view of the fact that development is defined as an objective of African investment treaties, as analysed in Section 5.3. The approach I adopt in this chapter allows the investment treaty regime to be held to account for the development that it is said it is capable of delivering. The goal is not to affirm the relevance of investment treaties for development.

[55] ibid.

[56] Beard, 'Representations of the Liberal State' (n 39) 10.

[57] Constitution of the Republic of Ghana 1992 arts 1(1), 40(a), and 73 (hereafter, Constitution of Ghana); Constitution of the Republic of Kenya 2010, art 2(6) (hereafter, Constitution of Kenya); Constitution of the Republic of Nigeria 1996, art 19(d); and Constitution of the Republic of South Africa 1996, art 231.

[58] Dominic Dagbanja, 'The Development Objective as an Imperative in Interpretation of International Investment Agreements' (2018) 44(2) University of Western Australia Law Review 145

5.2.2 The Constitutional Right to Development in Africa

This section establishes that the right to development is entrenched in a number of constitutions in Africa. A 'right' is defined as a 'legally enforceable claim'[59] or 'a recognized and protected interest the violation of which is wrong'.[60] I argue that the primary intent of the framers of the constitutions is to provide the frameworks for the states to advance the right to development in its broadest meaning.

In the preamble to the Constitution of Cameroon, the people of Cameroon '[r]esolved to harness' their 'natural resources in order to ensure the well-being of every citizen without discrimination, by raising living standards, proclaim our right to development'. This preamble shows that the right to development is established as an objective of constitutional governance in Cameroon. The preamble further sets out other principles, including a principle which imposes a corresponding obligation on Cameroon to the effect that the 'State shall provide all its citizens with the conditions necessary for their development'. Article 55(2) of the Constitution of Cameroon imposes a duty on the councils of regional and local authorities to promote economic, social, health, educational, and cultural development. The state also has a duty under Article 55(4) of the Constitution 'to ensure the harmonious development of all the regional and local authorities on the basis of national solidarity, regional potentials and inter-regional balance'.

On its part, the Constitution of Egypt variously refers to the quest for development and provides in Article 27 that the

> economic system aims at achieving prosperity in the country through sustainable development and social justice to guarantee an increase in the real growth rate of the national economy, raising the standard of living, increasing job opportunities, reducing unemployment rates and eliminating poverty.
>
> [The] economic system is socially committed to ensuring equal opportunities and a fair distribution of development returns, to reducing the gaps between incomes by setting a minimum wage and pension to ensure a decent life, and setting a maximum wage in state agencies for whoever works for a wage as per the law.

Under Article 38 of the Constitution of Egypt, the taxation system and other public levies are aimed at developing state resources and achieving 'social justice and economic development' and ensuring the 'promotion of heavy labor industries, and incentivizing their role in economic, social, and cultural development'. The state commits itself to maximize investment in human energy as to achieve sustainable development[61] and to develop and implement a plan for the

[59] Bryan Garner (ed in chief), *Black's Law Dictionary* (Thompson Reuters 2009) 1436.
[60] ibid.
[61] Constitution of the Arab Republic of Egypt 2014, art 41 (hereafter, Constitution of Egypt).

'comprehensive economic and urban development of border and underprivileged areas'.[62]

The preamble states that the Constitution of Ghana was enacted to 'establish a framework of government which shall secure for [the people of Ghana and] posterity the blessings of liberty, equality of opportunity and prosperity'.[63] Article 1(1) of the Constitution of Ghana states that '[t]he Sovereignty of Ghana resides in the people of Ghana in whose name and for whose welfare the powers of government are to be exercised in the manner and within the limits laid down in this Constitution'. The Constitution of Ghana also recognises and protects various fundamental human rights, including the right to life, right to own property,[64] and economic rights, especially those relating to work, and educational and cultural rights.[65] All of these constitute rights in and of themselves but they are also important attributes of the basic needs approach to development. By Article 12(1) of the Constitution of Ghana, these fundamental human rights are to be respected and upheld by the government and all legal persons in Ghana.

To give effect to the realisation of the right to development, the Constitution of Ghana in Article 86 establishes the National Development Planning Commission (NDPC). The Commission's role under Article 87 is to conduct strategic analyses of macro-economic and structural reform options, and to make proposals for the development of multi-year rolling plans and for the protection of the natural and physical environment. The NDPC is also required to make proposals for ensuring even development in Ghana, to monitor, evaluate, and coordinate development policies, programmes, and projects, and to perform other functions relating to development planning.[66] If development were peripheral and not central as a right in Ghana, the Constitution of Ghana would not have established the NDPC.

The Constitution of Ghana further provides for the Directive Principles of State Policy which, according to Article 34(1),

> shall guide all citizens, Parliament, the President, the Judiciary, the Council of State, the Cabinet, political parties and other bodies and persons in applying or interpreting this Constitution or any other law and in taking and implementing any policy decisions, for the establishment of a just and free society.

The Principles as enumerated in Articles 34–39 of the Constitution of Ghana cover a number of political, economic, social, educational, and cultural objectives that are pertinent to development in Ghana. In sum, they require the government to establish Ghana as a society that is just and free; a society of probity and accountability;

[62] ibid 236.
[63] Constitution of Ghana (n 57) preamble.
[64] ibid arts 18 and 20.
[65] ibid arts 13, 14, 16(1), 18, 20, and 24–26.
[66] ibid arts 86 and 87.

and a society in which the basic and essential needs of people can be met. By Article 36(1) of the Constitution of Ghana, the state must take all steps necessary to ensure that the economy is managed in a manner that leads to development, secures the maximum welfare, freedom, and happiness of every person in Ghana, and that adequate means of livelihood and suitable employment are provided.

The state must steps to ensure that individuals and the private sector bear their fair share of social and national responsibilities, including responsibilities to contribute to the overall development of Ghana.[67] Appropriate measures are to be taken to encourage foreign investment, subject to any existing law regulating investment in Ghana; afford equality of economic opportunity to all citizens; protect and safeguard the national environment; safeguard the health, safety, and welfare of all persons in employment; and encourage the participation of workers in the decision-making process at the workplace.[68]

The state must direct policies towards ensuring that every citizen has equality of rights, obligations, and opportunities before the law.[69] To meet the social goals in society, Article 37(2)(a) and (b) of the Constitution of Ghana says the 'State shall enact appropriate laws to assure ... the enjoyment of rights of effective participation in development processes' and 'the protection and promotion of all other basic human rights and freedoms, including the rights of ... vulnerable groups in development processes'. According to Article 37(3) of the Constitution of Ghana, in the discharge of these obligations the state is to be guided by international human rights instruments that recognise and apply particular categories of basic human rights to development processes, such as those specified in Subsection 5.2.3 later in this chapter.

Last but not least, the Constitution of Ghana attaches so much importance to development that it requires in Article 69 (b)(ii) that the President shall be removed from office if he is found to have conducted himself in 'a manner prejudicial to the economy ... of the State'. This provision can be read as consistent with Article 1(1) (obligation to promote the welfare of the people) and the development objective of managing the economy in Article 36(1). The requirement in Article 36(1) that the state 'shall take all necessary action' in the management of the economy suggests that governmental *actions* in the form of administration, legislation, policy-making and implementation, monitoring, and evaluation are all prerequisites for the realisation of development in Ghana. The government itself recognised

[67] ibid art 36(2)(a)–(e). On the enforceability of the directive principles of state policy see *New Patriotic Party v Attorney-General* [1993–94] 2 GLR 35 AT 65–66; *New Patriotic Party v Attorney-General (the CIBA case).* [1997–98] 1 GLR 378 at 393–94; *Ghana Lotto Operators Association v National Lottery Authority*, Ruling, Ref. No J6/1/2008, 23 July 2008; and Seth Yeboa Bimpong-Buta, *The Role of The Supreme Court in the Development of Constitutional Law in Ghana* (PhD thesis, Submitted in accordance with the requirements for the degree of Doctor of Law—LLD at the University of South Africa, 1 February 2005) at 187ff.

[68] Constitution of Ghana (n 57) art 36(4) and (6), (8)–(11).

[69] ibid art 37(1).

this when under the leadership of President John Atta Mills it stated in 2010 that policy on development must be guided by the 'imperative that it is through the execution of policies and programmes which bring about growth with equity that socio-economic development becomes inclusive and responsive to the needs of all Ghanaians'.[70] Development does not just happen on its own. In order for development to be attained, the state or someone must act. Development 'is not a mere evolutionary or natural process. If not managed, it remains a change process not capable of producing an improved quality of life'.[71]

The national values and principles of governance in Kenya include 'democracy and participation of the people'; 'human dignity, equity, social justice, inclusiveness, equality, human rights, non-discrimination and protection of the marginalised'; 'good governance, integrity, transparency and accountability'; and 'sustainable development'.[72] These values and principles reflect the meaning and scope of the concept of development as defined in Subsection 5.2.1.1 earlier in this chapter. These national values and principles of governance bind all state organs and government functionaries in Kenya when they apply or interpret the Constitution of Kenya; enact laws, apply and interpret them; and when they make and implement public policies.[73] Under Article 69(1)(a) of the Constitution of Kenya, Kenya 'shall ensure sustainable exploitation, utilisation, management and conservation of the environment and natural resources, and ensure the equitable sharing of the accruing benefits'. Individuals have an obligation to cooperate with state organs and other persons 'to protect and conserve the environment and ensure ecologically sustainable development and use of natural resources'.[74]

Article 174 of the Constitution of Kenya requires devolution of government with the object being to 'promote social and economic development and the provision of proximate, easily accessible services throughout Kenya'.[75] Article 201(b)(iii) of the Constitution of Kenya requires that public 'expenditure shall promote the equitable development of the country, including by making special provision for marginalised groups and areas'. The Constitution of Kenya also guarantees the right to a clean and healthy environment and highest attainable standards of health in Articles 42 and 43. The various constitutional provisions and the African Charter on Human and Peoples' Rights as analysed in Subsection 5.2.3 later in this chapter give rise to the right to development under the Constitution of Kenya.[76]

[70] Republic of Ghana, *Economic and Social Development Policies* (n 29) ii.

[71] Theo Scheepers, *A Practical Guide to Law and Development: An Introduction to the Law Applicable to Development and the Development Management Process in South Africa* (Juta & Co Ltd 2000) at 14.

[72] Constitution of Kenya (n 57) art 10(2)(a)–(d).

[73] ibid art 10(1)(a)–(d).

[74] ibid art 69(2).

[75] ibid art 174(f).

[76] See Joyce Miguda Majiwa, *Challenges Towards the Realization of the Right to Development in Kenya* (Mini dissertation, Submitted in Fulfilment of the requirement of the Degree Master of Laws, University of Pretoria, November 2013) 43–46. For general reading on the constitution, good governance, and development in Kenya see: Morris Kiwinda Mbondenyi and Osogo Ambani, *New Constitutional Law of*

According to its preamble, the Constitution of Nigeria was adopted 'for the purpose of promoting the good government and welfare of all persons' in Nigeria. Consistent with this broad principle, Section 14(2)(b) provides that 'security and welfare of the people shall be the primary purpose of government'. Fundamental objectives and directive principles of state policy in Sections 16(1)(b), 16(2)(a), and 17(3)(d) of the Constitution of Nigeria require the government of Nigeria to 'control the national economy in such manner as to secure the maximum welfare, freedom and happiness of every citizen'; 'direct its policy towards ensuring the promotion of a planned and balanced economic development'; and to ensure that '[t]here are adequate medical and health facilities for all persons'.

The Fourth Schedule to the Constitution of Nigeria spells out as the main function of a local government council 'the consideration and the making of recommendations to a State commission on economic planning and economic development of the State'. The Constitution of Nigeria is not explicit on the right to development but it does provide as reflected in Chapter II (fundamental objectives and directive principles of state policy) a normative framework to argue for the right to development in Nigeria. The fundamental rights in Chapter IV, including the right to property protected in Sections 43 and 44 of the Constitution of Nigeria and Nigeria's ratification of IHRTs such as the African Charter on Human and Peoples' Rights, guarantee a right to development in Nigeria.[77]

The right to development is reflected in Article 24 of the Constitution of South Africa, which provides for the right to an environment appropriate for health or well-being and corresponding obligation of the state to 'ensure ecologically sustainable development and use of natural resources while promoting justifiable economic and social development'. According to Article 152(1) of the Constitution of South Africa, a local government has to promote social and economic development and a safe and healthy environment.[78] Article 153 specifically deals with the developmental duties of South African municipalities. It states:

Kenya: Principles, Government and Human Rights (LawAfrica Publishing (K) Ltd 2012); and Patrick LO Lumumba, Morris Kiwinda Mbondenyi, and Steve O Odero *The Constitution of Kenya: Contemporary Readings* (LawAfrica Publishing (K) Ltd 2011).

[77] For a discussion of the nature of right to development see: Salim Bashir Magashi, *The Human Right to Development in Nigeria* (Dissertation presented for the Degree of Doctor of Laws in the Faculty of Law at Stellenbosch University March 2016); Olaitan Olusegun and Oyeniyi Ajigboye, 'Realizing the Right to Development in Nigeria: An Examination of Legal Barriers and Challenges' (2015) 6(1) Journal of Sustainable Development Law and Policy 145.

[78] On the right to development in South Africa see: Carol Chi Ngang, 'Radical Transformation and a Reading of the Right to Development in the South African Constitutional Order' (2019) 35(1) South African Journal on Human Rights 25; and Marius Pieterse, 'Possibilities and Pitfalls in the Domestic Enforcement of Social Rights: Contemplating the South African Experience' (2004) 26(4) Human Rights Quarterly 882.

> A municipality must—(a) structure and manage its administration and budgeting and planning processes to give priority to the basic needs of the community, and to promote the social and economic development of the community; and (b) participate in national and provincial development programmes.

These constitutions evidence the constitutionalisation of the right to development in Africa.

5.2.3 General International Law Right to Development in Africa

The General Assembly of the United Nations has made various instruments that address the subject of the right to development from social, political, cultural, and civil dimensions.[79] The right to development is *internationalised* in Africa to the extent that African countries have entered into IHRTs that recognise or guarantee the right to development. For example, African states are parties to the African Charter on Human and Peoples' Rights.[80] Article 22 of the Charter specifically recognises the right to development and the corresponding duty of the state parties in the following terms:

> All peoples shall have the right to their economic, social and cultural development with due regard to their freedom and identity and in the equal enjoyment of the common heritage of mankind.
>
> States shall have the duty, individually or collectively, to ensure the exercise of the right to development.

The African Commission on Human and Peoples' Rights has affirmed the right to development in a number of decisions.[81] The obligations of African states with respect to development policy-making and implementation also arise from a number of other regional treaties in Africa. For example, the objectives set out in Article 3 of the Constitutive Act of the African Union[82] adopted by African heads of state and government include the promotion and protection of human and peoples' rights; promotion of sustainable development; promotion of co-operation 'to

[79] Rolland, *Development at WTO* (n 1) 27.

[80] African Charter on Human and Peoples' Rights (27 June 1981, entered into force 21 October 1986) 21 ILM 58 (hereafter, African Charter).

[81] *Social and Economic Rights Action Centre v Nigeria*, African Commission on Human and Peoples' Rights, Comm No 155/96 (2001); *African Commission on Human and Peoples' Rights, Democratic Republic of the Congo v Burundi, Rwanda and Uganda*, (2004) AHRLR 19 (ACHPR 2003); Communication 227/99; 276/2003—*Centre for Minority Rights Development (Kenya) and Minority Rights Group International on behalf of Endorois Welfare Council v Kenya*.

[82] Constitutive Act of the African Union, adopted by the Thirty-Sixth Ordinary Session of the Assembly of Heads of State and Government at Lome, Togo, 11 July 2000.

raise the living standards' of Africans; and the advancement of the development of the African continent. Among the objectives of the Treaty Establishing the African Economic Community[83] stated in Article 4(a) is the need to 'promote economic, social and cultural development and the integration of African economies in order to increase economic self-reliance and promote an endogenous and self-sustained development'.

It also can be inferred from a rights-based approach to development that the right to development is recognised under the Charter of the United Nations,[84] the International Covenant on Civil and Political Rights,[85] and the International Covenant of Economic, Social and Cultural Rights,[86] because they are human-centred treaties and covenants specifically meant to advance the rights, interests, and welfare of human beings.[87] The Universal Declaration of Human Rights in Article 22 states that everyone 'has the right to social security and is entitled to realization, through national effort . . . of the economic, social and cultural rights indispensable for his dignity and the free development of his personality'.[88] According to the Declaration on the Right to Development,[89]

> Article 1(1): The right to development is an inalienable human right by virtue of which every human person and all peoples are entitled to participate in, contribute to, and enjoy economic, social, cultural and political development, in which all human rights and fundamental freedoms can be fully realized.
>
> Article 2(3): States have the right and the duty to formulate appropriate national development policies that aim at the constant improvement of the well-being of the entire population and of all individuals, on the basis of their active, free and meaningful participation in development and in the fair distribution of the benefits resulting therefrom.

[83] Treaty Establishing the African Economic Community (adopted 3 June 1991, entered into force 12 May 1994).

[84] Charter of the United Nations (signed 26 June 1945, entered into force 24 October 1945). 59 Stat 1031, TS 993 3 Bevans 1153 (hereafter UN Charter). See Ernst-Ulrich Petersmann, *Multilevel Constitutionalism for Multilevel Governance of Public Goods: Methodological Problems in International Law* (Hart Publishing2017).

[85] International Covenant on Civil and Political Rights (United Nations General Assembly Resolution 2200A (XXI) adopted,16 December 1966, entered into force 23 March 1976) 999 UNTS 171 (hereafter, ICCPR).

[86] International Covenant on Economic, Social and Cultural Rights (General Assembly resolution 2200A (XXI) adopted 16 December 1966, entered into force 3 January 1976). 993 UNTS 3 (hereafter, ICESCR).

[87] UN Charter (n 84); arts 55, 56, and preamble; Universal Declaration of Human Rights (UN GA Res. 217 A(III), UN Doc. A/810, adopted 10 December 1948) arts 22, 26(2), 28, and 29(1); ICCPR (n 85) art 1; and ICESCR (n 86) arts1(1), 2(1), and 11; and United Nations Declaration on the Right to Development UN GA Res 41/128 (4 December 1986).

[88] Universal Declaration of Human Rights (n 87) art 71.

[89] ibid.

Significantly, the constitutions of Cameroon,[90] Egypt,[91] Ghana,[92] Kenya,[93] Nigeria,[94] and South Africa[95] require their governments to adhere to international conventions such as the African Charter, thereby constitutionally domesticating international development law. From the perspective of the imperatives theory, the right to development and corresponding duties in Africa are *constitutional-general international law imperatives* because they are guaranteed by constitutions and general international law. The obligation with respect to development policy should, therefore, be treated as taking precedence over investment treaty obligations which are justified largely in investment treaties. Accordingly, based on the combined legal force of their constitutions and IHRTs, African states do not have the competence to conclude investment treaties that explicitly and directly prevent the adoption of measures for the realisation of the right to development.

5.3 Development, International Relations, and Politics of Investment Treaties in Africa

5.3.1 Foreign Direct Investment, Development, and Investment Treaties in Africa

The preambles to African investment treaties show that they seek to create favourable conditions for foreign investment because of the supposed role of foreign investment in development. The preambles explicitly link the protection of foreign investment to development cooperation, economic development, increased prosperity, and stimulation of the flow of capital and technology.[96] Strengthening cooperation between private enterprises of the contracting parties is also an important objective of the investment treaty framework in Africa. They adopt broadly similar wording. For example, the stated objective of the Ghana–United Kingdom investment treaty is 'to create favourable conditions for greater investments'. The parties assumed that the 'encouragement and reciprocal protection under

[90] Constitution of the Republic of Cameroon 1972 (with Amendments through 2008) art 5(2) and 45 (hereafter Constitution of Cameroon).

[91] Constitution of Egypt (n 61) art 93.

[92] Constitution of Ghana (n 57) arts 40(d) and 73.

[93] Constitution of Kenya (n 57) art 2(6).

[94] Constitution of Nigeria (n 57) arts 12(1) and 19(d). The African Charter on Human and Peoples' Rights (Ratification and Enforcement) Act No 2 of 1983 gives effect to the African Charter (n 80) in Nigeria.

[95] Constitution of South Africa (n 57) art 231.

[96] Belgo–Luxembourg Economic Union and United Republic of Cameroon Convention concerning the reciprocal promotion and protection of investments (signed 27 March 1980, entered into force 1 November 1981) preamble (hereafter, Cameroon–BLEU Investment Treaty).

international agreement of such investments will be conducive to the stimulation of individual business initiative and will increase prosperity'.[97]

The Ghana–Netherlands investment treaty was meant 'to strengthen the traditional ties of friendship' between the two countries and 'to extend and intensify the economic relations between them particularly with respect to investments'.[98] An agreement upon the treatment to be accorded to foreign investments was considered necessary to stimulate the flow of capital and technology for development. The South Africa–China investment treaty expressed the parties' intention to 'create favourable conditions for investments' based on their (i) recognition that 'the reciprocal encouragement, promotion, and protection of such investments will be conducive to stimulating business initiative of the investors and will increase prosperity in both States', and (ii) desire 'to intensify the economic cooperation of both States on the basis of equality and mutual benefits'.[99]

The investment treaties never pretend to present the protection of foreign investment as an end in itself, at least as reflected in the objectives stated in the preambles. Yet, the fact that the investment treaties articulate the objective of development in their preambles does not mean the contracting parties can confidently rely on an investment's lack of contribution to development as a defence in investment arbitration. The balance of arbitral decisions shows a state may not be relieved of liabilities arising from breach of an investment treaty obligation on the basis that the investment involved made no contribution to development. Most arbitral cases demonstrate that an investment's lack of contribution to development is not central to the definition of an investment.

In *Electrabel SA v Hungary*, the Tribunal identified profit and return as necessary and integral elements of an 'investment'. Although 'the economic development of the host State is one of the objectives'[100] of the Convention on the Settlement of Investment Disputes between States and Nationals of Other States (ICSID Convention) 'and a desirable consequence of the investment', the Tribunal held 'it

[97] Agreement between the Government of the United Kingdom of Great Britain and Northern Ireland and the Government of the Republic of Ghana for the Promotion and Protection of Investments (signed 22 March 1989, entered into force 25 October 1991) preamble; Agreement between the Government of Japan and the Government of the Republic of Kenya for the Promotion and Protection of Investment (signed 28 August 2016, entered into force 4 September 2017) preamble; Treaty between the Federal Republic of Germany and the Federal Republic of Nigeria Concerning the Encouragement and Reciprocal Protection of Investments, signed 28 March 2000, entered into force 20 September 2007) preamble; Agreement between the Government of the People's Republic of China and the Government of the Republic of South Africa concerning the Reciprocal Promotion and Protection of Investments (signed 3 November 1997, entered into force 1 April 1998) preamble.

[98] Agreement on Encouragement and Reciprocal Protection of Investments between the Kingdom of the Netherlands and the Republic of Ghana (signed 31 March 1989, entered into force 1 July 1991) preamble; and Agreement between the Government of Canada and the Government of the Arab Republic of Egypt for the Promotion and Protection of Investments (signed 13 November 1996, entered into force 3 November 1997) preamble.

[99] South Africa–China Investment Treaty (n 97) preamble.

[100] *Electrabel SA v Republic of Hungary*, ICSID Case No ARB/07/19, Decision on Jurisdiction, Applicable Law and Liability, 30 November 2012, [5.43].

is not necessarily an element of an investment'.[101] The Tribunal in *Saba Fakes v Turkey* reached the same conclusion, saying it was 'not convinced ... that a contribution to the host State's economic development constitutes a criterion of an investment within the framework of the ICSID Convention'.[102] Even when tribunals find that an investment treaty is aimed at promoting and protecting foreign investment to advance the well-being of people, they still place emphasis on the investment protection objective and gloss over the development objective. For example, in *Siemens A.G. v Argentina*, the Tribunal in interpreting the Argentina–Germany bilateral investment treaty (BIT)[103] stated that it[104]

> shall be guided by the purpose of the Treaty as expressed in its title and preamble. *It is a treaty 'to protect' and 'to promote' investments.* The preamble provides that the parties have agreed to the provisions of the Treaty for the purpose of creating favorable conditions for the investments of nationals or companies of one of the two States in the territory of the other State. Both parties recognize that the promotion and protection of these investments by a treaty may stimulate private economic initiative and increase the well-being of the peoples of both countries. *The intention of the parties is clear. It is to create favorable conditions for investments and to stimulate private initiative.*

Salini v Morocco[105] and *Fedax v Venezuela*[106] are cases which held the contrary view. They decided the contribution of an investment to the economic development of the host state is an element of the definition of an investment for purposes of deciding whether the investment is entitled to protection under an applicable investment treaty. *Mitchell v Democratic Republic of Congo*,[107] *Malaysian Historical Salvors SDN BHD v Malaysia*,[108] *Alex Genin Eastern Credit Ltd Inc v Estonia*,[109] *Pantechniki S.A. Contractors & Engineers (Greece) v The Republic of Albania*,[110]

[101] ibid [5.43].

[102] *Saba Fakes v Turkey*, ICSID Case No ARB/07/20, Award, 14 July 2010, [97].

[103] *Tratado entre la República Federal de Alemania y la Republica Argentina sobre Promoción y Protección Reciproca de Inversiones* (signed 9 April 1999, entered into force 8 November 1993).

[104] *Siemens A.G. v Argentina* ICSID Case No ARB/02/8, Decision on Jurisdiction, 3 August 2008, para 81 (emphasis added).

[105] *Salini Costruttori SpA & Italstrade SpA v Morocco*, ICSID Case No ARB/00/4, Decision on Jurisdiction, 23 July 2001.

[106] *Fedax NV v Republic of Venezuela*, ICSID Case No ARB/96/3, Decision of the Tribunal on Objection to Jurisdiction, 11 July 1997.

[107] *Patrick Mitchell v The Democratic Republic of Congo*, Case No ARB/99/7, Decision on the Application for Annulment of the Award, 1 November 2006 [27–41].

[108] *Malaysian Historical Salvors SDN BHD v The Government of Malaysia*, ICSID Case No ARB/05/10, Decision on the Application for Annulment, 16 April 2009 [56ff].

[109] *Alex Genin Eastern Credit Ltd Inc v The Republic of Estonia*, Case No ARB/99/2, Award, 25 June 2001 [348ff].

[110] *Pantechniki S.A. Contractors & Engineers (Greece) v The Republic of Albania*, ICSID Case No ARB/07/21, Award, 30 July 2009 [81]–[82].

Amoco Asia Corporation v Republic of Indonesia,[111] and *Joseph Charles Lemire v Ukraine*[112] also recognised contribution to the economic development of the host country as a characteristic of investment for the purpose of deciding if an investment is entitled to protection. Thus some tribunals recognise that the obligation to protect foreign investment is related to the host state's search for development.[113]

However, the predominant approach appears to be that contribution to a host country's development is not a mandatory element of the concept of investment.[114] The approach adopted by those tribunals raises a question as to what the consideration or *quid pro quo* is for states in return for the protections they accord to foreign investors. This question is most appropriately asked in light of *Société Générale*,[115] which held that the goals or purposes of investment treaties as reflected in their preambles are of less interpretive importance than their actual terms in treaty interpretation. Investment tribunals have effectively minimised the relevance of development in arbitration. The implication is that African countries would have difficulty using an investment's lack of contribution to development as a justification for not according an investment the required treatment under investment treaties.

As a matter of strategy, if African states have specific interests which need to be respected, they must make specific provisions to that effect in the substantive terms of investment treaties. African states could also provide a more specific definition of the concept of investment to include contribution to development in investment treaties, and this could limit the scope of application of the concept of investment.[116] Section 5.6 shows that Africa is moving towards this direction.

5.3.2 International Relations, Politics, and the Making of Investment Treaties in Africa

The analysis in Subsection 5.3.1 would seem to suggest investment treaties are entered into solely in the public interest. This may not really be the case.[117] Investment

[111] *Amoco Asia Corporation v Republic of Indonesia*, ICSID Case No ARB/06/18, Decision on Jurisdiction and Liability, 25 September 1983 [23].

[112] *Joseph Charles Lemire v Ukraine*, ICSID Case No ARB/O6/18, Decision on Jurisdiction and Liability, 14 January 2010 [272]–[273].

[113] See Schill, 'IIL as International Development Law' (n 2) 327 and 340–44.

[114] See Henckels, 'Balancing Investment Protection and Sustainable Development' (n 7), 305; and Caroline Henckels, 'Balancing Investment Protection and the Public Interest: The Role of the Standard of Review and the Importance of Deference in Investor–State Arbitration' (2014) Journal of International Dispute Settlement 197.

[115] *Société Générale v Dominican Republic*, LCIA Case No UN 7927, UNCITRAL Arbitration Rules, Award on Preliminary Objections to Jurisdiction, 19 September 2008.

[116] Dominic Dagbanja, 'Africa' in Markus Krajewski and Rhea Hoffmann (eds), *Research Handbook on Foreign Direct Investment* (Edward Elgar Publishing 2019) 336 (hereafter, Dagbanja, 'Africa').

[117] Lauge Poulsen, *Bounded Rationality and Economic Diplomacy: The Politics of Investment Treaties in Developing Countries* (CUP 2015) (hereafter, Poulsen, *Bounded Rationality and Economic Diplomacy*).

treaties have been inspired by 'capital-exporting states' increased concern for investment protection, given the scale, frequency, and volume of their foreign direct investment spurred by worldwide liberalization and globalization trends'.[118] The investment treaty regime thus originates and hinges primarily on the desire of governments in developed countries home to large multinational business entities to provide a secure legal regime for the protection of these businesses.[119] The internationalisation of foreign investment protection by treaty was primarily aimed at protecting the private business interests of investors from the developed world who invested abroad.[120] In that sense, investment treaties are a product of corporate influence operating on both the home and host countries of foreign investors and their investments.[121] According Thomas Pogge,[122]

> The governments of the more powerful developed countries, especially the so-called G-7, have played a dominant role in designing the post-Cold War global institutional order. In shaping this order, those governments have given much weight to the interests of their domestic business and financial elites and rather little weight to the interests of the poor and vulnerable populations of the less developed countries. The resulting global institutional order is arguably unjust insofar as the incidence of violence and severe poverty occurring under it is much greater than would have been the case under an alternative order whose design would have given greater weight to the interests of the poor and the vulnerable.

Thus, an analysis of the reasons for the signing of investment treaties can no longer be limited to the development argument, namely that investment treaties are designed to attract foreign investment for the development of the country receiving the investment.[123] Given in particular the 'double transformation of the traditional realm of international relations'[124] which involves the 'proliferation of international, supranational, and multinational actors, and the profound influence of

[118] Diane A Desierto, *Public Policy in International Economic Law: The ICESCR in Trade, Finance, and Investment* (OUP 2015) 314 (hereafter, Desierto, *Public Policy and International Economic Law*). See also Dagbanja, 'Limitation on Sovereign Regulatory Autonomy' (n 50).

[119] Zachary Elkins, Andrew T Guzman, and Beth A Simmons, 'Competing for Capital: The Diffusion of Bilateral Investment Treaties, 1960–2000' (2006) 60(4) International Organization 811, 817.

[120] Dagbanja, 'Limitation on Sovereign Regulatory Autonomy' (n 50) 4.

[121] It was on the basis that Multilateral Agreement on Investment was corporate inspired and was aimed at promoting corporate interests at the expense of sovereignty, environment, human rights, and development that the agreement received opposition among some scholars and a coalition of such as Amnesty International, the Australian Conservation Foundation, Friends of the Earth, Oxfam, Public Citizen, and Third World Network, among others. See Stephen J Kobrin, 'The MAI and the Clash of Globalizations' (1998) 112 Foreign Policy 112.

[122] Thomas Pogge, *Politics as Usual: What Lies Behind the Pro-Poor Rhetoric* (Polity Press 2010) 21–22 (hereafter, Pogge, *Politics as Usual*).

[123] For a refusal of investment attraction for development as the sole reason for the signing of investment treaties see Dagbanja, 'Limitation on Sovereign Regulatory Autonomy' (n 50) 20–22.

[124] Pogge, *Politics as Usual* (n 122) 14.

transnational rules and of the systematic activities of these actors deep into the domestic life of national societies',[125] investment treaties cannot be looked at from the perspective that they are simply instruments mutually agreed between two states for development purposes alone.

In light of the mirage of globalisation, an analysis of investment treaties focusing on the sole fact that African countries are looking for development in signing the treaties would ignore the profound effects of transnational actors on the domestic life of national societies and their decision-making.[126] The traditional conception of the world of international relations as inhabited only by states 'is rapidly losing its *explanatory* adequacy—through the emergence and increasing importance of transnational rules, and through the creation and increasing stature on the international stage of non-state actors, such as multinational corporations, international agencies, regional organizations, and NGOs'.[127] Central to globalisation and global justice rhetoric 'is the causal impact of the design of the transnational institutional arrangements upon the conditions of life experienced by human beings worldwide'.[128] Thus, individual states' diplomatic and international relations with treaty partners may have influenced investment treaties in Africa. Desierto articulates the reasons other than the public interest in development that may underlie the signing of particular investment treaties (which may be applicable to Africa):[129]

> Whether viewed from the normative or functionalist perspective, the proliferation of IIAs bears testament to how States value the need to maintain and guarantee regulatory predictability, at least sufficiently enough for these States to accept the trade-off that future exercises of regulatory powers could be subjected to claims against the State for alleged international responsibility. The State's authoritative decision-makers may choose to incur this trade-off not just for supposed ability of an IIA to attract foreign investment from new capital-exporting sources, but also for the fact that these decision-makers might also stand to reap other immediate *indirect* political and economic gains from choosing to entrench regulatory predictability through an IIA … [T]hese collateral or indirect benefits from successfully negotiating an IIA … include: 1) obtaining favorable counterpart international lending or sovereign financing terms as part of a basket of international commitments with an IIA partner; 2) opening new market access through a broader free trade agreement that includes the IIA; 3) garnering favorable perceptions and increased support from domestic constituencies and local businesses; 4) institutionalizing an international investment regulatory policy

[125] ibid 14.
[126] ibid 17.
[127] ibid.
[128] ibid 19.
[129] Desierto, *Public Policy and International Economic Law* (n 118) 314–15.

that is consistent with the decision-maker's political views on resource allocation and development strategies; and 5) paving the way for other additional strategic cooperation in the future with the new State partner under the IIA. Moreover, it is also possible that a State's authoritative decision-makers see few costs in entering into an IIA—where the duration of an IIA's applicability stands to outlast politicians' electoral terms, these decision making elites could be less concerned with the possibility of any future political fallout if the State were to be held internationally responsible under the IIA for regulatory actions that injure foreign investors. Under these circumstances, the functional gains from concluding an IIA make it only more politically expedient to do so than otherwise.

Thus, each African state's decision to enter into investment treaties at the time may have been aimed at a number of objectives other development *per se*. These may include putting the country concerned on par with other African countries in terms of competition without a real focus on the actual benefits that will derive from signing the investment treaties. The decision may also have been influenced by corporate lobbying even if the entering into the treaty coincided with a development objective. The investment treaties may also be a deliberate global agenda pushed by global economic institutions and multinational business entities making or interested in making investments in Africa.[130] Most African countries often receive development aid and budgetary support from the United Kingdom, the European Union, and now China. It may be that African states entered into some of these treaties to meet the demands of their so-called development partners who may insist on such treaties to secure legal protection for their investors in return for financial aid or loans.

The benefits that members of the signing governments stand to gain could also be part of the explanatory variables. Again, the investment treaties may be seen as a way of promoting the political objectives of the political party in power on privatisation and liberalisation. For example, the government of President John Kufuor of Ghana placed emphasis on privatisation and liberalisation and set up a branch of a ministry responsible for private sector development. This was done even though the Ghana Investment Promotion Centre, which is primarily responsible for foreign investment promotion, was already in existence. Most of Ghana's investment treaties came into force during John Kufuor's administration.

Investment treaties are used to 'liberalize the economies of developing counties'.[131] According to Ofodile, 'it is not clear the extent to which factors such as resource constraint, lack of legal and technical capacity, and official corruption really

[130] ibid 314. See also Andrew T Guzman, 'Why LDCs Sign Treaties That Hurt Them: Explaining the Popularity of Bilateral Investment Treaties' (1997) 38 Virginia Journal of Transnational Law 639.

[131] Uche Ewelukwa Ofodile, 'Africa–China Bilateral Investment Treaties: A Critique' (2013) 35 Michigan Journal of International Law 131, 139.

influence the outcome of negotiation of land lease agreements'[132] and by extension, investment treaties in Africa. Many governments of the developing countries are 'autocratic, corrupt, brutal and unresponsive to the interests of the poor majority. They are greatly at fault for not representing the interests of the poor in international negotiations and for consenting to treaties that benefit themselves and foreigners at the expense of their impoverished populations.'[133]

The point then is that there are other possible explanations than the public interest for the signing of investment treaties in Africa as the preambles may suggest.[134] With the potential for governments signing these agreements and contracts to benefit themselves, out of political expediency or to meet borrowing conditions rather than solely in order that investment might be attracted to meet the needs of the people, Pogge says:[135]

> We must then ask ourselves whether it is morally acceptable that the existing international order recognizes rulers—merely because they exercise effective power within a country and regardless of how they acquired or exercise such power—as entitled to confer legally valid property rights in this country's resources and to dispose of the proceeds of such sale, to borrow in the country's name and thereby to impose debt service obligations upon it, to sign treaties on the country's behalf and thus to bind its present and future population, and to use state revenues to buy the means of internal repression. Such recognition accords international resource, borrowing, treaty, and arms privileges to many governments that are plainly illegitimate. These privileges are *impoverishing*, because their exercise often dispossesses a country's people who are excluded from political participation as well as from the benefits of their government's borrowing or resource sales. These privileges are moreover *oppressive*, because they often give illegitimate rulers access to the funds they need to keep themselves in power even against the will of the majority. And these privileges are *disruptive*, because they provide strong incentives toward the democratic acquisition and exercise of political power.

However, there are those who see nothing wrong with transnational rules governing private foreign investment promotion and protection. The argument in support of investment treaties is that states are willing parties to them.[136] In this

[132] Uche Ewelukwa Ofodile, 'Managing Foreign Investment in Agricultural Land in Africa: The Role of Bilateral Investment Treaties and International Investment Contracts' (2014) 7(2) The Law and Development Review 329, 332.

[133] Thomas Pogge, *World Poverty and Human Rights: Cosmopolitan Responsibilities and Reforms* (Polity Press 2002) at 22.

[134] Poulsen, *Bounded Rationality and Economic Diplomacy* (n 117).

[135] Pogge, *Politics as Usual* (n 122) 18–19.

[136] For this debate see for example Muthucumaraswamy Sornarajah and Leo Trakman, 'A Polemic: The Cases for and Against Investment Liberalization' in Leon A Trakman and Nicola W Ranieri (eds), *Regionalism in International Investment Law* (OUP 2013) 499 (hereafter, Sornarajah

regard, an investment treaty is seen as reflecting 'the mutual decision of its States Parties to bind themselves ... a strategy which helps the problem of enforcing government promises during the inevitable intervening time between a government promise and its performance'.[137] The state

> is implicated by participating in the construction of the rules and structures governing international economic relations and, in turn, committing itself to abide by the scope of state law-making jurisdiction imposed by those same rules. States, in other words, are the authors of the very legal regime that is realigning the bounds of permissible state action.[138]

Such an argument is legally justified in terms of the *pacta sunt servanda* principle codified in Article 26 of the VCLT,[139] namely that a treaty in force binds the parties and they must perform the treaty in good faith. In this sense, investment treaties are 'precommitments, in the sense of giving up future choices to guard against preference shifts'[140] and must be respected and observed at all times.

However, the argument that consent makes and justifies a treaty binding on states in all circumstances is refutable because 'consent cannot defeat a charge of human rights violations given that, on the usual understanding of moral and legal human rights, they are inalienable and thus cannot be waived by consent'.[141] Moreover,

> an appeal to consent cannot justify the severe impoverishment of children who are greatly overrepresented among those who suffer severe poverty and its effects. Insofar as the present global order is, foreseeably, greatly suboptimal in terms of avoiding severe poverty of children, the claim that this order violates their human rights cannot be blocked by any plausible appeal to consent.[142]

and Trakman, 'A Polemic'); and Muthucumaraswamy Sornarajah, 'The Case against a Regime on International Investment Law' in Leon Trackman and Nicola Ranieri (eds), *Regionalism in International Investment Law* (OUP 2013) 475.

137 Desierto, *Public Policy and International Economic Law* (n 118) 312–13.

138 David Schneiderman, 'Investment Rules and the New Constitutionalism' (2000) 25 Law and Society Inquiry 757, 758.

139 Vienna Convention on the Law of Treaties (opened for signature 23 May 1969, entered into force 27 January 1980) 1155 UNTS 331 (hereafter, VCLT).

140 Tom Ginsburg, Svitlana Chernykh, and Zachary Elkins, 'Commitment and Diffusion: How and Why National Constitutions Incorporate International Law' (2008) University of Illinois Law Review 201, 212.

141 Pogge, *Politics as Usual* (n 122) 40.

142 ibid 41.

Above all, Pogge forcibly and cogently argues that

> insofar as very poor people do not consent, through a meaningful democratic process, to some global institutional arrangements, the justificatory force of such consent is typically weakened by their having no other tolerable option, and often weakened even further by the fact that their calamitous circumstances are partly due to those whose conduct this consent is meant to justify.[143]

Any argument that host developing states are 'willing' parties to investment treaties is effectively undermined by the use of model investment agreements, and especially when unequal bargaining power is inherent in the nature of the investment treaty negotiation process involved.[144] In an investment treaty negotiation process characterised by unequal bargaining power, bilateral treaties become a basis to protect investments in the same way as would have been imposed without a treaty by a state in a power position.[145]

Thus the binding effect of an investment treaty should be looked at not just in terms of consent but also the totality of the surrounding circumstances governing the conclusion of the treaty including any conditions that may defeat free consent and the negotiation process as envisaged under Articles 31 and 32 of the VCLT. The 'overall coherence of national and international economic law necessary for an efficient functioning of international markets depends not only on coherent legal principles of international private and public law, but also on their democratic recognition and support as legitimate and just'.[146] Such democratic recognition and support is further justified because '[e]conomies, finance and markets' that underlie the investment treaty regime 'are all social phenomena. They frame, and are framed by, relationships among people, families ... and the other diverse communities that make up society, and by relationships with other nations. They are also shaped by—and generate—unequal distributions of wealth and power.'[147] Therefore, where an investment treaty can be entered into only in accordance with a national constitution and general international law for public interest purposes, then the binding effect of the treaty should have regard to those legal norms which underlie the conclusion of the treaty.

[143] ibid.

[144] Dagbanja, 'Limitation on Sovereign Regulatory Autonomy' (n 50) 22–23.

[145] Kojo Yelpaala 'Fundamentalism in public health and safety in bilateral investment treaties [Part I]' (2008) 3(1) Asian Journal of WTO and International Health Law and Policy 242, 249.

[146] Ernst-Ulrich Petersman, 'Why Rational Choice Theory Requires a Multilevel Constitutional Approach to International Economic Law: A Response to The Case Against Reforming the WTO Enforcement Mechanism' (2008) University of Illinois Law Review 359, 371.

[147] Jane Kelsey, *The Fire Economy: New Zealand's Reckoning* (Bridget Williams Books with New Zealand Law Foundation 2015) 82.

5.4 Investment Treaties, Investor–State Arbitration, and Development Policy-making in Africa: Case Studies

5.4.1 Targeted Industrial and Social Policies in Africa

As established in Subsections 5.2.2 and 5.2.3, the constitutions and various IHRTs require African states to take measures to protect citizens and vulnerable groups in particular. Such measures could contravene the national treatment and most-favoured-nation (MFN) treatment principles of investment treaties, whereby the same or similar treatment must be extended to foreign investors or African states must compensate them. States have the discretion to decline the admission of foreign investors into those sectors because it is within their sovereign and constitutional rights to do so. However, if states choose to admit them, the discretion to give preferential treatment to domestic investors would be impaired by the national treatment and MFN standards of investment protection.

Investment treaty provisions that substantively and expressly limit states from implementing such measures, or require the states to extend the measures to parties that the various constitutions do not require, conflict with the states' constitutional duties to make and implement development policies in favour of special groups or individual citizens.

The Constitution of Ghana in Article 12(2) provides that '[e]very person in Ghana . . . shall be entitled to the fundamental human rights and freedoms of the individual'. One such fundamental human right is freedom from discrimination. The Constitution of Ghana prohibits discrimination on grounds of gender, race, colour, ethnic origin, religion, creed, or social or economic status.[148] Discrimination is defined as giving different treatment to different persons attributable only or mainly to their respective descriptions, 'whereby persons of one description are subjected to disabilities or restrictions to which persons of another description are not made subject or are granted privileges or advantages which are not granted to persons of another description'.[149] A person must not be discriminated against by reason, among others, of the place of origin.[150] In *Commission on Human Rights and Administrative Justice v Norvor*, the High Court of Ghana held that freedom from discrimination 'knows no bounds but is to be enjoyed by every person in Ghana'.[151]

It might be argued that the national treatment and MFN obligations are consistent with the constitutional protection of freedom from discrimination and that investment treaties and the Constitution of Ghana do not conflict. However, the Constitution of Ghana provides in Article 17(4)(c) that the protection against

[148] Constitution of Ghana (n 57) art 17(1).
[149] ibid art 17(2).
[150] ibid art 17(3).
[151] *Commission on Human Rights and Administrative Justice v Norvor* [2001–2002] 1 The Ghana Law Reports 78, 90.

discrimination and the guarantee of equality before the law shall not 'prevent Parliament from enacting laws that are reasonably necessary to provide for the imposition of restrictions on the acquisition of land by persons who are not citizens of Ghana or on the political and economic activities of such persons and for other matters relating to such persons'. The Constitution of Ghana in Article 36(2)(a) requires the state to afford ample opportunity for individual initiative and creativity in economic activities and to foster an enabling environment for a pronounced role of the private sector in the economy. Article 36(2)(b) of the Constitution further requires the state to ensure that individuals and the private sector bear their fair share of social and national responsibilities, including responsibilities to contribute to the overall development of Ghana.

Article 65(1) and (3) of the Constitution of Kenya places similar restrictions on the acquisition of land by non-citizens, requiring them to hold only a leasehold interest in land for ninety-nine years and that for purposes of landholding a body corporate would be treated as a citizen only if it is wholly owned by one or more citizens. Article 65(4) of the Constitution of Kenya empowers Parliament to make legislation for the operation of this provision on landholding. Parliament in accordance with Article 66(2) of the Constitution of Kenya can enact legislation that ensures that 'investments in property benefit local communities and their economies'.

The Constitution of Nigeria in Section 16(1)(b) requires the state to control the national economy in a manner that secures the maximum welfare of citizens. Section 217(2) of the Constitution of South Africa[152] provides that when organs of government contract for goods or services, they may implement a procurement policy that provides for 'categories of preference in the allocation of contracts' and for 'the protection or advancement of persons, or categories of persons, disadvantaged by unfair discrimination'.

By these provisions, the Parliaments of Ghana, Kenya, Nigeria, and South Africa can enact laws restricting foreign investors' economic activities. By these constitutions, foreign investors may be treated or regulated differently from the way domestic investors are treated or regulated for the public good. The states can take measures that they consider reasonably necessary to advance the interests of citizens that may not be available to non-citizens engaged in the same or similar business activities. These are the sorts of measures the national treatment standard prohibits. Based on these and other constitutional and legislative provisions, African states have the authority and discretion to choose to pursue industrial policies specifically targeted at local businesses so that they can grow and contribute to development which might turn out to conflict with investment treaty commitments.

[152] Constitution of South Africa (n 57).

5.4.1.1 Investment Treaties, Investor–State Arbitration, and Industrial Policies in Africa

The concept of industrial policy is contentious. It may be defined in general term as 'any policy that affects the evolution of industry'[153] such as manufacturing, mining, energy, and electricity. An industrial policy may be *selective* or *targeted*, that is a policy that 'deliberately favours particular industries—or even firms—over others, against market signals, usually to enhance efficiency and to promote productivity growth for the targeted industries as well as for the whole economy, but also to manage the industries' decline smoothly'.[154] The industrial sector 'is crucial for the structural transformation of African economies. Industry, manufacturing in particular, has traditionally been a source of substantial employment generation in developed and developing countries alike.'[155]

Different countries in Africa have different industrial policies and the relationship between industrial policies and investment treaty regime will differ from country to country. For example, the purpose of Cameroon's Mining Code 'is to boost, encourage and promote investments in the mining sector that can contribute to the economic and social development of the country'.[156] The law and regulation of the mining sector are thus tied to the development needs of Cameroon. Therefore, Cameroon can tie the grant of a mining title, royalty and tax regimes in the mining industry to the contribution the mining will make to development. The imposition of tax on investment operations can be a subject of investor–state dispute settlement.[157] Section 44(3) of the Mining Code states that a mining agreement signed between an exploration permit holder and the state to develop and mine or finance a new mineral deposit 'shall comprise'

> provisions relating to the local content of the projects to be implemented under the mining agreement, notably training, employment and protection of Cameroonian labour, outsourcing to local small-and medium-sized enterprises (SMEs), development and upgrading of local enterprises to enable them take part in the construction or operation of the plants or infrastructure provided for in the mining agreement, as well as in the social projects aimed at developing the neighbouring or indigenous populations.

[153] United Nations Economic Commission for Africa, *Transformative Industrial Policy for Africa by the Economic Commission for Africa* (UNECA 2016) 28

[154] ibid.

[155] United Nations Economic Commission for Africa, *Dynamic Industrial Policy in Africa: Innovative Institutions, Effective Processes and Flexible Mechanisms Institutional Dynamics* (Policy Brief No 11 2014) 1.

[156] Cameroon Mining Code Law No 2016/017 of 14 December 2016, s 2.

[157] *Cargill, Incorporated v United Mexican States*, ICSID Case No ARB(AF)/05/2, Award, 18 September 2009; and *Feldman v Mexico*, ICSID Case No ARB (AF)/99/1, Award, 16 December 2002.

Requirements on local content constitute a performance requirement under investment treaties.[158] These requirements in Section 44(3) of the Mining Code could be challenged under Article 3(2) of the Cameroon–BLEU investment treaty which provides that investments 'shall be safeguarded and protected at all times and shall not be subject to any unreasonable or discriminatory measure that might, *de jure* or *de facto*, impede their management, maintenance, use, enjoyment or liquidation, with the exception of measures necessary for the maintenance of public policy'. Imposing the requirements on foreign investors which might not be imposed on domestic investors might be challenged as discriminatory or they may simply be challenged as unreasonable.

In Ukraine, a law that required 50 per cent of a television station's broadcasting time to be reserved for music produced in Ukraine was challenged in the case of *Lemire v Ukraine*.[159] In 2004, on the recommendation of a public auditor, Canada developed guidelines setting a fixed amount for research and development spending which affected the exploration, development, and production phases of the oil industry. The guideline required investors to buy goods and services in Newfoundland and Labrador.[160] This measure was successfully challenged in *Mobil Oil v Canada*.[161] The Tribunal found that the guideline was in breach of Article 1106.1.c of the North America Free Trade Agreement. Similar cases have been brought against the introduction of performance requirements.[162]

Egyptian investment law is to similar effect as in Cameroon as regards the use of investment law as a tool to promote industry and national development. Thus, Article 2 of Investment Law, Law No 72 of 2017 states that investment in Egypt 'aims at improving the national economic growth rates and the domestic production rates, as well as provision of employment opportunities, promotion of exports, and boosting of competitiveness which contribute to achieving the comprehensive and sustainable development'. Article 68 of the Law empowers the Supreme Council for Investment to adopt the policies and investment plans which 'prioritize the target investment projects, in line with the State's general policy, the economic and social development plan, and the applicable investment regimes'.

[158] Suzy H Nikièma, *Performance Requirements in Investment Treaties* (IISD Best Practices Series—December 2014) (hereafter, Nikièma, *Performance Requirements*).

[159] *Joseph Charles Lemire v Ukraine*, ICSID Case No ARB/06/18, Award of 14 January 2010.

[160] Nikièma, *Performance Requirements* (n 158).

[161] *Mobil Investments Canada Inc and Murphy Oil Corporation v Government of Canada*, ICSID Case No ARB(AF)/07/4, Decision of 22 May 2012.

[162] *Pope & Talbot Inc v Government of Canada*, UNCITRAL, Interim ruling of 26 June 2000; *SD Myers Inc v Canada*, UNCITRAL, partial award of 13 November 2000; *ADF Group Inc v United States of America*, ICSID Case No ARB (AF)/00/1, award of 9 January 2003; *Archer Daniels Midland Company and Tate & Lyle Ingredients Americas, Inc v United Mexican States*, ICSID Case No ARB (AF)/04/5, award of 21 November, *Corn Products International Inc v United States of America*, ICSID, Case No ARB (AF)/04/1, award of 15 January 2008; *Cargill, Incorporated v United Mexican States*, ICSID Case No ARB(AF)/05/2, award of 18 September 2009; and *Merrill & Ring Forestry LP v Government of Canada*, UNCITRAL, ICSID, Award of 31 March 2010.

Article 8 of the Law requires employment and training of local labour, and Article 41 imposes various fees on the commodity value upon ingress for the storage projects, on commodity value upon egress for manufacturing and assembly projects, and on the total revenues for projects the main activity of which does not require the ingress or egress of goods for projects established in public free zones. For projects established in private free zones similar fees are imposed on the total revenues realised for the manufacturing and assembly projects upon the goods being exported abroad as well as fees on the total revenues realized by these projects upon the ingress of the commodities into Egypt. Investors must also pay fees on the total revenues realized in relation to projects whose main activity does not require the ingress or egress of goods.

Article 2 of Egypt's Executive Regulations of the Investment Law No 72 of 2017 provides that an investor 'may' allocate a percentage of 'profits … to social development by participating in any or all fields as follows', taking measures necessary to safeguard and improve the environment; providing services or programmes in fields of health, social, or culture care, or any other field of development including by creating job opportunities to persons with special needs; supporting technical education or funding research, studies, and awareness-raising campaigns aimed at developing and improving production; and undertaking training and scientific research to update technology used in production, and studies aimed at to improve the environment and prevent adverse environmental impacts. These stipulations would seem to be optional with the use of the word 'may' which does not import obligation. However, Article 3 of the Executive Regulations says that an investor allocating a part of profits to establish this social responsibility system 'shall' provide the General Authority for Investment and Free Zones (GAFI) with an annual report evidencing documents as prescribed by GAFI.

These requirements are all potential candidates for investor–state suits if implemented. They could be challenged as being in breach of performance requirements and right to transfer funds. For example, Article IX(1) of the Egypt–Canada investment treaty, guarantees investors 'the unrestricted transfer of investments and returns', and the impositions of social responsibilities on investors in these Executive Regulations do not fall within the exceptions in Article IX(3) of the investment treaty. Article V(2)(b) of the Egypt–Canada investment treaty prohibits performance requirements on domestic content. Under Article V(1)(a) of the treaty, a contracting party shall not require an enterprise to appoint to senior management positions individuals of any particular nationality. Under Article V(1)(b) of the investment treaty, a contracting party may require that a majority of the board of directors or any committee of an enterprise be of a particular nationality, or resident in the territory of the contracting party, only if such requirement 'does not materially impair the ability of the investor to exercise control over its investment'. In *Wena Hotels Limited v Egypt*, that country's policies of subsidising domestic users of gas and electricity, encouraging local industries to convert to gas and pricing and other policies that were said to restrict the further development by local gas producers of Egypt's natural gas resources in which a foreign investor made investments were found to be discriminatory and in breach of the fair and equitable treatment and legitimate expectations of the investor contrary to the Egypt–Spain BIT.[163]

Similar issues confront Ghana. The Ghana Investment Promotion Centre Act 2013 (Act 865) says in Section 34(3)(b) that an investor can employ non-managerial staff of any nationality but a Ghanaian of similar qualification and experience 'shall have the first option'. There are also policies in Ghana that are largely aimed at promoting the domestic industry. The government developed the Ghana Industrial Policy in 2010 in response to the challenges facing the manufacturing sector, such as increased competition in domestic and export markets and high production and distribution costs arising from high interest rates, aged and obsolete equipment, inefficient infrastructural services, and low productivity.[164] The aim was to 'develop requisite skills, ensure adequate and cost-competitive production inputs and services, and provide needed finance for industrial development'.[165]

The Industrial Policy provided guidelines for the implementation of the government's industrial development agenda 'with particular respect to the growth, diversification, upgrading and competitiveness of Ghana's manufacturing sector',[166] some of which could be owned solely by Ghanaians or by Ghanaians and foreign citizens. The key development objectives of the Industrial Policy were to expand productive employment and technological capacity in the manufacturing sector, and to promote agro-based industrial development and spatial distribution of industries to achieve reduction in poverty and income inequalities.[167] While foreign investors in the manufacturing sector may be entitled to the benefits under the policy, the state is under no obligation to extend them to business entities owned solely by foreign investors. Since the focus of the policy is the growth and capacity of local manufacturers, the state may choose to favour domestic businesses only. Such preferential treatment may be held to be inconsistent with national treatment. If the Industrial Policy were applied to favour third state investors but not those investors protected under Ghana's investment treaties, the latter could institute investor–state dispute claims against Ghana for breach of MFN since the treaty obligations require protections accorded to third state investors to be extended to treaty partner investors.

[163] *Unión Fenosa Gas SA v Arab Republic of Egypt* (ICSID Case No ARB/14/4), Award, 31 August 2018 paras 9.40 and 9.144–9.146

[164] On the evolution of industrial policy in Ghana see: Charles Ackah, Charles Adjasi, and Festus Turkson, 'Industrial Policy in Ghana' in Carol Newman and others (eds), *Manufacturing Transformation: Comparative Studies of Industrial Development in Africa and Emerging Asia* (OUP 2016); and United Nations Industrial Development Organisation, *The Industrial Policy Process in Ghana* (Development Policy, Statistics and Research Branch Working Paper 2 2013).

[165] Government of Ghana, *Ghana Industrial Policy* (Ministry of Trade and Industry 2010) 4 <https://www.moti.gov.gh/docs/Industrial%20Policy.pdf> accessed 8 February 2022.

[166] ibid 3.

[167] ibid 4.

The Public Procurement Act 2003 (Act 663) in section 3(t) requires the Public Procurement Authority of Ghana to assist the local business community to become competitive and efficient suppliers to the public sector.[168] The Act also allows for the use of national competitive tendering whereby only domestic prospective tenderers may be invited to participate in the procurement process.[169] The implementation of these policies and laws specifically targeted at the domestic investors could be found to conflict with national treatment and MFN.[170]

Domestic law in Ghana also makes provision for other special assistance to domestic businesses that may create conflict with the national treatment standard. The National Board for Small-Scale Industries Act 1981 (Act 434) and the Ghana Export Promotion Authority Act 1969 (Act 396) require the executive directors of the National Board for Small-scale Industries and Ghana Export Promotion Authority to provide assistance to domestic businesses that may not be available to foreign investors in like circumstances. In particular, section 4 of the Ghana Export Promotion Authority Act requires the Authority to organise an insurance credit guarantee scheme for the protection of the interest of Ghanaian exports. If foreign investors are engaged in the same export industry as domestic investors, they may seek compensation under the investment treaties in the event that the government introduces credit schemes that advantage domestic investors or which threaten the market share of foreign investors.[171]

Investment treaties exhibit a dual nature when it comes to industrial policy: they can 'be potentially supporting and potentially constraining of industrial policies'.[172] By creating a legal framework for investment protection, they may attract investment into sectors of the economy in which the host state does not have the needed domestic capacity. For example, although Ghana is endowed with natural resources in the form of minerals and oil, it has limited technological capacity and know-how to explore and exploit them. Foreign investment in these industries is necessary for the state to extract these resources and the development of these industrial sectors in general.

[168] See Dominic Dagbanja, 'Promoting a Competitive Local Business Community in Ghana: The Role of the Legal Framework for Public Procurement' (2014) 58(2) Journal of African Law 1.

[169] Dominic Dagbanja, *The Law of Public Procurement in Ghana: Law, Policy and Practice* (Lap Lambert Academic Publishing AG & Co Kg 2011) 151.

[170] Agreement between the Kingdom of Denmark and the Government of the Republic of Ghana Concerning the Promotion and Protection of Investments (signed 13 January 1992, entered into force 6 January 1995) art 3(2); Ghana–Netherlands Investment Treaty (n 98) art 3(1); and Ghana–United Kingdom Investment Treaty (n 97) art 3(2).

[171] Luke Eric Peterson, *Bilateral Investment Treaties and Development Policy-Making* (International Institute for Sustainable Development 2004) 30.

[172] Wolfgang Alschner and Elisabeth Tuerk, 'The Role of International Investment Agreements in Fostering Sustainable Development' in Freya Baetebs (ed), *Investment Law within International Law: Integrationist Perspectives* (CUP 2013) 217, 224 (hereafter, Alschner and Tuerk, 'Role of IIAs in Fostering Sustainable Development').

However, investment treaties can also constrain industrial policy if a state wants to protect domestic investors from invasion by foreign investors or simply wants to protect infant or strategic domestic investors for development purposes.[173] For example, under section 27 of Ghana Investment Promotion Centre Act 2013 (Act 865) (GIPCA) non-citizens and enterprises not wholly owned by a citizen are not permitted to invest or participate in the sale of goods or provision of services in a market;[174] operation of a taxi or car hire service in an enterprise that has a fleet of less than twenty-five vehicles; printing of recharge scratch cards; production of exercise books and other basic stationary; and the retail of finished pharmaceutical products. Only citizens and enterprises wholly owned by citizens may invest in these areas. Investment treaties are potential barriers to the attainment of these legislative goals. Upon admission, foreign investors can challenge such provision as discriminatory and unreasonably restricting their investment opportunities and market share in the prohibited areas.

South Africa is in a similar position as other African countries analysed in terms of conflict between investment treaties and industrial and socio-economic policies. Section 217(2) of the Constitution of South Africa grants organs of the state and other institutions identified in national legislation power relating to 'implementing a procurement policy providing for (a) categories of preference in the allocation of contracts; and (b) the protection or advancement of persons, or categories of persons, disadvantaged by unfair discrimination'. Section 217(3) of the Constitution of South Africa requires the enactment of legislation to 'prescribe a framework within which' this preferential policy 'must be implemented'. Consequently, South Africa has a large body of legislation and policies that seeks to give preferential treatment in the areas of procurement and the employment of black people and other marginalised groups to regulate ownership structures of businesses to promote black people's interest in those businesses and to provide special assistance to domestic businesses. There are industrial and social-economic legislation and policies said to be aimed at addressing historically disadvantaged people including black people and Indians or helping domestic businesses.[175]

The Broad-based Socio-economic Empowerment Charter for the Mining and Minerals Industry, 2018[176] (the Mining Charter) was made pursuant to section

[173] ibid.

[174] The Ghana Investment Promotion Centre Act defines a market in section 43 as 'a public place whether open or enclosed, established and managed by local custom, or specifically designated by the appropriate local government authority or its agents and which has selling sites in the nature of stores and stalls among others for the purpose of selling and buying'.

[175] Preferential Procurement Policy Framework Act 2000 (No 5); National Empowerment Fund Act (1998) (No 105); Employment Equity Act 1998 (No 55); Broadbased Black Economic Empowerment Act 2003 (No 53); Industrial Development Corporation Act 1940 (No 22); and Codes of Good Practice on Broadbased Black Economic Empowerment (August 2017) <https://www.thedti.gov.za/gazzettes/41024.pdf> accessed 19 December 2021.

[176] Department of Mineral Resources, Broad-based Socio-economic Empowerment Charter for the Mining and Minerals Industry, 2018 (No 1002, 27 September 2018) (hereafter, 'Mining Charter').

100 (2) of the Mineral and Petroleum Resources Development Act 2002 (Act No 28 of 2002) (MPRDA herein) for the mining and minerals industry. The object of this Act is 'to redress historical socio- economic inequalities, to ensure broad-based economic empowerment and the meaningful participation of Historically Disadvantaged Persons in the mining and minerals industry'.[177] To further this object of the Act, the Mining Charter is aimed, among other things, at enabling 'growth and development of the local mining inputs sector by leveraging the procurement spend of the mining industry'.[178]

The Charter requires inclusive procurement. To achieve inclusive procurement, a mining right holder is required to identify goods and services that will be required in its operations and ensure that its procurement policies adhere to specified criteria.[179] In the case of the procurement of *mining goods*,[180] inclusivity is met if a minimum of 70 per cent of total mining goods procurement spend is on South African manufactured goods.[181] In the case of services, a minimum of 80 per cent of the total spend on services must be sourced from a South African-based company.[182] The Protection of Investment Act 2015 (No 22) is also very explicit on the right to regulate on social and economic policies in section 12.

The investment treaties African countries are parties to, except a few of the most recent ones as analysed in Section 5.6, do not include exceptions to ensure that positive discriminatory measures taken in favour of designated businesses are protected from investment treaty claims for the payment of compensation. Therefore, existing targeted policies or future ones stand the risk of being challenged as being in breach of the national treatment standard. In fact, in *Foresti v Republic of South Africa*[183] the foreign investors sued South Africa based on investment treaties due to the adverse impact of its Black Economic Empowerment legislation on their assets. This case, fully discussed in Section 5.6.1 later in this chapter, was eventually settled when South Africa granted the claimants new order mineral rights based on other conditions without requiring them to sell off a percentage of their shares. The case could have ended with much weightier consequences for South Africa but it also exemplifies how the international investment treaty framework provides foreign investors with a cause of action to challenge domestic human rights-based laws and policies that are otherwise lawful under national constitutions.[184]

[177] ibid. The Mineral and Petroleum Resources Development Act, 2002 (Act No 28 of 2002) defines 'historically disadvantaged person as "any person, category of persons or community, disadvantaged by unfair discrimination before the Constitution took effect"

[178] Mining Charter (n 176) item 1(h).

[179] ibid.

[180] The Mining Charter (n 176) defines mining goods as referring to 'to capital goods and consumables used by a right holder or by a contractor on behalf of a right holder'.

[181] ibid item 2.2.1.

[182] ibid 2.2.2.

[183] *Piero Foresti v The Republic of South Africa*, ICSID Case No ARB(AF)/07/1, Award, 4 August 2010.

[184] Megan Wells Sheffer, Bilateral Investment Treaties: A Friend or Foe to Human Rights? (2011) 39 Denver Journal of International Law and Policy 483.

Another African-specific case is *Funnekotter v Zimbabwe*.[185] The investors made direct or indirect investments in large commercial farms in Zimbabwe. The claimants said the Lancaster House Constitution of Zimbabwe 1979 was amended in 2000 and 2005 in response to land reforms. In implementing the amended Constitution of Zimbabwe, all the agricultural land owned by the claimants were acquired by and vested in the state with full title. According to the investors, they had effectively been deprived of their properties by this amendment and other legislative measures and the invasion of their farms by war veterans and settlers in violation of the bilateral investment treaty concluded between the Netherlands and Zimbabwe.[186] They requested the Tribunal to declare Zimbabwe responsible for its unlawful action and to order Zimbabwe to compensate them for all the damages suffered.

Zimbabwe invoked the state of necessity to justify the measures of expropriation it took in the public interest. Zimbabwe contended that the measures it took in depriving investors of their properties were taken in conformity with the Land Acquisition Act 2002 and its Constitution which permitted the government to acquire lands in question and vest them in the rightful owners. Moreover, the measures were taken in the public interest and under due process of law.[187] The land was acquired to address the need of the landless and liberation war veterans.

The undertakings in the investment treaty, according to Zimbabwe, did not preclude Zimbabwe from acquiring land at any time as long as it was in the public interest to do so.[188] The Tribunal was of the opinion that Zimbabwe never explained why such a state of necessity prevented it from calculating and paying the compensation due to the farmers in conformity with the investment treaty.[189] Moreover, the Tribunal concluded that during the period 2000–2005 when the measures complained of were taken, there had been no state of emergency declared in Zimbabwe.[190] The Tribunal held that the deprivation of properties complained of was not accompanied by the provision of payment of compensation as contemplated under the investment treaty. Therefore, Zimbabwe was in breach of the expropriation provision of the BIT and liable to pay compensation to the investors.[191]

Another case illustrating how an industrial policy may be challenged by foreign investors is *Nusa Tenggara Partnership BV v Indonesia*.[192] Newmont Nusa Tenggara

185 *Funnekotter v Republic of Zimbabwe*, ICSID Case No ARB/05/6, Award, 22 April 2009 (hereafter, *Funnekotter v Zimbabwe*).

186 Agreement on Encouragement and Reciprocal protection of Investments between the Republic of Zimbabwe and the Kingdom of the Netherlands, signed 11 December 1996, entered into force 1 May 1998.

187 *Funnekotter v Zimbabwe* (n 185) [61]–[62].

188 ibid [84].

189 ibid [106].

190 ibid [103].

191 ibid [107] and [148].

192 *Nusa Tenggara Partnership BV v Indonesia*, ICSID Case No ARB/14/15, Order of the Secretary-General Taking Note of the Discontinuance of the Proceedings, 29 August 2014 (hereafter, *NT Partnership v Indonesia*).

was engaged in the mining of copper in Indonesia. The company was largely co-owned by Newmont Mining Corporation in the United States and Japan's Nusa Tenggara Mining Corporation. The source of the dispute between Indonesia and Newmont was Indonesia's introduction of a ban on the exports of ore concentrates in which Newmont had invested. The export ban was part of the Law 4/2009 on Mineral and Coal Mining, which required mining companies to 'downstream' production (to refine and process minerals by establishing a smelter) in the country prior to export. The law allowed exports of semi-finished mineral products, such as copper concentrate, until 2017, but only with a progressive export tax which ranged between 20 per cent and 60 per cent.

This was part of a strategy of the Indonesian government to reduce its dependency on the export of raw materials and to assert control over the management of its resources, consistent with the Declaration on Permanent Sovereignty over Permanent Sovereignty Natural Resources.[193] The progressive tax rate was intended to force miners to develop mineral processing facilities in Indonesia, as part of a broader goal to get a larger share return from its mineral resources. The law also aimed to limit foreign ownership of mining companies by obliging foreign-owned mining industries to divest ownership share progressively to become a minority shareholder within ten years. The Indonesian government further hoped to spur development of domestic downstream processing industries in order to produce value-added products and generate more revenue. The government wanted to boost domestic employment and the local economy and help Indonesia to be less dependent on the export of raw materials. The requirements would seem to be consistent with the conventional wisdom that foreign investment leads to development.

However, mining companies active in extractive industry opposed the law. According to Newmont, it had led them to halt work a copper and gold mine, which created hardship and economic loss.[194] The company instituted arbitration proceedings against Indonesia in June 2014 under the Indonesia–Netherlands investment treaty,[195] arguing that the plan to implement a ban on unprocessed mineral exports would violate the treaty. Newmont later withdrew the case following a settlement reached with Indonesia to give the company special exemptions from the mining law.[196] This case is[197]

[193] Declaration on Permanent Sovereignty over Permanent Sovereignty Natural Resource (GA Res 1803 (XVII), 17 UN GAOR Supp (No 17) at 15, UN Doc A/5217 (1962) art 1.

[194] Hilde van der Pas and Riza Damanik, *The Case of Newmont Mining vs Indonesia* (EU–SEAN FTA Network Briefing, 12 November 2014) <https://www.tni.org/en/briefing/netherlands-indonesia-bit-rolls-back-implementation-new-indonesian-mining-law> accessed 29 November 2020 (hereafter, Pas and Damanik, 'Case of Newmont Mining').

[195] Agreement on Economic Cooperation between the Government of the Kingdom of The Netherlands and the Government of the Republic of Indonesia, signed 7 July 1968, entered 17 July 1978. This BIT has been terminated.

[196] *NT Partnership v Indonesia* (n 192).

[197] Pas and Damanik, 'Case of Newmont Mining' (n 194).

> a powerful example of how investment agreements ... are used by companies to get exemptions from government regulations and legislation, undermining democracy and development. It also illustrates the long-term dangers of governments signing investment agreements, which continue to be enforced even when subsequent governments try to re-establish sovereign control over investment in their countries.

Indonesia's experience illustrates how taxation and export processing requirements could create problems with the investment treaty regime in Africa. For example, Article 174 of the Constitution of Ghana authorises Parliament to regulate taxation by way of legislation. The Internal Revenue Act 2000 (Act 592) was enacted pursuant to this provision. The Act empowers the state to impose taxes on individuals and businesses. Taxation is one legal means through which the state can generate revenue to meet its development needs. The use of export taxes and local processing requirements is justified to give effect to the development provisions in the Constitution of Ghana.

The Ghana Export Promotion Authority Act empowers the Authority in section 4(2)(e) 'to create interest in, and goodwill for, Ghanaian products'. Under Section 12 of the Export and Import Act 1995 (Act 503), the Minister of Trade and Industry 'may, by legislative instrument, prohibit or restrict the exportation or importation of the goods specified in the instrument'. This gives a wide discretion to the Minister to regulate export and import, which discretion may be exercised to meet local processing requirements as part of Ghana's development strategy.

The South African Industrial Development Corporation Act 1940 (No 22) similarly established the Industrial Development Corporation of South Africa Ltd and empowers it to facilitate, promote, and assist in the financing of new industries and industrial undertakings, foster the development of small and medium enterprises, and leverage foreign direct investment in South Africa.[198] These measures are in the same category as the Indonesian measures that were challenged in *Nusa Tenggara v Indonesia*.[199]

5.4.1.2 Reconciling Treaty-based Standards of Investment Protection with Industrial Policy Objectives in Africa

There are scholars who think targeted social and economic policies may not be justifiable. In making a case for national treatment, Jan Paulsson suggests that '[h]otheaded politicians may seek public favour by advancing narrow conceptions of the national interest by law or decree'.[200] However, Paulsson failed to tell the reader what the national interest is, what amounts to 'narrow conceptions of national

[198] Industrial Development Corporation Act 1940 (No 22) s 3.

[199] *NT Partnership v Indonesia* (n 192).

[200] Jan Paulsson, *Denial of Justice in International Law* (CUP 2005) 147.

interest', and by what standard 'narrow conceptions of national interest' will be measured. If Paulsson had explained these concepts, his claims could have been better evaluated. Governments exist to advance the interests of the public they represent and this may require the taking of both immediate and long-term positions that they consider are in the national interest, in accordance with their constitutional and general international law obligations.

In a world where states 'compete with and oppose each other for power, the foreign policies of all nations must necessarily refer to their survival as their minimum requirement',[201] including on foreign investment protection by treaty. Hans Morgenthau points out that 'no nation can have a sure guide as to what it must do and what it need not do in foreign policy without accepting the national interest as that guide'.[202] Therefore, respect and space must be given to each nation state to define its national interest. A 'philosophy, very much alive ... which, while it recognizes the national interest and its importance, defines it in terms which take the heart out of the concept and out of the policies intended to support it'[203] must, therefore, be avoided in international investment rulemaking.

The 'legitimacy of the national interest must be determined in the face of possible usurpation by subnational, other-national, and supranational interest',[204] and not just in terms of how it affects a supranational interest, such as foreign investment. There is no nation that has the resources to promote all desirable objectives with equal vigour. Therefore, all nations must be allowed to allocate their scarce resources as rationally as they deem fit,[205] and to define their national interests against usurpation by non-national interests.[206] In a bilateral and multinational world it is imperative that 'the national interest of a nation which is conscious not only of its own interests but also of that of other nations must be defined in terms compatible with the latter'.[207] The point remains, nevertheless, that each nation state must be the judge of its national interest, such as protecting local businesses. At least, the protection of the businesses of citizens is consistent with the protection of the national interest. National treatment in investment treaties tends to screw African states in terms of determining what serves their national interests and allocating scarce resources accordingly.

The African constitutions analysed in this chapter require or permit all constitutional measures necessary to protect the public interest. This will include assisting domestic investors without having to extend the same or similar treatment

[201] Hans Morgenthau, 'Another 'Great Debate': The National Interest of the United States' (1952) 46(4) The American Political Science Review 961, 972 (hereafter, Morgenthau, 'Great Debate').

[202] Hans Morgenthau, 'What Is the National Interest of the United States?' (1952) 282 The Annals of the American Academy of Political and Social Science 1, 6.

[203] ibid.

[204] Morgenthau, 'Great Debate' (n 201) 973.

[205] ibid 977.

[206] ibid 976.

[207] ibid 971.

to foreign investors. These constitutions specifically permit restrictions on non-citizens' economic activities. Any such restrictions stand to be challenged under investment treaties.

Thus, there is the need to safeguard industrial policy and development policy in investment treaties. Arbitral tribunals derive their mandate from the terms of investment treaties which substantively focus on investor and investment protection. Investment treaties are mostly silent on development and states' development policy-making autonomy and do not impose any obligations on foreign investors in terms of the contribution they should make to the development of their host countries. Accordingly, arbitral tribunals have interpreted and will continue to interpret investment treaties in a manner that advances investment interests to the neglect of development and development objectives.[208]

Given pro-investor interpretive approaches, states must assert their authority over the application of investment treaties by providing for substantive obligations in investment treaties on corporate legal responsibilities of foreign investors. The contribution of the proposed business undertaking to development must be specified as an essential characteristic of investment. This will ensure that an investment is not entitled to protection if it does not make such contribution.[209] This has already been envisaged by Article 12 of Ghana Model BIT of 2008,[210] which states that nationals and companies of contracting states in the territory of the other shall be bound by the laws and regulations in force in the host state, including the host states laws and regulations on labour, health, and the environment. The provision also states that nationals and companies of one contracting party in the territory of the other contracting party 'shall to the extent possible, encourage human capital formation, local capacity building through close co-operation with the local community, create employment opportunities and facilitate training opportunities for employees, and the transfer of technology'.

The Kenya–Japan investment treaty also states in the preamble that the treaty 'is designed to allow each Contracting Party to regulate, and to introduce new measures relating to, investments in its Area in order to meet national public policy objectives'.[211] Article 4(3) of this investment treaty specifically exempts measures related to the acquisition of land, subsidies, and government procurement from the MFN obligation. Similar exceptions to the national treatment and MFN are provided for in Article 4 of the 2012 Southern Africa Development Community Model BIT.[212] The African states should go further and revise existing investment

[208] *MTD Equity Sdn. Bhd and MTD Chile SA v Republic of Chile*, Decision on Jurisdiction, at para 104; and *SGS Société Générale de Surveillance SA v Philippines*, Case No ARB/02/6, Decision of the Tribunal on Objections to Jurisdiction, 29 January 2004, [116].

[209] Alschner and Tuerk, 'Role of IIAs in Fostering Sustainable Development' (n 172) 230.

[210] Ghana Model BIT <https://investmentpolicy.unctad.org/international-investment-agreements/treaty-files/2866/download> accessed 29 September 2020.

[211] Japan–Kenya Investment Treaty (n 97).

[212] SADC Model Bilateral Investment Treaty Template with Commentary (Southern African Development Community, 2012).

treaties to exclude industrial policy tools such as taxation, subsidies, and government procurement from the purview of future investment treaties. Reservations should be made for selected industries and the possibility of adopting non-conforming measures in future in the reserved areas.[213]

5.4.2 Foreign Exchange Transactions Regulation in Africa

5.4.2.1 Capital Controls as a Development Tool in Africa

A common substantive provision in investment treaties is the requirement on transfer of investment capital, returns, and associated funds. Transfer of funds is a right to make international payments and to move money out of host country to home country or to other countries for various purposes. Some treaties use *repatriation*, which refers to the movement of investment funds from the host country to the investor's home country. *Transfer* is broader as it covers movement of money or making payments to the host state and from the host state to the home or any other country.[214] The right to transfer funds is necessary to enable foreign investors to make monetary transfers for their business and other purposes.[215] However, depending on how that right is articulated in an investment treaty, the duty of the host state to regulate the movement of capital can be extinguished or effectively curtailed when alleged violations of guarantees on transfer of funds or international payments are subject to investor–state arbitration. Abba Kolo articulated the dilemma this creates:[216]

> From the point of view of the foreign investor, the essence of making an investment is to make profits and distribute same to its shareholders who might reside in its home country or in several countries. Repatriation of funds might

[213] Alschner and Tuerk, 'Role of IIAs in Fostering Sustainable Development' (n 172) 225.

[214] Jeswald Salacuse, *The Law of Investment Treaties* (2nd edn, OUP 2015) 286 (hereafter, Salacuse, Law of Investment Treaties).

[215] According to Salacuse,

> The ability of a foreign investor to make international monetary payments freely both into and out of a host country is crucial to the success of any foreign investment. Investors need to transfer funds into the host country in order to establish an investment, operate it, expand it, and support it during economic hard times. They need to transfer funds out of the country in order to purchase raw materials and spare parts, make royalty and technology payments, service debts, distribute profits made by the enterprise, and repatriate capital when the investment is sold. The aim of all foreign investors is not just to make a profit, but to make a profit that can be freely transferred to its home country or elsewhere. Investors want the freedom to engage in these monetary transactions whenever they see fit in response to market conditions and without the need to secure government approvals for them. They thus consider the rights granted to them by the host country with respect to international monetary transactions as important matters affecting their treatment. ibid 284.

[216] Abba Kolo, 'Investor Protection vs Host State Regulatory Autonomy during Economic Crisis: Treatment of Capital Transfers and Restrictions under Modern Investment Treaties' (2007) 8(4) Journal of World Investment and Trade 457, 471.

> also be needed by the foreign investor for other purposes such as to service external loans, pay license fees and royalties, purchase raw materials and machinery for production and pay for other services. These are critical for the success of an investment. Hence, the importance of the repatriation provision in investment treaties. On the other hand, a host state might be concerned about the depletion of its foreign reserves through such transfers and the adverse effect it might have on the economy especially during times of economic difficulties. Therefore it will not want to curtail its discretion to adopt measures including exchange restrictions in order to deal with economic difficulties.

Capital controls can help avoid or prevent capital flight when there are difficulties in a country. The imposition of capital controls is an important element of fiscal sovereignty.[217] During periodic economic, social, and political crises, monetary and exchange rate regimes have often been renegotiated.[218] The International Monetary Fund (IMF) suggests that countries often tighten monetary policy during crisis.[219] In this respect, monetary policy (defined in terms of money, interest, and exchange rates)[220] and regulation, both as crisis response measures and the rehabilitation of capital controls as a pre-emptive tool, are important aspects of development policy. Kelsey rightly argues that[221]

> [m]oney is not simply a commodity. Nor are national currencies merely the symbols of a (presumed) national identity. In an economic system based on

[217] ibid at 460.Writing on this subject, Salacuse stated:

> States ...... have the right under international law to control the transfer of all funds into and out of their territory. While host country governments understand that giving foreign investors the right to make international payments freely is important for the promotion of investment, they also know that granting them total freedom to transfer funds poses certain risks. Sudden large infusions of foreign capital can lead to inflation and appreciation of a country's currency, which in turn may have negative effects on the export of its goods and the country's overall macroeconomic situation. Large outflows of funds can dangerously reduce monetary reserves, create undesirable volatility in exchange rates, inhibit a country's ability to secure goods and services needed for the public welfare, and negatively affect the host government's ability to meet its international financial obligations. Moreover, governments also perceive that supervision and control over international payments are necessary to prevent crime and security threats, to facilitate the collection of taxes, and to protect creditors. As a result of these considerations, host governments, while seeking to promote foreign investment through treaties, are also concerned with maintaining their ability to regulate monetary transactions so as to protect these important interests. Salacuse, *Law of Investment Treaties* (n 213) 284.

[218] Jane Kelsey, 'The Denationalization of Money: Embedded Neo-Liberalism and the Risks of Implosion' (2003) 12(2) Social & Legal Studies 155–76, 156 (hereafter, Kelsey, 'Denationalization of Money').

[219] IMF, *Recent Experiences in Managing Capital Inflows—Cross-Cutting Themes and Possible Policy Framework* (14 February 2014) [5] <http://www.imf.org/external/np/pp/eng/2011/021411a.pdf> accessed 29 September 2020.

[220] Jane Kelsey, *The New Zealand Experiment: A World Model for Structural Adjustment?* (Auckland University Press 1995) 150.

[221] Kelsey, 'Denationalization of Money' (n 218) 156.

> commodity capitalism, money is the medium for exercising power. It serves as the means of payment, store of value and unit of account, and as a commodity in its own right. Monetary policy and exchange rates are the vehicles through which national governments control the creation of money and influence its value so as to distribute resources among competing interests. Their ability to adjust the value and price of money in response to internal and external economic shocks impacts on the affordability of goods and services, the viability and profitability of businesses, the level of wages and unemployment, the sustainability of regions and pressures to migrate. These, in turn, affect people's wellbeing, the cohesion and stability of the society and citizens' confidence in their government.

The United Nations Task Team on the Post-2015 UN Development Agenda highlighted the importance of the state's autonomy in light of the global financial crisis:[222]

> The recent financial crisis has highlighted the damaging impacts on living standards that can result from macroeconomic instability. Large swings in economic activity, high inflation, unsustainable debt levels and volatility in exchange rates and financial markets can all contribute to job losses and increasing poverty... The broad objective of macroeconomic policy is to contribute to economic and social wellbeing in an equitable and sustainable manner.
>
> Continued and sustained economic growth is not only a precondition for employment generation, but also provides countries the fiscal space to address other critical social concerns, such as access to health services, sanitation and safe drinking water, and others ... Accordingly, the primary goal of macroeconomic stabilization policies should be to achieve stable economic growth. This key policy objective is complemented by the need to stabilize intermediate variables that can have a strong impact on growth. Price stability and external balances in particular play an important role through their impact on investment decisions. To achieve these intermediate goals, countries need policy space to use macroeconomic tools flexibly, including counter-cyclical fiscal and/or monetary policies, appropriate investment and exchange rate regimes, and strong financial sector regulation and supervision.

There is a link between macroeconomic stability and meeting the essential and basic needs of people, which I argue is central to African development. These authorities also point to the central importance of regulation by the state for a stable

[222] United Nations Task Team on the Post-2015 UN Development Agenda, *Macroeconomic Stability, Inclusive Growth and Employment: Thematic Think Piece* (United Nations May 2012) 3 and 4 <http://www.un.org/millenniumgoals/pdf/Think%20Pieces/12_macroeconomics.pdf> accessed 29 September 2020.

financial system to be attained. The IMF also argues that 'capital controls may be useful in addressing both macroeconomic and financial-stability concerns'.[223] Prudential regulations and capital controls can also help to 'reduce the buildup of vulnerabilities on balance sheets and the emergence of credit booms'.[224] In fact, 'monetary policies have been effective in driving economic development in Nigeria'.[225] The 'exchange rate, money supply and interest rate were all significant in explaining GDP [gross domestic product]'.[226]

The capital controls toolkit encompasses a broad spectrum of instruments, including administrative taxes on certain inflows and outflows, minimum holding periods, and currency-specific reserve requirements.[227] For capital control measures to have their desired effects, they should be targeted at the specific risks at hand and tailored to country circumstances because 'there is no "one-size-fits-all" approach to capital control design'.[228] Capital controls, by their nature, 'limit the rights of residents or non-residents to enter into capital transactions or to effect the transfers and payments associated with these transactions'.[229] Investment treaties commonly prohibit capital control measures, such as restriction on transfer of funds. Investment treaty provisions can prevent governments from taking 'pre-emptive or remedial action in relation to future crises including the application of capital controls and restructuring of sovereign debt'.[230]

5.4.2.2 Transfer of Investment Funds and Foreign Exchange Transactions Regulation in Africa

The Cameroon–BLEU investment treaty guarantees national and MFN for transfer of investment and returns without exception.[231] The Egypt–Canada BIT guarantees investors, unrestricted right to transfer capital and returns.[232] However, a contracting party may prevent a transfer 'through the equitable, non-discriminatory and good faith application of its laws relating to bankruptcy, insolvency or the protection of the rights of creditors; issuing, trading or dealing in securities; criminal

[223] Jonathan D Ostry, Atish R Ghosh, Karl Habermeier, and Luc Laeven, *Managing Capital Inflows: What Tools to Use?* (SDN/11/06, IMF, 5 April 2011) 4, <http://www.imf.org/external/pubs/ft/sdn/2011/sdn1106.pdf> accessed 29 September 2020.

[224] ibid 6.

[225] Akinjare Victoria, AA Babajide, Isibor Areghan Akhanolu, and Okafor Tochukwu, 'Monetary Policy and its Effectiveness on Economic Development in Nigeria' (2016) 10(22) International Business Management 5336, 5340

[226] ibid.

[227] IMF, *Recent Experiences in Managing Capital Inflows—Cross-Cutting Themes and Possible Policy Framework* (14 February 2014) [5] and [7] <http://www.imf.org/external/np/pp/eng/2011/021411a.pdf> accessed 29 September 2020.

[228] Jonathan D Ostry and others, *Managing Capital Inflows* (n 223) 7

[229] ibid 11.

[230] Jane Kelsey, 'How the Trans-Pacific Partnership Agreement Could Heighten Financial Instability and Foreclose Governments' Regulatory Autonomy' (2010) 8 New Zealand Yearbook of International Law 3.

[231] Cameroon–BLEU Investment Treaty (n 96) art 5.

[232] Egypt–Canada Investment Treaty (n 98) art IX(1).

or penal offenses; reports of transfers of currency or other monetary instruments; or ensuring the satisfaction of judgments in adjudicatory proceedings'.[233]

All the investment treaties of Ghana provide in various ways for transfer of investment and returns. The Ghana–China and Ghana–Malaysia investment treaties make the transfer subject to domestic laws and regulations.[234] The Ghana–Denmark investment treaty similarly requires transfer subject to the right of each state party to exercise 'equitably, in good faith and on a non-discriminatory basis the powers conferred by its laws'.[235] The Ghana–Netherlands investment treaty requires transfers in a freely convertible currency, 'without undue restriction or delay'.[236] The Ghana–United Kingdom and Ghana–Netherland investment treaties do not subject the right to repatriation of investment and returns to regulation under municipal law. The Ghana–United Kingdom investment treaty is the most absolute. It guarantees foreign investors the right of 'unrestricted transfer' of investments and returns.[237]

The Kenya–Japan, Nigeria–Germany, and South Africa–China investment treaties oblige the contracting parties to ensure that transfers relating investments are made freely into and out of a contracting party's territory without delay. Such transfers include initial capital and any additional amounts made later, profits, interest, capital gains, dividends, royalties, fees, the proceeds from liquidation, payments made pursuant to a loan agreement, and earnings and remuneration of personnel.[238]

A failure or refusal to permit the transfer of funds may breach not only the specific provisions on transfer of investment and returns in an investment treaty, but the obligations to provide foreign investors with fair and equitable treatment and full protection and security as well. Some of the treaties do not make provision for balance of payment exceptions. On the contrary, they require that foreign investors be accorded national treatment and MFN treatment in the event of a national emergency.[239]

The Constitution of Ghana requires the Bank of Ghana to promote and maintain the stability of the currency and to 'direct and regulate the currency system in the interest

233 ibid art IX(3).

234 Agreement between the People's Republic of China and the Government of the Republic of Ghana Concerning the Encouragement and Reciprocal Protection of Investments (signed 12 October 1989, entered into force on 22 November 1991 art 5; and Protection of Investments (signed on 8 November 1996, entered into force18 April 1997) art 6.

235 Ghana–Denmark Investment Treaty (n 170) art 8.

236 Ghana–Netherlands Investment Treaty (n 98) art 5.

237 Ghana–United Kingdom Investment Treaty (n 97) art 8.

238 Kenya–Japan Investment Treaty (n 97) art 13; Nigeria–Germany Investment Treaty (n 97) art 6; and South Africa–China Investment Treaty (n 97) art 6.

239 Ghana–China Investment Treaty (n 234) art 4; Agreement between the Government of the Republic of Ghana and the Government of Malaysia for the Promotion and Protection of Investments (signed on 8 November 1996, entered into force 18 April 1997) art 4; Ghana–Denmark Investment Treaty (n 170) art 7; Ghana–Netherlands Investment Treaty (n 98) art 7. Ghana–United Kingdom Investment Treaty (n 97) art 5.

of the economic progress of Ghana'.[240] The Bank is also required to 'encourage and promote economic development and the efficient utilisation of the resources of Ghana through effective and efficient operation of a banking and credit system in Ghana'.[241] The Constitution of Ghana expressly relates monetary policy and regulation to development in Ghana. The Constitution of South Africa is to similar effect. Section 228(2)(a) of the Constitution of South Africa states that the 'power of a provincial legislature to impose taxes, levies, duties and surcharges—may not be exercised in a way that materially and unreasonably prejudices national economic policies, economic activities across provincial boundaries, or the national mobility of goods, services, capital or labour'. Therefore, signing an investment treaty that prevents or limits the space for foreign exchange regulation may well be inconsistent with these constitutions.

Article 13(1)(a) of the Kenya–Japan investment treaty requires repatriation of the 'initial capital and additional amounts to maintain or increase investments'. This could potentially conflict with Section 7(b)(ii) of Foreign Investments Protection Act 1964 (No 35, Cap. 518). Section 7(b)(i) of this Act and Article 13(1)(a) of the investment treaty can operate together without conflict because this section allows for an amended or a varied amount to be substituted for the original capital amount and that such capital can be repatriated. However, any other addition to the capital after a certificate is issued recognising the varied or amended capital is not allowed to be repatriated as part of the capital. This is the effect of Section 7(b)(ii) of the Foreign Investments Protection Act which says 'no additional amount or sum shall be added to the capital specified in the certificate (as amended or varied) to represent any increase in the capital value of the investment since the issue of the certificate or since the last amendment or variation of the certificate'.

Section 7(c) of the Foreign Investments Protection Act allows transfer of 'the principal and interest of any loan specified in the certificate' to invest foreign assets in Kenya. The requirement that the principal and interest be specified in the certificate means that if either or both are not so specified, they might not be transferable. While Section 7(a) of the Act allows transfers of 'profits' it might have a narrower view of what constitutes profits than may be interpreted under the Kenya–Japan investment treaty which allows transfer of profits but does not define the concept. Under Section 7(a) of the Act, 'any increase in the capital value of the investment arising out of the sale of the whole or any part of the capital assets of the enterprise or revaluation of capital assets shall not be deemed to be profit arising from or out of the investment for the purposes of this Act'.

The Foreign Exchange Act 2006 (Act 723) of Ghana empowers the Bank of Ghana to 'make rules to prescribe the conditions required to carry out the business of foreign exchange transfers'.[242] The Act also permits the imposition of temporary

[240] Constitution of Ghana (n 57) art 183(2)(a).
[241] ibid art 183(2)(c).
[242] Foreign Exchange Act (Ghana) s 19.

restrictions where the Governor of the Bank of Ghana 'determines that the country is experiencing or has experienced a severe deterioration in its balance of payments that requires the temporary imposition of exchange controls beyond'[243] ordinary measures relating to foreign exchange control.

Specifically, where the country is experiencing or has experienced a severe deterioration in its balance of payments, the Governor in consultation with the Minister responsible for Finance and Economic Planning may make rules to restrict payments between residents and non-residents or between non-residents; payments to or from the country; the acquisition, holding, and use in the country of foreign currency or travellers' cheques; and the frequency at which the acts of purchase and sale of foreign exchange may be effected in the country.[244] The Governor of the Reserve Bank of South Africa has similar powers under Financial Sector Regulation Act 2017 (No 9) when a 'systemic event', meaning 'an event or circumstance, including one that occurs or arises outside the Republic, that may reasonably be expected to have a substantial adverse effect on the financial system or on economic activity in the Republic'.[245] The Governor has the duties and powers under Sections 14, 15, and 18 of the Act to minimise adverse effects on financial stability and economic activity of a systemic event or to prevent or reduce the spread of risk posed to the financial system by a systemic event. The Governor can limit transfer of funds to address issues arising from a systemic event, powers which might conflict with South Africa's investment treaties since not all of them make exception for such regulation.

The constitutional and statutory provisions on limiting transfers during financial emergencies analysed in this chapter do not make any distinction between nationals and non-nationals or between foreign investors and domestic investors. Everybody is to be subject to the regulations if the specified conditions are met. They are therefore consistent with Ghana–China and South Africa–China investment treaties which allow transfers subject to domestic law. However, the provisions of the Ghana–United Kingdom, Ghana–Netherlands, Kenya–Japan, and Nigeria–Germany investment treaties seek to exempt foreign investors from such foreign exchange regulation by granting unqualified rights to transfer funds. While the Ghana–China, Ghana–Malaysia, and Ghana–Denmark investment treaties make guarantees as to transfer of funds subject to domestic law, they also specify the rate and currency of exchange, and even the times that transfers are to be done. These specifics can conflict with contrary requirements in relevant statutes such as the Foreign Exchange Act of Ghana. Under Article 6(1) of the South Africa–China investment treaty, transfer of funds is subject to the requirements of domestic law.

[243] ibid s 20(1).

[244] ibid 20(1)(a)–(d).

[245] Financial Sector Regulation Act 2017 (No 9) s 1. Other relevant legislation in South Africa on this issue include Banks Act 1990 (No 94); Banking Institutions Act 1946 (No 25); and Financial Markets Act 2012 (No 19).

This qualification to the right to transfer of funds is an important way of preserving some measure of space for state regulation. This means, for example, that transfer of funds from South Africa will be subject to the Protection of Investment Act 2015 (No 22) which says transfer of funds must be subject to taxation and other applicable legislation.[246]

As discussed in Section 5.3, these African investment treaties were entered into, in part, for development and by implication form part of policies to prevent or mitigate a crisis that would impact on the poor. The restrictions of these investment treaties on capital controls can have a direct impact on development because they limit foreign exchange regulation and prevent the adoption of policies to address crisis in the interests of the poor in Africa. This possibility is not just hypothetical. In early 2014 the currency of Ghana, the Cedi, seriously depreciated against major foreign currencies, with 7.8 per cent depreciation against the US dollar.[247] The Bank of Ghana in February 2014 issued a new set of foreign exchange regulations and a code of conduct to guide the operations in the foreign exchange market.[248] The new measures consisted of revisions to the 2007 rules for the operation of foreign exchange and foreign currency accounts, restrictions on foreign currency-denominated loans and transfer of export proceeds to foreign countries, and revision of operating procedures for foreign exchange bureaux.[249] These measures were intended to reduce the country's vulnerability to shocks, stabilise the local currency, re-anchor inflation expectations, and sustain macroeconomic stability.[250]

The measures were, therefore, consistent with the Bank of Ghana's constitutional mandate to promote and maintain the stability of the currency of Ghana and direct and regulate the currency system in the interest of the economic progress of Ghana. Nevertheless President John Mahama, in the same month, reassured foreign investors that 'all agreements governing their investments remain in force and transfer of profits and dividends are guaranteed'.[251] This assurance shows the continued emphasis on, and preferential treatment of, foreign investment in Africa even when there was the need to enforce just-announced measures to check the decline of the cedi. It also highlights the fact that a country with international legal commitments to protect foreign investment, such as under an investment treaty,

[246] Protection of Investment Act 2015 (Act No 22) (Government Gazette Vol 606, No 39514, 15 December 2015) s 11 (hereafter, PIA).

[247] Bank of Ghana, *Monetary Policy Committee: Press Release* (February 2014) [10]; and Bank of Ghana, *Notice to Banks and the General Public: Revised Rules on the Operation of Foreign Exchange Accounts and Foreign Currency Accounts* (Notice No BG/GOV/SEC/2014/02, 4 February 2014).

[248] ibid [13].

[249] ibid [14].

[250] ibid [12].

[251] Republic of Ghana, *State of the Nation Address: Structural Transformation—Rising to the Challenge* (Delivered to the 6th Parliament of the 4th Republic of Ghana on Thursday, 25 February 2014) 10.

can feel compelled to make exceptions to the implementation of domestic measures so as to keep to the international commitments.

It is particularly important for African countries to be concerned about absolute guarantees of monetary transfers and foreign exchange in the investment treaties. The fact that a country is experiencing or has experienced a severe deterioration in its balance of payments or other financial crisis will not necessarily relieve it from compliance with these investment treaty obligations.

While investment 'is an important ingredient for economic growth, and ... capital flows may under certain conditions be a valuable supplement to domestic savings for financing such investment',[252] 'certain capital flows (such as short-term debt) can have de-stabilizing effects in developing countries'.[253] During financial and currency crises countries need room for manoeuvre to experiment with a variety of capital account regulations.[254] Capital regulations are used to manage exchange rate volatility, to avoid currency mismatches, limit speculative activity in the economy, and provide room for manoeuvre for monetary policy. Measures may be either price based or quantity based. Measures are price-based when they alter the price of foreign capital, such as with a tax on inflows or outflows. Quantity-based measures include prohibitions or caps on minimum stay periods for capital that comes into the country.[255] Capital account regulations of capital inflows may include tax on foreign exchange derivatives, limits or taxes on net liability position in foreign currency of financial intermediaries, and mandatory approvals for capital transactions. Capital outflow regulatory measures may include prohibition or limits on sectors in which foreigners can invest, restrictions on amounts of principal or capital income that foreign investors can send abroad, and taxes on capital outflows.[256]

The Argentine experience shows that some of these measures can be the subject of investor–state arbitration. In *Continental Casualty Company v Argentina*[257] the Tribunal found that the Argentina–United States investment treaty,[258] like the Ghana–United Kingdom investment treaty, prohibited all restrictions on transfer of funds. This, according to the Tribunal, limited the state's prerogatives to impose

[252] Kevin Gallagher, Stephany Griffith-Jones, and José Antonio Ocampo, 'Capital Account Regulations for Stability and Development: A New Approach' in Kevin Gallagher Stephany Griffith-Jones, and José Antonio Ocampo (eds), *Regulating Global Capital Flows for Long-Run Development* (The Frederick S. Pardee Centre for the Study of Longer-Range Future Task Force Report, Boston University Creative Services March 2012) 1.

[253] ibid.

[254] ibid.

[255] ibid 4.

[256] ibid.

[257] *Continental Casualty Company v Argentina, ICSID Case No ARB/03/9*, Award, 5 September 2008 (hereafter, *CCC v Argentina*).

[258] Treaty between United States of America and the Argentine Republic Concerning the Reciprocal Encouragement and Protection of Investment, signed 14 November 1991, entered into force 20 October 1994.

currency exchange restrictions.[259] A law enacted by Argentina in response to the economic crisis limited cash withdrawals from bank accounts and transfers of funds out of Argentina, with the exception of certain current transactions. The law was presented as a short-term emergency measure until the conversion of the public debt could be completed so as to avoid any instability in the level of deposits in the financial system. The foreign investor argued that the legislative restriction imposed by Argentina breached the applicable investment treaty provision on transfer of investment and returns. Argentina argued that the regulations of monetary transfers conformed to customary international law consistent with the exercise of monetary sovereignty by states. Argentina also justified the restriction as necessary under the essential security provision of the investment treaty given the severe difficulties in the balance-of-payment,[260] an argument not available to African countries under study because there is no such provision in their investment treaties. Where investment treaties lack public interest exceptions, tribunals will exclude public interest regulation from the treaties' scope of application.[261]

The Tribunal held that the guarantee regarding transfer of investment is fundamental to the freedom to make foreign investment and that it was an essential element of the promotional role of investment treaties.[262] However, the Tribunal rejected the investor's claim because the type of transfer at issue did not specifically represent the proceeds from the sale or liquidation of all or any part of an investment and, therefore, was not a transfer related to protected investment as required by the applicable investment treaty.[263] The Tribunal concluded that it was unnecessary to examine whether in view of the acute foreign exchange crisis Argentina was encountering, the country was allowed, notwithstanding treaty obligations, to introduce the exchange restrictions law.[264] In *Enron Corporation v Argentine Republic*,[265] it was held that economic and financial crises or other major crises 'do not in themselves amount to a legal excuse'[266] for breach of investment treaty obligations. However, *LG&E Energy Corporation v Argentina*[267] reached a contrary decision when it accepted Argentina's defence of necessity.

Africa's investment treaties' provisions allowing free, unrestricted transfer of funds can limit the space for capital control regulation in Africa to the extent that such regulation can be challenged before investment tribunals. This is particularly the case as some of the investment treaties require that even in emergency

[259] *CCC v Argentina* (n 257) [240].
[260] ibid [82].
[261] Bradly Condon, 'Treaty Structure and Public Interest Regulation in International Economic Law' (2014) 17(2) Journal of International Economic Law 333.
[262] *CCC v Argentina* (n 257) [239].
[263] ibid [241] and [244].
[264] ibid [245].
[265] *Enron Corporation v Argentina ICSID Case No ARB/01/3*, Award, 22 May 2007.
[266] ibid para 232.
[267] *LG & E Energy Corporation v Argentina*, Decision on Liability, ICSID Case No ARB 02/1, 3 October 2006.

situations investors must be accorded national treatment and MFN treatment. As Kelsey has argued, 'binding and enforceable financial services and investment agreements tie governments' to the regime of high liberalisation and light regulation of financial markets. Governments that adopt alternative strategies to that orthodoxy 'risk legal challenges for breaching their trade obligations',[268] such as national treatment and guarantees on capital movements, if they adopt currency controls measures such as capping currency forward trading and derivatives trading of domestic banks, imposition of a limit on forward foreign exchange contracts between bankers and exporters, and restrictions on bank loans in foreign currency to local companies.

5.5 Aligning Investment Treaties with the Right to Development and Corresponding Duties of Africa States

There are constitutional and IHRT rights of citizens to development in Africa and corresponding duties of African states to make and implement development policies. Domestic measures, whether in economic or financial crises, intended to address public interest concerns risk being challenged through investment treaty arbitration. I argue that the validity and legal effect of an investment treaty should be premised on the nature of its conflict with pre-existing norms which determine the making and coming into force of that treaty or on norms which later come into force and determine the continued validity of the treaty. The right and the duty of a state in Africa under its constitution and general international law to formulate appropriate national development policies to improve the well-being and livelihoods of the people are such norms. These norms limit the competence of African states in making investment treaties and inform their interpretation.

African states (eg Cameroon, Egypt, Ghana, Kenya, Nigeria, and South Africa) do not have interests of their own to pursue in entering into investment treaties, other than to enable them to meet their basic public interest obligations towards citizens. One of the strategies African states have adopted to meet their development obligations is to enter into various investment treaties to guarantee foreign businesses willing to invest within their territories protections against non-commercial risks. In this sense, foreign investments 'are ... means to finance the development of the recipient State'.[269]

The absolute limitations the investment treaties place on governmental regulation to secure the protection of foreign investment could be justified if there were

[268] Jane Kelsey, 'The Conundrum of Shifting Orthodoxies: FTAs and Korea's Currency Controls' (2011) 14(4) Journal of International Economic Law 485.

[269] Omar Garćia-Bolívar, 'Economic Development at the Core of the International Investment Regime' in Chester Brown and Kate Miles (eds) *Evolution in Investment Treaty Law and Arbitration* (CUP 2011) 586, 588 (hereafter, Garćia-Bolívar, 'Economic Development at the Core of II Regime').

only one path towards development and that path were proven to be foreign investment. In theory and practice this is not so.[270] The theory that foreign investment leads to development is highly contested because in spite of the liberalisation of foreign investment regulation, 'there is nothing to show that the benefits of foreign investment have resulted in the economic progress of the least developed countries. The correlation between liberalization and development cannot be cogently demonstrated to establish the theory of neo-liberalism that foreign investment should be given protection through legal instruments.'.[271] Thus, without further assurance of how the promotion and protection of foreign investment *per se* brings or will lead to development in Africa, absolute restrictions that investment treaties impose, even on general governmental regulation meant to contribute to the realisation of development, cannot be constitutionally justified.

Investment treaties need to be aligned with overall development policy, constitutions, and general international law which are the foundation of development policies in Africa. To enhance coherence between investment protection obligations in investment treaties and national development objectives, the legal duties to make and implement development policies must limit the power of African states in terms of investment treaty obligations they can undertake. There is the need to make provision in future investment treaties for an investment to be entitled to protection only if it makes contribution to development as contemplated under the Draft Pan-African Investment Code.[272]

The substantive obligations in existing treaties to protect foreign investment must be interpreted and enforced in a manner that takes account of that development objective and the legal duties of African states to make and implement development policies. Where the states parties manifest their intent to benefit themselves by way of development (as reflected in the preambles to investment treaties), it becomes important that that intent is taken into consideration in the interpretation of the investment treaties.[273] Where the objectives and purposes of investment treaties are contained in their preambles and these objects include an expectation that foreign investment will contribute to development based on the protection accorded to foreign investment,[274] the investment's contribution to development must equally be relevant in determining whether the investment is entitled to the protection. Indeed, the obligation to protect foreign investment must

[270] Sornarajah and Trakman, 'A Polemic' (n 136) 504.

[271] Muthucumaraswamy Sornarajah, 'The Clash of Globalizations and the International Law on Foreign Investment' (2003) 10(2) Canadian Foreign Policy Journal 1, 15 (hereafter, Sornarajah, 'Clash of Globalizations').

[272] African Union, Draft Pan-African Investment Code (December 2016) art 22(3). <https://au.int/sites/default/files/documents/32844-doc-draft_pan-african_investment_code_december_2016_en.pdf> accessed 29 September 2020 (hereafter, PAfIC).

[273] Garćia-Bolívar, 'Economic Development at the Core of II Regime' (n 269) 588 and 589–90.

[274] Sornarajah, *Law on Foreign Investment Law* (n 3) at 50.

not be enforceable if it was undertaken on the basis that an investment will contribute to development and the investment fails to contribute to development.

Every law has a purpose. The substantive provisions of a law have their own purposes too, but those purposes are commonly intended to advance the primary purpose for which the law is made in the first place. The substantive provisions of a law do not have ends independent of the primary enactment in which they are contained. Therefore, it is inaccurate to interpret a provision of an enactment without reference to the overarching objective of the enactment containing the provision it is intended to advance. Unless the preamble or provision of an investment treaty shows in clear and unambiguous terms that its primary and sole purpose is the protection of foreign investment, it will be out of the context of the treaty to interpret it in disregard of its development implications if the treaty's preamble or provision states that it is aimed at attracting foreign investment for development.

The issue here is not whether a preamble prevails over substantive provisions in law but whether preambles contain purposes of the law which the substantive terms of the law must be interpreted to advance. This distinction is often not made in the literature. The imperative to interpret investment treaties in accordance with their objectives contained in their preambles, and not just in terms of their substantive standards of investment of protection, is consistent with Article 31(1) and (2) of the VCLT wherein it is stated a treaty shall be interpreted 'in the light of its object and purpose. The context for the purpose of the interpretation of a treaty shall comprise, in addition to the text, including its preamble and annexes.' The position advanced here is supported by Sornarajah who argues that[275]

> [t]he present instruments on investment are premised on the assumption that foreign investment promotes the economic development of the states into which the investment flows. All bilateral investment treaties and regional treaties on investment contain a prefatory statement to the effect that such development takes place as a result of investment flows. It may be implied from this that multinational corporations which make investments in host states should promote economic development or, at the least, should not conduct themselves in such a manner as to hinder such development. If there is clear evidence that a multinational corporation has hindered development, the argument may be made that the rules of investment protection are not applicable to that investment and therefore that the investment will not be protected. After all, all investment instruments insist that economic development is the objective of foreign investment.

Sornarajah argues in similar terms that[276]

[275] ibid 153.
[276] Sornarajah, 'Clash of Globalizations' (n 271) 18–19.

> [t]he re-emergence of the right to development as a means of articulating the aims of the least developed nations in the alleviation of hunger and poverty ... will have to be taken into account in balancing the call for absolute freedom of pre-entry rights of establishment, national standard, and full protection for foreign investment. It cannot any longer be argued with conviction that foreign investment that does not address the developmental needs of the poor is entitled to the standards of protection demanded by neo-liberal theory.

It has been argued that the concept of 'development' is amorphous and very broad since it can contain many elements. This situation can make it difficult for investment tribunals to define and measure development and the contribution of an investment to the development of the host state.[277] However, investment promotion and protection by treaty is premised on the conventional wisdom that '[w]ith its enormous potential to create jobs, raise productivity, enhance exports and transfer technology, foreign direct investment is a vital factor in the long-term economic development of the world's developing countries'.[278]

According to those who support investment protection by treaty, outward investment offers additional avenue for developing countries to link up to global markets and production systems. These investments could help firms to access markets, natural resources, foreign capital, technology, or various intangible assets that are essential to their competitiveness that may not be readily available in their home countries.[279] These stated benefits of the legal commitment to protect foreign investment can form the starting point for a tribunal to determine whether the investment at stake has made or can make contribution to the host state's development.

Thus, in making an assessment of an investment's contribution to the development of the host state, account should be taken of what foreign investment is said to be capable of bringing to the host state, namely the extent to which the investment benefits the public interest in terms of transfers technology or know-how to the host state, employment, and the overall positive impact of the investment on the host state's development.[280] This is particularly so in the case of African countries such as Ghana, Nigeria, Kenya, and South Africa because their constitutions require that the private sector bears its fair share of social and national responsibilities, including responsibilities to contribute to development. This suggests that the protection of private sector interests must be tied to national development priorities. These African states can insist that a foreign investor is not entitled to any rights under investment treaties if the investment does not meet specified

[277] Desierto, *Investment Agreement Applicability* (n 10) 250.

[278] Kofi Annan, 'Foreword' in UNCTAD *World Investment Report 2003. FDI Policies for Development: National and International Perspectives*, (United Nations, 2003) at iii.

[279] ibid.

[280] Garćia-Bolívar, 'Economic Development at the Core of II Regime' (n 269) at 603.

developmental goals at the time of the admission of the investment or expressly stated developmental objectives in the investment treaties. It must follow that[281]

> [i]f an investment is contrary to the public interest, has not generated any knowledge transfer to the host State, has not enhanced the economy or its productivity, has not increased the standards of living of the host country or the labour conditions, it almost certainly has not made a contribution to the economic development of that country... [T]hat investment should be denied protection.

The standards of investment protection, such as fair and equitable treatment and full protection and security, among others, do not have fixed and determinable meanings and scope that investment tribunals can readily pick and apply in investment dispute settlement in a predictable manner. Also, there are no fixed ways of determining the standards of compensation payment in investment arbitration. Investment tribunals have never been deterred by their inability to give fixed meanings to these standards. They are able to find their way through these ill-defined standards to determine states' liability in the interest of protecting foreign investment under investment treaties. As tribunals are able to do this in favour of foreign investors, they should be willing to consider the merits of a state's assertion about a purported investment's lack of contribution to development for which the investment may or may not be entitled to protection. An inability precisely to define development and the contribution of an investment to the host state's development should not deter investment tribunals from considering a state's argument that an investment should be not entitled to protection because it has made no contribution to its development. If an investment treaty has development as an objective, that objective becomes important for consideration in interpreting the treaty.

5.6 Development Objectives in Domestic Investment Laws and Investment Treaty Reforms in Africa

5.6.1 The Reform of Municipal Investment Law in South Africa

South Africa's experience with investor–state arbitration and the effect of investment treaties contributed to the reform of its municipal investment legislation and the termination of a number of investment treaties. A case in point is *Foresti v South Africa*.[282] Italian investors in South Africa[283] initiated arbitral proceedings against

[281] Garćia-Bolívar, 'Economic Development at the Core of II Regime' (n 269) 695.

[282] *Piero Foresti v The Republic of South Africa* ICSID Case No ARB (AF)/07/1, Award, 4 August 2010 (hereafter, *Foresti v South Africa*).

[283] ibid [1].

South Africa in 2006 alleging breach of both the 1999 South Africa–Italy BIT[284] and the 2003 South Africa– Luxembourg BIT[285] provisions on expropriation by the enactment of the MPRDA and the Mining Charter dated 13 August 2004.[286] This legislation and implementing policy instrument introduced compulsory equity divestiture requirements with respect to the investors' shares in the operating companies belonging to the investors.[287]

The investors argued that the Mining Charter was aimed at encouraging greater ownership of the mining industry assets by historically disadvantaged South Africans ('HDSAs'). This was reflected in the requirements in the Mining Charter that mining companies achieve 26 per cent HDSA ownership of mining assets. The Charter further required mining companies to publish employment equity plans directed towards achieving a baseline of 40 per cent HDSA participation in management.[288] The investors owned the mineral rights, which constituted the investments, indirectly through intermediaries and subsidiaries, which were not parties to the arbitral proceedings.[289]

The investors argued that their shares in the operating companies were expropriated by the operation of the Black Economic Empowerment equity divestiture requirements under the Mining Charter and the MPRDA. They noted that the Mining Charter required them to sell 26 per cent of their shares in the mining companies to HDSAs. They argued that the equity divestiture scheme constituted a direct, indirect, or partial expropriation of their shares in the operating companies. These measures amounted to expropriation because of the alleged failure of South Africa to pay compensation, lack of due process, and discrimination.[290] The investors also claimed that the MPRDA and the Mining Charter breached South Africa's fair and equitable treatment and national treatment obligations under the two BITS.[291]

The case was ultimately discontinued at the request of the investors because pursuant to an agreement, South Africa granted their operating companies new order mineral rights without requiring the investors to sell 26 per cent of their shares to HDSAs. Based on an offset agreement, the operating companies were to be 'deemed to have complied with the Mining Charter' if they made a 21 per cent beneficiation offset, that is process and add value to 21 per cent quarried stone in South Africa. The divestiture was also 'deemed' to have been met if the operating

[284] Agreement between the Government of the Republic of South Africa and the Government of the Italian Republic for the Promotion and Protection of Investments, signed in Rome on 9 June 1997.

[285] Agreement between the Republic of South Africa and the Belgo–Luxembourg Economic Union on the Reciprocal Promotion and Protection of Investments, signed in Pretoria on 14 August 1998.

[286] *Piero Foresti v South Africa* (n 282) [54].

[287] ibid.

[288] ibid [56].

[289] Department of Trade and Industry, 'Bilateral Investment Treaty Policy Framework Review' (Government Position Paper 0001, June 2009) 10 (hereafter, DTI, 'BIT Policy Framework Review').

[290] *Piero Foresti v South Africa* (n 282) [64].

[291] ibid [78].

companies provided a 5 per cent employee ownership programme for their employees. In effect, South Africa, like Indonesia, effectively abandoned the full effect of its domestic legislation and implementing policy (the MPRDA and Mining Charter) because of investment treaty and arbitration commitments. According to Malebakeng Forere,[292]

> [t]he facts of this case indicate what awaited South Africa in its endeavour to balance two competing interests – growing the economy by attracting FDI and complying with the constitutional mandate to address past injustices.

Meanwhile in 2005, the South African Department of Trade and Industry (DTI herein) initiated a review of South African BITs. The review effectively started in 2008.[293] According to Forere, the review 'was a result of pressure from developed nations seeking compensation from South Africa for its failure to observe treaty obligations. Specifically, the *Foresti* case is the motivation behind the investment policy shift in South Africa.'[294] South Africa subsequently terminated the two BITs on which the case was based. The review points to the conflict between national strategic plans and the realms of development policy and investment treaty terms.[295] The main concerns of South Africa were that[296]

> [i]nvestment dispute settlement has now embarked on a course that effectively assigns arbitral panels an active role in implementation and interpretation of BITs. Investors have become aware of the attractive *status quo* under the global investment regime—literally hundreds of long-ignored investment treaties offer investors access to an investor–state dispute settlement mechanism, allowing them to take their disputes directly to international arbitration—leapfrogging domestic legal systems (and thus, any safeguards designed to protect important public goods). Some investors are using bilateral investment treaties to challenge treatment of foreign investments in various sensitive areas, including water and sewage provision, oil and gas exploitation and mining concessions. Major law firms are using BITs as the tool of choice for challenging host state regulation of public services.
>
> BITs extend far into developing countries' policy space, imposing damaging binding investment rules with far-reaching consequences for sustainable development. New investment rules in BITs prevent developing country governments

[292] Malebakeng Agnes Forere, 'The New South African Protection of Investment Act: Striking a Balance between Attraction of FDI and Redressing the Apartheid Legacies' in Fabio Morosini (ed), *Reconceptualizing International Investment Law from the Global South* (CUP 2017) 251, 262 (hereafter, Forere, 'New South African Protection of Investment Act').

[293] ibid 260

[294] ibid.

[295] ibid

[296] DTI, 'BIT Policy Framework Review' (n 289) 10–11 and 46.

> from requiring foreign companies to transfer technology, train local workers, or source inputs locally. Under such conditions, investment fails to encourage or enhance sustainable development. There are many who question whether BITs in fact attract FDI at all. Various countries are reviewing their BIT regimes . . . Whilst a revised BIT will go a long way in resolving critical problems . . . it will not, however, be a panacea for all other FDI problems. These problems can only be tackled by proper policy integration, co-ordination and implementation.
>
> Trade and investment are essential for sustainable development, and the imbalances that characterise and distorted global trade and investment flows must be addressed as a matter of urgency. Unequal and exploitative investment agreements, which prohibit the very policies developing countries need to fight poverty, is no way to put trade and investment at the service of sustainable development.

Following the completion of the *Bilateral Investment Treaty Policy Framework Review*, the South African government enacted the Protection of Investment Act 2015 (Act No 22) (PIA herein) to regulate future investments.[297] The PIA has a number of important features for regulatory autonomy and development policy. First, the PIA focuses on investment protection rather than promotion. The PIA does not contain 'incentives or guarantees at the pre- establishment stage as a way of promoting or attracting investment into South Africa'.[298] The PIA is applicable only to covered investments; that is, investments that have been admitted and established in accordance with South African law.[299] Section 7 of the PIA specifically provides that '[a]ll investments must be established in compliance with the laws' of South Africa, and that the Act 'does not create a right for a foreign investor or prospective foreign investor to establish an investment' in South Africa. This means that South Africa gets to decide which investor and investment to admit and which not to admit in accordance with its laws. While the pre-establishment protection is important in investment decision-making by foreign investors, it has been suggested that its exclusion 'cannot be said to be scaring investors away'.[300]

However, some of South Africa's existing BITs contain an obligation to promote and create conditions favourable for investment that might be interpreted as imposing pre-establishment obligation. For example, Article 2(1) of the South Africa–Korea BIT provides that each contracting party 'shall encourage the creation of favourable conditions for investors of the other Contracting Party to make investments in its territory and shall admit such investments in accordance with its laws and regulations'.[301] The obligation to 'encourage the creation of favourable

297 Forere, 'New South African Protection of Investment Act' (n 292) 263

298 ibid 267.

299 ibid.

300 ibid.

301 Agreement between the Government of the Republic of Korea and The Government of the Republic of South Africa on the Promotion and Protection of Investments, signed 7 July 1995, entered into force 28 June 1997.

conditions for investors to make investments' is essentially a pre-establishment provision. An equivalent provision is contained in South Africa–Nigeria BIT.[302] Therefore, while the PIA has made way for policies on the question of admission of investors, those possible policies are not fully guaranteed in practical terms because investment treaties such as South Africa–Korea BIT and South Africa–Nigeria BIT can encroach upon it.

Second, the PIA seeks specifically to reconcile the obligations to protect foreign investment with the constitutional obligations to protect the public interest. The purpose of the PIA is to protect investment in 'accordance with and subject to the Constitution, in a manner which balances the public interest and the rights and obligations of investors'.[303] The purpose is also to affirm South Africa's 'sovereign right to regulate investments in the public interest'[304] and to affirm the Bill of Rights in the Constitution of South Africa and the laws 'that apply to all investors and their investments in the Republic'.[305] Specifically under section 12(1) of the PIA, the government and organs of state have the right to regulate and may 'in accordance with the Constitution and applicable legislation, take measures'[306] to

1. redress injustices and inequalities that are historical, social and economic nature.
2. uphold democratic values and principles including accountability, transparency and impartial, fair, equitable provision of services in accordance with the Constitution of South Africa.
3. uphold constitutionally guaranteed rights.
4. promote and preserve cultural and national heritage and practices, indigenous knowledge, and related biological resources.
5. foster economic development, industrialisation and beneficiation
6. realise socio-economic rights.
7. protect the environment, conserve and achieve sustainable use of natural resources.
8. protect the security interests and financial stability of the South Africa.

Third, while the PIA provides for national treatment,[307] it does limit the scope of the national treatment in terms of comparative factors to use when making in 'like circumstances' determination and in of terms the subject matter, that is the measures to which national treatment apples. Investment treaties generally do not

[302] Agreement between the Government of the Republic of South Africa and the Government of the Federal Republic of Nigeria for the Reciprocal Promotion and Protection of Investments, signed 29 April 2000, entered into force 27 July 2005, art 3(1) (hereafter, South Africa–Nigeria Investment Treaty).

[303] PIA (n 246) s 4(a).

[304] ibid s 4(b).

[305] ibid s 4(c).

[306] ibid s 12(1) and (2).

[307] ibid s 12(1).

provide for limitation as to the scope of national treatment. Under the PIA, 'like circumstances' are defined as requiring 'an overall examination of the merits of the case by taking into account all the terms of a foreign investment'.[308] These terms include the effect of the foreign investment in South Africa and the cumulative effects of all investments, the sector of the foreign investments, *the* aim of the measure, the effect on third persons including the local community and employment, and direct and indirect effect on the environment.[309] An examination of in like circumstances 'must not be limited to or be biased towards any one factor'.[310]

However, the right of foreign investors and their investments to be treated no less favourably than South African investors and investments in like circumstances does not oblige South Africa to extend to foreign investors and their covered investments the benefit of specified treatment, preference or privilege. Thus, national treatment does not cover[311]

1. taxation provisions in international agreements or arrangements and in South African law.
2. government procurement.
3. government subsidies and grants.
4. laws and other measures intended to promote the achievement of equality in South Africa and to protect persons or categories of persons, historically disadvantaged by unfair discrimination on grounds of race, gender or disability.
5. laws and other measures designed to promote and preserve cultural and national heritage and practices, indigenous knowledge and biological resources.
6. special advantages accorded by development finance institutions in the form of development assistance.
7. special advantages accorded by development finance institutions to develop small and medium businesses and new industries.

Fourth, the PIA grants foreign investors the right to property in accordance with the Constitution[312] and the right to transfer investment funds subject to taxation and applicable legislation.[313] Investments may also be accorded 'a level of physical security as may be generally provided to domestic investors in accordance with minimum standards of customary international law and subject to available resources and capacity'.[314] It is worth noting that South Africa chose to include the minimum standard of customary international law in its domestic law. This is

[308] ibid s 8(2).
[309] ibid.
[310] ibid s 8(3).
[311] ibid s 812(4).
[312] ibid s 10.
[313] ibid s 11.
[314] ibid s 9.

because in the report leading to the PIA, the DTI wondered what the content of the standard was, noting that[315]

> [i]n many instances it has been contended that an international minimum standard exists. Apart from the rule relating to compensation for expropriation and the settlement of such issues through a tribunal that sits outside the host state, there does not seem to be any guidance as to what the content of the standard is. The existence of a minimum international customary law standard has long been disputed. Such standards impact on the ability of governments to prefer its own nationals on grounds of past discrimination or on the basis of economic considerations. Greater balance must be injected into relationships governed by BITs.

These features do make the PIA a unique and innovative piece of municipal foreign investment legislation, when compared to other domestic legislation studied in this book such as Ghana Investment Promotion Centre Act. As analysed in Chapter 3, the PIA does away with investor–state arbitration as the default dispute settlement mechanism and replaces it with state-to-state arbitration which the government may only consent to upon exhaustion of local remedies. The PIA expressly addresses the right of South Africa to regulate in the public interest in accordance with the Constitution of South Africa. It defines the factors that must be used in making in 'like circumstances' determination when interpreting national treatment and specifies measures of public interest and essential security to which national treatment is not applicable. This approach is crucial to limit the scope of national treatment which, as it stands under investment treaties, is very broad. It should go a long way to allow South Africa to regulate foreign investment the way it should under municipal law and to pursue measures required or permitted under the Constitution of South Africa without having to account to foreign investors through investor–state arbitration.

However, South Africa remains party to investment treaties that do not necessarily accommodate these flexibilities. In the event of conflict, these investment treaties may prevail over the requirements in the PIA and may erode the autonomy that was intended to be achieved by enacting the legislation.

Also, it is quite unusual that a national piece of legislation would provide for national treatment, physical security of property, and an international minimum standard of customary international law, standards of investment protection that have hitherto been predominantly available either under investment treaties or customary international law. While it may promote fairness to grant foreign investors and investments national treatment under national legislation, it is questionable whether it is prudent to do so. By requiring that foreign investors and their

[315] DTI, 'BIT Policy Framework Review' (n 289) 10.

investments to be accorded the same treatment and nationals of the host state, national treatment essentially gives foreign investors an automatic, *de facto* right of citizenship without the foreign investors having to acquire citizenship *per se*.

In most parts of the *developed* world such as in Australia, New Zealand, and the United Kingdom, it takes years of residence to acquire citizenship by foreign nationals already living and working in these countries and contributing to their economies.[316] These non-citizens, for as long as they remain on temporary visas in these countries, are not accorded national treatment in relation to even a basic human right such as access to public health services, except perhaps in an emergency situation or as may be prescribed by regulations. Non-citizens are not entitled to national health insurance coverage even though their contributions to the national economies in terms of labour and payment of taxes may be the same as those made by citizens. Temporary visa holders in Australia are required to maintain their own health insurance. For example, it is a requirement for Subclass 482 (Temporary Skill Shortage) that an applicant "has adequate arrangements for health insurance during the period of the applicant's intended stay in Australia."[317] A temporary visa holder or a class of temporary visa holders may only enjoy the health insurance if the Minister for health so prescribes by regulations.[318] This may be supported by the argument that differential treatment between nationals and non-nationals based on *municipal law* is inevitable. Why should there be an exception to this in the context of foreign investment? It is unfair and inequitable to 'poor' host African states and their citizens that foreign investors and investments from 'rich' and 'developed' countries should have an automatic right of national treatment upon admission and establishment. This is particularly the case in situations where the foreign investors and investments are yet to contribute to the development of the host states (if such contribution will ever be made at all) and the reciprocal benefit of granting national treatment is neither certain nor guaranteed.

Presumably the extension of national treatment to foreign investors is about the contribution their investments stand to make to the national economy of the host state. Should national treatment be extended then to non-citizens and other foreign business entities who or which may be making the same contribution to the development of the host states as foreign investors and foreign investment do? The appropriateness of extending national treatment to foreign businesses in Africa is questionable. African countries and developing countries in general must have the freedom to decide who to extend measures aimed at domestic businesses to and should not limit that domestic policy by providing for national treatment under domestic law and international trade and investment treaties.

[316] Australian Citizenship Act 2007 (No 20) ss 20 and 22; Citizenship Act 1977 (New Zealand, Public Act No 61) s 8(2); and British Nationality Act 1981 s 18 and Sch 1[1(2)].

[317] Migration Regulations 1994 (Cth), clause 482.214 of Schedule 2.

[318] Health Insurance Act 1973 (Cth), s 6A.

African nations must not take measures positively and directly intended to disadvantage foreign business merely because of their foreign status. However, African states must be free to design policies targeted at domestic businesses and their citizens because the primary responsibilities of African states are owed first to their citizens such as appertain under the constitutions in this book. Moreover, it may be that the gains and costs to the national economy for[319] extending the measures to foreign investors and foreign investment cannot be measured and would never be realised anyway, if those gains and costs will be ascertained at all at the time of extending the treatment. Thus, if national treatment would be extended to foreign investors and their investment, it could be conditional upon an assessment, at the point of implementation, of the gains and costs of extending the treatment. Comparative lessons could be drawn from national immigration and citizenship laws of the developed world where noncitizens must live and/or work in the host country for years before they become eligible to apply for permanent residency or citizenship.

5.6.2 The Reform of Investment Treaties in Africa

Efforts at reforming the investment treaty and arbitration framework to accommodate states' right to regulate are taking place globally as well.[320] At the United Nations level, the United Nations Conference on Trade and Development (UNCTAD) is leading the way by developing frameworks to guide investment treaty and arbitration reforms. This is reflected in UNCTAD's *Investment Policy Framework for Sustainable Development*.[321]

Africa is awake on this matter. Upon reviewing a number of recent investment treaties, Hamed El-Kady and Mustaqeem De Gama concluded that Africa was now 'taking a more active approach in the formulation of their international investment commitments at the national, bilateral and regional levels. Africa is becoming a laboratory for innovative and sustainable development-oriented investment policymaking'.[322] There is no need to rewrite much of what has been written on Africa and the reform of investment treaties.[323]

[319] Dominic Dagbanja, 'The Case Against National Treatment in Africa' (Afronomicslaw.org blog, 4 June 2020) <https://www.afronomicslaw.org/2020/06/03/the-case-against-national-treatment-in-africa/> accessed 30 September 2020.

[320] UNCTAD, *World Investment Report 2019: Special Economic Zones* (United Nations 2019) 99–102 (hereafter, *World Investment Report 2019*).

[321] UNCTAD, *Investment Policy Framework for Sustainable Development* (United Nations 2015).

[322] Hamed El-Kady and Mustaqeem De Gama 'The Reform of the International Investment Regime: An African Perspective' (2019) 34(2) ICSID Review –Foreign Investment Law Journal 482 (hereafter, El-Kady and Gama, 'Reform of II Regime').

[323] ibid; Makane Moïse Mbengue, 'Africa's Voice in the Formation, Shaping and Redesign of International Investment Law' (2019) 34(2) ICSID Review—Foreign Investment Law Journal 455 (hereafter, Mbengue, Africa's Voice'); Antonio R Parra, 'The Participation of African States in the Making of the ICSID Convention'(2019) 34(2) ICSID Review –Foreign Investment Law Journal 270; Won Kidane,

5.6.2.1 Development in Bilateral Investment Treaty Reforms

At the bilateral level, African countries have negotiated new BITs that contain innovative and flexible provisions to accommodate development policy and the states' right to regulate in the public interest.[324] For example, South Africa–Nigeria BIT narrows the scope of application of national treatment and MFN stating these standards are not applicable to domestic law and international agreements relating to taxation and laws and other measures aimed achieving equality and protecting persons or categories of persons who have been disadvantaged by unfair discrimination.[325]

The Cameroon–Canada BIT provides that the parties 'shall encourage the creation of jobs in Canada through Cameroonian investments and the creation of jobs in the Republic of Cameroon through Canadian investments'.[326] The provisions on performance requirements, expropriation, and transfer of funds do not guarantee absolute right to foreign investors and provision is made to accommodate some flexibility in the area of taxation.[327] For Cameroon, national treatment, MFN and performance requirement obligations do not apply to (i) social services (such as public law enforcement, social and income security or insurance; social welfare; public education; public training; health and child care); (ii) the rights or preferences provided to aboriginal peoples; and (iii) the rights or preferences provided to socially or economically disadvantaged minorities.[328] Similar general exemptions can be found in the Kenya–Japan BIT[329] and Egypt–Mauritius BIT[330] in respect of national treatment and MFN.

The efficacy of these exemptions as defences is yet to tested in investor–state arbitration. The qualifications or provisos in the texts of some of these general exceptions might defeat their purposes concerning preserving the right to regulate. For example, Article 3(2) of the Kenya–Japan BIT provides that the obligation of national treatment 'shall not be construed so as to prevent' contracting parties 'from adopting

'The Culture of Investment Arbitration: An African Perspective' (2019) 34(2) ICSID Review—Foreign Investment Law Journal 411; Meg Kinnear and Paul Jean Le Cannu, 'Concluding Remarks: ICSID and African States Leading International Investment Law Reform' (2019) 34(2) ICSID Review—Foreign Investment Law Journal 542 (hereafter, Kinnear and Cannu, 'Concluding Remarks'); 'Makane Moïse Mbengue, Africa and the Reform of the International Investment Regime' (2017) 18 Journal of World Investment and Trade 371; and Okechukwu Ejims, 'The 2016 Morocco–Nigeria Bilateral Investment Treaty: More Practical Reality in Providing a Balanced Investment Treaty?' (2019) 34(1) ICSID Review—Foreign Investment Law Journal 62.

[324] El-Kady and Gama, 'Reform of II Regime' (n 320).

[325] South Africa–Nigeria Investment Treaty (n 302) art 4.

[326] Agreement between Canada and the Republic of Cameroon for the Promotion and Protection of Investments, signed 3 March 2014, art 3(2).

[327] ibid arts 9, 10 11, 14, and 16.

[328] ibid art 16 and Schedule II.

[329] Japan–Kenya Investment Treaty (n 97) arts 3–5.

[330] Agreement between the Government of the Republic of Mauritius and the Government of the Arab Republic of Egypt on the Reciprocal Promotion and Protection of Investments, signed 25 June 2014, entered into force 17 October 2014 art 5(4).

or maintaining a measure that prescribes special formalities in connection with investment activities of foreign investors in its Area in accordance with its laws and regulations, *provided that such special formalities do not impair the substance of the rights of investors*' (emphasis added). By this qualification or proviso, measures that prescribe special formalities in connection with investment activities of foreign investors may not be adopted if the measures will impair the substance of investors' rights, even though they may not be aimed directly at impairing the investments. The measures may be adopted at the risk of an investor–state suit. Therefore, the scope left for this exemption to apply could be very narrow depending on the nature of the effect of the measure on the rights of foreign investors.

5.6.2.2 Development in Regional and Continental Investment Treaty Reforms

Regional and continental investment treaties and model investment treaties have also undergone some reform in Africa. Many of them are friendly towards development policy, but some are templates or model investment treaties and the extent of their influence in the making of investment treaties actually entered into has not been researched as yet. James Gathii has fully treated the subject of regional trade and investment law in Africa.[331]

The Southern African Development Community Protocol on Finance and Investment (SADC FIP) is one search regional multilateral investment agreement. It was signed by SADC Member States on 18 August 2006 and entered into force on 16 April 2010. The SADC FIP is aimed at bringing about harmonisation of investment policies among Member States of the SADC to promote the region's economic integration objective. Twelve members of SADC signed the Agreement Amending Annex 1 (Cooperation on Investment) of the Protocol on Finance and Investment on 31 August 2016[332] (Agreement Amending SADC FIP).

The Agreement Amending SADC FIP prohibits nationalisation or expropriation of investment.[333] However, measures of general application do not constitute expropriation of a debt security or loan even if they imposed costs on the debtor that caused the debtor to default on its debt.[334] Also, measures of general application by a state party 'designed and applied to protect or enhance legitimate public welfare objectives, such as public health, safety and the environment, shall not constitute an indirect expropriation'.[335] To limit the factors that must be taken into consideration when determining whether foreign investors and domestic

[331] James Gathii *African Regional Trade Agreements as Legal Regimes* (CUP 2011).

[332] Agreement Amending Annex 1 (Cooperation on Investment) of the Protocol on Finance and Investment on signed 31 August 2016 <https://investmentpolicy.unctad.org/international-investment-agreements/treaty-files/5527/download> accessed 29 September 2020.

[333] ibid art 5(1).

[334] ibid art 5(6).

[335] ibid art 5(7).

investment are in like circumstances for purposes the national treatment standard, the Agreement Amending SADC FIP provides that such a determination shall be done on a case-by-case basis based on specified factors.[336] Furthermore, notwithstanding the national treatment standard, a state party may, in accordance with 'domestic legislation grant preferential treatment to domestic investments and investors in order to achieve national development objectives'.[337] Above all, investors and their investments 'shall abide by the laws, regulations, administrative guidelines and policies of the Host State for the full life cycle of those investments'.[338]

The 2012 SADC Model BIT specifically addresses the issue of the right of states to pursue development goals. Article 21 of the Model BIT provides that '[n]notwithstanding any other provision'[339] of the agreement, a state party may grant preferential treatment based on domestic legislation 'in order to achieve national or sub-national regional development goals'.[340] State parties may also take measures that[341]

1. support the development of local entrepreneurs.
2. increase employment.
3. increase human resource capacity and training.
4. are necessary to address historically based economic disparities suffered by identifiable ethnic or cultural groups due to discriminatory or oppressive measures.

The Economic Community of West African States (ECOWAS) has Community Rules on Investment (CRI), which have been in force since 2009.[342] The objective of the CRI 'is to promote investment that supports sustainable development' in the ECOWAS region.[343] Like the Agreement Amending SADC FIP, the CRI provide that a measure of general application does not constitute expropriation of a debt security or loan even if it imposed costs on the debtor and made the debtor to default on its debt.[344] The right to transfer funds is not absolute as it may be limited in specified circumstances.[345] Investors and their covered investments 'are subject to the laws and regulations'[346] of the host state and 'shall strive through their management policies and practices, to contribute to the development objectives of the

336 ibid art 6(2).
337 ibid art 6(3).
338 ibid art 8.
339 SADC Model Bilateral Investment Treaty Template with Commentary 2012, art 21.1.
340 ibid art 21.1.
341 ibid art 21.2–21.3.
342 Supplementary Act A/SA.03/12/08 Adopting Community Rules on Investment and Modalities for Their Implementation with ECOWAS (signed 19 December 2008, entered into force 19 January 2009).
343 ibid art 2.
344 ibid art 8(7).
345 ibid art 10.
346 ibid art 11(1).

host States and the local levels of government where the investment is located'.[347] The CRI imposes pre-establishment obligations on investors and investments to conduct social impact assessment of the potential investment and comply with minimum standards on socio-cultural impact of the assessment.[348] In addition, investors 'shall be subject to civil actions for liability in the judicial process of their host State for acts or decisions made in relation to the investment where such acts or decisions lead to significant damage, personal injuries or loss of life in the host State'.[349] The ECOWAS Common Investment Code of July 2018, a soft instrument, contains similar provisions as the ECOWAS CRI.[350]

At the continental level, an important soft law instrument the African Union (AU) has put in place in furtherance of the objectives of the AU primary treaty, especially on economic integration, is the 2016 Draft Pan-African Investment Code (PAfIC).[351] The PAfIC seeks 'to promote, facilitate and protect investments that foster the sustainable development of each Member State'.[352] It provides for various qualifications to the usual standards of investment protection to limit the scope of their application[353] and abandons standard investment treaty terms such as full protection and security and fair and equitable treatment.

The PAfIC provides that in order to qualify as an investment, the business undertaking must, among other factors, make 'a significant contribution to the host State's economic development'.[354] The addition of contribution to the development of the host state as an element of investment in the PAfIC should help settle the issue whether or not an investment is entitled to protection under an IIA if it does not make a contribution to the development of the host state.[355] Arbitral tribunals are divided on the subject into those that support contribution to development as an element of investment[356] and those that do not.[357] The position adopted

[347] ibid art 11(3).
[348] ibid art 12(1).
[349] ibid art 17
[350] ECOWAS Common Investment Code (July 2018) arts 31–32.
[351] PAfIC (n 272).
[352] ibid art 1.
[353] ibid arts 7–12 and 15–17.
[354] ibid art 4(4)(vi).
[355] Dominic Dagbanja, 'The Development Objective as an Imperative in Interpretation of International Investment Agreements' (2018) 44(2) University of Western Australia Law Review 144
[356] *Salini Costruttori SpA & Italstrade SpA v Morocco*, ICSID Case No ARB/00/4, Decision on Jurisdiction (23 July 2001); *Fedax NV v Republic of Venezuela*, ICSID Case No ARB/96/3, Decision of the Tribunal on Objection to Jurisdiction (11 July 1997); *Patrick Mitchell v The Democratic Republic of Congo*, Case No ARB/99/7, Decision on the Application for Annulment of the Award, 1 November 2006; *Malaysian Historical Salvors Sdn, BHD v Malaysia*, ICSID Case No ARB/05/10, Award on Jurisdiction, 17 May 2007; *Alex Genin Eastern Credit Ltd Inc v The Republic of Estonia*, Case No ARB/99/2, Award, 25 June 2001; *Pantechniki S.A. Contractors & Engineers (Greece) v The Republic of Albania*, ICSID Case No ARB/07/21, Award, 30 July 2009; *Amoco Asia Corporation v Republic of Indonesia*, ICSID Case No ARB/06/18, Decision on Jurisdiction and Liability, 25 September 1983; and *Joseph Charles Lemire v Ukraine*, ICSID Case No ARB/O6/18, Decision on Jurisdiction and Liability, 14 January 2010.
[357] *Société Générale v Dominican Republic*, LCIA Case No UN 7927, UNCITRAL Arbitration Rules, Award on Preliminary Objections to Jurisdiction, 19 September 2008; *Consorzio Groupement LESI-DIPENTA v Algeria*, ICSID Case No ARB/03/08, Award (10 January 2005); and *Electrabel SA v Republic*

by the AU is in accord with the very conventional wisdom underlying the making of BITs and other IIAs, namely that they are necessary to attract investment for development. Importantly, the PAfIC also has provisions specifically on the obligations of investors.[358]

Thus, the PAfIC was designed to assure investment promotion and protection within the context of Member States' right to regulate in the public interest and to ensure that investment ultimately contributes to the development of the host state. The terms of the PAfIC give effect to its drafters' recognition in the preamble that the AU Member States have the right 'to regulate all the aspects relating to investments within their territories with a view to meeting national policy objectives and to promote sustainable development objectives'.[359] The PAfIC now provides a framework for ongoing negotiation of the Investment Protocol to the Agreement Establishing African Continental Free Trade Area.[360]

These reform efforts point to Africa giving primary consideration to sustainable development as an overarching objective of investment treaties, defining investment in terms of its contribution to the development of host states, abandoning or qualifying the usual standards of investment protection and providing for binding obligations on investors.[361] However, the 'effectiveness of these new treaty obligations, including new obligations weighing on investors, will depend in large part on the tools used for their enforcement'.[362]

It is also important to note that African countries remain parties to a large number of investment treaties concluded with developed countries in the 1960s and early 2000s that do not contain these flexibilities for development policy and the right to regulate.[363] For example, Cameroon–Netherlands BIT (1966),[364] Cameroon–Switzerland BIT (1964),[365] Cameroon–Germany BIT (1962),[366]

of Hungary, ICSID Case No ARB/07/19, Decision on Jurisdiction, Applicable Law and Liability (30 November 2012).

358 PAfIC (n 272) arts 19–24.

359 The analysis on PAfIC is taken from Dominic Dagbanja, 'Africa' (n 116); 354–55. See also Mbengue, 'Africa's Voice (n 319) 471–73.

360 Mbengue, 'Africa's Voice' (n 319) 473.

361 ibid 18; Kinnear and Cannu, 'Concluding Remarks' (n 321) 544; and African Society of International Law, *2016 AFSIL Principles on International Investment for Sustainable Development in Africa* <https://www.unil.ch/investmentafrica/files/live/sites/investmentafrica/files/Events/AfSIL%20 28-29.10.2016/2016%20AFSIL%20Principles%20Investment.pdf> accessed 19 December 2021.

362 Kinnear and Cannu, 'Concluding Remarks' (n 321) 545.

363 See Dagbanja 'Africa' (n 116) 340 and 343–44.

364 *Accord de coopération économique et technique entre le Gouvernement du Royaume des Pays-Bas et le Gouvernement de la République Fédérale du Cameroun*, signed 6 July 1965, entered into force 7 May 1966.

365 *Accord de commerce, de protectiondes investissements et de coopération techniqueentre la Confédération suisse et la République fédérale du Cameroun*, signed 28 January 1963, entered into force 6 April 1964.

366 *Traite entre la République Fédérale d' Allemagne et la République Fédérale du Cameroun relatif á l' encouragement des investissements de capitaux*, signed 29 June 1962, entered into force 21 November 1963.

Egypt–United Kingdom BIT (1976),[367] and Egypt–Romania BIT (1977)[368] are all still in force.[369] According to UNCTAD, 'the stock of old-generation treaties is 10 times larger than the number of modern, reform-oriented treaties. Investors continue to resort to old-generation treaties'.[370] More specifically, about '60 per cent of investment arbitrations in 2018 were brought under BITs'[371] and treaties with investment provisions such as free trade agreements 'signed in the 1990s or earlier. The remaining cases were based on treaties signed between 2000 and 2011.'[372] Thus, while the most recent investment treaties do make some space for the right to regulate and development policy-making, that regulatory autonomy cannot be guaranteed under the older investment treaties which mostly contain absolute, unqualified rights for foreign investors and their covered investments and impose corresponding obligations on host states.

These reforms may not also be directly aligned with the requirements of national constitutions from which the right to regulate derives. Except in the case of South Africa, where specific reference has been made to the Constitution in the investment treaty reform efforts, these reforms in Africa are general and based on the challenge posed by investor–state arbitration. It does not seem the reform efforts have been informed by the specific dictates of national constitutions. Investment treaty reforms to accommodate development policy in Africa must be informed by the nature of the constitutional right to development and corresponding obligations of African states. Unless the reforms are done in the context of specific constitutional rights and obligations, the terms agreed to and flexibilities incorporated into investment treaties may not lead to compatibility between the right to regulate under national constitutions and obligations under those investment treaties. Thus, the extent of constitutional obligations must determine treaty negotiation and conclusion as along as national constitutions retain supremacy in the hierarchy of legal norms and dictate international economic relations.

[367] *Agreement between the Government of the United Kingdom of Great Britain and Northern Ireland and the Government of the Arab Republic of Egypt for the Promotion and Protection of Investments*, signed 11 June 1975, entered into force 24 February 1976.

[368] *Agreement between the Socialist Republic of Romania and the Arab Republic of Egypt on the Promotion and Mutual Guarantee of Capital Investments*, signed 10 May 1076, entered into force 2 January 1977.

[369] UNCTAD, International Investment Agreements Navigator: Cameroon <https://investmentpolicy.unctad.org/international-investment-agreements/countries/34/cameroon> accessed 29 September 2020; and UNCTAD, International Investment Agreements Navigator: Egypt <https://investmentpolicy.unctad.org/international-investment-agreements/countries/62/egypt> accessed 29 September 2020.

[370] UNCTAD, *World Investment Report 2019* (n 318) xii.

[371] ibid at 103.

[372] ibid.

5.7 Conclusion

African constitutions represented in this book specifically assign to the respective governments the duties to make and implement development policies. Most of the investment treaties of African countries are aimed at limiting regulation that might affect foreign investment even if the regulation is required by constitutions and meant to advance development. African countries are parties to IHRTs, which expressly recognise the right to development and impose corresponding duties on the states. The powers of African governments are to be exercised first and foremost to promote the welfare of the people. The standards of investment protection, such as national treatment and unrestricted right to transfer investment and returns, are incompatible with the constitutions to the extent that they prevent or limit regulation in the public interest and require that treatment accorded to domestic investors should be extended to foreign investors when the constitutions require the contrary. Governments in Africa must not have the competence to enter into a treaty that abridges their powers to make and implement development policies for the public good if by such abridgement the states cannot take measures required by their constitutions in the public interest.

The absolute limitations the investment treaties place on governmental regulations to secure the protection of foreign investment could be justified if there were only one path towards development and that sole path were proven to be foreign investment. This is not so.[373] The theory that foreign investment leads to development is highly contested because the liberalisation of foreign investment regulation, foreign investment has not resulted in any 'developing' country attaining the status of a 'developed' country.[374] Thus, without further assurance of how the promotion and protection of foreign investment *per se* brings or will lead to development in Africa, the absolute restrictions that investment treaties impose even on general governmental regulation meant to contribute to the realisation of development cannot be constitutionally and reasonably justified.

There is the need for investment treaties and domestic investment laws and policies to be aligned with the constitutional right to development and corresponding duties in constitutions and general international law in Africa. To enhance coherence between investment protection obligations and national development objectives, the legal duties to make and implement development policies must limit the power of the African states in terms of investment treaty obligations they can undertake. Future investment treaties should make

373 Sornarajah and Trakman, 'A Polemic' (n 136) 504.
374 Sornarajah, 'Clash of Globalizations' (n 271) 15.

provision for an investment to be entitled to protection only if it makes contribution to development. The substantive obligations in existing treaties to protect foreign investment must be interpreted and enforced in a manner that takes account of that development objective and the legal duties of African states to make and implement development policies.

6

The Necessity, Making and Reform of Investment Treaties and Investor-State Arbitration in Africa

6.1 Introduction

Investment treaties are playing an increasingly prominent role in shaping the domestic regulatory decisions of states in ways that were not anticipated when they were signed, especially in Africa and other 'developing' countries. Investment Treaties have also become important instruments for the promotion of international economic relations between and among developed countries. As a result, a number of investor-state claims has been brought against them, much to their dislike.

The search for development has played an important role in the expansion and growth of this investment treaty regime in Africa. Explanations as to the best way forward for a country to improve its chances for development and the role of foreign investment therein have been expressed in various languages, including in the form of classical economic, dependency and middle path theories.[1] The neo-liberal theory in particular has influenced the liberalisation of foreign investment regimes worldwide.

Investment treaties, underpinned by neo-liberalism,[2] are intended to provide the legal basis for the treatment of foreign investment. Their terms and processes reflect the predominant ideas of less government intervention and regulation in favour of free markets and increased private sector activities; belief in and emphasis on the liberalisation of foreign investment inflows on the assumption that such inflows are fundamental to economic development and justify absolute protection of foreign investment; safeguards of property rights of (particularly private) foreign investors; external arbitration as the supposedly effective

[1] Muthucumaraswamy Sornarajah, *The International Law on Foreign Investment* (3rd edn, CUP 2010) 47–61.

[2] Muthucumaraswamy Sornarajah, *Resistance and Change in the International Law on Foreign Investment* (CUP 2015) 10–15; Jane Kelsey, *The Fire Economic: New Zealand's Reckoning* (Bridget Williams Books Ltd 2015) 121–49; and Jane Kelsey, *Reclaiming the Future: New Zealand and the Global Economy* (Bridget Williams Books Ltd 2000) 121–60.

The Investment Treaty Regime and Public Interest Regulation in Africa. Dominic Npoanlari Dagbanja, Oxford University Press.
 DOI: 10.1093/oso/9780192896179.003.0006

and neutral mechanism for resolving disputes between foreign investors and host states; and the consequential call for a realignment of legal systems to suit these neo-liberal ideals.[3]

The protection of foreign investment by treaty is achieved by substantive standards of investment protection and investor–state arbitration. These are reflected in African investment treaties. Although these treaties pre-date the neo-liberal period, the detailed study of development, environment, human rights, and judicial autonomy in this book shows that they can be used to achieve its objectives and limit states' ability to fulfil their duties under their constitutions and general international law to act in the public interest. In this regard, the objectives of neo-liberalism as reflected in the terms of investment treaties are unbalanced since the treaties seek to restrain public interest regulation in order to attain investment protection objectives.

Investment treaties entitle foreign investors to claim that legislative, policy, and administrative measures or even judicial decisions have breached states' obligations towards them and to bring regulatory actions under the scrutiny of arbitral tribunals. The various legislative and administrative measures of states that have been challenged in recent years include environmental policies, banking sector reforms, legislative and policy measures in response to economic crises, revocations of licences and permits, application of tax laws, judicial decisions, and water concessions.[4] The standards of investment protection are primarily aimed at restricting governmental regulation that might adversely affect the activities of foreign investors and the value of their investments and to compensate them for such adverse effects, whether the regulation is in the public interest or not.

International investment law scholarship that is critical of this trend has focused on how investor–state suits might limit states' regulatory autonomy or the adoption of particular governmental measures. The restraining effect of investment treaties has led to some scholars likening these treaties to national constitutions because they pre-commit future governments to certain norms and policies, they are difficult to amend, include binding enforcement mechanisms, and serve a different constituency by 'conferring privileged rights of citizenship on corporate capital, while constraining the power of the nation state and the democratic rights of its citizens'.[5]

Scholarly works on the role of constitutional law and general international law norms (the very norms which define the functions of governments in the public interest and

[3] Muthucumaraswamy Sornarajah, 'The Retreat of Neo-Liberalism in Investment Treaty Arbitration' in Catherine Rogers and Roger Alford (eds), *The Future of Investment Arbitration* (New York University Press 2009) 273, 274–75.

[4] Gus Van Harten, *Sovereign Choices and Sovereign Constraints: Judicial Restraint in Investment Treaty Arbitration* (OUP 2013) 10–13; and Santiago Montt, *State Liability in Investment Treaty Arbitration: Global Constitutional and Administrative Law in the BIT Generation* (Hart Publishing 2009) 2.

[5] Jane Kelsey 'Global Economic Policy-Making: A New Constitutionalism?' (1999–2000) 9 Otago Law Review 535, 545; see also David Schneiderman, *Constitutionalizing Economic Globalization: Investment Rules and Democracy's Promise* (CUP 2008) 69.

justify states' claim for regulatory autonomy in investment treaty arbitration) in the making and interpretation of investment treaties are not common in the literature. Indeed, the subject has not been explored systematically. In particular, country-specific studies on whether states can sign on to the type of obligations they undertake in investment treaties in light of their obligations towards their own citizens, and how agreements that do not conform to those standards should be treated, are wanting.

This book has addressed that lacuna, with specific reference to Africa. The book argues that the African states' obligations to protect the public interest are central under their constitutions and general international law as the powers of government must be exercised both to promote the welfare of the people and within constitutional limits. Moreover, investment treaties presuppose the existence of norms necessary for them to come into existence and to have legal effect, and the states' obligations to comply with them. These factors limit the investment treaty obligations African states can assume in the future and raise difficult legal questions about the validity of existing treaties that conflict with the states' public interest obligations. If they are treated as valid, their interpretation must be informed by those constitutional and general international law obligations. This book developed this proposition through the imperatives theory. It argues that the autonomy to regulate in the public interest cannot be retained or effectively recaptured without ensuring that the norms pertaining to human rights, environment, development, and the jurisdiction of the domestic courts remain paramount bases for determining what states can or cannot do with public powers, both domestically and in international economic relations. The obligation to protect foreign investment must be made to coexist, and not displace, the public interest objectives especially development for which African states have entered into investment treaties.

6.2 Reconciling Standards of Investment Protection with Public Interest Regulation in Africa

Three scenarios are considered as to how to reconcile the standards of investment protection with the obligations of African states towards the public: the framework for making future treaties, renegotiation of existing treaties, and interpretation of current treaties that remain unchanged.

6.2.1 The Framework for Making Future Investment Treaties in Africa

The duties of African states to regulate in the public interest, the difficulties of voiding treaties, and the narrow room for escaping from a treaty's binding effect under the Vienna Convention on the Law of Treaties (VCLT) support the need to rethink the terms of future investment treaties. Existing investment treaties that prevent or limit governmental regulation because of their effect on foreign investors and give rise to liability to pay compensation for regulation mandated in the public interest are incompatible with the states' public interest obligations based on national laws (constitutions in particular) and general international law.

The admission and coming into force of African investment treaties were conditioned upon the states parties complying with the constitutional and internal legal procedures and requirements.[6] The object of requiring compliance with municipal law in the admission of investment and for the entry into force of the investment treaties was to ensure that the procedures and fundamental interests under municipal law are not rendered otiose by the entry into force of the treaties. That objective will be defeated if investment treaties remain valid or have binding effect even when the admission of investment or coming into force of the treaties did not comply with the African constitutions and legislation.

African constitutions set the terms for the making and entry into force of investment treaties. In this book, I distinguish between procedural and substantive compliance, and between procedural constitutionality and substantive constitutionality. Those treaties which purportedly entered into force without having complied with the procedural requirements under the constitutions are invalid (procedural unconstitutionality) and unenforceable. The constitutions equally require African governments to conduct their international affairs, such as entering into investment treaties, in a manner that is consistent with the national interest. Those treaties that validly entered into force are substantively inconsistent with the constitutions (substantive unconstitutionality) and general international law to the extent that they prevent or limit public interest regulation. If a treaty has not been validly made, it has no effect and the principle that international law overrides municipal law in the event of conflict does not apply accordingly.

The dilemma is how procedural and substantive invalidity should be treated. The domestic courts in Africa could determine that an investment treaty is invalid. However, a declaration of invalidity under municipal law by municipal courts does not have effect in international law. Since these are bilateral treaties, issues as to their invalidity are better resolved through diplomatic discussion. The investment treaties provide for the settlement of state-to-state disputes regarding the application or interpretation of investment treaties by consultation through diplomatic channels or by a state-to-state arbitral tribunal specifically set up for that purpose. Such a tribunal may be constituted by each contracting party appointing

[6] Agreement between the People's Republic of China and the Government of the Republic of Ghana Concerning the Encouragement and Reciprocal Protection of Investments (signed 12 October 1989, entered into force on 22 November 1991), arts 1 and 14; and Agreement Between the Government of the Republic of Mauritius and the Government of the Arab Republic of Egypt on the Reciprocal Promotion and Protection of Investments (signed 25 June 2014, entered into force 17 October 2014), art 3(1) and (3).

an arbitrator and the two arbitrators appointing a third person. Where the contracting parties are unable to constitute a tribunal within the specific periods, then either contracting party may apply to the President of the International Court of Justice (ICJ) to appoint the arbitrators.[7]

Since such a tribunal is to be constituted by the states parties themselves, it is more likely to be vested with the powers of those states that will enable it to resolve a dispute on the validity, unlike investor–state tribunals whose jurisdiction is limited to resolving investment disputes with no power to adjudicate upon matters involving public law and policy. The problem is that the scope of this power is limited to the application or interpretation of investment treaties. A dispute over the validity of an investment treaty is not an investment dispute because it concerns whether the treaty is legally valid and can bind the parties.

Therefore, it is for the parties to resolve such a dispute and they may do so through diplomatic channels or state-to-state dispute resolution tribunal. If one of the parties is still not satisfied with the decision of this tribunal, they may have a dispute over the validity of an investment treaty resolved by the ICJ. The jurisdiction of the ICJ, comprises all cases which the parties refer to it. Under Article 36(1) and (6) of the Statute of the ICJ,[8] the states parties may at any time declare that they recognise as compulsory *ipso facto* and without special agreement the jurisdiction of the Court in all legal disputes concerning any question of international law or the existence of any fact which, if established, would constitute a breach of an international obligation.

If these avenues fail to resolve the procedural or substantive invalidity of an investment treaty there is very limited scope to void it under the VCLT. The status of existing investment treaties becomes a matter of legal argument once an action is taken to enforce it. The solution to the difficulty of voiding treaties under the constitutions and the VCLT would require fresh legal arguments in an international legal environment that is receptive to concerns that states should not be able to enter into treaties that prevent them from fulfilling their public interest obligations. It is conceivable that the parties might agree, or the ICJ might rule, in the future to void a treaty on the basis that the core duties of states prevented them from entering into the treaty. This is envisaged under Article 46 of the VCLT.

That is not the situation now. Given the need to maximise the space to regulate in the public interest, and recognising the limited scope to void a treaty or escape its binding effect under current interpretations of the VCLT, the following specific proposals would severely restrict the scope of investment treaties to make them compatible with the imperatives theory.

First, 'investment' should only be entitled to coverage and protection under an investment treaty where it has made a tangible contribution to the development in

[7] Ghana–China Investment Treaty, art 9; and Egypt–Mauritius Investment Treaty, art 9.

[8] United Nations, Statute of International Court of Justice, 18 April 1946.

one of the ways identified in African constitutions and as defined by the parties in the investment treaty.

Second, indirect expropriation must be done away with completely. There are several reasons for this. One is specific to African constitutions: the requirement for payment of compensation for indirect expropriation under the investment treaties conflicts for example with the Constitutions of Egypt, Cameroon, Ghana, Kenya, Nigeria, and South Africa which recognise payment of compensation only for *compulsory taking possession* or *acquisition* of property *by law*, that is direct expropriation.

A more general principled reason is that the rule on indirect expropriation does not respect the objective underlying *general* governmental regulation and its indirect nature indicates no intent of such regulation to harm the investor. Losses arising from indirect regulation must be seen as incidental to the doing of business with or in a state. Foreign investors should be entitled to protection against only direct expropriation, which is explicitly aimed at taking away a right, returning to the original objective of investment treaties. The effect of direct expropriation and indirect expropriation may be the same, and it might be argued that a state should not achieve indirectly what it cannot do directly. However, against the backdrop of the right to regulate in the public interest, treating them as one and the same thing does not preserve the necessary room for regulation justified by domestic law and international law. States have a legitimate expectation to exercise their freedom to regulate and that foreign investors will not seek to profit from the exercise of that freedom when it adversely affects the value of their investments. Therefore, if there is not a confiscation or explicit taking of an investment, a right to remedy should not arise. Some investment treaties provide that measures for public health and environmental protection do not constitute indirect expropriation except in rare circumstances and provided the measures are not used as a disguised restriction on international trade and investment.[9] This is an improved version of the absolute right of foreign investors against indirect expropriation in older investment treaties. However, the provisos or qualifications to this exception against indirect expropriation weaken its potency.

It may well be argued that the recommendation against indirect expropriation provisions being included in future investment treaties or being removed from existing investment treaties would deny foreign investors the ability to challenge measures that are outright takings of investments and are not arguably for public purposes, but are for other purposes. The recommendation may seem to shield measures extending well beyond the protection of human rights and the environment. It is the case that the proposal for excluding indirect expropriation from

[9] For example, Agreement between the Government of the Republic of Kazakhstan and the Government of the Republic of Singapore on the Promotion and Mutual Protection of Investments, signed 21 November 2018, art 19; and Ghana Model BIT 2008 art 7(6).

investment treaties is about safeguarding measures which are aimed at protecting human rights, the environment, and the right to development but which have adverse indirect effects on investment even though they were never aimed at expropriating investment. Where measures are not directly and primarily aimed at protecting human rights or other public interest under state laws but are manifestly used to excuse their adverse effects on the investment, those laws may well achieve the effect of direct expropriation. Such measures ought to be treated differently from those aimed at the protection of the public interest but which have an indirect adverse effect on investment.

However, the case against indirect expropriation may still be appropriate even with respect to non-public interest measures having the effect of expropriation. Some constitutions in Africa only recognise direct expropriation whether for public purposes or for non-public purposes such as is the case in Kenya,[10] Nigeria,[11] and Ghana.[12] Indeed, some constitutions in Africa directly permit indirect expropriation by general law, that is law not specifically aimed at compulsorily acquiring property.[13] Thus, there are constitutional issues with indirect expropriation and thus a legitimate case against indirect expropriation even in the case of measures of non-public nature adopted by states which have the effect of expropriation.

Third, I argue against the inclusion of national treatment and most-favoured-nation treatment (MFN) in future investment treaties of African. The African states exist or must exist first for their own citizens and should not place foreigners and citizens on the same level in terms of economic protection. African states should be able to initiate and implement measures solely in the interests of citizens whether they are engaged in the same or similar business as foreign investors without having to incur investment treaty liability. Therefore, national treatment must never be included in future investment treaties. Deciding whether particular measures serve the national interest is the prerogative of African states. So national treatment should be a choice and not an obligation giving rise to compensation. The developed countries use their immigration laws and policies selectively to advance their national interests in a manner that is arguably exploitative. African countries can learn from this and use international economic agreements purposely and selectively to advance their economic interests rather than merely being appendages and incidental beneficiaries to the regime.

The case against the MFN rule is that it can indirectly defeat the very purpose for which a state did not agree to a particular investment treaty term with a particular treaty partner. Put another way, a country that is not able to negotiate a desired standard with a treaty partner may gain the protection of that

[10] Constitution of the Republic of Kenya 2010, arts 24(2) and 40(2) and (3).
[11] Constitution of the Federal Republic of Nigeria 1999, s 44(1)
[12] Constitution of the Republic of Ghana 1992, art 20(1) and (2).
[13] Constitution of Nigeria (n 11) s 44(2) and Constitution of Ghana (n 12) art 20(4).

standard for its investors and their investments if the treaty partner grants that higher standard of protection to investors and investment of a third country in another treaty. There may be a special public interest reason why particular treatment may have to be accorded to investors of one treaty partner instead of another. African states should not be burdened with additional responsibility to extend such special treatment to third state investors if it does not serve the public interest to do so. Like the national treatment standard, MFN should be a choice to be made by African states and not an obligation under an international treaty. If national treatment and MFN standards are retained or continued to be included in investment treaties, the *Most-Favoured-Home-Third States Clause* (MFHT Clause) must be included in investment treaties. The MFHT Clause will impose obligations on foreign investors to carry on their businesses and operations accordance with the most favourable environmental, human rights, and other operating and performance standards and obligations applicable in the home state or in third states.

Fourth, the fair and equitable treatment (FET) protection has become one of the most controversial in international investment law because its precise contours are indeterminate. Like indirect expropriation, it has become a powerful and flexible test for foreign investors to use to challenge regulatory actions. For African countries, such a term cannot continue to be agreed to in its current amorphous form. Its continued use is conditional on limiting its scope or demarcating its boundaries to preserve regulatory autonomy. To be fair and equitable, this standard must operate to protect the interests of the state too. It cannot be said to be *fair and equitable* in situations where the standard is interpreted and applied as an obligation of the state alone but not that of the foreign investor. Fairness and equity do not exist in one-sidedness. They exist in reciprocity.

Fifth, provisions on transfer of investment and returns would need to preserve the right of African governments to restrict transfers in the interest of financial stability and economic development. There must be absolute freedom to restrict transfers for purposes of stabilizing the economy in cases of economic and financial crises and the existence of that situation must be self-judging.

The terms that may appropriately be included in investment treaties then are direct expropriation and full protection and security (FPS) which reflect what investment protection by treaty was originally about. There is doubt in the literature whether full protection and security covers protection against physical injury and non-physical injury to investment. This would need clarification in future investment treaties too.

In future, African states must not enter into treaties that contain investor–state dispute settlement. The supremacy of national courts under national constitutions counsels against such arbitration. African states should require the use of national courts to resolve investment disputes or develop alternative inter-state mechanisms that are more legitimate and accountable in terms of effectively protecting public and private interests than the current system of investment tribunals that have narrow jurisdiction over investment disputes do. The dispute settlement mechanism must be clear in investment treaties themselves that judicial decisions and constitutional issues cannot be challenged in arbitration and limit remedies to actual loss and simple interest.

This case for the narrowing of investment protection in several core rules, and removing investor–state arbitration, raises the question of whether investment treaties are actually needed to provide protection for foreign investors. This question is particularly relevant as foreign investors can seek protection under African constitutions and legislation for expropriation, transfer of investment and returns, investment incentives, and for breach of other specific commitments. Moreover, ongoing reforms of investment treaties and investor–state arbitration to accommodate states' right to regulate reinforce the relevance of the question whether investment treaties are necessary and needed at all. If investment treaties and investment arbitration are not bringing about the neutrality and efficiency that underlie them, the question arises to why their reform is necessary and must be pursued at all costs but a return to municipal law and domestic courts for investment protection must never be raised or considered.

A state-to-state dispute settlement body should work for investment disputes as it does for trade disputes in the case of World Trade Organization dispute settlement and appellate bodies. Given the interconnection between trade and investment, a state-to-state dispute settlement body should be able to resolve both investment and trade disputes efficiently rather than maintaining separate disputes settlement mechanisms, one for trade and another for investment.[14]

Thus, to the extent that states continue to enter into investment treaties and agree to investor–state arbitration, a rethink of the terms of those treaties and the role of arbitral tribunals becomes necessary. This book provides a basis for such rethinking.

6.2.2 Renegotiation of Existing Investment Treaties in Africa

The parties to investment treaties are free to renegotiate the terms of their treaties just as they 'freely' entered into them. The starting point for such renegotiation is an important soft law instrument the African Union (AU) has put in place in

[14] Yenkong Ngangjoh-Hodu has argued that from 'a human and financial resource capacity perspective, a joint dispute settlement for both will generally make more sense. In the case of PICs [Pacific Island Countries] which face a myriad of challenges, including small administrations having a dual system would be burdensome financially and also in terms of human resources', Yenkong Ngangjoh-Hodu, 'Re-constructing Dispute Settlement Mechanism in Trade and Investment Agreements: Key Considerations for the PACER Plus Negotiating Parties' (2015) 10(9) Global Trade and Customs Journal 191, 295.

furtherance of the objectives of the AU's primary treaty, especially on economic integration, is the 2016 Draft Pan-African Investment Code (PAfIC)[15] which is intended to guide AU Member States as they negotiate investment treaties and the investment chapter of the African Continental Free Trade Agreement.[16] The PAfIC seeks 'to promote, facilitate and protect investments that foster the sustainable development of each Member State'.[17] The PAfIC is quite revolutionary because it abandons standard investment treaty terms such as FPS and FET. Other standard investment treatment terms such national treatment,[18] MFN,[19] expropriation,[20] transfer of investment and returns,[21] and performance requirements[22] are qualified so as to make room for the adoption of measures that would otherwise be contrary to these standards. The efficacy of these exceptions would need to be assessed before they are introduced into investment treaties.

The PAfIC retains the usual broad definition of investment in Article 4(4) but it also provides quite uniquely that in order to qualify as an investment, the investment must be a substantial business activity and involve commitment of capital or other resources, gain or profit must be expected, risk must be assumed and the investment must make 'a significant contribution to the host State's economic development'. The addition of contribution to the development of the host state as an element of investment should settle the issue whether or not an investment is entitled to protection under an investment treaty if it does not make contribution to the development of the host state. Arbitral tribunals are divided on the subject, those which support contribution to development as an element of investment[23] and those which do not.[24]

[15] Draft Pan-African Investment Code, E/ECA/C OE/3 5/18, AU/STC/FMEPI/EXP/18(II), 25 March 216.

[16] UNCTAD, *World Investment Report 2017: Investment and the Digital Economy* (United Nations 2017) 113.

[17] Pan-African Investment Code (n 15) art 1.

[18] ibid arts 9 and 10.

[19] ibid arts and 8.

[20] ibid arts 11 and 12.

[21] ibid arts 15 and 16.

[22] ibid art 17.

[23] *Salini Costruttori SpA & Italstrade SpA v Morocco*, ICSID Case No ARB/00/4, Decision on Jurisdiction (23 July 2001); *Fedax NV v Republic of Venezuela*, ICSID Case No ARB/96/3, Decision of the Tribunal on Objection to Jurisdiction (11 July 1997; *Patrick Mitchell v The Democratic Republic of Congo*, Case No ARB/99/7, Decision on the Application for Annulment of the Award, 1 November 2006; *Malaysian Historical Salvors Sdn, BHD v Malaysia*, ICSID Case No ARB/05/10, Award on Jurisdiction, 17 May 2007; *Alex Genin Eastern Credit Ltd Inc v The Republic of Estonia*, Case No ARB/99/2, Award, 25 June 2001; *Pantechniki S.A. Contractors & Engineers (Greece) v The Republic of Albania*, ICSID Case No ARB/07/21, Award, 30 July 2009; *Amoco Asia Corporation v Republic of Indonesia*, ICSID Case No ARB/06/18, Decision on Jurisdiction and Liability, 25 September 1983; and. *Joseph Charles Lemire v Ukraine*, ICSID Case No ARB/O6/18, Decision on Jurisdiction and Liability, 14 January 2010.

[24] *Société Générale v Dominican Republic*, LCIA Case No UN 7927, UNCITRAL Arbitration Rules, Award on Preliminary Objections to Jurisdiction 19 September 2008; *Consorzio Groupement LESI-DIPENTA v Algeria*, ICSID Case No ARB/03/08, Award (10 January 2005); and *Electrabel SA v Republic of Hungary*, ICSID Case No ARB/07/19, Decision on Jurisdiction, Applicable Law and

The position adopted by the African Union on the contribution of investment to development is in accord with the very conventional wisdom underlying the making of investment treaties, namely that they are necessary to attract investment for development. Also, importantly the PAfIC has provisions specifically on the obligations of investors.[25] The PAfIC was thus designed to ensure investment promotion without compromising Member States' right to regulate in the public interest and to ensure that investment ultimately makes contribution to the development of the host state. The terms of the PAfIC give effect to its drafters' recognition in the preamble that AU Member States have the right 'to regulate all the aspects relating to investments within their territories with a view to meeting national policy objectives and to promote sustainable development objectives'.

There is an alternative. The approach under the PAfIC and similar moves by many other countries to preserve regulatory autonomy[26] raises a legitimate question of whether the time has come to return to the protection of foreign investment under municipal law. Ongoing reforms of the investment treaty regime challenge the need to continue with them. Enforcing a narrower range of investor protections through domestic courts would also ensure that foreign investors can be effectively made subject to the laws of the host country in which they invest and not seek to evade that accountability by challenging new regulations or even judgments before international investment tribunals. African states need to engage seriously with the prudence in being parties to such investment treaties. It cannot be that without investment treaties, no credible guarantees can be provided for investment protection or that without investment tribunals, no credible alternative dispute resolution mechanisms can be relied on to solve investment disputes.

6.2.3 The Interpretation of Existing Investment Treaties

If a dispute arises under existing investment treaties with African countries, it must be interpreted having regard to the public interest obligations of the contracting parties and the specific legal justification for the exercise of the right to regulate in the public interest. Where the particular right to regulate is justified under both constitutions and general international law, then normative priority should be given to the public interest regulation obligations. They should prevail over

Liability (30 November 2012). See Dominic Dagbanja, 'The Development Objective as an Imperative in Interpretation of International Investment Agreements' (2018) 44(2) University of Western Australia Law Review 144 (hereafter, Dagbanja, 'Development Objective and IIA Interpretation').

[25] Pan-African Investment Code (n 14) arts 19–24.

[26] UNCTAD, *World Investment Report 2012: Towards a New Generation of Investment Policies* (United Nations 2012).

investment treaty obligations, since in such a case the rule that international law prevails over municipal law in the event of conflict should be inapplicable. A 'balance' cannot be achieved in the international investment regime if the legal justification for the adoption of a measure giving rise to a treaty claim is irrelevant in decisions on liability and award of damages. To justify their legitimacy as neutral and efficient forums for the resolution of investor–state disputes, investment tribunals must begin to give due consideration to the public interest justification of a challenged measure. There would be the need to consider the design and structure of investment tribunals if they are to play this new role.

6.3 Protecting Public Interest Regulation in Future Investment Treaties: Specific Considerations

The examination of four different and fundamental arenas of public interest—the national judicial system, the environment, human rights, and development—shows how these scenarios might be applied in the future.

6.3.1 Preserving and Reclaiming the Jurisdiction of Municipal Courts

The foundation of international arbitration for the resolution of investment disputes is the presumed inefficiency and possible bias of municipal courts in the settlement of disputes between a host state and alien multinational business entities. International arbitration was seen as a mechanism that would provide foreign business entities and states alike with a neutral, independent, and competent forum for the efficient, swift, cheap, and flexible resolution of disputes relating to investments. However, the actual functioning of this mechanism reveals systemic and endemic deficiencies. Not only has international arbitration been used by foreign investors to challenge public interest regulation, it has also become a mechanism through which judicial decisions have been challenged before private arbitrators. Such investor–state suits pose serious challenges to the authority of municipal courts and the sanctity of their decisions.[27]

There are substantial academic and policy debates over the wisdom and efficacy of the investor–state dispute settlement mechanism. The legitimacy, independence, transparency, impartiality, and accountability of arbitral tribunals have been credibly questioned in the literature. A more foundational question which this book addressed is the competence of states to agree to a mechanism that enables

27 For the intersection of judicial decisions and investor-state arbitration, see Berk Demirkol, *Judicial Acts and Investment Treaty Arbitration* (CUP 2018).

foreign investors to bypass the jurisdictions of the courts, using legal rules that do not apply in domestic law, and potentially enables international tribunals to override the municipal courts whose jurisdictions under national constitutions are supreme, original, appellate, and final. The decisions of municipal courts in Africa have been challenged by foreign investors before investment tribunals which proceeded to make conflicting decisions and sought to replace the decisions of the courts with their own, without showing the courts were legally wrong or had failed to administer justice. In this respect, international arbitration can undermine the rule of law and the administration of justice in Africa.

In this book, I made a number of arguments and proposals. First, I challenged the notion that national legal systems are incompetent to resolve investment disputes given (i) the structure of municipal courts with their self-correcting mechanisms of appeals and reviews of their decisions to ensure effective administration of justice; and (ii) the role of municipal courts in the recognition and enforcement of foreign arbitral awards.

Second, I argued that the investment tribunals' presumed competence to resolve substantive investment disputes under the investment treaties does not empower them to review municipal judicial decisions, nor do the tribunals have the legitimacy under constitutional law to do so.

Third, the fundamental principles of African legal systems in which the courts have original, appellate, and final jurisdictions over all legal disputes and persons, and in which the principles of probity, separation of powers, rule of law, accountability, and transparency are entrenched and paramount, militate against African states agreeing to international arbitration, surrendering all judicial powers to this mechanism merely because foreign investors are involved.

In relation to existing investment treaties, I questioned the legality of a general agreement to arbitrate given the original, appellate, and final judicial powers of the courts under African constitutions. I also argued against agreeing to international arbitration in light of the fact that customary international law does not grant foreign investors an automatic right to an international dispute resolution body. In customary international law resort to a foreign forum is justified if domestic remedies are not available at all or if they prove ineffective.[28] Accordingly, it is proposed that the right to international arbitration under existing investment treaties must be interpreted as accruing only when an investor has had recourse to municipal courts and has not found a remedy, and that international forum can and should be a state-to-state, not investor–state forum, which requires the investor to have the endorsement of their parent state to pursue the dispute. This proposal will ensure that foreign investors have recourse to municipal courts before any attempt to have recourse to an international forum can be made. This procedure will

[28] *Elettronica Sicula SPA (ELSI)*, Judgment, ICJ Reports (1989) 15 [55], [56], and [59].

help give effect to the provision on the original jurisdiction of the courts under the various constitutions considered in this book. Any agreement in future to investment treaty arbitration has to take into consideration the arbitrability of the subject matter of a dispute in light of national constitutions and general international law and the ability of the foreign forum to 'balance' both public and private interests.

Proposals to reform investment treaty arbitration are founded on criticisms of the system for bias and lack of legitimacy. In the same way that the limitations of investment treaty arbitration justify the reform of the system, it is time to revisit the role of domestic courts and the sort of reforms that are necessary to enable them effectively to discharge their duties in settling these disputes. Pursuing investor–state arbitration reforms,[29] including the suggestion for an international investment court, without looking at the possible role of domestic courts in investment disputes settlement entrenches the view that only investment tribunals can resolve investment disputes and must be stuck to at all costs. Such an entrenched view suggests that the courts can never be placed in a position to resolve investment disputes even though the same states that champion investor–state arbitration and invest in them are responsible for ensuring that the courts function properly and efficiently even in relation to foreign investors and investments.

6.3.2 Preserving and Reclaiming Environmental and Human Rights Regulatory Autonomy

Environmental regulation of foreign investments in such countries as Canada, the United States, Mexico, Indonesia, and Germany, have been challenged by foreign investors through investor–state dispute settlement for allegedly breaching the substantive standards of investment protection. Measures that have been challenged include orders banning the export of chemicals and products that affect environmental quality, water, and health; denial and revocation of environmental permits; legislation and regulations prohibiting the use of pesticides on environmental and public health grounds; expropriation of property for natural resources conservation purposes; imposition of conditions on environmental permits; and amendment of legislation to phase out nuclear power plant operation.[30]

Investor claims challenging environmental and human rights measures have raised academic and policy debates on how states might recapture environmental

[29] On reforms of investor–state arbitration see: Gabrielle Kaufmann-Kohler and Michele Potestà, Special Issue: 'Investor–state Dispute Settlement and National Courts: Current Framework and Reform Options' in Gabrielle Kaufmann-Kohler and Michele Potestà (eds) *European Yearbook of International Economic Law* (Springer 2020) 1; and Katia Fach Gómez, *Key Duties of International Investment Arbitrators: A Transnational Study of Legal and Ethical Dilemmas* (Springer 20019).

[30] Jorge Viñuales, *Foreign Investment and the Environment in International Law* (CUP 2012) 17–23.

and human rights regulatory autonomy. Again, the contribution of this book has been to assess the implications of the constitutional and general international law duties of African states to protect the environment and human rights in the making and interpretation of investment treaties. I showed that key aspects of the legal regime for environmental and human rights protection in Africa, such as the cancellation and termination of environmental permits and regulation of the import, export, or use of environmentally hazardous substances, could potentially be challenged by foreign investors under African investment treaties. I argued that because environmental treaties and human rights treaties promote the protection of the environment and human rights in the same manner as do African constitutions, their combined legal force take or should take precedence when there is a conflict with investment treaties, dictating the standards of investment protection the states can undertake and informing the interpretation of investment treaties.

It is only by entering into investment treaties whose terms respect constitutional and general international law norms on human rights and environmental rights, the protection of the environment, and conservation of natural resources that the states can retain policy-making capacity and regulatory autonomy. *Chemtura v Canada*[31] and *Methanex v United States*[32] have endorsed the principle that where environmental regulation is justified in the public interest under domestic legislation and international law liability does not arise from the regulation. Also, where the activities of foreign investors pose a direct risk of damaging the environment and a state intervenes within the law to avoid or remove the risk, then due consideration should be given to the regulation and the legal justification in support. Enforceable obligations to respect, observe, and uphold human rights and environmental rights must be imposed on foreign investors in investment treaties. It is not enough merely to affirm or recognise the right to regulate in investment treaties nor merely to state that contracting parties to investment treaties should encourage foreign investors to incorporate international corporate social responsibility practices in their policies and operations. The language in investment treaties, which comes with substantive and enforceable standards of investment protection, must be one of the corporate *legal* responsibilities of foreign investors. The soft law approach of corporate *social* responsibilities which comes with the language that foreign investors may be encouraged to voluntarily adopt relevant principles on business and human rights does not ensure that foreign investors effectively account for the violations of human rights and environmental degradations that come with their activities.

[31] *Chemtura Corporation v Canada*, NAFTA/UNCITRAL, Award, 2 August 2010.
[32] *Methanex Corporation v United States of America*, NAFTA/UNCITRAL, Final Award, 7 August 2005.

6.3.3 Preserving and Reclaiming Development Policy Autonomy

The relationship between African states' investment treaty obligations and their development policymaking and implementation obligations was illustrated with reference to industrial policy and capital control regulation. A number of arguments have been advanced. The states have constitutional and general international law duties to make and implement development policies for the realisation of the legal right to development in Africa, which means they must only enter into treaties that are consistent with and promote a national interest, such as development, and in particular, the human right to development.

Investment treaties with African countries were or are aimed at establishing standards of investment protection to attract foreign investment for development and not merely to protect foreign investment as an end in itself. The interpretation of the investment treaties must take account of that development objective, as well as the constitutional and general international law duties of the states to make and implement measures for the realisation of the right to development in Africa.[33] Where an investment has made no contribution to development it must not be entitled to protection. The challenge posed to development by international investment law cannot be addressed effectively unless investment treaties are made subject to states' regulatory powers under both their constitutions and general international law to make and implement development policies for the interests of citizens, from whom the powers of states derive.

Given that foreign investment is not the panacea for all development problems in Africa, a restricted approach to investment protection must ensure the role of African states in development is not underestimated or undermined, and foreign investment is not given absolute protection above everything else. To reconcile investment treaty terms with the primary obligations of the states, investment treaties must be made and interpreted in a manner consistent with or to accommodate public interest regulation. There is the need to make provision in future investment treaties for an investment to be entitled to protection only if it contributes to development, which means for example performance requirements must not be allowed under investment treaties (or they must be effectively qualified) because imposing performance requirements is one of the ways to ensure that an investment actually makes contribution to the host state. A prohibition against performance requirements cannot be reconciled with the development objective contained in investment treaties, whether in the substantive terms or preambles or both. What Africa needs for the realisation of its development goals is strong governance systems that respect rights, including domestic legal systems that work for both domestic

33 Dagbanja, 'Development Objective and IIA Interpretation' (n 24).

investors and foreign investors, not an international legal and institutional regime that favours, pampers, and privileges foreign investors.

6.4 Conclusion

This book has focused on the capacity of African states to conclude investment treaties and the terms the states can or cannot agree to under those treaties in light their public interest obligations. It equally addressed the issue of how the limitation public interest obligation places on the treaty-making capacity of states should inform treaty interpretation. In doing so, the book provides a basis for how the challenge the investment treaty regime poses to regulatory autonomy might be addressed in future rather than providing an exact roadmap of how they should look like. This is an issue that should engage the attention of Africa now and in the future, as it should other developing countries and beyond. A constitutional, general international law and principled basis for that reflection is crucial and this book is a contribution to that.

Index

For the benefit of digital users, indexed terms that span two pages (e.g., 52–53) may, on occasion, appear on only one of those pages.